Innovative Interventions to Reduce Dementia Caregiver Distress

A Clinical Guide

David W. Coon, PhD, is a licensed psychologist and Research Scientist/ Project Director at Institute on Aging (formerly, Goldman Institute on Aging) in San Francisco, where he serves as a project director and investigator on a number of social and behavioral intervention and education programs targeting seniors and their informal caregivers. He also currently serves as the Associate Director of the Older Adult & Family Center of the VA Palo Alto Health Care System and Stanford University School of Medicine. Dr. Coon received his doctorate in counseling psychology from Stanford University in 1996; and his postgraduate training in geropsychology at Veteran's Administration Palo Alto Health Care System and Stanford University. Dr. Coon's professional interests and publications have focused on the experience of family caregivers among diverse groups, and the development of effective psychosocial interventions to meet the needs of today's midlife and older populations.

Dolores Gallagher-Thompson, PhD, ABPP, is Associate Professor of Research in the Department of Psychiatry and Behavioral Sciences at Stanford University School of Medicine and Director of the Older Adult & Family Center of the VA Palo Alto Health Care System and Stanford University. Her career has focused on clinical and research issues in the field of geropsychology for over 20 years, as well as on the training of psychology students, interns, and postdoctoral Fellows. She has devoted most of the past decade to developing and scientifically evaluating a series of small group, psychoeducational intervention programs for family caregivers of elders with Alzheimer's disease or a related form of dementia. Most recently, her work has focused on the complex issues facing ethnically and culturally diverse caregiving families. Her research has been funded by the National Institute on Aging and the Alzheimer's Association, and she has authored over 100 publications on these and related topics.

Larry W. Thompson, PhD, is Professor Emeritus, Stanford University School of Medicine, and currently is also the Goldman Family Professor of Psychology at Pacific Graduate School of Psychology in Palo Alto, CA. He was Director of the Older Adult and Family Center until his retirement from the VA 5 years ago. Dr. Thompson headed a multidisciplinary research team that recently completed one of the first studies to compare the effectiveness of cognitive/behavioral therapy and antidepressant medication—both alone and in combination. He has spent over 30 years training psychology students, interns, and postdoctoral Fellows at Duke University, the University of Southern California, Stanford, and now PGSP. He has over 100 publications in the field of geropsychology, as well as several other edited books. He is currently studying the effectiveness of cognitive/behavioral therapy for the treatment of bipolar disorders.

Innovative Interventions to Reduce Dementia Caregiver Distress

A Clinical Guide

David W. Coon, PhD
Dolores Gallagher-Thompson, PhD, ABPP
Larry W. Thompson, PhD, Editors

 Springer Publishing Company

Springer Publishing Company, Inc.
536 Broadway
New York, NY 10012-3955

Acquisitions Editor: Helvi Gold
Production Editor: Jeanne W. Libby
Cover design by Joanne E. Honigman

03 04 05 06 07/5 4 3 2 1

Coon, David W.
  Innovative interventions to reduce dementia caregiver distress : a clinical guide / David W. Coon, Dolores Gallagher-Thompson, Larry, W. Thompson
       p. ; cm.
    Includes bibliographical references and index.
    ISBN 0-8261-4801-8
    1. Dementia—Patients—Care—Psychological aspects. 2. Dementia—Patients—Family relationships. 3. Caregivers—Mental health services.
  4. Caregivers—Mental health. I. Gallagher-Thompson, Dolores.
  II. Thompson, Larry W. III. Title
    [DNLM: 1. Dementia—nursing. 2. Caregivers—psychology. 3. Home Nursing—psychology. 4. Stress, Psychological—therapy. WM 220 C775i 2003]
  RC521 .C665 2003
  362.1'9683—dc21   2002030438
                                                                            CIP

Printed in the United States of America by Maple-Vail.

Contents

Contributors

Soledad Argüelles, PhD
Center on Adult Development
and Aging
University of Miami
Miami, FL

Trinidad Argüelles, PhD
Center on Adult Development
and Aging
University of Miami
Miami, FL

Patricia Arean, PhD
University of California,
San Francisco
Department of Psychiatry,
Psychiatry Care Clinic
San Francisco, CA

Michelle Bourgeois, PhD
Department of Communication
Disorders
Florida State University
Tallahassee, FL

Louis Burgio, PhD
The University of Alabama
Applied Gerontology Program
Tuscaloosa, AL

Robert Burns, MD
VA Medical Center (11H)
Memphis, TN

James A. D'Andrea, PhD
VISN 21, Mental Illness Research
and Education Clinical Center
(MIRECC)
VA Palo Alto Health Care System
Menlo Park, CA

Helen Davies, MS, RN
Stanford/VA Alzheimer's Disease
Research Center of California
Palo Alto, CA

Elizabeth Edgerly, PhD
Alzheimer's Association of
Northern California, Greater
San Francisco Bay Area Chapter
Mountain View, CA

Susan E. Fisher
University of Alabama
Tuscaloosa, AL

Laura N. Gitlin, PhD
Community and Homecare
Research Division
Thomas Jefferson University
Senior Health Institute
Jefferson Health System
Philadelphia, PA

Benjamin H. Gottlieb, PhD
Psychology Department
University of Guelph
Guelph, Ontario
Canada

Delois Guy, DSN, RN
Gerontology and Geriatric Medicine
Dementia Care Research Program
University of Alabama
  at Birmingham
Birmingham, AL

Lisa P. Gwyther, MSW
Duke University
Duke Medical Center
Durham, NC

William E. Haley, PhD
Department of Gerontology
College of Arts and Sciences
University of South Florida
Tampa, FL

Rita Hargrave, MD
Department of Veterans Affairs
Northern California Health Care
  System
Martinez Veterans Administration
Martinez, CA

Ladson Hinton, MD
University of California, Davis
Department of Psychiatry
Sacramento, CA

Gayle Iwamasa, PhD
Department of Psychology
University of Indianapolis
Indianapolis, IN

Julia Kasl-Godley, PhD
VA Palo Alto Health Care System
Palo Alto, CA

Kathleen Kelly, MPA
Family Caregiver Alliance
San Francisco, CA

Ellen J. Klausner, PhD
Department of Psychiatry
Cornell University Medical Center
White Plains, NY

Sean A. Lauderdale, MA
Aging Treatment Studies Program
VA Palo Alto Health Care System
  and
Stanford University School of
  Medicine
Menlo Park, CA

Diane Feeney Mahoney, PhD, RN
HRCA Research and Training
  Institute
Hebrew Rehabilitation Center
  for Aged
Boston, MA

Jennifer Martindale-Adams, EdD
VA Medical Center
Memphis, TN

Katie Maslow, MSW
Alzheimer's Association
Washington, DC

Mary Mittelman, DrPH
Silberstein Aging & Dementia
  Research Center
New York University Medical
  Center
New York, NY

Lisa Montes, BA
Alzheimer's Association of
  Northern California, Greater
  San Francisco Bay Area Chapter
Mountain View, CA

Linda Nichols, PhD
VA Medical Center (11H)
Memphis, TN

Marcia G. Ory, PhD
Department of Social and
    Behavioral Health
School of Rural Public Health
Texas A & M University
    System—Health Sciences Center
University Park Plaza
College Station, TX

Darlyne Redd, MSW
University Alzheimer Center
Fairhill Center for Aging
Cleveland, OH

Richard Schulz, PhD
University Center for Social and
    Urban Research
University of Pittsburgh
Pittsburgh, PA

John Selstad, BA
National Chronic Care Consortium
Bloomington, MN

Nancy Solano, PhD
Older Adult and Family Center
VA Palo Alto Health Care System
    and
Stanford University School of
    Medicine
Menlo Park, CA

Ann Steffen, PhD
Department of Psychology
University of Missouri-St. Louis
St. Louis, MO

Alan Stevens, PhD
Division of Gerontology/Geriatric
    Medicine
The University of Alabama
    at Birmingham
School of Medicine
Birmingham, AL

Sandy Chen Stokes, MSN, RN
John XXIII Multi-Service Center
San Jose, CA

Edith Yau, MA
Alzheimer's Association of
    Northern California, Greater
    San Francisco Bay Area Chapter
Mountain View, CA

Antonette Zeiss, PhD
VA Palo Alto Health Care System
    (116 B)
Palo Alto, CA

L. McKenzie Zeiss, MA
University of California Irvine
Irvine, CA

Preface

E vidence is continuing to accumulate that family caregivers who experience increased stress and strain due to their participation in care activities are more likely to have higher morbidity and mortality than caregivers who report little or no difficulty (e.g., Schulz & Beach, 1999). It also is becoming increasingly clear that a pivotal factor in making the decision to place a relative in an institutional setting is the caregiver's appraisal of his or her incapability to continue to provide high-quality care for a loved one in the family setting. As concerned caregivers continue periodically to wrestle with the dilemma of placement, they invariably must consider the delicate balance between their capabilities versus the ever-changing requirements for maintaining high-quality care. The decision to place comes when the balance between these two is eroded. It is clearly understood by researchers, practitioners, and policy makers alike that at the point in caregiving when this occurs, there is a monumental economic impact on both family and societal resources. Perhaps the two most important factors in this equation are perceived decline in their own health status along with increasingly demanding and complex health care and behavioral management requirements with regard to their care-receiver. Because stress and strain are proving to be important determinants of health status, efforts to alleviate these not only may improve quality of life in the family unit, but also may be extremely cost-effective in terms of economic resources by delaying or permanently avoiding institutionalization.

Against this backdrop, it is reasonable to consider any and all assistance programs that might serve this end. However, without careful scrutiny the end-point of such reasoning could be wasteful "shotgun" intervention programs. It behooves interested professionals to expand their notions of what might be considered potential interventions and begin to implement evaluations of their efficacy and effectiveness in alleviating caregiver stress. Furthermore, as one considers the magnitude of factors that potentially aggravate the tasks of care-giving, one could ask if intervention programs at multiple levels (from the individual to the family system and even to the larger community) may operate symbiotically to enhance quality of life for caregivers or antagonistically to increase the burden and stresses confronting them. At the present time we have limited empirical data to address such questions, and even fewer models that have been developed to guide us in our efforts to evaluate the interaction of multilevel, multifaceted intervention programs.

As our thinking along these lines took shape, we learned that the editorial staff at Springer Publishing Company also perceived a need to publish a volume on intervention programs for dementia caregivers. We were encouraged by Springer to address these issues in an edited book that would include contributions from prominent researchers, practitioners, and policy makers who are focusing on the challenges of developing cost-effective interventions with a variety of different caregiving populations.

The three chapters in part 1 outline emerging themes and pose challenges that require continued theoretical exploration and development. In contrast, in part 2 we have included seven chapters that present a broad array of practical intervention strategies developed by individuals from different professional disciplines (including, for example, medicine, social work, occupational therapy, nursing, psychology, and geropsychiatry). Several novel approaches are presented, such as the use of technological advances to help distressed caregivers and the value of partnering with primary care physicians to improve quality of life for both patient and caregiver.

Part 3 presents innovative interventions with specific populations that have received relatively little attention in the caregiving literature to date. These are racial and ethnic minority caregivers, male caregivers, and caregivers who self-identify as lesbian, gay, bisexual, or transgender. Finally, we conclude by recommending several directions for future research.

In this volume, we have sought to provide an overview of the current state of the art with respect to dementia caregiving intervention research. We have also included theoretical developments that we hope will be beneficial to all professionals interested in working with caregivers, whether they be researchers, clinicians, or policy makers. We anticipate that casual readers will find this information useful as well as they pursue their professional careers; perhaps they will even be encouraged to join us in addressing the future challenges of developing and refining multilevel, multifaceted interventions.

We are grateful to the authors for the breadth and depth of their contributions, and for their remarkable cooperation in the editing process. We would like to thank especially Helvi Gold, our section editor, for her patience and encouragement in the development of this book. Without her support and the support of others in Springer Publishing Company, the final completion of this work would never have been realized.

LARRY W. THOMPSON,
DOLORES GALLAGHER-THOMPSON,
AND DAVID W. COON

REFERENCE

Schulz, R., & Beach, S. (1999). Caregiving as a risk factor for mortality: The caregiver health effects study. *Journal of the American Medical Association, 282,* 2215–2219.

1

Background Issues

1

Family Caregivers: Enduring and Emergent Themes

David W. Coon, Marcia G. Ory, and Richard Schulz

The dramatic aging of the American population has focused attention on chronic illnesses and their societal impact (Administration on Aging, 2000a; Federal Interagency Forum, 2000; Robert Wood Johnson Foundation, 2001). The realities of chronic illness not only impact the older persons themselves, but also drive the need for informal care from families and friends. However, this growing need is emerging just as societal shifts such as smaller family sizes, rising divorce rates, and growing numbers of dual income families are attenuating the number of informal caregivers readily available to assist current and future cohorts of impaired older adults (National Health Council, 2001; Schulz, O'Brien, Bookwala, & Fleissner, 1995). Yet caregiving currently remains very much a "family affair," with the majority of informal care being shouldered by family and friends. A recent national telephone survey found that nearly one in four U.S. households included at least one caregiver who provided unpaid care to help someone at least 50 years of age take care of himself or herself. Overall, these findings translate into approximately 22 million caregiving households nationwide (National Alliance for Caregiving and the American Association of Retired Persons [NAC/AARP, 1997]). Caregiving tasks and burdens are often numerous and varied and frequently change across the course of an illness. They can range from the simple running of errands and provision of emotional support to assisting with bathing, feeding, or other activities of daily living and the management of disruptive behaviors. Family and friends typically have to juggle their lives to encompass these care responsibilities and their related stressors while at the same time trying to fulfill other substantive familial and social roles (e.g., spouse, parent, and friend, employee, volunteer, and community member). These caregiving responsibilities and the need to balance roles often come with a price—a substantial amount of caregiver stress and distress. As a result, many family caregivers become our "hidden patients" struggling with their own mental and physical health concerns (Administration on Aging, 2000b; Bookwala, Yee, & Schulz, 2000; Coon, Schulz, & Ory, 1999; Fengler & Goodrich, 1979; Schulz & Quittner, 1998).

Caring for a family member or friend with Alzheimer's disease or a related progressive dementia appears to come with a special set of challenges. Numerous studies illustrate the deleterious personal, health, and social impacts of dementia care including its astounding economic costs (e.g., Harrow et al., 2002; Leon, Cheng, & Neumann, 1998; Ory, Hoffman, Lee, Tennstedt, & Schulz, 1999; Schulz et al., 1995). Today's caregivers of people with dementia provide care for longer than ever before and more frequently experience greater emotional distress, higher use of psychotropic medications, poorer self-reported physical health, and compromised immune function than their noncaregiving counterparts (e.g., Schulz et al., 1995; Zarit, Johansson, & Jarrott, 1998). Moreover, caregivers of persons with dementia in comparison to caregivers of nondementia persons spend more time providing care, report more physical and mental health problems and caregiver strain, and describe additional employment complications, greater family conflict, and more family and leisure time constraints (Ory et al., 1999). These points not only illustrate the importance of acknowledging the needs of both these types of caregivers relative to noncaregivers, but also stress that service providers, program developers, researchers, and policy makers learn to identify the best ways to assist caregivers in each group, because the two groups may differ with regard to their stressors, perceived stress, and need for informal and formal support to help maintain their physical and mental health (Coon et al., 1999; Ory et al., 1999).

This chapter extends our own prior work by presenting a key set of ongoing and emergent themes in family caregiving of persons with dementia that we find particularly relevant for the development of interventions designed to address the needs of these caregivers (e.g., Coon & Thompson, 2002; Ory et al., 1999; Schulz, 2000; Schulz et al., in press). Many of these themes are pertinent to other types of caregivers and may be extended or modified in consideration of their particular needs and situations. In addition, a number of our themes are interwoven among the remaining chapters of this book, exemplifying the significant strides made in recent years in interventions designed to address the needs of diverse groups of family caregivers of persons with dementia.

BUILDING AND TRANSPORTING FRAMEWORKS FOR CAREGIVER INTERVENTIONS

Although the stressors and strains associated with dementia care are well documented, the majority of interventions described in caregiver intervention research are still not explicitly theory-based or theory-driven. This practice often generates intervention methods, designs, and measurement strategies that are disconnected from one another and leads to results that are in conflict with one another (Bourgeois, Schulz, & Burgio, 1996). Even for those interventions that are unequivocally theory-driven, descriptions of their theoretical frameworks and their relationship to intervention components is frequently lacking, leaving service providers and policy makers without frameworks that help translate significant findings into viable programs and services at local levels. Effective frameworks and their relevant intervention protocols that are easily transportable into service settings are needed for the overall caregiving process as well as for caregiving interventions themselves. Involving service providers, program administrators, and policy makers in the development or refinement of models can help maximize their utility in the service or practice arena. This is a critical step for translating research-based programs into intervention strategies, programs, and services that can reach large numbers of people in real-world settings. The chapters in this book describe a variety of steps taken to develop theory-based innovative interventions that are transferable to numerous organizations and community settings that serve today's family caregivers.

Expanding Models to Capture the Dynamics of Caregiving

Most current caregiving research is built on stress and coping or stress-process models (e.g., Haley, Levine, Brown, & Bartolucci, 1987; Lazarus & Folkman, 1984; Pearlin, Mullan, Semple, & Skaff, 1990); however, ongoing investigations into dementia caregiving continue to uncover its multidimensional nature. These complexities of dementia caregiving suggest that new models or modifications to existing models are needed to help us better understand the dynamic relationships among caregiver, care recipient, and social and physical environmental variables, as well as the critical linkages between these relationships and caregiver outcomes. It is particularly important that clinical researchers, service providers, and policy makers have useful frameworks to conceptualize effectively the caregiving needs of tomorrow's diverse caregiving families. We need to understand how caregiving processes and outcomes are influenced by the growing numbers of caregivers from blended and other nontraditional families, long-distance family caregivers, and families with divergent cultural views of the definitions and meanings of dementia, caregiver stress, and family caregiving itself. Different causes of stress and distress among distinct populations of caregivers may require new models or building flexibility into current models to incorporate some uniquely tailored prevention or treatment components. However, both approaches will require increasing our understanding of caregiving dynamics, especially with regard to the unique patterns of care among caregivers from different populations, such as different ethnic and racial minority caregivers, gay and lesbian caregivers who are navigating discriminatory care arenas, and rural families providing care in service-poor regions (Coon et al., 1999; Fredriksen-Goldsen & Scharlach, 2001; Gallagher-Thompson, Solano, Coon, & Árean, in press; Gallagher-Thompson, Haley, et al., 2002).

Models of caregiver service utilization as part of the caregiving process are also warranted, including those that help identify and overcome barriers to service utilization such as lack of awareness, lack of recognition that services are needed, time and cost constraints, and language or cultural barriers, as well as concerns about discrimination by groups of minority caregivers. Such models are particularly timely given the recent allocation of family caregiving monies to state area agencies on aging through the National Family Caregiver Support Program (Administration on Aging, 2000b). The development and investigation of service utilization models in turn could be expanded with explorations of social marketing principles (e.g., Nichols, Malone, Tarlowe, & Loewenstein, 2000) or other strategies that help service providers, program developers and policy makers to design and disseminate more effectively available intervention programs and services to caregiving families.

In response to these issues, new models are emerging in the caregiving literature that attempt to address the dynamics of caregiving and service utilization. For example, Montgomery and Kosloski's marker framework looks at the developmental phases of caregiving process as determined by the needs of different types of caregivers (Montgomery & Kosloski, 1999), and rests on two premises: (a) there is no single, generic caregiver role, but rather caregiving emerges from prior role relationships and is integrated with other roles; and (b) caregiving is a dynamic process that unfolds over time with variable durations for different caregivers. The process encompasses seven key "markers" or important points in the caregiving trajectory that mark significant shifts in the caregiving process (e.g., defining oneself as a caregiver, seeking assistance and formal service use, and placement). Moreover, distinct groups of caregivers (e.g., spouses versus adult children) are assumed to experience markers differently and at different intervals, leading to alternate caregiving trajectories that require unique types of services. Similarly, Caron's model (Caron, Pattee, & Otteson, 2000) emphasizes phases of caregiving, rather than stage of disease, whereby caregiving is defined in terms of tasks and challenges faced by families along a continuum of caregiving, which ranges from prediagnosis, diagnosis, role change, and chronic caregiving to the transition to alternative care and end-of-life issues. The use of the framework by the Chronic Care Network for Alzheimer's Disease project (a national demonstration project described in chapter 8; and Maslow & Selstad, 2001) led to the development of a grid that lists objectives for each caregiving phase and specific local information, programs, and services available to reach those objectives. However, whatever the models and theories used to guide our understanding of the caregiver process including caregiver service utilization, it will be very important to consider how effectively these frameworks characterize the needs of diverse caregivers at different points along their caregiving careers.

Differentiating and Characterizing Intervention Models

In addition to the theories of caregiving process, service providers and clinical researchers alike would benefit from more explicit descriptions of the theories and models that guide the development and implementation of successful caregiver interventions. For example, is the intervention framed within an environmental-press theory that emphasizes alterations or modifications of the living environment? Or is it driven by psychologically oriented theories of behavior change from cognitive or behavioral traditions that focus on reducing caregiver emotional distress or care recipient problem behaviors? or is it derived from a family systems tradition that extends beyond the caregiver-care recipient dyad? In addition, descriptions of theory-based interventions and their outcome data need to identify more clearly the underlying pathways through which positive change is proposed to occur. Such information will help lead to a greater understanding of which caregiver interventions work for whom. The diverse sociocultural histories and other individual differences of caregivers including the particular points when interventions are accessed suggest that a combination of theoretical frameworks may be necessary to explain how positive change unfolds (Coon et al., 1999; Gitlan et al., 2000).

Recent discussions of stepped care models in the psychological literature (e.g., Davison, 2000; Haaga, 2000) are pertinent to the exploration of individual difference variables as well as to the tailoring of interventions to meet the unique needs of divergent groups of caregivers. If applied to family caregivers, stepped care models would be built on the assumption that not all caregivers would need the same type and intensity of intervention. Moreover, interventionists would want to begin with the most minimally intensive and intrusive intervention that a given group of caregivers (e.g., wives or daughters) would most likely respond to favorably. In stepped care models, treatment monitoring provides an essential guide to intervention continuation or alteration and ultimately serves as a tool to minimize costs. Interventionists only begin to implement more intensive, and potentially more intrusive, interventions when the less intensive interventions have failed or when those interventions are not in the best interest of the caregiver. For example, ongoing failure to respond to a lower level of care could ultimately discourage future help-seeking by the caregiver or undermine positive treatment response to other levels or types of interventions. Ideally, screens or initial assessments ultimately would be developed to match caregivers with appropriate intervention type and intensity based on empirically supported linkages among initial and ongoing assessments, treatment steps, and outcomes. Still, even with such tools, clinical judgment will often be required to implement these general principles with specific cases of caregivers (Davison, 2000; Haaga, 2000).

Finally, Schulz and his colleagues recently developed a conceptual model with utility for both providers and researchers that helps characterize caregiver interventions, their content, process, and goals. The framework uses the following intervention components in its classification scheme:

1. *the primary entity targeted* (e.g., the caregiver, the care recipient, or the social or physical environment)
2. *the primary domain targeted* (such as one's knowledge, behavior, or affect)
3. the *intensity* of the intervention, including the amount and frequency of interventionist contact with the intervention participant
4. *personalization*, or the extent to which the intervention is tailored to the individual needs of the participant (Czaja, Schulz, Lee, & Belle, 2001; Schulz, Gallagher-Thompson, Haley, & Czaja, 2000).

This taxonomy can be used as a tool where interventions can be classified and identified as fitting the parameters needed by the caregivers served within particular programs or by identifying areas where additional caregiver intervention research is needed. Thus, it may prove useful in the development, description, and translation of models and their interventions into service arenas.

IN PURSUIT OF INTERVENTION OUTCOMES

Caregiving intervention studies to date have included (with varying degrees of success) a myriad of outcomes ranging from caregiver mental health and distress to care-recipient behavior problems and institutionalization. The appropriate identification of outcomes rests in the clear identification of both the proximal and distal outcomes of the intervention (Kennet, Burgio, & Schulz, 2000). The taxonomy described in the previous section can help researchers and program evaluators link relevant primary and secondary outcomes to the parameters of their particular interventions. Too often, interventions fail to assess their proximal goals, focusing instead on the big-ticket distal outcomes like service utilization, time to institution-alization, or reduction of depression. However, proximal outcomes are essential in helping us understand how interventions work. For example, an intervention designed to reduce caregiver depression by increasing their engagement in pleas-ant activities needs to measure both the distal outcome of depression as well as the proximal outcome of caregiver pleasant activities. Without a measure of pleasant activities, we muddy our understanding of how or why the intervention does or doesn't work. This also raises the issue of targeting interventions to appropriate groups of caregivers. Caregivers who are not reporting depressive symptoms and a constriction of pleasant activities, but rather are struggling with anger as a result of care-recipient problem behaviors, are unlikely to benefit from this intervention or be able to report even fewer depressive symptoms.

Intervention researchers also need to consider incorporating outcome measures that can easily be adopted by service providers and program staff in the transfer of interventions to the community for ongoing monitoring and evaluation. How-ever, a tension exists between the various stakeholders interested in caregiver interventions. Policy makers and other researchers often want to see outcome measures commonly used with other populations to facilitate comparisons be-tween caregivers and noncaregivers. Yet those outcomes do not always reflect the desired outcomes of intervention participants themselves or their service providers, which suggests the need for explorations beyond traditional outcome measures. This exploration may prove particularly important for nonmajority caregivers. Gottlieb and his colleagues in chapter 2 expand upon this debate and raise important issues regarding the development and application of measures to assess the extent to which interventions are implemented as intended, because problems with implementation erode confidence in both the intervention and its outcomes.

Extending Outcomes

Most outcomes in caregiver intervention research have focused on the mental health or psychosocial consequences of caregiving. However, caregiving can also negatively affect caregivers' physical health and health behaviors (Schulz et al., 1995). For example, recent data from the Caregiver Health Effects Study showed that older adults caring for a disabled spouse who experienced strain as a result of their caregiving role were 63% more likely to die within 4 years than noncare-givers (Schulz & Beach, 1999). Similarly, caregivers also appear less likely than their noncaregiving counterparts to practice preventive health behaviors that are important in chronic disease prevention and control (Burton, Newsom, Schulz, Hirsch, & German, 1997; King & Brassington, 1997; Scharlach, Midanik, Run-kle, & Soghikian, 1997). These findings underscore that health care and other service providers might need to see caregiver/care-recipient dyads as a unit to assess both the care recipient's and the caregiver's risk for negative physical health outcomes (Schulz & Beach, 1999). The American Medical Association's recent addition to its Web site of a Caregiver Health Assessment section— including a caregiver self-assessment tool, resources for caregivers, and a dementia guide—serves as another indicator of growing interest in caregiver physical-health outcomes. These recent research findings also underscore the importance of developing and testing interventions that help caregivers maintain as many healthy lifestyle behaviors as possible while facing the arduous demands of family caregiving. As an initial step, the first systematic investigation of a physical-activity intervention tailored to caregivers of persons with dementia demonstrated that female caregivers could indeed benefit from a regular moderate-intensity exercise program in terms of reductions in stress-induced cardiovascular reactivity and improvements in sleep quality (King, Baumann, O'Sullivan, Wilcox, & Castro, 2002).

Although the vast majority of research delineates negative effects of caregiving, an expanding literature suggests that caregiver stress and burden may be counterbalanced in part by the positive aspects of caregiving, or caregiver gain, including such aspects as the opportunity to serve as a role model for others or give back to the care recipient, prevention of further care-recipient deterioration, increased self-esteem, an enhanced sense of meaning or purpose, and feeling appreciated or other feelings of pleasure (e.g., Farran, Keane-Hagerty, Salloway, Kupferer, & Wilken, 1991; Kramer, 1997a; Lawton, Rajagopal, Brody, & Kleban, 1992; Miller & Lawton, 1997; NAC/AARP, 1997). This relatively new caregiver literature provides increasing support for the "gains" perspective as a particularly meaningful arena for research and intervention development, especially given several studies suggesting that individual difference variables such as race, ethnicity, gender or education may be related to perceived rewards from caregiving (e.g., Kramer, 1997b; Lawton et al., 1992; Picot, Debanne, Namazi, & Wykle, 1997). These positive aspects may affect the quality of care as well, having beneficial effects for both caregivers and care recipients.

Quality of care as an intervention outcome has received relatively little attention in the caregiving literature (Schulz & Williamson, 1997) but is deserving of future consideration. For example, some research suggests that certain caregivers may be at particular risk for abuse, including caregivers who experience violence from their care recipient, experience a lack of adequate help from their informal or formal supports, or report certain care-recipient behavior problems like verbal or physical aggression, embarrassing public displays, or refusal to eat or take medications (e.g., Anetzberger, 1987; Compton, Flanagan, & Gregg, 1997; Pillemer & Suitor, 1992). These findings suggest not only the need for measures to capture quality of care for use in caregiving intervention programs, but also intervention strategies designed to target various points along the spectrum of care. These strategies might be designed to support the potential enhancement of exemplary caregiving activities and the maintenance of current satisfactory care activities or to prevent physical, psychological, or financial harm to the care recipient.

Studies that further explore physical health and health behaviors, positive aspects of caregiving, and quality of care within the caregiving process can benefit theories or frameworks of caregiver adaptation that are useful in the development and evaluation of caregiver interventions. Service providers and program developers, in turn, can benefit from intervention studies designed to have an impact on these specific outcomes.

A Move Toward Clinical Significance

As a complement to the outcome issues presented thus far, a recent review of dementia caregiver interventions extends the traditional discussion of caregiver outcomes beyond statistical significance to include issues of clinical significance or the *practical importance* of the intervention effects (Schulz et al., in press). This recent review echoes our position that researchers, program evaluators, and policy makers need to examine the extent to which an intervention makes a "real" difference in the everyday lives of caregivers, their care recipients, or their families (e.g., Kazdin, 1999; Kendall, 1999). Schulz and colleagues broaden the relevance of clinical significance beyond just the traditional psychotherapeutic view of change in symptomatology and categorize clinical significance of caregiver intervention outcomes into four domains believed to be important to the individual or society: *symptomatology, quality of life, social significance,* and *social validity.* Table 1.1 lists these domains and provides their definitions and relevant examples. In sum, recent caregiving intervention studies demonstrate increasing promise in affecting symptomatology, including the treatment of depression, as well as social significance, particularly with regard to delayed institutionalization of the care recipient. In addition, caregivers in most studies rate the interventions as beneficial or valuable, which adds clinical significance support in terms of social validity. However, researchers, policy makers, service providers, and caregivers themselves may hold different views on the relative importance of these domains. The need to examine intervention outcomes in these domains is obviously formidable, given that most outcome measures have been normed on predominantly Caucasian female samples. We recommend further evaluation and potential adaptation to accurately capture the experiences of other caregiving groups. Cultural proscriptions may also encourage different groups of caregivers to hold divergent views on the relative importance of these domains. Still, a recognition of the clinical significance of outcomes and an attempt to measure at least some aspect of each domain will not only help advance caregiver intervention

TABLE 1.1   Domains of Clinical Significance

Domain of Significance	Definition	Examples
Symptom-atology	Extent to which an individual returns to normal functioning or moves from one diagnostic category to a less severe one.	Measures of depression, anxiety, anger, psychological morbidity, physical health symptoms, clinical health assessments (e.g., blood pressure, exercise stress tests).
Quality of Life	Extent to which interventions broadly improve the quality of life of an individual as measured by multidimensional instruments or indicators.	Life satisfaction, morale or marital satisfaction, caregiver burden, social support.
Social Significance	Extent to which outcomes are important to society.	Amount of service utilization, patient functional status, time to care recipient placement or time spent on caregiving tasks.
Social Validity	Extent to which treatment goals, procedures and outcomes are acceptable to caregivers, care recipients, caregiving families.	Caregiver or expert ratings of the interventions and their impact on their lives and those they care about (their care recipients, their families). Caregiver recommendation of intervention program to others.

research, but can also help us bridge the translation gap between clinical research, practice, and policy by exploring outcomes in at least some domains relevant to each group of stakeholders.

PROMISING INTERVENTIONS AT THE MILLENNIUM

Over the years, several types of caregiver interventions and support services have proven useful to caregivers of persons with dementia. However, the magnitude of their utility depends not only on the outcomes measured and their related domains of clinical significance, but also on the care recipient's level of impairment and the caregiver's background characteristics, including their psychosocial strengths and vulnerabilities. Still, numerous literature reviews have been unable to identify *the* antidote to alleviate caregiver stress and its sequelae (e.g., Bourgeois et al., 1996; Dunkin & Anderson-Hanley, 1998; Kennet et al., 2000; Knight, Lutzky, & Macofsky-Urban, 1993; Pusey & Richards, 2001; Schulz et al., in press). Clearly, no single, easily implemented and consistently effective method exists for achieving the same clinically significant outcomes across caregivers. This is especially true when considering racial and ethnic diversity as it is overly simplistic to assume that interventions successful with caregivers from one background will automatically achieve the same results with another significantly different group of caregivers. Yet these reviews do support the claim that comprehensive, intensive, and individually tailored interventions appear more likely to be effective than interventions without similar characteristics. These characteristics may support in part the successful outcomes associated with multicomponent approaches (e.g., Mittelman, Ferris, Shulman, Steinberg, & Levin, 1996; Ostwald, Hepburn, Caron, Burns, & Mantell, 1999), which through their assortment of intervention techniques may create caregiving interventions that address a wider variety of concerns for more diverse groups of caregivers.

Knowledge and Skill Training

In general, caregivers are likely to benefit from enhanced knowledge about disease, the caregiving role, and resources available to assist them in that role. But many caregivers may have additional education and training needs, especially in terms of specific skills necessary to effectively handle care-recipient behavior problems (e.g., Burgio et al., 2002; Teri, Logsdon, Uomoto, & McCurry, 1997) or manage their own thoughts, feelings, and behavior in response to caregiving (e.g., Gallagher-Thompson, Lovett, et al., 2000; Oswalt et al., 1999). Emerging work indicates that such skill programs can be culturally tailored to meet the needs of different racial or ethnic groups, suggesting that further development of skill-training interventions that attend to the special needs of minority caregivers is also necessary (e.g., Burgio et al., 2002; Gallagher-Thompson, Árean, Rivera, & Thompson, 2001; Gallagher-Thompson, Coon, et al., 2002).

Technological and Environmental Approaches

Similarly, the role of technology in assisting family caregivers of the new century has gained considerable attention—from telephone-based technologies to Web-based education and support—with some intervention studies that examine the successful combination of skill-focused technological interventions, including telephone-based linkages, video training, and computer screen phones as modalities to deliver therapeutic content for stress management (e.g., Czaja & Rubert, in press; Mahoney, Tarlow, & Sandaire, 1998; Steffen, 2000). As described in chapter 5, preliminary results of family caregiving intervention that combines technological support for linking family caregivers to other family members and to community resources demonstrated positive mental health outcomes, especially for Cuban American caregivers (Czaja & Rubert, in press). As technological advances, including telemedicine, more frequently permeate caregivers' lives, these combined approaches will require shifts in the caregiving models used by researchers and in the skill sets considered necessary for professionals who serve caregiving families. There is also growing evidence of the benefits achieved by simultaneously treating the caregiver and the care recipient (e.g., providing medications or memory retraining in the early stages of impairment), as well as by modifying the social and physical environment so it is supportive of caregiver and patient activities (Gitlin, Corcoran, Winter, Boyce, & Hauck, 2001; Schulz et al., in press). Furthermore, the field could benefit from investigations of interventions that are focused "upstream" in the caregiving process, intervening with patients and caregivers from a prevention perspective before caregivers are already saddled with depression, overwhelmed with patient behavioral disturbances, or embroiled in caregiving crises.

Although the complexity and rigor of interventions studies continue to improve, sample sizes are often too small to detect effects and several methodological concerns remain, including a lack of randomized controlled trials and very little treatment implementation data being collected or reported (Bourgeois et al., 1996; Burgio et al., 2001; Schulz et al., in press). In addition, multicomponent interventions have yet to provide information about the relative effectiveness of their components (Bourgeois et al., 1996; Zarit et al., 1998), fueling questions about the mechanisms that drive their successful outcomes and making it difficult to determine how to maximize the benefits for different groups of caregivers (e.g., different cultural groups, caregivers of individuals with different impairments, employed caregivers, etc.) while minimizing costs to both caregivers and service agencies. Thus, a thorough investigation of the central mechanisms of various multicomponent interventions could help in the development of stepped care approaches that are individualized to meet the needs of diverse groups of caregivers.

BUILDING SUSTAINABLE PARTNERSHIPS

The formation and maintenance of strong organizational and community partnerships is essential to our goal of identifying and accessing family caregivers and effectively addressing their needs and concerns through proven intervention programs. Partners themselves can be defined as organizations or organizational departments that come together in a social change effort and thereby serve as conduits to target audiences (Nichols et al., 2000; Nichols et al., 2002), whether the partnership occurs across or within research, university, health care, or community-based systems.

For example, the National Institute on Aging and the National Institutes for Nursing Research provided sponsorship for a unique, multisite research project entitled Resources for Enhancing Alzheimer's Caregiver Health (REACH). The primary goal of this effort was to test systematically well-specified and theory-based caregiver intervention approaches that were culturally tailored to meet the needs of racial and ethnic majority and minority caregiving populations (Coon et al., 1999). All six REACH sites, based on their local environments and target populations, formed key partnerships with an array of organizations such as local Alzheimer's Association chapters, community centers, churches, Alzheimer's day-care centers, physician offices, and home health agencies and included sites actively partnering with community-based organizations that served the racial and ethnic populations targeted. Similarly, the Chronic Care Network for Alzheimer's disease demonstration project, mentioned previously, is sponsored by the Alzheimer's Association and the National Chronic Care Consortium and spans seven national sites. Each site in the initiative sought to foster and strengthen partnerships among managed care systems, Alzheimer's Association chapters, and other community agencies. From the outset, the CCN/AD partnerships worked together to develop and put into practice user-friendly tools designed to facilitate the identification and care management of patients with dementia and their family caregivers across the disease trajectory (Maslow & Selstad, 2001).

Partnerships and the Social Marketing of Interventions

Relevant to the discussion of strong partnerships is the social marketing approach to recruitment and retention of caregivers of persons with dementia in clinical research that has recently emerged in the literature (Nichols, Malone, Tarlow, & Loewenstein, 2000; Nichols et al., 2002). Although social marketing is usually used in public health initiatives to change health behavior, this framework warrants serious consideration in the marketing of interventions, programs and services to family caregivers. Social marketing not only incorporates the concepts of *product, price, place,* and *promotion* into the successful design and marketing of intervention programs, but also emphasizes the important role of *partners* in their successful development, delivery, and continuation. This framework stresses the need to clearly identify and address the needs, perceptions, and values of the intervention's target audience (e.g., family caregivers). Therefore, caregiver interventions (our *product*) must also meet the needs, interests, and values of caregivers at a *price* in terms of time, money, and effort acceptable to the specific group of caregivers targeted (e.g., male caregivers or family caregivers in the

Latino community). In addition, serious attention needs to be given to *place*, *promotion*, and *partners*, including the intervention's accessibility for caregivers, the advertising and incentives necessary to interest the caregiving groups targeted, and the invaluable role of partners in accessing and referring caregivers for continued program enrollment and success. When research, practice, and policy partners work in tandem to develop models that describe caregiving dynamics as well as the intervention frameworks investigated and implemented, it translates to effective programs based on these models that are more likely to garner support for continuance. If an organization's administrators, clinicians, and services providers are viewed as vital members of these partnerships from the partnership's inception, they can, in turn, facilitate both the initial integration and the ongoing maintenance of effective caregiver interventions within their organizations and across the partnership. Unfortunately, well-meaning professionals too often have assumed "if we build it, they will come," rather than taking the time to gather input systematically from other partners and their constituents about these marketing components prior to developing caregiving interventions.

Partnerships like REACH and CCN/AD have already integrated several social marketing components into their projects. They naturally call for multiple disciplines working together as teams to design, develop, and improve caregiver interventions across the continuum of care from prediagnosis and early stages of a disease through end-of-life issues and caregiver bereavement. In addition, these partnerships share recruitment and retention activities for caregiver interventions, programs, and services and plan for ongoing caregiver assistance and the sustainability of successful intervention activities after initial research or other sponsored funding ends. Numerous possibilities exist to form partnerships between various caregiving organizations, religious institutions, local employers, senior centers, and other community agencies to help translate effective caregiver education, training, and support programs from research settings into our communities. Moreover, community partners who provide services to underserved and minority caregivers could help play a central role in disseminating information and translating appropriate interventions into these communities (e.g., Gallagher-Thompson, Árean, et al., 2000; Navaie-Waliser et al., 2001). Chapters by Burgio, Burns, Argüelles and their colleagues in this volume provide additional insight into caregiver interventions that were investigated as part of the REACH and CCN/AD projects.

A CALL FOR INTERVENTIONS AT MULTIPLE LEVELS

The needs of care recipients and their caregivers and families vary across the course of dementia, as well as in response to the vicissitudes of life, such that information, interventions, and services that are useful at one point in the caregiving career may not prove helpful at another. These changes imply that at least periodic if not ongoing assistance is warranted. The future of social and behavioral intervention research with older adults and their families suggests the need for multiple levels of intervention ranging from the *individual* and the *interpersonal* levels to the *organizational, community,* and *policy* levels in order to achieve effective behavior change (Emmons, 2001). Just as there are many pathways to various caregiving outcomes, a diverse collection of proven intervention strategies or techniques at each of these levels will be needed to address the complex needs of caregivers and care recipients in our pluralistic society (Coon & Thompson, 2002). For instance, skill-based interventions that focus on the caregiver (e.g., Gallagher-Thompson, Lovett, et al., 2000) would typify the individual level, whereas skill-based interventions that work with caregiver/care recipient dyads (e.g., Teri et al., 1997) or interventions that include family counseling or integrate family meetings (e.g., Mittelman et al., 1996) would be considered interpersonal in nature.

Establishing Multilevel Linkages

Such a framework also implies that purposeful linkages must be established between successful intervention components identified at each level in order to help maximize and sustain positive behavior change. Thus, successful caregiver interventions delivered at the individual or interpersonal levels will need to be partnered not only with interventions focused at the organizational level (e.g., interventions directed at or through health care systems, senior centers, or faith-based organizations), but also with interventions disseminated through communities (e.g., within retirement communities, assisted-living centers, or public service areas) and more broadly based policy levels. This approach requires the identification and strengthening of existing partnerships or the creation of new partnerships like those described in the previous section. These partnerships should be designed to help caregivers across the course of dementia by taking into consideration both short- and long-term impacts of caregiving on mental, physical, and social health, such as personal and professional role changes and losses, issues associated with anticipatory grief, transitional stressors related to respite care and institutionalization, and end-of-life issues and caregiver bereavement (e.g., Aneshensel, Pearlin, Mullan, Zarit, & Whitlatch, 1995; Schulz & Beach, 1999). For example, the $125 million in fiscal year 2001 for the National Family Caregiver Support Program allocates $113 million from the federal government to the states to work in partnership with their area agencies on aging and local community-service providers in order to provide five basic services for family caregivers (see Table 1.2). This shift in policy may foster new and ongoing partnerships between providers that have the potential to impact not only the individual and interper-

TABLE 1.2   National Family Caregiver Support Program's Five Basic Services

Service	Brief Description
1. Information and Referral	Information to caregivers about available services.
2. Access Assistance	Assistance to caregivers in gaining access to available services.
3. Caregiver Support and Training	Individual counseling, organization of support groups, and caregiver training to assist caregivers in making decisions and solving problems relating to their caregiving roles.
4. Respite	Respite care to enable caregivers to be temporarily relieved from their caregiving responsibilities.
5. Supplemental Services	Supplemental services, on a limited basis, to complement the care provided by caregivers.

sonal levels, but also the organizational and community levels as well. Table 1.3 provides only a handful of basic examples of possible interventions that could be useful to caregivers at each of the five levels.

Successful development of these partnerships and linkages will also call for a shift from the discrete stances taken by individual providers or organizations to acting as change agents within emerging change agencies or up-and-coming partnerships that are focused on systemic change and connections. Thus, service providers and program directors working with caregivers will need to consider expanding their mission beyond the individual or interpersonal intervention levels and look for new ways to facilitate successful linkages across the range of intervention levels from practice to policy.

Moreover, additional agencies need to develop research initiatives and demonstration grant programs for fostering research and community-based partnerships that will explore linkages between these levels. Agencies can do this by following the lead of community-based organizations like the Alzheimer's Association and government agencies within the Department of Health and Human Services, such as the National Institute on Aging, the National Institute for Nursing Research, and the Administration on Aging. Initial support of this kind not only helps identify efficacious and effective caregiver interventions, but also assists service providers who face the realties of limited resources. Translating research into practice is aided by (a) providing assistance to expand their services to meet the needs of the most prevalent groups of caregivers of patients with dementia within a service area, (b) helping to appropriately tailor and then disseminate existing tools and programs to meet the needs of smaller groups of caregivers, and (c)

TABLE 1.3 Multiple Levels of Caregiver Interventions

Level	Examples
Individual	• Caregiver education regarding dementia and its progression. • Individual counseling or support groups for caregivers. • Caregiver relaxation training to manage caregiver stress. • Caregiver skill training to manage their own depression or anger. • Caregiver respite.
Interpersonal	• Caregiver skill training to help manage care recipient behavior problems. • Caregiver and care recipient early stage dementia groups for spouses.
Organizational	• Faith based organizations pooling resources for congregation education on dementia and caregiving, and the development of friendly visitor and respite programs for caregivers. • Partnerships between community-based organizations and primary care setting to create pathways of care for caregivers and care recipients.
Community	• Media and community/service campaigns to increase dementia and caregiving awareness. • Continuous care retirement community education, training and support interventions for the entire community to teach both caregivers and their neighbors and friends about dementia and dementia caregiving.
Policy	• National Family Caregiver Support Program funding allocated to states for their area agencies on aging. • American Medical Association addition of Caregiver Health Assessment and related caregiving material on its web site. • Government and private foundation support for caregiver intervention research and demonstration projects.

supporting the design and development of new intervention programs for diverse groups of caregivers. This support can be designed in ways that strengthen partnerships across multiple intervention levels to increase the likelihood of transportability and sustainability beyond the grant period. Another way to further the translation of research into practice and policy across intervention levels is to encourage interdisciplinary partnership training that includes current and future cost considerations and their evaluation from the outset (Mahoney, Burns, & Harrow, 2000).

However, we must exercise caution in attributing costs solely to the partnership. Interventions must be affordable to caregivers, too; that is, caregivers must be able to reconcile the perceived costs of service utilization with their perceived benefits. Caregivers consideration of the affordability of services includes not only financial costs, but also costs in terms of time, effort, potential family conflict, potential loss of confidentiality, and the like. Stepped care models or approaches that incorporate components from multiple levels of intervention as needed by groups of caregivers or individual caregivers may help minimize these costs, which should increase the likelihood of caregiver service utilization.

Undoubtedly, key challenges remain in the development and dissemination of effective family caregiver interventions. Given the complexity of caregiving issues and the scope and diversity of caregiving, our solutions must now be comprehensive in level and scope and yet flexible enough to be effectively tailored to meet the needs of families within their particular sociocultural contexts (Coon & Thompson, 2002). A multilevel framework should also encourage family caregiver education and intervention to encompass multiple settings and life domains, take advantage of various delivery points for intervention messages, and deliver interventions through multiple modes and communication channels. This approach should encourage us to pinpoint effective ways to embed interventions within ongoing community programs and services as another way to keep costs down and increase transportability. Messages and interventions at multiple levels could go a long way in helping "normalize" the experience of family caregiving in our society. This normalization might in turn foster the readiness of caregivers to accept change (e.g., Keller & White, 1997; Prochaska, Norcross, & DiClemente, 1994)—a readiness that is needed for constructive engagement in service utilization and the adoption of effective intervention strategies.

CAREGIVING INTERVENTIONS FOR A PLURALISTIC SOCIETY

The pluralistic nature of our society is reflected in the variety of beliefs that distinct groups of family caregivers hold about the etiology of dementia, the responsibilities of family caregiving, and the role of formal and informal social support in dementia care. And even though more published literature is emerging that expands our understanding of the needs and experiences of diverse types of family caregivers (e.g., Hinton, Fox, & Leukoff, 1999; Janevic & Connell, 2001; NAC/AARP, 1997; Yeo & Gallagher-Thompson, 1996), the vast majority of today's research on caregiver interventions focuses on the intervention experiences of Caucasian female caregivers. However, family caregivers enter intervention programs with individual histories shaped by multiple layers of social influence, including years of family expectations and peer pressure, social class standing, racial and ethnic identifications, and other cultural influences. These factors help form a complex set of beliefs, values, and expectations regarding dementia and family caregiving that influence the proper courses of action to take, including the appropriateness of help-seeking for caregiving concerns and the suitability of particular intervention strategies prescribed by caregiver programs.

Initial research with caregivers from different racial and ethnic groups confirms that caregiving can vary significantly among groups, including differing levels of reported emotional distress and positive aspects of caregiving (for example, see Aranda & Knight, 1997; Connell & Gibson, 1997; Gonzalez, Gitlin, & Lyons, 1995, for reviews). In contrast, differences in coping resources and social support are less clear, with recent work suggesting that minority caregivers may not have more social support than White caregivers, as was once assumed (Gallagher-Thompson, Árean, et al., 2000; Haley et al., 1995; Janevic & Connell, 2001; Roth, Haley, Owen, Clay, & Goode, 2001). Differences also have been found between other caregiver groups such as men and women and caregiving spouses versus adult children caring for impaired parents (e.g., Gallagher-Thompson, Coon, Rivera, Powers, & Zeiss, 1998; Kramer, 1997b; NAC/AARP, 1997). Much more empirical research is needed to clarify patterns of differences between and within various groups, which could assist with the design or modification of interventions. Substantial qualitative research could prove particularly useful in both measurement and intervention development by capturing group members' own conceptualization of disease, the caregiving role and its relevant outcomes, and broadening investigations beyond just the primary caregiver to the extended family (Gallagher-Thompson, Árean, et al., 2000; Janevic & Connell, 2001). Moreover, similarities across caregiving groups are as important to identify as differences (Aranda, 2001), because shared needs, beliefs, values, coping strategies, and the like might serve as building blocks of interventions applicable to multiple caregiving groups.

Thus, the complexity of the caregiving experience, especially in terms of the variability of caregivers' sociocontexts and their psychosocial resources, suggests the need to develop effective interventions that can be suitably targeted to individuals, with modifications built in to maximize their relevance to more than just one of today's many caregiving constituencies. Still, researchers, service providers, and program developers must exercise caution. The failure to recognize distinctions between groups of caregivers as well as the heterogeneity within groups often results in misinformation, excludes constituent groups of caregivers, and can lead to the development of less successful community services, programs, and policies. Building partnerships with community leaders and gatekeepers at agencies that serve the targeted communities and involving community members from the inception of a project can prove invaluable in creating interventions that are accessible as well as culturally appropriate and acceptable (Gallagher-Thompson et al., in press; Valle, 1998).

The diversity of today's family caregivers should permeate our decision-making throughout the intervention process, including the identification of theoretical models and their components, the development of partnerships, the selection of measures to capture outcomes, and the design and delivery of the intervention, as well as its evaluation and dissemination. Several chapters in this volume, including those by Gallagher-Thompson, Edgerly, Lauderdale, Coon, and their colleagues, encourage professionals to expand their thinking beyond the traditional caregiving "majority" to develop innovative interventions tailored to meet the specific needs and caregiving situations of smaller yet distinct groups of caregiver.

SUMMARY

The goal of this chapter was to present a set of key themes for consideration by researchers, practitioners, and policy makers interested in the development, implementation, evaluation, and dissemination of family caregiver interventions, with particular attention paid to dementia care. These themes encompassed the development and transfer of theory-driven models of care into research and practice, improved measurement of pertinent outcomes and their clinical significance for various stakeholders, the formation of partnerships to sustain interventions and related programs, the development of promising interventions targeted at multiple levels of impact, and the consideration of caregiver diversity in intervention design and delivery. Clearly, numerous substantive challenges remain, including a central charge to identify and disseminate clinically significant and cost-effective caregiver interventions that are applicable to diverse caregiving groups and easily transferable from research settings to the front lines of our communities. We believe consideration of the chapter's themes will help strengthen forthcoming interventions designed to meet this challenge. Our goal is to raise substantive issues to help guide research, practice, and policy discussions to meet the needs of our growing caregiver population.

REFERENCES

Administration on Aging. (2000a). *A profile of older Americans: 2000*. Washington, DC: U.S. Department of Health and Human Services.

Administration on Aging. (2000b). *America's families care: A report on the needs of America's family caregivers*. [On-line]. Available: www.aoa.dhhs.gov/carenetwork/report.html

Aneshensel, C. S., Pearlin, L. I., Mullan, J. T., Zarit, S. H., & Whitlatch, C. J. (1995). *Profiles in caregiving: The unexpected career*. San Diego, CA: Academic Press.

Anetzberger, G. J. (1987). *The etiology of elder abuse by adult offspring*. Springfield, IL: Charles C. Thomas.

Aranda, M. P. (2001). Racial and ethnic factors in dementia care-giving research in the US. *Aging and Mental Health, 5,* S116–S123.

Aranda, M. P., & Knight, B. G. (1997). The influence of ethnicity and culture on the caregiver stress and coping process: A sociocultural review and analysis. *Gerontologist, 37,* 342–254.

Bookwala, J., Yee, J. L., & Schulz, R. (2000). Caregiving and detrimental mental and physical health outcomes. In G. M. Williamson, P. A. Parmelee, & D. R. Shaffer (Eds.), *Physical illness and depression in older adults: A handbook of theory, research, and practice* (pp. 93–131). New York: Plenum Press.

Bourgeois, M. S., Schulz, R., & Burgio, L. (1996). Intervention for caregivers of patients with Alzheimer's disease: A review and analysis of content, process, and outcomes. *International Journal of Human Development, 43,* 35–92.

Burgio, L., Corcoran, M., Lichstein, K. L., Nichols, L., Czaja, S., Gallagher-Thompson, D., Bourgeois, M., Stevens, A., Ory, M., & Schulz, R. (2001). Judging outcomes in psychosocial interventions for dementia caregivers: The problem of treatment implementation. *Gerontologist, 41,* 481–487.

Burgio, L., Stevens, A., Guy, D., Roth, D. L., & Haley, W. F. (2002). *Impact of two psychosocial interventions on White and African American family caregivers of individuals with dementia.* Manuscript submitted for publication.

Burton, L. C., Newsom, J. T., Schulz, R., Hirsch, C., & German, P. S. (1997). Preventive health behaviors among spousal caregivers. *Preventive Medicine, 26,* 162–169.

Caron, W. A., Pattee, J. J., & Otteson, O. J. (2000). *Alzheimer's disease: The family journey.* Plymouth, MN: North Ridge Press.

Compton, S. A., Flanagan, P., & Gregg, W. (1997). Elder abuse in people with dementia in Northern Ireland: Prevalence and predictors in cases referred to a psychiatry of old age service. *International Journal of Geriatric Psychiatry, 12,* 632–635.

Connell, C. M., & Gibson, G. D. (1997). Racial, ethnic and cultural differences in dementia caregiving: Review and analysis. *Gerontologist, 37,* 355–364.

Coon, D. W., & Thompson, L. (2002). Family caregiving for older adults: Emergent and ongoing themes for the behavior therapist. *Behavior Therapist, 25,* 17–20.

Coon, D. W., Schulz, R., & Ory, M. G. (1999). Innovative intervention approaches with Alzheimer's disease caregivers. In D. Biegel & A. Blum (Eds.), *Innovations in practice and service delivery across the lifespan* (pp. 295–325). New York: Oxford University Press.

Czaja, S. J., & Rubert, M. (in press). Telecommunications technology as an aid to family caregivers of persons with dementia. *Psychosomatic Medicine.*

Czaja, S. J., Schulz, R., Lee, C. C., & Belle, S. (2001). *A methodology for describing and decomposing complex psychosocial and behavioral interventions.* Manuscript submitted for publication.

Davison, G. (2000). Stepped care: Doing more with less. *Journal of Consulting and Clinical Psychology, 68,* 580–585.

Dunkin, J. J., & Anderson-Hanley, C. (1998). Dementia caregiver burden: A review of the literature and guidelines for assessment and intervention. *Neurology, 51*(Suppl. 1), S53–S60.

Emmons, K. M. (2001). Behavioral and social science contributions to the health of adults in the United States. In B. D. Smedley & S. L. Syme (Eds.), *Promoting health:*

Intervention strategies from social and behavioral research (pp. 254–321). Washington, DC: National Academy Press.

Farran, C. J., Keane-Hagerty, E., Salloway, S., Kupferer, S., & Wilken, C. S. (1991). Finding meaning: An alternative paradigm for Alzheimer's disease family caregivers. *Gerontologist, 31,* 483–489.

Federal Interagency Forum on Aging Related Statistics (2000). *Older Americans 2000: Key indicators of well-being.* Washington, DC: U.S. Department of Health and Human Services.

Fengler, A. P., & Goodrich, N. (1979). Wives of elderly disabled men: The hidden patients. *Gerontologist, 19,* 175–183.

Fredriksen-Goldsen, K. I., & Scharlach, A. E. (2001). *Families and work: New directions in the 21st century.* New York: Oxford University Press.

Gallagher-Thompson, D., Árean, P., Coon, D., Menéndez, A., Takagi, K., Haley, W., Argüelles, T., Rubert, M., Loewenstein, D., & Szapocznik, J. (2000). Development and implementation of intervention strategies for culturally diverse caregiving populations. In R. Schulz (Ed.), *Handbook on dementia caregiving: Evidence-based interventions for family caregivers* (pp. 151–185). New York: Springer.

Gallagher-Thompson, D., Árean, P., Rivera, P., & Thompson, L. W. (2001). Reducing distress in Hispanic family caregivers using a psychoeducational intervention. *Clinical Gerontologist, 23,* 17–32.

Gallagher-Thompson, D., Coon, D. W., Rivera, P., Powers, D., & Zeiss, A. M. (1998). Family caregiving: Stress, coping and intervention. In M. Hersen & V. B. Van Hasselt (Eds.), *Handbook of clinical geropsychology* (pp. 469–493). New York: Plenum Press.

Gallagher-Thompson, D., Coon, D., Solano, N., Ambler, C., Rabinowitz, R., & Thompson, L. (2002). *Change in indices of distress among Caucasian and Latina caregivers of elderly relatives with dementia: Site specific results from the REACH National Collaborative Study.* Manuscript submitted for publication.

Gallagher-Thompson, D., Haley, W., Guy, D., Rubert, M., Argüelles, T., Zeiss, L. M., Tennstedt, S., & Ory, M. (In press). *Tailoring psychological interventions for ethnically diverse dementia caregivers. Clinical Psychology: Science and Practice.*

Gallagher-Thompson, D., Lovett, S., Rose, J., McKibbin, C., Coon, D. W., Futterman, A., & Thompson, L. W. (2000). Impact of psychoeducational interventions on distressed family caregivers. *Journal of Clinical Geropsychology, 6,* 91–110.

Gallagher-Thompson, D., Solano, N., Coon, D., & Árean, P. (in press). Recruitment and retention of Latina dementia family caregivers in intervention research: Issues to face, lessons to learn. *Gerontologist.*

Gitlan, L. N., Corcoran, M., Martindale-Adams, J., Malone, C., Stevens, A., & Winter, L. (2000). Identifying mechanisms of action: Why and how does intervention work? In R. Schulz (Ed.), *Handbook on dementia caregiving: Evidence-based interventions for family caregivers* (pp. 225–248). New York: Springer.

Gitlan, L. N., Corcoran, M., Winter, L., Bouyce, A., & Hauck, W. W. (2001). A randomized, controlled trial of a home environmental intervention: Effect on efficacy and upset in caregivers and on daily function of persons with dementia. *Gerontologist, 41,* 4–14.

Gonzalez, E., Gitlin, L., & Lyons, K. J. (1995). Review of the literature on African American caregivers of individuals with dementia. *Journal of Cultural Diversity, 2*(2), 40–48.

Haaga, D. A. (2000). Introduction to the special section on stepped care models in psychotherapy. *Journal of Consulting and Clinical Psychology, 68,* 547–548.

Haley, W. E., Levine, E. G., Brown, S. L., & Bartolucci, A. A. (1987). Stress, appraisal, coping and social support as predictors of adaptational outcome among dementia caregivers. *Psychology and Aging, 2,* 323–330.

Haley, W. E., West, C. A., Wadley, V. G., Ford, G. R., White, F. A., Barrett, J. J., Harrell, L. E., & Roth, D. L. (1995). Psychological, social, and health impact of caregiving: A comparison of Black and White dementia caregivers and noncaregivers. *Psychology and Aging, 10,* 540–552.

Harrow, B., Mahoney, D. F., Mendelsohn, A. B., Ory, M. G., Coon, D. W., Belle, S. H., & Nichols, L. O. (2002). *The cost of informal caregiving and formal service use for people with Alzheimer's disease.* Manuscript submitted for publication.

Hinton, W. L., Fox, K., & Levkoff, S. (1999). Introduction: Exploring the relationships among aging, ethnicity and family dementia caregiving. *Culture, Medicine and Psychiatry, 23,* 403–413.

Janevic, M. R., & Connell, C. M. (2001). Racial, ethnic and cultural differences in the dementia caregiving experience: Recent findings. *Gerontologist, 41,* 334–347.

Kazdin, A. E. (1999). The meanings and measurement of clinical significance. *Journal of Consulting and Clinical Psychology, 67,* 332–339.

Keller, V. F., & White, M. K. (1997). Choices and changes: A new model for influencing patient health behavior. *Journal of Clinical Outcomes Management, 4,* 33–36.

Kendall, P. C. (1999). Clinical significance. *Journal of Consulting and Clinical Psychology, 67,* 283–284.

Kennet, J., Burgio, L., & Schulz, R. (2000). Interventions for in-home caregivers: A review of research 1990 to present. In R. Schulz (Ed.), *Handbook on dementia caregiving: Evidence-based interventions for family caregivers* (pp. 61–125). New York: Springer.

King, A. C., Baumann, K., O'Sullivan, P., Wilcox, S., & Castro, C. (2002). Effects of moderate-intensity exercise on physiological, behavioral, and emotional responses to family caregiving: A randomized controlled trial. *Journal of Gerontology: Medical Sciences, 57A,* M26–M36.

King, A. C., & Brassington, G. (1997). Enhancing physical and psychological functioning in older family caregivers: The role of regular physical activity. *Annals of Behavioral Medicine, 19,* 91–100.

Knight, B. G., Lutzky, S. M., & Macofsky-Urban, F. (1993). A meta-analytic review of interventions for caregiver distress: Recommendations for future research. *Gerontologist, 33,* 240–248.

Kramer, B. J. (1997a). Gain in the caregiving experience: Where are we? What next? *Gerontologist, 37,* 218–232.

Kramer, B. (1997b). Differential predictors of strain and gain among husbands caring for wives with dementia. *Gerontologist, 37,* 239–249.

Lawton, M. P., Rajagopal, D., Brody, E., & Kleban, M. (1992). The dynamics of caregiving for a demented elder among Black and White families. *Journal of Gerontology: Social Sciences, 47,* S156–S164.

Lazarus, R., & Folkman, S. (1984). *Stress, appraisal, and coping.* New York: Springer.

Leon, J., Cheng, C. K., & Neumann, P. J. (1998). Health service utilization costs and potential savings for mild, moderate and severely impaired Alzheimer's disease patients. *Health Affairs, 17,* 206–216.

Mahoney, D. F., Burns, R., & Harrow, B. (2000). From intervention studies to public policy: Translating research into practice. In R. Schulz (Ed.), *Handbook on dementia caregiving: Evidence-based interventions for family caregivers* (pp. 249–281). New York: Springer.

Mahoney, D. F., Tarlow, B., & Sandaire, M. S. (1998). A computer-mediated intervention for Alzheimer's caregivers. *Computers in Nursing, 16,* 208–215.

Maslow, K., & Selstad, J. (2001). Chronic care networks for Alzheimer's disease: Approaches for involving and supporting family caregivers in an innovative model of dementia care. *Alzheimer's Care Quarterly, 2,* 33–46.

Miller, B., & Lawton, P. (1997). Symposium: Positive aspects of caregiving. *Gerontologist, 37,* 216–217.

Mittelman, M. S., Ferris, S. H., Shulman, E., Steinberg, G., & Levin, B. (1996). A family intervention to delay nursing home placement of patients with Alzheimer's disease: A randomized controlled trial. *Journal of the American Medical Association, 276,* 1725–1731.

Montgomery, R. J. V., & Kosloski, K. D. (1999). Family caregiving: Change, continuity, and diversity. In R. L. Rubinstein & P. Lawton (Eds.), *Alzheimer's disease and related dementias: Strategies in care and research.* New York: Springer.

National Alliance for Caregiving and the American Association of Retired Persons. (1997). *Family caregiving in the US: Findings from a national survey. Final Report.* Bethesda, MD: National Alliance for Caregiving.

National Health Council. (2001). *Family caregiving agenda for action: 2001 interim report on progress.* Washington, DC: Author.

Navaie-Waliser, M., Feldman, P. H., Gould, D. A., Levine, C., Kuerbis, A. N., & Donelan, K. (2001). The experiences and challenges of informal caregivers: Common themes and differences among Whites, Blacks and Hispanics. *Gerontologist, 41,* 733–741.

Nichols, L. O., Malone, C., Tarlow, B., & Loewenstein, D. (2000). The pragmatics of implementing intervention studies in the community. In R. Schulz (Ed.), *Handbook on dementia caregiving: Evidence-based interventions for family caregivers* (pp. 127–150). New York: Springer.

Nichols, L., Martindale-Adams, J., Burns, R., Coon, D., Ory, M., Mahoney, D., Tarlow, B., Burgio, L., Gallagher-Thompson, D., Guy, D., Arguelles, T., & Winter, L. (2002). A social marketing approach to recruitment: The Resources for Enhancing Alzheimer's Caregiving Health (REACH) Study. Manuscript submitted for publication.

Ory, M. G., Hoffman, R. R., Yee, J. L., Tennstedt, S., & Schulz, R. (1999). Prevalence and impact of caregiving: A detailed comparison between dementia and nondementia caregivers. *Gerontologist, 39,* 177–185.

Ostwald, S. K., Hepburn, K. W., Caron, W., Burns, T., & Mantell, R. (1999). Reducing caregiver burden: A randomized psychoeducational intervention for caregivers of persons with dementia. *Gerontologist, 39,* 299–308.

Pearlin, L. I., Mullan, J. T., Semple, S. J., & Skaff, M. M. (1990). Caregiving and the stress process. An overview of concepts and their measures. *Gerontologist, 30,* 583–594.

Picot, S. J., Debanne, S. M., Namazi, K. H., & Wykle, M. L. (1997). Religiosity and perceived rewards of Black and White caregivers. *Gerontologist, 37,* 89–101.

Pillemer, K. A., & Suitor, J. J. (1992). Violence and violent feelings: What causes them among family caregivers? *Journal of Gerontology: Social Sciences, 47,* 165–172.

Prochaska, J. O., Norcross, J. D., & DiClemente, C. C. (1994). *Changing for good.* New York: William Morrow.

Pusey, H., & Richards, D. (2001). A systematic review of the effectiveness of psychosocial interventions for carers of people with dementia. *Aging and Mental Health, 5,* 107–119.

Robert Wood Johnson Foundation. (2001). National blueprint for increasing physical activity among adults 50 and older: Creating a strategic framework and enhancing organizational capacity for change. *Journal of Aging and Physical Activity, 9*(Suppl.), S5–S28.

Roth, D. L., Haley, W. E., Owen, J. E., Clay, O. J., & Goode, K. T. (2001). Latent growth models of the longitudinal effects of dementia caregiving: A comparison of African-American and White family caregivers. *Psychology and Aging, 16,* 427–436.

Scharlach, A. E., Midanik, L. T., Runkle, C. M., & Soghikian, K. (1997). Health practices in adults with elder care responsibilities. *Preventive Medicine, 26,* 155–161.

Schulz, R. (Ed.). (2000). *Handbook on dementia caregiving: Evidence-based interventions for family caregivers.* New York: Springer.

Schulz, R., & Beach, S. R. (1999). Caregiving as a risk factor for mortality: The caregiver health effects study. *Journal of the American Medical Association, 282,* 2215–2219.

Schulz, R., Gallagher-Thompson, D., Haley, W., & Czaja, S. (2000). Understanding the interventions process; a theoretical/conceptual framework for intervention approaches to caregiving. In R. Schulz (Ed.), *Handbook on dementia caregiving: Evidence-based interventions for family caregivers* (pp. 33–60). New York: Springer.

Schulz, R., O'Brien, A. T., Bookwala, J., & Fleissner, K. (1995). Psychiatric and physical morbidity effects of dementia caregiving: Prevalence, correlates, and causes. *Gerontologist, 35,* 771–791.

Schulz, R., O'Brien, A., Czaja, S., Ory, M., Norris, R., Martire, L. M., Belle, S., Burgio, L., Gitlin, L., Coon, D., Burns, R., Gallagher-Thompson, D., & Stevens, A. (in press). Dementia caregiver intervention research: In search of clinical significance. *The Gerontologist.*

Schulz, R., & Quittner, A. L. (1998). Caregiving through the lifespan: An overview and future directions. *Health Psychology, 17,* 107–111.

Schulz, R., & Williamson, G. M. (1997). The measurement of caregiver outcomes in Alzheimer disease research. *Alzheimer Disease and Associated Disorders, 11,* 117–124.

Steffen, A. M. (2000). Anger management for dementia caregivers: A preliminary study using video and telephone interventions. *Behavior Therapy, 31,* 281–299.

Teri, L., Logsdon, R. G., Uomoto, J., & McCurry, S. M. (1997). Behavioral treatment of depression in dementia patients: A controlled clinical trial. *Journal of Gerontology B: Psychological Science and Social Science, 52,* 159–166.

Valle, R. (1998). *Caregiving across cultures.* Washington, DC: Taylor & Francis.

Yeo, G., & Gallagher-Thompson, D. (Eds.). (1996). *Ethnicity and the dementias.* Washington, DC: Taylor & Francis.

Zarit, S. H., Johansson, L., & Jarrott, S. E. (1998). In I. H. Nordhus, G. R. VandenBos, S. Berg, & P. Fromholt (Eds.), *Clinical geropsychology* (pp. 345–360). Washington, DC: American Psychological Association.

2

Monitoring and Evaluating Interventions

Benjamin H. Gottlieb, Larry W. Thompson, and Michelle Bourgeois

The purpose of this chapter is to present ideas about appropriate measures for evaluating the process and outcomes of various kinds of interventions offered to family caregivers of older adults. Outcome evaluation is needed to inform service planners and policy makers who are responsible for developing new institutional programs. It is also needed by the practitioners involved in implementing specific strategies in their therapy modalities, and by clinical researchers attempting to develop more effective interventions or evaluate specific theoretical models that explain various mechanisms of change implicated in the caregiving process. Understandably, professionals coming from different perspectives will want to focus on the outcomes of family caregiving that are most relevant to their own interests and responsibilities. For example, policy makers would be impressed with information about whether the intervention delays institutionalization of the care recipient and whether it helps or hinders the delivery of other community services. Practitioners would be more concerned with whether or not particular caregivers (and possibly their family as well) benefited from the intervention program in which they participated and whether they will continue to use the program as needed in the future. For clinical researchers the endpoints that traditionally seem to matter the most focus on the caregivers' mental health status, such as their levels of depression, anxiety, and anger, or other measures of adjustment and function that are conventionally employed in clinical outcome studies.

THE STRESSFUL CONTEXT OF CAREGIVING

Any consideration of the outcomes of family caregiving must be predicated on a firm understanding of the stressful demands and repercussions associated with the care of an older adult affected by dementia. Fortunately, there are a number of reports in the literature that carefully document this, with consensus among them regarding the paramount role of behavioral disturbances and evidence of depressive affect displayed by the relatives in the stressed caregivers' experience (cf. Schulz, O'Brien, Bookwala, & Fleissner, 1995, for a review; Gallagher, Rose, Rivera, Lovett, & Thompson, 1989). Specifically, caregivers are distressed by the belligerence, lack of cooperation, oppositional behaviors, and nighttime wakefulness of their relatives, as well as by their relatives' apparent sadness, listlessness, and vegetative behavior. The actual work of caregiving, while tiring, does not seem to have as powerful an impact on the caregivers' emotional lives. However, one additional source of stress that can undermine the caregivers' morale is their *role captivity* (Pearlin, Mullan, Semple, & Skaff, 1990), a term that aptly reflects the necessity of monitoring and supervising the relative on a round-the-clock basis. This in turn means that family caregivers who cannot find or afford substitute caregivers must relinquish much if not all of their other responsibilities and pursuits, with an associated narrowing of their social field and social roles. For example, there is evidence that family caregivers must either reduce their hours of paid employment or withdraw from the workplace (Gottlieb, Kelloway, & Fraboni, 1994; Scharlach, Sobel, & Roberts, 1991). A final source of stress for family caregivers is the gradual loss of communication and rapport with their relatives. Naturally, the extent of stress this produces varies as a function of the historic relationship between the two parties, yet it is hard to imagine anyone's responding with affective neutrality to the deterioration and demise of a parental or spousal attachment figure. Overlaid on these particular stressors is the reality that family care of persons with dementia is a relatively enduring responsibility and therefore qualifies as a chronic stressor. Perhaps for this reason, Pearlin and Aneshensel (1994) discuss the vicissitudes of the caregivers' "careers," involving changes in the nature and intensity of the demands they face over the course of caregiving.

Moreover, recognizing that the demands on family caregivers are unrelenting, service planners have extended various types of respite arrangements to the caregivers, hoping that such episodic relief will moderate feelings of overload and postpone placement of the relative in long-term care (Gottlieb & Johnson, 2000). Other types of interventions, based on treatment models, have also been frequently employed, including such procedures as support groups, individual skill training, group psychoeducational programs, and various forms of individual psychotherapy (Bourgeois, Schulz, & Burgio, 1996; Gallagher-Thompson et al., 2000; Steffen, Gallagher-Thompson & Thompson, 1997; Gallagher-Thompson,

Coon, Rivera, Powers, & Zeiss, 1998). As illustrated in other chapters of this volume, interventions at multiple levels have been mounted to address stressful elements of the caregiving process, ranging from far-reaching governmental policy changes and community actions to one-on-one direct observation and instruction of family members with specific caregiver problems and specific home modifications for safety and practical ease of care issues. In our work with caregivers over the years, we have found that many of them routinely report they have benefited substantially from many different types of interventions and that they would continue to participate if the interventions were available. It is not uncommon, for example, to hear caregivers make exit statements like "I'm so glad that I found this help," "You came along at just the right time and I got just what I needed to deal with my situation," or "Will you continue this for us? It's so helpful." Although such responses are encouraging to researchers and practitioners alike, it is also common to find that this positive impact is not reflected to the same degree in other conventional outcome measures. This often presents a dilemma for professionals who focus on the development and evaluation of programs for caregivers undergoing stress, knowing full well that their particular program may be extremely helpful to caregivers, yet not being able to demonstrate this convincingly when using the standard measures of outcomes in randomized clinical trials.

What sorts of outcomes have been examined to evaluate interventions, and how appropriate are they? Our focus in this chapter is not on the psychometric strengths and weaknesses of the measures that have been employed, nor is it on the comparative effectiveness of alternative interventions in achieving these outcomes. Instead, our goal concerns issues of "goodness of fit"—that is, the fit between the intervention outcomes that have been adopted and the needs and concerns of family caregivers; the fit between the intervention technology and the outcomes that are examined; and the fit or correspondence between the intervention blueprint and the program that is actually delivered. Consideration of these three aspects of program design will pave the way for a new generation of interventions that are based on a stronger theoretical and analytic foundation.

THE FIT BETWEEN INTERVENTION OUTCOMES AND THE NEEDS OF CAREGIVERS

Of all the outcomes examined in caregiver intervention studies, by far the most prevalent are measures of psychiatric symptomatology, especially clinical depression or depressive affect. This is probably because depression has been the most widely studied outcome in investigations of the health consequences of caring for a family member with dementia. For example, in their review of the literature on the morbidity associated with caregiving of persons with dementia, Schulz and colleagues (1995) observe: "Virtually all studies report elevated levels of depressive symptomatology among caregivers, and studies using diagnostic interviews report a higher prevalence of clinical depression and anxiety among caregivers when compared to population norms or control groups" (p. 787).

Given the multiple demands and stressful challenges involved in caring for a relative with dementia, and given the future threat that accompanies knowledge of the deteriorative course of this disease, is it any wonder that caregivers experience depressive affect? More important, should we approach the task of intervention development for caregivers with the implicit goal of treating a psychiatric disorder, or rather approach it as an enterprise devoted to assisting individuals with a burdensome and prolonged life task? If our aim is to treat clinically significant depression, then we ought to follow established and well-documented treatment protocols that call for a specified dosage of medication to be taken over a specified period of time or participation in empirically validated psychotherapies for this disorder, or a combination of both in particularly complex cases (Schneider, Reynolds, Leibowitz, & Friedhoff, 1994). From this perspective, the focus on symptom changes does indeed have high priority. However, if we conceive of our interventions as ways of delivering supplemental resources to caregivers and safeguarding their well-being, then we need to ensure that we understand the aspects of their well-being that matter to them and the resources they might put to good use.

There are several reasons why depression and other psychiatric outcomes such as anxiety may not always stand as important indicators of caregivers' well-being. Caregivers themselves rarely come to programs because they are depressed, rarely state that they hope the program will alleviate their depression, and rarely comment on this contribution of the program when asked to list its benefits when the program concludes. In fact, the following comments are more typical of the reactions of caregivers when asked about the program's effects on their mental health. In this instance, the remarks were made during exit interviews that followed the conclusion of a series of psychoeducational group sessions conducted by two of the editors (DGT, LWT). One older man asked, "Did you really expect me not to be sad, when day after day I watch my wife go downhill, and I never know if or when she's going to be incontinent?" In another interview, a woman asks, "How can I not be anxious when I never know if he's going to do something crazy? Pinch one of my friends on the bottom or something just as bad!" Yet another respondent observes, "My mother loves to go out to eat, so I try to take her out as often as I can. But I know that almost every time we're out, just the slightest thing will happen and she'll get so upset we'll have to leave. It's so embarrassing." Anyone working with family caregivers has no doubt heard similar accounts and might therefore be prompted to ask themselves whether it is reasonable to expect caregivers to come away from intervention programs feeling less sadness about their relative or feeling less anxious about present and future developments. Indeed, it would be reasonable to expect dysphoria and anxiety as normal accompaniments of these caregivers' chronically stressful circumstances, and it would be unreasonable to try to sanitize their emotions. In fact, a more realistic and perhaps even healthy outcome of programs for family caregivers would be for the participants to come away with these feelings validated, normalized, and accepted.

In our experience, caregivers rarely say that any specific intervention has substantially mitigated their psychological distress or their feelings of loss. Yet often they will volunteer that they feel better because they have learned some type of skill or have acquired information that will improve their effectiveness as a caregiver. Many say that sharing with others has helped them realize their reactions are normal and they're not "going crazy." Most report that they have learned to do some concrete activities with their loved one that they believe contribute to their relative's quality of life. Others tell us they are learning to be more patient and loving toward their relative despite the ongoing memory and behavioral problems, because they have learned to attribute problematic behaviors to the disease itself, rather than to the individual with the disease. In short, we have found that caregivers tend to emphasize outcomes that enhance their sense of self-worth in the caregiving role, while at the same time increase their skill level for handling the varied demands of this role.

Why does the emphasis on mental-illness outcome measures continue? As coauthors with extensive experience working with family caregivers, and as academic researchers who regularly apply for grant support, we have come to the point where we actually feel tyrannized by these measures of psychiatric symptomatology, knowing of course that if we do not include them in a grant proposal, all will be lost. If we fail to hitch our wagons to illness-related outcomes and instead justify our interventions in terms of some quasi-medical standard, then we are likely to incur the wrath of the reviewers. Moreover, we believe that the standards that have been adopted have been absolute rather than being considered in relation to what might be normal, and even healthy, emotional functioning in individuals undergoing exceptionally harsh circumstances. Hence, if these measures are to be included at all, the evidence they yield should be evaluated in a contextually relative manner that takes into account what is normative for persons in those circumstances, not what is normative for members of the general population. A larger issue that we have grappled with is whether as researchers and practitioners we have been seduced onto another discipline's playing field, judging the success of our programs far too exclusively in terms of disease and pathology rather than in terms of the social and psychological gains these programs have produced.

At the same time one must realize that extreme feelings of depression or anxiety do occur at higher prevalence rates in caregivers than in the population at large and do warrant treatment. If untreated, they can interfere with the caregiver's ability to function adequately. And although it is true that caregivers generally do not seek treatment for their depression or other psychiatric symptoms, alleviation of psychological distress is a positive outcome if it occurs. However, instruments assessing the intensity of affect are not the most meaningful outcome tools in many instances, and change in these instruments should not be considered the gold standard by which all interventions are valued or compared.

If symptom measures should not automatically be viewed as the gold standard when evaluating the efficacy or effectiveness of interventions for family caregivers, what then would be a more appropriate set of outcome measures? First, we believe the measures ought to reflect what caregivers themselves view as desirable outcomes. This involves getting closer to the people who participate in these interventions and asking them directly what would make a difference to their well-being. The evidence we have gained from speaking to caregivers is that their own morale and sense of well-being are closely tied to three factors. The first is their relative's well-being, that is, caregivers seem to feel better when they believe their relative is content and well cared for. For example, if caregivers believe their relatives are not enjoying a day program, then the caregivers will be distressed too. The second factor is that caregivers want feedback telling them they are doing the best job they can; they want reassurance that they compare equally or favorably to other caregivers in the same situation, with respect to both their current handling of the situation and their planning for the future. The third factor is that they want to believe they are making some progress in adapting to the caregiver role; that despite the unrelenting demands and the future uncertainty they face, their coping skills have improved or at least they are not as vulnerable as they were when they started out. For example, they have learned to expend less energy when they need to manage their relative's behavior, and they have learned when to stop trying to manage the behavior in one particular way and shift to other strategies they have discovered over time. More generally, in the future investigators should consider inserting more positive measures of the proximal and distal outcomes of their interventions, such as optimism, hope, self-efficacy, and positive emotional states. As Ryff, Singer, Love, and Essex (1998) point out, "Elevating the side of strengths, we propose a conceptualization of *resilience,* which speaks to the capacities of some aging persons to stay well, recover, or even improve, in the face of cumulating challenge" (p. 69).

When these three factors or domains of well-being are translated into more specific constructs for outcome assessment, the following measures could be adopted. Whereas validated instruments exist to tap some of these constructs, others await instrument development:

• The belief that the care recipient is as comfortable and content as possible
• The belief that the relationship is as positive as it can be, given the disease process and the historic relationship between the parties

• Acquisition of specific skills to manage troublesome day-to-day behavioral problems with their loved one more effectively

• Acquisition of information and skills on how to obtain resources from both formal community services and informal support systems of importance to both current demands and future planning for themselves and their care recipient

• A sense of mastery over various caregiving domains, including behavior management, the provision of direct care, and the identification, utilization, and orchestration of community services

• A sense of mastery over their own self-care, including physical health matters and issues pertaining to effective psychological organization, control, and functioning

More on consideration of specific measures will be provided later. However, with respect to mastery we would like to mention here that two separate and distinct measures can be adopted to tap this broad construct, one gauging coping efficacy—defined as the caregivers' own evaluation of the effectiveness of their coping (Gignac & Gottlieb, 1996)—and the other gauging caregiving self-efficacy, which is defined as the caregivers' confidence in their ability to successfully perform particular tasks (Gottlieb & Rooney, in press; Steffen, McKibbin, Zeiss, Gallagher-Thompson, & Bandura, 2002).

THE FIT BETWEEN INTERVENTION TECHNOLOGY AND OUTCOMES

Once program planners have identified the outcomes they wish to attain, it is essential that they identify existing or invent new theoretical models that explain change in these outcomes. A strong intervention design would allow researchers to uncover reasons for its success or failure in achieving these outcomes by tracing the links between the intervention strategies, the intervening changes that occurred, and the final outcomes. The fact is that the vast majority of psychosocial intervention programs have adopted a "black-box" approach, meaning they implement one or more intervention components that they believe stand a good chance of turning things around and then they examine whether indeed the hoped for changes have occurred. What they usually omit from their planning process is the specification of the proximal variables that must be impacted if change in the distal variables is to occur. These proximal variables, which can be any one or a combination of knowledge, affect, behaviors, or cognitions, are the mediating processes or mechanisms of change, and if they are not specified and actually measured, then it is impossible to know how or why the intervention worked or failed to work. For example, if a given intervention proved particularly successful in lowering depressive affect or subjective burden but showed no evidence of change in the antecedent or proximal variables that were targeted (such as knowledge and skills), then the theory underlying the intervention strategy would need to be modified. Clearly, either other kinds of knowledge and skills had changed, or something other than knowledge and skills must have changed to produce the desired outcomes. In short, the success of interventions depends on (a) one's power to effect change in the mediating variables through the intervention strategy, and (b) the strength of the link from the mediating variables to the desired outcomes. It follows that the more mediating mechanisms specified on the basis of theory, the more options for intervention. However, it should be emphasized that knowledge of the mechanisms to be targeted does not imply knowledge of how to intervene effectively. For example, knowing that perceived social support is a stress buffer, we may make it the mediating variable in an intervention we are planning. However, we may find ourselves in the dark about how to alter perceived support because we don't know whether it is predicated on interaction with certain peers, personality characteristics, self-presentation needs, or some combination of these variables.

One additional point should be underscored: One should never assume that change in the mediator(s) guarantees change in the outcomes. For example, just because behavioral training brings about an increase in caregivers' skills does not mean it reduces their feelings of burden and depression. The point is that one may be very successful in changing one or more mediating variables, but find that they have little impact on the outcomes of interest. For example, from the support group literature, we know that caregivers exchange support, vent their feelings, get validation for their roles, and engage in social comparisons, but most studies have found that change in these mediators has not had much impact on caregivers' depression, rates of institutionalizing their relatives, or their quality of life (Thompson & Gallagher-Thompson, 1996).

If a sound conceptual framework guides the particular intervention that is being employed or evaluated, then questionnaires or observational measures can be selected or constructed to measure the intervening mechanisms of change as well as the distal outcomes. In this way, linkages can be made between model and measures, and each can inform the other as intervention refinement progresses. Many researchers have used a variation of the Stress-Process Model (Lazarus & Folkman, 1984) as a conceptual backdrop in their exploration of factors and mechanisms responsible for caregivers' adjustment. This model views appraisals and coping resources as dynamic and interacting processes that are activated in responding to specific external stressors. Numerous studies have shown that several constructs derived from this model are relevant predictors or moderators of well-being and quality of life for caregivers (see review in Lee, 1999). They include the primary appraisal process itself (How threatening is the stressor? Is it viewed primarily as positive or negative?); the process of secondary appraisal of the stressor, including an assessment of one's own and the social environment's resources for dealing with stress (e.g., one's perceived sense of mastery and self-efficacy for coping with it); and the actual employment of a range of cognitive and behavioral coping efforts.

Our review of the caregiving literature reveals that most of the measurement tools that have been employed are *generic*, that is, they were developed for use in studies or in clinical work dealing with a diversity of client populations and stressors. Relatively few measures have been tailored to the particular aspects of caregiving that we have been describing. Yet the many challenges inherent in the caregiving role call for contextually relevant measures of coping processes and outcomes, measures that may not necessarily be relevant to other groups. Many generic scales designed to assess constructs relevant to their theoretical model or their outcome goals may not be sensitive to variations that are meaningful for caregivers (cf. Bell, Araki, & Newmann, 2001, for example). Whenever possible, practitioners and researchers are advised to use measures developed expressly for caregivers, rather than generic measures.

Another apt illustration of the benefits of tailor-made or domain-specific measurement tools is a recent study that documented the domain specificity of coping on the part of family caregivers of persons with dementia. Gottlieb and Gignac (1996) conducted in-depth interviews with a sample of 51 family caregivers, asking them five broad questions designed to elicit descriptions of cognitive coping, escape/avoidance coping, support-seeking, emotion-focused coping, and problem-focused coping. Their coping efforts were described for two specific stressors, one being the symptom of the disease that the caregivers found most stressful or upsetting, and the other a deprivation occasioned by caregiving, such as the loss of freedom and independence or the cancellation of retirement plans. The investigators then conducted a rigorous content analysis of the transcripts, resulting in the development of a classification scheme consisting of 53 categories of coping, which they organized into 11 classes of coping. These authors not only showed that certain classes of coping are particularly relevant to each of the two types of stressors they asked about, but also that there were numerous kinds of coping efforts that were not represented in generic coping instruments. Equally important, they emphasized that the prediction of caregiver outcomes is likely to be improved by assessing coping with items that are specific to the stressor domain being studied. In addition, clinical intervention is improved when knowledge is based on contextually specific ways of coping rather than on generic coping items.

THE FIT BETWEEN THE INTERVENTION'S BLUEPRINT AND ITS IMPLEMENTATION

It is generally assumed that intervention programs that are grounded in prior research or substantial clinical experience, that are theory-driven, and that have reasonable face validity will achieve the intended effect. When results are marginal or equivocal, however, there are many reasons why the specific outcome measures used may not really reflect the treatment provided (Bourgeois, Schulz, Burgio, & Beach, in press). For example, the measures may not have been sensitive to caregiving issues or appropriately tailored for use with family caregivers. An alternative explanation for equivocal or relatively modest results is that the intervention itself may not have been delivered in the best possible way or it may not have been delivered as intended. Thus, more needs to be known about the intervention process itself.

Moncher and Prinz (1991) proposed that the significance or power of research results, while unequivocally influenced by the adequacy of the research design and the outcome measures, may be undermined by the lack of verification of the treatment process. Without confirmation that manipulation of the independent variable occurred as planned, the internal validity, external validity, construct validity, and statistical power of the research outcomes can all be questioned. Furthermore, inadequate descriptions of the intervention strategies, stemming from lack of a protocol manual or idiosyncratic application, can lead to replication failures. When comparing different intervention strategies, or an intervention compared to control conditions, their specific objectives and procedures must be understood and correctly implemented in order to ensure construct validity (Moncher & Prinz, 1991). Clear differentiation between intervention protocols is needed to prevent overlap and confounding of the intervention process with other variables, such as session length and therapist style (Derer, 1985). Finally, methodological soundness and statistical power in outcome studies are highly correlated (Happe, 1983; Smith, Glass, & Miller, 1980). It cannot be assumed that all subjects received identical exposure to the intervention unless the process has been monitored for potency and content. Failure to address these issues may result in decreased power to detect intervention effects (Frances, Sweeney, & Clarkin, 1985).

Historically, the measurement of the treatment process was first advocated in the 1950s and 1960s to address accountability issues in psychotherapy (Eysenck, 1952). In the ensuing years and through the next decade, no more than 20% of studies assessed any sort of treatment variable (Billingsley, White, & Munson, 1980; Peterson, Homer, & Wonderlich, 1982). The 1980s were somewhat better, with 45% of treatment studies across clinical psychology, behavior therapy, psychiatry, and marital and family therapy measuring some aspect of adherence to a treatment protocol (Moncher & Prinz, 1991). In the emergent caregiver intervention literature there has been less than 5% incidence of reports of treatment process measures (Bourgeois et al., 1996). Clearly, there is a need to assess the treatment process and the fidelity of treatment in a timely and cost-effective manner.

Several workers who are concerned with intervention research have provided useful discussions regarding this problem. For example, both Yeaton and Sechrest (1981) and Kazdin (1986a, 1986b) defined treatment fidelity as encompassing two related concepts: treatment integrity and treatment differentiation. Treatment integrity refers to the degree to which a treatment or treatment condition is implemented as intended. Differentiation refers to the degree to which treatment conditions differ from one another. These researchers proposed that treatment integrity can be improved by better descriptions of interventions. The identification of intervention characteristics, such as strength (i.e., amount and intensity of treatment), sequence of procedures, training content, and clinician variables, would result in better and more accurate monitoring of the treatment process. This would enhance the replicability, generalizability, and interpretation of research results. The danger in not determining treatment integrity is that a partially administered treatment could result in less than efficacious outcomes that would be attributed to the intended treatment.

Lichstein, Riedel, and Grieve (1994) have expanded upon the concepts of treatment integrity and fidelity in their model of treatment implementation. They argue that treatment must be tracked from the presentation of the treatment by the clinician to its utilization by the client. Previous attention to this topic stopped at what Lichstein and his colleagues labeled the *delivery* of the intended treatment and did not account for a variety of client variables that could impact the intended outcome, such as the client's understanding, acceptance, and action due to the treatment. Lichstein and colleagues described these additional constructs as treatment *receipt* and treatment *enactment*. They postulated further that these components are prerequisites to valid conclusions about study outcomes and that failure to completely implement any one of these components would result in diminished treatment outcomes. Thus, when designing the evaluation of any intervention for caregivers, researchers are encouraged to plan for and assess these three implementation components as follows:

1.   *Delivery* of the intended treatment involves the careful planning and description of all aspects of the treatment, including the skills and actions of the therapist. A manual of specific procedures has become the industry standard for ensuring accurate treatment delivery. Manuals often include the background information on the treatment, an outline of the correct procedures, a step-by-step timeline for delivery of all treatment activities, and examples of correction procedures for improper behaviors. The training of the intervention agent, the therapist, should also be well specified. It should include review and mastery of the procedures manual, role playing, and practice with and supervision by an "expert" in conducting the selected intervention. Review of audio- and videotapes of the treatment implementation with pilot clients or actors enhances standardization of treatment delivery.

To ensure that the trained therapists deliver the intended treatment, procedures for assessing treatment delivery must be implemented. These include directly assessing the therapist's skills by having an independent rater score positive and negative therapist behaviors from audio- or videotapes of actual treatment sessions. Indirect methods of assessing treatment delivery include therapist self-reports, but these may unintentionally misrepresent protocol compliance. Therapists can make errors of omission or commission by failing to include intended components or adding components that are not intended.

2. *Receipt* of the treatment involves the client's comprehension of the treatment goals and educational materials provided by the therapist to assist in reaching those goals. Formal receipt techniques include having the client role play (with feedback) and repeat and summarize important points. The therapist's use of informal strategies such as simple verbal cues, instructions, and reminders can supplement the formal techniques. The assessment of treatment receipt is crucial for determining that the therapy has been successfully implemented. When working with caregivers, direct observation of them exhibiting desired behaviors is the clearest way to assess receipt. When this is not possible, indirect methods such as the use of questionnaires to ascertain comprehension or perceived self-efficacy in the use of the behaviors are preferable to none. Documentation of attendance at scheduled sessions, as well as all other client contacts, allows for measurement of amount and duration of therapist contact, which no doubt interacts with the particular intervention being used, to influence receipt independently.

3. *Enactment* refers to the client's compliance with treatment. Because it would be impossible to follow each client home to monitor treatment enactment, formal enactment strategies range from written reminder cards, forms for recording home practice, behavior logs or diaries, checklists or rating scales, contracting for homework assignment completion, self-monitoring, reinforcement, and family or peer support. Informal strategies that are often used include verbal persuasion, positive reinforcement, and motivational speeches. An illustration of the use of this model within a multisite, cooperative research study of caregiving interventions—Resources for Enhancing Alzheimer's Caregiver Health (REACH)—was recently published (Burgio et al., 2001).

CONSIDERATIONS IN THE SELECTION OF OUTCOME MEASURES

Although our emphasis has been on the need to develop new and more contextually tailored outcome measures, we would be remiss if we did not provide information concerning some of the pioneering efforts by researchers in assessment areas relevant to caregiving. Rather than include an exhaustive list of measures, we will highlight selected conceptual and methodological issues relevant to the development of measures for this population and also identify several scales that have been developed specifically with this population in mind. Readers who have had limited experience with assessment may also find it helpful to review measures and issues more generally involved in the assessment of elderly populations (Lawton & Teresi, 1994), as well as ethnically diverse older populations (Skinner, Teresi, Holmes, Stahl, & Sterwart, 2001).

1. *Measures of symptoms and psychiatric disorders.* Although we recommend that less emphasis be placed on measures of psychopathology in this research area, if the design calls for inclusion of symptom measures, one of the most informative resources available is the *Handbook of Psychiatric Measures* (American Psychiatric Association, 2000). This book provides a comprehensive review of a wide array of interview and self-report measures of symptoms and diagnoses, including detailed psychometric references, and a CD that contains copies of many of the public domain instruments.

2. *Positive aspects of caregiving.* This dimension is often overlooked, yet its importance to the development of useful models of adjustment in caregivers has been emphasized recently (Kramer, 1997; Noonan & Tennstedt, 1997). Farran, Miller, Kaufman, Donner, and Fogg (1999) have also presented theoretical discussions focused on the meaningfulness of caregiving, along with a scale developed specifically for use with caregivers of family members with dementia. Instruments for assessing positive aspects of caregiving have also been developed for use with caregivers of cancer victims (Nijboer, Triemstra, Tempelaar, Sanderman, & van den Bos, 1999). A measure is also available that has been developed specifically for use with caregivers of frail elders, which has been used with both Caucasian and African American populations (Picot, Youngblut, & Zeller, 1997). Lawton and colleagues included a five-item scale measuring caregiver satisfaction in the Philadelphia Geriatric Center Appraisal Scales (PGCAS; Lawton, Kleban, Moss, Rovine, & Glicksman, 1989). These scales have been used widely in caregiver research and program evaluation studies and are available for use with Spanish-speaking caregivers as well (Harwood et al., 2000a).

Watson, Clark, and Tellegen (1988) have developed a widely used measure of positive and negative affect that could serve as an informative indicator of short-term changes in mood. The positive affect measure in particular could be adopted as a way of determining whether the personal and coping resources that caregivers actually employ or perceive to be available to them boost positive moods or whether they dampen negative moods. Another similar measure is Bradburn's Affect Balance Scale (Bradburn, 1969) which yields three scores: positive affect, negative affect, and affect balance (positive minus negative scores).

3. *Coping with specific stressful demands of caregiving.* There is an extensive literature focusing on the implications of stress-adaptation models for explaining

physical and mental health factors in numerous populations, and caregiving has been no exception (Williamson & Schulz, 1993). The PGCAS mentioned earlier included one of the earlier attempts to focus on the importance of appraisal and coping in caregivers. Gottlieb and Gignac (1996) have developed a coping measure that is specific to caregivers' handling of the symptoms of dementia and the "deprivations" it occasions. Vitaliano and colleagues have developed a generic scale, the Revised Ways of Coping Scale, that has been used in a number of studies with caregivers (Vitaliano, Russo, Carr, Mairuro, & Becker, 1985). This scale categorizes coping into different strategies that might be used to deal with stressful situations, such as seeking support, blaming oneself, blaming others, being problem-focused, using cognitive restructuring, counting one's blessings, and avoiding the situation and issues.

4. *Religious coping.* Interest is increasing in the use of religion as a means of coping with health-related problems and other life stressors. Evidence is accumulating that emphasizes the importance of religion as a coping mechanism among caregivers, particularly in ethnic minority groups (Haley et al., 1996). Caregivers often spontaneously comment on the importance of their spiritual and religious beliefs in helping them find meaning in the drudgery of caregiving activities, and specific items included in interviews or self-report measures that pertain to the role of religion are frequently endorsed. Within the context of coping appraisal models, the argument is often made that a caregiver's ability to deal constructively with new problems and challenges is likely to be associated with the extent to which they are able to construct positive or negative meanings for any given situation. For some individuals, religious or spiritual beliefs and practices clearly facilitate such appraisals. Thus, assessment of these beliefs and practices may be used to determine whether religious coping serves as a useful moderator or mediating factor in predicting intervention outcomes. There are only a few instruments available to use in the assessment of religious coping for which reliability and validity have been documented, and to our knowledge none is specifically designed for use with caregivers. Pargament, Koenig, and Perez (2000) have developed a theoretically based measure to assess a wide range of religious coping methods, including both helpful and harmful religious expressions. They also have developed a short form to evaluate positive and negative aspects of religious coping. The short form is currently being used in several outcome studies connected with the REACH project referred to elsewhere in this chapter, but no data concerning reliability, validity, or sensitivity to change in this population are yet available.

5. *Mastery in the caregiving role.* The PGCAS (Lawton et al., 1989) includes a caregiver mastery scale that has been used in numerous research settings with caregivers. It focuses on the sense of how much the caregiver feels in control of the many problems arising in caregiving. Steffen and associates (2002) have developed a reliable and valid measure of self-efficacy for caregivers in three

specific areas related to caregiving: How effective the caregiver feels (a) in managing difficult behaviors; (b) in managing negative thoughts about the care recipient and caregiving per se that might develop; and (c) in taking care of their own mental and physical health. This interviewer-administered scale is available in both English and Spanish from the editor (DGT). Gottlieb and Rooney (in press) have also developed and validated a three-dimensional measure of caregiving self-efficacy, which taps the caregivers' confidence that they can perform the instrumental tasks associated with the care of their relatives, that they can maintain a harmonious relationship with the care recipient, and that they can engage in the self-care necessary to maintain relatively good spirits over the course of caregiving.

6. *Perceived burden.* This domain refers to the extent to which problems commonly seen in caregiving situations are rated as distressing or troublesome to the caregiver. One of the most common measures of this construct in use today is the Revised Memory and Behavior Problem Checklist (RMBPC; Teri et al., 1992). This scale measures two different features: objective burden, referring to the actual frequency of various problems; and subjective burden, referring to the amount of distress each problem causes the caregiver. The items can be grouped into three subscales pertaining to memory problems, general disruptive behaviors, and depression. The authors reported adequate reliability and validity for this measure; however, its sensitivity to change may be questionable. Some members of ethnic minorities object to the concept, arguing that caring for a loved one cannot be a burden. In our experience, some Caucasians also have difficulty framing caregiving as a role that should burden or bother them. Recent evaluations of the effect of behavioral interventions on this measure have shown minimal change in African Americans (Burgio, 2001) and Latinas (Gallagher-Thompson, 2001). A modified version of this scale that includes only items pertaining to disruptive behaviors and depression in care recipients is available in Spanish (Harwood et al., 2000b).

7. *Quality of life.* Recently there has been a resurgence of interest in quality of life measures, particularly health-related quality of life. Most attempts to evaluate these constructs in caregivers have used generic measures. One such measure that is receiving some attention is the Quality of Life Inventory (QOLI) (Frisch, 1992). This inventory measures the importance and degree of satisfaction for a number of factors cutting across finances, living conditions, instrumental and social support systems and general well being. The Caregiver Well-Being Scale (Tebb, 1995) focuses on the assessment of caregiver basic needs and satisfaction with activities of daily living, with a view to enhancing potential strengths. A recent evaluation of its psychometric properties (Berg-Weger, Rubio, & Tebb, 2000) revealed good internal consistency and construct validity. The basic needs subscale has three principal factors: expression of feelings, physical needs, and self-security. The activities of living subscale includes the

following: leisure time, maintenance of functions outside the home, family support, and household maintenance and tasks. Although originally viewed as a guide to assist caregivers in improving their quality of life and general well-being, the measure is one of the few designed specifically for this group and may be sensitive to change in intervention studies.

Health-related quality of life measures are currently being developed and evaluated in a number of research settings. The emphasis in this area appears to be on the development of measures that are highly specific for different disorders. To our knowledge, there are no instruments pertaining to health-related quality of life that have been developed specifically for use with caregivers. For the interested reader, there are useful resources that discuss issues and problems in developing such instruments (cf. O'Connor, 1993; Rook, 1994).

8. *Target complaints.* Another novel strategy for clinicians and researchers to consider is the "target complaints" approach (TC; Battle et al., 1966), which has the advantage of customizing the outcome assessment process for each individual. Because simple rating scales are employed to determine the severity of complaints at any point in time, this methodology can be used effectively to evaluate responses of groups of caregivers, such as those participating in a randomized clinical trial. The methodology involves asking individuals to explain the main complaints for which they are seeking assistance and then asking for a rating of how much each problem is bothering them now on a Likert scale ranging from "not at all bothersome" to "could not be worse." At the conclusion of the intervention program the individual completes the same rating scales. They are also asked how much the problem has changed since treatment began. They could also be asked what they attribute the change to, what their contribution to the change was versus the contribution of other factors (such as a change in resources), what specifically they did to cope with the problem, and other questions depending on the specific interests and theoretical model of the interventionist.

TCs are relatively easy to obtain from the individual, typically have high relevance to functional problem areas that can be targeted in interventions, are sensitive to change in treatment programs, and show high correlations with generic symptom measures (Koss et al., 1983; Pilkonis, Imber, Lewis, & Rubinsky, 1984). This approach offers an easy and quick assessment that is well received by caregivers, primarily because it reflects directly on matters of importance to them and communicates that the investigator is interested in their situation. Moreover, because TCs usually are focused on valid indicators of functioning, they do bridge the gap between clinical symptom measures and real-life issues. Additionally, there is every reason to think that assessment of TC change could be incorporated within an appraisal-coping matrix.

An example of how this strategy works can be seen in the following case illustration of a caregiver who sought assistance from the author (LWT): KW, a 71-year-old married female, was a caregiver for her husband who had been diagnosed with early-stage dementia approximately 2 years prior to her contacting the clinic. She came in response to a notice in the local newspaper that was soliciting participants for a depression treatment study. KW was diagnosed as having a dysthymic disorder with mild to moderate anxiety and depression. She reported that she was sad almost all the time with low energy and concentration problems. She complained of being irritable with others, particularly her two middle-aged married daughters. She also felt unattractive because she was eating too much and gaining weight. After explaining the rationale for the proposed intervention, her specific TCs to work on were elicited. The TC most bothersome to KW was that she missed contacts with friends and felt isolated and lonely. Her rating on this complaint was "couldn't be worse." A second TC, which was nearly as discomforting, was that her husband was untidy and she had to spend enormous amounts of time continually cleaning up after him. A third less bothersome TC was focused on her problem in controlling her angry feelings towards her husband. Specific interventions to assist her in developing skills to minimize these problems were successful. KW developed assertion skills that enabled her to obtain assistance from her daughters so that she could have some free time for socialization. She learned how to view her husband's untidiness as less catastrophic and was able to develop a more practical strategy for cleaning. Finally, she learned to attribute his unruly behavior to his disease rather than to his contrary nature, which lessened her anger. From her perspective, the outcome of the intervention was extremely successful; this was reflected in the decreased severity ratings for the TCs after treatment. It is noteworthy, however, that even though she felt more comfortable and confident in her role as a caregiver and was less pessimistic about the future, her scores on the clinical scales of depression and anxiety had decreased only slightly and still were above the recommended normal range cutoff scores for adult noncaregivers.

In her exit interview, KW reported that the intervention had improved her sense of effectiveness and comfort in her role as caregiver. She understood more clearly how important it was to take care of herself as well as her husband and believed she now had tools to help her do this. Nevertheless, she was still sad about her situation and the plight of her husband, and she experienced apprehension about each coming day, knowing full well that her state of affairs and her husband's condition would be no better or even worse than the last. Thus, we can see that the intervention helped KW in handling her present dilemmas, and it laid an optimistic backdrop for future problem solving. However, the link between these improvements and her emotional state was not clearly evident.

Such data raise interesting questions for building new models. As noted earlier, should we necessarily expect to see major changes in affect in individuals confronted with this unique and chronic strain? How important is an individual's affective state in determining their general sense of well-being or quality of life while they are in the caregiving role? Among other questions, what factors might be responsible for the linkage between these two domains?

CONCLUDING COMMENTS

In summary, we recommend careful selection of outcome measures that are informed in part by caregivers themselves and in part by knowledge of the risk and protective factors that may influence the quality of life and well-being of family caregivers. We also encourage other investigators to choose or create outcome measures that are sensitive to the particular demands and context of caregiving, one example being coping strategies that are tailored to this stressful domain. We recommend that clinicians and researchers consider an idiographic rather than a nomothetic approach in selecting measuring tools and questionnaires. We believe that one needs to focus more on individual goals and what is important to the particular caregiver, and then monitor the extent to which these goals are achieved as the intervention progresses. We also emphasize the importance of measuring the process during the intervention itself to ensure that treatment is delivered as intended.

In our view and that of others prominent in this field (Light & Lebowitz, 1989), there is still much to be done. Very few appropriate measures have been evaluated for gender or ethnicity effects. Also, most measures do not take into account the stage of the caregiving process the person has reached at the time of the intervention. Finally, at the present time we have few measures of the impact of caregiving on the family as a unit. This is an area clearly deserving of more attention in the future.

REFERENCES

American Psychiatric Association. (2000). *Handbook of psychiatric measures.* Washington, DC: American Psychiatric Association.

Battle, C. C., Imber, S. D., Hoen-Saric, R., Stone, A. R., Nash, E. R., & Frank, J. D. (1966). Targets complaints as criteria of improvement. *American Journal of Psychotherapy, 20,* 184–192.

Bell, C. M., Araki, S. S., & Newmann, P. J. (2001). The association between caregiver burden and caregiver health-related quality of life in Alzheimer's disease. *Alzheimer Disease and Related Disorders, 15,* 129–136.

Berg-Weger, M., Rubio, D. M., & Tebb, S. S. (2000). The caregiver well-being scale revisited. *Health and Social Work, 25,* 255–263.

Billingsley, F., White, O., & Munson, R. (1980). Procedural reliability: A rationale and an example. *Behavioral Assessment, 2,* 229–241.

Bourgeois, M., Schulz, R., & Burgio, L. (1996). Intervention for caregivers of patients with Alzheimer's disease: A review and analysis of content, process, and outcomes. *International Journal of Human Development, 43,* 35–92.

Bourgeois, M., Schulz, R., Burgio, L., & Beach, S. (in press). Skills training for spouses of patients with Alzheimer's disease: Outcomes of an intervention study. *Journal of Clinical Geropsychology.*

Bradburn, N. (1969). *The structure of psychological well-being.* Chicago: Aldine.

Burgio, L. (2001, August). *Differential effects of skills training and minimal support interventions.* Paper presented at the American Psychological Association Meetings, San Francisco.

Burgio, L., Corcoran, M., Lichstein, K., Nichols, L., Czaja, S., Gallagher-Thompson, D., Bourgeois, M., Stevens, A., Ory, M., & Schulz, R. (2001). Judging outcomes in psychosocial interventions for dementia caregivers: The problem of treatment implementation. *Gerontologist, 41,* 481–489.

Derer, K. (1985). Operational specificity: Implications for field-based replications. *Journal of Behavior Therapy and Experimental Psychiatry, 16,* 9–14.

Eysenck, H. (1952). The effects of psychotherapy, and evaluation. *Journal of Consulting Psychology, 16,* 319–324.

Farran, C. J., Miller, B. H., Kaufman, J. E., Donner, E., & Fogg, L. (1999). Finding meaning thru caregiving: Development of an instrument for family caregivers of persons with Alzheimer's disease. *Journal of Clinical Psychology, 55,* 1107–1125.

Frances, A., Sweeney, J., & Clarkin, J. (1985). Do psychotherapies have specific effects? *American Journal of Psychotherapy, 39,* 159–174.

Frisch, M. B. (1992). Clinical validation of the quality of life inventory. A measure of life satisfaction for use in treatment planning and outcome assessment. *Psychological Assessment, 4,* 92–101.

Gallagher-Thompson, D. (2001). Dementia caregiving interventions. In D. Gallagher-Thompson (Chair), *The impact of gender, ethnicity and sexual orientation.* Symposium presentation at the American Psychological Association Convention, San Francisco.

Gallagher-Thompson, D., Coon, D. W., Rivera, P., Powers, D., & Zeiss, A. M. (1998). Family caregiving: Stress, coping and intervention. In M. Hersen & V. Van Hasselt (Eds.), *Handbook of clinical geropsychology* (pp. 469–493). New York: Plenum Press.

Gallagher-Thompson, D., Lovett, S., Rose, J., McKibbin, C., Coon, D., Futterman, A., & Thompson, L. W. (2000). Impact of psychoeducational interventions on distressed family caregivers. *Journal of Clinical Geropsychology, 6,* 91–110.

Gallagher, D., Rose, J., Rivera, P., Lovett, S., & Thompson, L. W. (1989). Prevalence of depression in family caregivers. *Gerontologist, 29,* 449–456.

Gignac, M. A., & Gottlieb, B. H. (1996). Caregivers' appraisals of efficacy in coping with dementia. *Psychology and Aging, 11,* 214–225.

Gottlieb, B. H., & Gignac, M. A. (1996). Content and domain specificity of coping among family caregivers of persons with dementia. *Journal of Aging Studies, 10,* 137–155.

Gottlieb, B. H., & Johnson, J. (2000). Respite programs for caregivers of persons with dementia: A review with practice implications. *Aging and Mental Health, 4*(2), 119–129.

Gottlieb, B. H., Kelloway, E. K., & Fraboni, M. (1994). Aspects of eldercare that place employees at risk. *Gerontologist, 34,* 815–821.

Gottlieb, B. H., & Rooney, J. (in press). Validation of the RIS eldercare self-efficacy scale. *Canadian Journal on Aging.*

Gottlieb, B. H., & Wagner, F. (1991). Stress and support processes in close relationships. In J. Eckenrode (Ed.), *The social context of coping* (pp. 165–188). New York: Plenum Press.

Happe, D. (1983). Behavioral intervention: It doesn't do any good in your briefcase. In J. Grimes (Ed.), *Psychological approaches* (pp. 15–45). Des Moines, IA: Iowa State Department of Education.

Haley, W. E., Roth, D. L., Coleton, M. I., Ford, G. R., West, C. A. C., Collins, R. R., & Isobe, T. L. (1996). Appraisal, coping, and social support as mediators of well-being in Black and White family caregivers of patients with Alzheimer's disease. *Journal of Consulting and Clinical Psychology, 64,* 121–129.

Harwood, D. G., Barker, W. W., Ownby, R. L., Bravo, M., Aguero, H., & Duara, R. (2000a). Predictors of positive and negative appraisal among Cuban American caregivers of Alzheimer's disease patients. *International Journal of Geriatric Psychiatry, 15,* 481–487.

Harwood, D. G., Barker, W. W., Ownby, R. L., Bravo, M., Aguero, H., & Duara, R. (2000b). The behavior problems checklist-Spanish: A preliminary study of a new scale for the assessment of depressive symptoms and disruptive behaviors in Hispanic patients with dementia. *International Psychogeriatrics, 13,* 23–35.

Kazdin, A. (1986a). Comparative outcome studies of psychotherapy: Methodological issues and strategies. *Journal of Consulting and Clinical Psychology, 54,* 95–105.

Kazdin, A. (1986b). The evaluation of psychotherapy: Research, design and methodology. In S. L. Garfield & A. E. Bergin (Eds.), *Handbook of psychotherapy and behavior change* (3rd ed., pp. 23–68). New York: Wiley.

Koss, M. P., Graham, J. R., Kirkhart, K., Post, G., Kirkhart, R. O., & Silverberg, R. S. (1983). Outcome of eclectic psychotherapy in private psychological practice. *American Journal of Psychotherapy, 3,* 400–410.

Kramer, B. J. (1997). Gain in the caregiving experience: Where are we? What next? *Gerontologist, 37,* 218–232.

Lawton, M. P., Kleban, M. H., Moss, M., Rovine, & Glicksman, A. (1989). Measuring caregiving appraisal. *Journal of Gerontology: Psychological Sciences, 44,* P61–P71.

Lawton, M. P., & Teresi, J. A. (Eds.). (1994). *Annual review of gerontology and geriatrics: Focus on assessment techniques.* New York: Springer.

Lazarus, R. S., & Folkman, S. (1984). *Stress, appraisal and coping.* New York: Springer.

Lee, C. (1999). Health, stress and coping among women caregivers: A review. *Journal of Health Psychology, 4*(1), 27–40.

Lichstein, K., Riedel, B., & Grieve, R. (1994). Fair tests of clinical trials: A treatment implementation model. *Advances in Behavior Research and Therapy, 16,* 1–29.

Light, E., & Lebowitz, B. D. (Eds.). (1989). *Alzheimer's disease treatment and family stress: Directions for research.* Rockville, MD: National Institute of Mental Health.

Moncher, F., & Prinz, R. (1991). Treatment fidelity in outcome studies. *Clinical Psychology Review, 11,* 247–266.

Nijboer, C., Triemstra, M., Tempelaar, R., Sanderman, R., & van den Bos, G. A. M. (1999). Measuring both negative and positive reactions to giving care to cancer patients: Psychometric qualities of the caregiver reaction assessment (CRA). *Social Sciences and Medicine, 48,* 1259–1269.

Noonan, A. E., & Tennstedt, S. I. (1997). Meaning in caregiving and its contribution to caregiver well-being. *Gerontologist, 37,* 785–794.

O'Connor, R. (1993). *Issues in the measurement of health-related quality of life.* NHMRC National Centre for Health Program Evaluation, Melbourne, Australia. Available: www.RodOConnorAssoc.com.

Pargament, K. I., Koenig, H. G., & Perez, L. M. (2000). The many methods of religious coping: Development and initial validation of the RCOPE. *Journal of Clinical Psychology, 56,* 519–543.

Pearlin, L. E., & Aneshensel, C. S. (1994). Caregiving: The unexpected career. *Social Justice Research, 7,* 373–390.

Pearlin, L. I., Mullan, J. T., Semple, S. J., & Skaff, M. M. (1990). Caregiving and the stress process: An overview of concepts and their measures. *Gerontologist, 30,* 583–594.

Peterson, L., Homer, A., & Wonderlich, S. (1982). The integrity of independent variables in behavior analysis. *Journal of Applied Behavior Analysis, 15,* 477–492.

Picot, S. J., Youngblut, J., & Zeller, R. (1997). Development and testing of a measure of perceived caregiver rewards in adults. *Journal of Nursing Measurement, 5,* 33–52.

Pilkonis, P. A., Imber, S. D., Lewis, P., & Rubinsky, P. (1984). A comparative outcome study of individual, group, and conjoint psychotherapy. *Archives of General Psychiatry, 41,* 431–437.

Rook, K. S. (1994). Assessing the health-related dimensions of older adults' social relationships. In M. P. Lawton & J. A. Teresi (Eds.), *Annual review of gerontology and geriatrics: Focus on assessment techniques* (pp. 142–182). New York: Springer.

Ryff, C. D., Singer, B., Love, G. D., & Essex, M. J. (1998). Resilience in adulthood and later life. In J. Lomranz (Ed.), *Handbook of aging and mental health: An integrative approach* (pp. 69–96). New York: Plenum Press.

Scharlach, A. E., Sobel, E. L., & Roberts, R. E. L. (1991). Employment and caregiver strain: An integrative model. *Gerontologist, 31,* 778–787.

Schneider, L. S., Reynolds, C. F., Lebowitz, B. D., & Friedhoff, A. J. (Eds.). (1994). *Diagnosis and treatment of depression in late life.* Washington, DC: American Psychiatric Press.

Schulz, R., O'Brien, A. T., Bookwala, J., & Fleissner, K. (1995). Psychiatric and physical morbidity effect of dementia caregiving: Prevalence, correlates and causes. *Gerontologist, 35,* 771–791.

Skinner, J. H., Teresi, J. A., Holmes, D., Stahl, S. M., & Sterwart, A. L. (Guest Editors). (2001). Measurement in older ethnically diverse populations. *Journal of Mental Health and Aging, 7,* 5–200.

Smith, M., Glass, G., & Miller, T. (1980). *The benefits of psychotherapy.* Baltimore: Johns Hopkins University Press.

Steffen, A. M., Gallagher-Thompson, D., & Thompson, L. W. (1997). Distress levels and coping in female caregivers and non-caregivers with major depressive disorder. *Journal of Clinical Geropsychology, 3,* 101–110.

Steffen, A. M., McKibbin, C., Zeiss, A. M., Gallagher-Thompson, D., & Bandura, A. (2002). Revised scale for caregiving self-efficacy: Reliability and validity studies. *Journal of Gerontology: Psychological Sciences, 57B,* P74–P86.

Tebb, S. S. (1995). An aid to empowerment: A caregiver well-being scale. *Health and Social Work, 20,* 87–92.

Teri, L., Truax, P., Logsdon, R., Uomoto, J., Zarit, S., & Vitaliano, P. P. (1992). Assessment of behavioral problems in dementia: The revised memory and behavior problem checklist. *Psychology and Aging, 7,* 622–631.

Thompson, L. W., & Gallagher-Thompson, D. (1996). Practical issues related to maintenance of mental health and positive well-being in family caregivers. In L. Carstensen, B. Edelstein, & L. Dornbrand (Eds.), *The practical handbook of clinical gerontology* (pp. 129–150). Los Angeles: Sage.

Vitaliano, P. P., Russo, J., Carr, J. E., Mairuro, R. D., & Becker, J. (1985). The ways of coping checklist: Revision and psychometric properties. *Multivariate Behavioral Research, 20,* 3–26.

Watson, D., Clark, L. A., & Tellegen, A. (1988). Development and validation of brief measures of positive and negative affect: The PANAS scales. *Journal of Personality and Social Psychology, 54,* 1063–1070.

Williamson, G. M., & Schulz, R. (1993). Coping with specific stressors in Alzheimer's disease caregiving. *Gerontologist, 33,* 747–755.

Yeaton, W., & Sechrest, L. (1981). Critical dimensions in the choice and maintenance of successful treatments: Strength, integrity, and effectiveness. *Journal of Consulting and Clinical Psychology, 49,* 156–167.

3

Interventions for a Multicultural Society

Dolores Gallagher-Thompson, Rita Hargrave, Ladson Hinton, Patricia Árean, Gayle Iwamasa, and L. McKenzie Zeiss

In the United States at present, a dramatic increase is occurring in the proportion of both the oldest-old (those aged 80 and above) and elders of color, who represent a wide array of culturally, racially, and ethnically distinct groups. According to relatively recent census data, growth in these two categories is expected to be tremendous in the next 20 to 30 years. In fact, it is expected that more than 25% of the population in this country will be age 65 or greater within the next decade or so as the baby boomers advance; and that the overall proportion of non-Hispanic Whites will drop from the current 90% to approximately 60% of the total U.S. population by the year 2030. Hispanic/Latino and Asian American elders are expected to increase at the most rapid rates, while growth in the African American and Native American populations is expected to be much slower (U.S. Bureau of the Census, 1992). What this means for clinicians and researchers working with older adults is that there will be more of them to treat; they will generally be older, due to improved health care that is prolonging life (along with increasing access to health care and related insurance amongst all older people); and they are more likely to be non-Caucasian (or non European American, if that term is preferred) than is the case at present. For these reasons, it is imperative that health care personnel begin to appreciate the tremendous heterogeneity of these groups and its implications for clinical and research practice.

More specifically, there are now a number of qualitative studies, conducted in the U.S. and in other countries, indicating how diverse cultural orientations may lead to ways of understanding dementia—and its associated impact on both the patient and other family members—that are significantly different from the biomedically based view of dementia that dominates the field today (Elliott, Di Minno, Lam, & Tu, 1996; Hinton, Fox, & Levkoff, 1999). These diverse "explanatory models," as they are referred to by Kleinman (1980), are of crucial importance to understanding how cultural differences influence the caregiving process. As Connell and Gibson (1997) have noted, culture is the lens through which events and experiences are perceived. How the tasks of caregiving are evaluated (e.g., how stressful they are deemed to be) and what impact (positive and negative) they have on key family caregivers is highly affected by culturally based explanatory models of health, illness, disease, wellness, and coping.

Thus, the primary goal of this chapter is to provide contextual background information about what is known regarding how cultural differences influence the dementia caregiving process in three major groups: African Americans, Hispanic/ Latino Americans, and Japanese Americans. We selected these groups not because other cultural, racial, or ethnic groups are less prevalent or less important, but because more research has been conducted, comparatively speaking, with individuals who self-identify as being a member of one of these particular groups. Before proceeding, however, a strong disclaimer is needed: We are aware that by using the named categories, which are derived from U.S. Census data and in common use in our society today, we may be accused of being insensitive to the tremendous within-group heterogeneity that is present (Kramer & Barker, 1994). That is to say, "Hispanics/Latinos" are not a homogeneous group at all, nor are "Asian/Pacific Islanders" or any of the other broad categorizations used to describe people of color. Rather, within each category or grouping, multiple cultures are represented, each with different patterns of immigration, periods of longevity in this country, variable access to services (depending in part on their educational attainments and social class in the country of origin, as well as on the degree of acculturation to the dominant society), and preferred language use, which may even differ in specific circumstances (such as speaking in one's native language to discuss personal matters, but in English for commerce and communication outside the immediate cultural group). This notable heterogeneity makes it easy for stereotypes to develop and be used: They are a way to simplify and make sense of the great variety that confronts health care professionals. However, the authors of this chapter agree that within-group diversity is just as important to understand, appreciate, and study as between-group differences are and perhaps more so. As argued so cogently by Whitfield and Baker-Thomas (1999), by gathering groups under one ethnic umbrella and then comparing them to Caucasians, important differences within each group are lost; yet these may be crucial for interpreting the phenomenon of caregiving stress and for the development of culturally appropriate interventions for caregivers of particular ethnic and cultural backgrounds.

In order to facilitate the reader's understanding of what follows, we have organized the available information under several headings that are used throughout; for example, unique explanatory models, how they might impact the development of programs for caregivers, and other factors affecting the caregiving situation and related help-seeking.

AFRICAN AMERICAN CAREGIVING: EXPLANATORY MODELS AND CULTURAL BELIEFS ABOUT DEMENTIA

As indicated earlier, there is much gerontological research to suggest that health care behaviors of ethnic minority elders are shaped by culturally mediated perceptions, beliefs, definitions, and responses to disease (Picot, 1995a, 1995b; Wenger, 1993). Explanatory models (EMs) of disease help describe illness behavior and service utilization patterns in ethnic minority patients and their caregivers. EMs include cultural beliefs about disease etiology, symptom severity, patterns of illness behavior, treatment alternatives, style of medical decision making, and assessment of treatment options (Kleinman, 1980). Current literature on EMs among African American elders and caregivers suggest that they characterize dementia as either (a) an aspect of normal aging, (b) a form of mental illness, (c) an expression of culture-specific deficits, or (d) a disruption in social functioning.

Dementia as Normal Aging

Many African American caregivers view memory loss as a consequence of normal aging. Symptoms of dementia may evoke limited concern among caregivers until the disease is in the advanced stage (Valle, 1989). Other authors suggest that African American caregivers may be reluctant to participate in research or clinical services that put a medical label on the family member (Gonzales, Gitlin, & Lyons, 1995).

Dementia as a Type of Mental Illness

Neuropsychiatric symptoms and behavioral problems associated with dementia may be viewed by African American families as a form of mental illness and be associated with substantial stigma and denial (Cox & Monk, 1996).

Dementia as a Culture-Specific Syndrome

Symptoms of dementia are similar to African American culture-specific syndromes of "worriation" and "spells" (Gaines, 2000). *Worriation* is a combination of anxiety and preservative thinking that can cause brain damage (Gaines 2000). It may resemble the anxiety, agitation, and obsessional thinking observed in some dementia patients. *Spells* are episodes of unusual consciousness consisting of extreme anger or irritability, fugue states, trances, or waking visions (e.g., when someone is awake and believes that he sees a dead relative) (American Psychiatric Association, *Diagnostic and Statistical Manual of Mental Disorders* [DSM-IV], 1994; Gaines, 2000). The fluctuations in mood and cognition and the perceptual distortions characteristic of dementia may be interpreted by the caregiver as spells.

Dementia as a Disruption in Social Functioning

Some authors suggest that Southern Black cultures place greater emphasis on performance of social role functions and affective functioning within the family than on cognitive functioning (Gaines, 2000). Therefore, African American caregivers may not acknowledge that symptoms of dementia are problematic until the patient cannot fulfill his usual family or social roles.

Medical anthropological research, on the other hand, reveals that "An elder might have shown clear and concerning symptoms of memory loss for a long time, but the caretaker [*sic*] recalls that something really dangerous was wrong when the elder began to hide things and accuse people of stealing money from him or her" (Fox, Hinton, & Levkoff, 1999). This study found that wrongful accusations directed at the caregiver were more commonly discussed than folk illnesses such as worriation or spells. The authors propose that the prevalence of themes of financial loss and betrayal are the result of the African American's lifelong experience of economic inequality, institutional racism, and social humiliation. This perspective is supported by the fact that the poverty rate in 1990 among African American elders was 34%, compared to 10.1% for elderly Whites.

ATTITUDES TOWARDS FAMILY CAREGIVING AMONG AFRICAN AMERICANS

Because African American elders maintain substantial status in their families, churches, and communities, family caregiving is highly socially valued and strongly encouraged. Lawton, Rajagopal, Brody, and Kleban (1992) report that African Americans subscribe more strongly than Whites to traditional values about caregiving. Traditional caregiving values include repaying the debt of being cared for as a child, continuing family tradition of mutual concern, fulfilling personal values, and setting an example for one's children.

Current social gerontology research describing ethnic minority caregivers often uses the *ethnic compensation model* as a theoretical framework. This model focuses on the ways that people reframe racial and ethnic identities as strengths or benefits that support health or protect people from harm caused by discrimination (Cool, 1987). Some authors suggest that the extensive use of this model has produced many studies that erroneously equate racial and ethnic differences with socioeconomic and social structural inequality (Fox et al., 1999). Much of the social gerontology literature has described African American caregivers as unassuming, unconditionally loyal, self-satisfied, less burdened, and less taxed servants. "However, the experiences of racialized subordination within a political economy, so central to an understanding of [African American] caregiver/family stories, are difficult to find represented in much of the comparative literature in social gerontology on caregiver burden" (Fox et al., 1999).

EXPLANATORY MODELS OF CAREGIVING AMONG AFRICAN AMERICANS

Several studies (Morcyz, Malloy, Bozick, & Martz, 1987; Mui, 1992) employ the scarcity hypothesis of role theory to examine the experiences of African American caregivers. The scarcity hypothesis suggests that people lack adequate time and resources to fulfill their multiple role obligations. These multiple role commitments promote role strain, resulting in role-demand overload and role conflict (Goode, 1960). In Morcyz's (1985) study, caregiver role strain was produced from the interaction of three variables: patient characteristics, caregiver characteristics, and environment (e.g., the physical layout of living space, financial resources, and availability of social support). The scarcity model predicted a positive relationship between role strain and the desire to institutionalize elders who have dementia. Because this relationship did not predict the behavior of African American caregivers, Morcyz concluded that the model was more salient for White than for African American caregivers.

Pearlin's conceptual model of caregiver stress has been the basis of other studies of African American and White caregivers (Cox & Monk, 1990). Pearlin describes caregiver stress as the result of the interaction of four factors: the background and context of stress, the stressors themselves, various mediators of stress, and the outcome or manifestation of stress (Pearlin, Mullan, Semple, & Skaff, 1990). The background and context of stressors consist of the socioeconomic status of the caregiver and the number of hours devoted to caregiving. Actual stressors include the patient's cognitive, physical and social functioning, disruptive behaviors, and family and job conflicts of the caregiver. Mediators are social supports, sense of competency as a caregiver, and coping mechanisms, such as prayer and religion, that protect the caregiver against negative effects of the stressors. Outcomes include activity limitations, relationship strain, personal strain, and role strain.

IMPLICATIONS FOR CAREGIVERS

Caregiver research has identified several key issues that affect African American families dealing with dementia and caregiving. These issues are caregiver demographics, caregiver health status, and caregiver burden.

Caregiver Demographics

African American compared to White caregivers are less likely to be spouses (Lawton et al., 1992) and are more likely to be the adult children of their care recipients (Hinrichsen & Ramirez, 1992). African American caregivers are often unmarried and as a result have fewer financial resources available to them; they also tend to be younger and have less formal education and lower incomes than White caregivers (Haley et al., 1993; Hinrichsen & Ramirez, 1992). Most African American caregivers are actively managing more than one person and may be responsible for the well being of children and other family members (National Alliance on Caregiving and the American Association of Retired Persons, 1997; Wood & Parham, 1990).

Studies of African American families suggest that caregiving is not restricted to a single person or the immediate family (Gibson & Jackson, 1987). Adult children are the most preferred caregivers, but siblings, other relatives, and friends also provide assistance when children are not available (Taylor, 1988). Other investigators (Cox & Monk, 1996) state that previous research may have overestimated the availability and extent of assistance rendered by African American adult children and other family caregivers. They suggest that adult children may be affected by strains and commitments in their own lives, which may severely limit the amount of assistance they can offer frail African American elders.

African American caregiver interviews reveal that in some cases extended families have disappointed caregivers and actually added to their daily burdens. Many caregivers reported that there were few instances of shared decision-making and often the primary caregiver was the sole decision-maker (Fox et al., 1999).

Health Status

Little is known about the health status of African American caregivers, though many are in an age group (45–64 years) that experiences significant health problems (Gibson, 1986; Horton & Smith, 1990). African American caregivers may be particularly vulnerable to poor health because they take on the bulk of the care (Taylor & Chatters, 1991; Yee, 1990), compared to White caregivers in the same age group (U.S. Dept of Health and Human Services, 1991). Some investigators suggest that African American caregivers more often report poor health and have higher mortality rates (Dilworth-Anderson & Anderson, 1994).

Caregiver Burden

Caregiving for a frail elder may lead to changes and conflicts in an individual's personal life, social interactions, and work life. These restrictions and changes, coupled with the overall emotional, physical, and financial impact of caregiving, in general lead to increased stress and burden (Brody, 1981, 1985). *Burden* has been defined as the negative psychological, economic, and physical effects of caring for a person who is impaired (Fredman, Daly, & Lazur, 1995). Caregiver burden is associated with greater functional and cognitive impairment in the patient and is a significant predictor of institutionalization. Studies of ethnic differences in caregiver burden have revealed conflicting results: Some have found that White compared to African American caregivers are more burdened (Fredman et al., 1995; Hinrichsen & Ramirez, 1992; Lawton et al., 1992; Mui, 1992), while others did not (cf. Morcyz et al., 1987). Yet some who have content-analyzed African American caregiver interviews have found themes of burden, loss, and alienation that have not been captured in the comparative social gerontology literature (Fox et al., 1999). Possible reasons for the conflicting results are differences in sampling strategies, decreased sensitivity of measures of burden among ethnic minority caregivers, and increased discomfort in African American caregivers about revealing personal feelings to interviewers who are of a different race.

RECOMMENDATIONS FOR COMMUNICATING WITH AFRICAN AMERICAN CAREGIVERS

For an individual African American patient with dementia, the health care professional will often interact with a network of caregivers who vary greatly in their educational backgrounds and levels of comfort with medical systems. Recommendations that can help to establish a productive working relationship with African American caregivers include the following:

1. Develop rapport with available members of the caregiver network. Identify one or two key informants who will consult with other family members to minimize confusion, multiple phone calls, and miscommunication.

2. Clarify with the caregivers what degree of detail that they want to know about the elder's condition. Some families will want a clearly articulated medical diagnosis such as Alzheimer's disease. Other families will feel uneasy about a medical label and are more concerned with management of problem behaviors.

3. Educate the caregivers about the etiology and disease progression of dementia.

4. Collaborate with the caregivers on the frequency and manner in which they would like to have updates on the patient's condition. Encourage caregivers to come to appointments with a written list of concerns and questions.

5. Provide the family with books, pamphlets, videos, and Internet sites that are informative and enlightening. Encourage the use of cognitive enhancers (e.g., Aricept) with African American patients with dementia. Encourage African American patients and caregivers to participate in dementia research.

6. Inform African American caregivers about the availability of long-term care services such as day care, respite care, home care, support groups, and individual and family counseling. Recommendations concerning these treatment options may need to be repeated several times over the course of months and years.

7. When indicated, encourage African American caregivers to engage in psychotherapy that focuses on the impact of caregiving on their emotional well-being and that helps them to develop strategies to manage the role conflicts between caregiving, work, family, and other responsibilities.

IMPLICATIONS FOR SERVICE UTILIZATION AND THE DEVELOPMENT OF EFFECTIVE INTERVENTIONS

Numerous barriers to health service utilization contribute to the underrepresentation of African Americans in dementia assessment clinics, long-term care services, and caregiver resources. Health services research has documented long-standing ethnic inequalities in access to, and quality of, care (Belgrave, Wykle, & Choi, 1993; Falcone & Broyles, 1994; Geiger, 1996). Because African American elders are often economically disadvantaged and uninsured, their health care may be limited to overcrowded, underfunded public and county health-care systems (Davis, 1985). African American elderly patients are more likely to have serious or chronic illnesses, more likely to use emergency rooms, and less likely to have a regular source of health care such as a primary medical doctor (Butler, 1988; Davis, 1985).

African American caregivers may be less knowledgeable about dementia assessment centers and the full array of available services. Even when they are aware of available resources, African American patients may mistrust Whites and traditional medical institutions (Terrell & Terrell, 1981). The lack of cultural relevance of existing programs and their inability to meet unique culturally defined needs of patients and caregivers may further alienate and discourage African American elders (Valle, 1989). Dissatisfaction with formal health care systems may be one of the factors promoting the continued use of informal caregivers and alternative health care providers (e.g., folk healers).

Many investigators have developed recommendations to improve dementia care-service utilization by African American elders and caregivers. For example, dementia-related programs need to be located within the target community (Valle, 1989) and should utilize staff who are culturally compatible with the target population. Agencies should be encouraged to conduct sensitivity training for staff when ethnic minority staff is not available (Valle, 1998). In addition, culturally relevant outreach and educational programs should be offered as part of the service package (Valle, 1989). African American national and community organizations should be encouraged to participate in dementia education and outreach to African American elders. Many authors have described the need for the validation of existing standardized tests among African American and other ethnic elders (Teng, Chui, & Sapevia, 1990). Additional resources need to be devoted toward the development of new, culture-free assessment instruments with increased sensitivity and specificity and of alternative strategies for detecting dementia in diverse ethnic populations (Teng et al., 1990).

Because African American and other ethnic minority caregivers usually do not attend support groups, several investigators have developed a multistage process to improve African American participation in these services. In their work with African American and Hispanic caregivers, Henderson and colleagues (Henderson, Gutierrez-Mayka, Garcia, & Boyd, 1993) outlined a four-stage process consisting of the following steps: (a) implement a targeted ethnographic survey and repeated interviews of key public figures to assess the concerns and lifestyles of the African American community; (b) initiate repeated contacts with African American caregivers through letters, telephone calls, home visits, and provision of staff persons to broker community resources; (c) conduct support group meetings in culturally neutral locations (e.g., churches); and (d) maintain an ongoing presence in the community over time. By using culture-friendly methods such as these, and others outlined by Young, Edevie, Young, and Peters (1996) that focus on enhancing enrollment of African Americans into research, African American caregivers are more likely to feel comfortable participating in intervention programs that were developed with input and support from their community.

LATINO/HISPANIC AMERICAN CAREGIVING: EXPLANATORY MODELS AND CULTURAL BELIEFS ABOUT DEMENTIA AND FAMILY CAREGIVING

Although Latino culture is comprised of a variety of subcultures with differing attitudes and norms, the one consistent feature that crosses all Latino subcultures is the strength of, and reliance on, family. Perhaps more than any other cultural group in the U.S., Latinos live in multigenerational homes and rely on extended family for social, financial, and instrumental support when coping with psychosocial stress (Cox & Monk, 1993b). The care of people who have dementia in the Latino community is primarily the responsibility of the family and rests largely on female members of the family and community. A study by Hendersen and Gutierrez-Mayka (1992) found the rank of preferences for family caregiving for a patient with dementia to be the wife first; a sister or female blood relative second; a female nonrelative third; male blood relatives fourth; and male in-laws last. Thus female resources are exhausted before attempts are made to engage men in this role.

Though women in this culture accept the caregiver role as their duty to family, the strain it places on them can be extraordinary. According to cultural mores, reliance on outside support is viewed as shirking one's responsibility and placing undue demands on outsiders. Research has shown that this particular cultural belief is an unhealthy one: Latina caregivers report more depression and more severe levels of depression when directly compared with other ethnic groups (Adams, Aranda, Kemp, & Takagi, in press). Also, those who fail to use outside supports and who view the care of the family member as their sole responsibility are most depressed and distressed (Cox & Monk, 1993a, 1996). The association between depression and adherence to traditional caregiving norms is largely related to the feeling that the caregiver is not doing her job well; despite all her efforts, the family member she is caring for becomes more difficult to manage. This sense of failure is fueled by the fact that dementia is poorly understood among the Latino community (Gallagher-Thompson, Talamantes, Ramirez, & Valverde, 1996). Because the cognitive decline in AD is associated with marked behavioral disturbance, Latinos often view AD as a form of mental illness, which from the Latino perspective should be controllable by a diligent family member (Gallagher-Thompson et al., 1996).

A lack of understanding of dementia creates additional stress for the family and caregiver. Because dementia is thought of as a mental disorder, family members are more likely to hide the problem from others. This is done out of respect for the affected family member and because the *concepto de familia* prevalent in the Latino community specifies that if one person has a stigmatized disease, the whole family shares the stigma. Admission that a family member has a mental illness results in feelings of shame and embarrassment on the part of family members. This shame further discourages family members and caregivers from seeking support, thus isolating the Latino caregiver even more (Connell & Gibson, 1997).

IMPLICATIONS FOR CAREGIVERS

Because of the need to protect the family and patient from stigma, Latinos are often more reluctant to use supportive services for the caregiver and for themselves. Even though there is now some research supporting the effectiveness of various interventions, such as psychoeducational programs and support groups, for reducing caregiver distress among Latinos (see Gallagher-Thompson, Árean, Rivera, & Thompson, 2001), many tend to be fearful of such psychologically based programs. This may be due in part to the cultural norm of not sharing family secrets with strangers, as well as to the role overload so common in this situation. There literally may be no time to spare—for many, caregiving is a full time job, and services such as in-home supportive care or day or overnight respite, which are typically used by stressed Caucasian caregivers when finances permit, would not be seen as culturally appropriate for Latinas. Although one study found that when surveyed many Latinos indicate there are other family members who can care for the patient for short periods of time (Cox & Monk, 1993a), utilization of those supports tends to be infrequent.

In attempting to link a caregiver to supportive services, a provider may do best by appealing to the caregiver's sense of responsibility. Indicating that improved health will help the caregiver be more efficient and productive as a caregiver is often a compelling argument. In addition, telling the caregiver that she will learn strategies for better managing the family member's illness provides a strong rationale for attending supportive services (Gallagher-Thompson et al., 1997). When possible, it is best to involve other family members in the education. Caregivers are more likely to receive support for taking breaks or using formal assistance if the family is informed about the illness.

CARE RECIPIENT AND CAREGIVER ASSESSMENT ISSUES

Most providers are going to be faced with problems in assessing a patient who potentially has dementia and engaging the family members in use of outside support services. Issues such as the availability of bilingual and bicultural staff to provide assessment and treatment, as well as resolution of such practical problems as securing transportation to and from the site of the evaluation or treatment, all need to be addressed to ensure successful experiences (Árean &

Gallagher-Thompson, 1996). Out of respect for the family member who is ill, the caregiver will try her best to minimize the patient's disability so as not to embarrass him or her in front of other respected people, such as doctors. In addition, the caregiver will minimize the extent of burden she is under. As John and McMillian (1998) discovered in their focus-group study of burden among Mexican Americans, the term "burden" was not widely endorsed, though the experiences reported by these caregivers—such as frustration and resentment due to lack of involvement in caregiving by other family members—were certainly burdensome. To the Latino community, admitting burden implies that the caregiver does not accept her role and thus is ungrateful for all the caregiving she received when she needed help from the family. After all, didn't her husband work hard to make sure she had a home? Didn't her mother change her diapers and clean up her messes when she could not care for herself? Why should she feel burdened by what is essentially her reciprocal duty?

The level of acculturation can further complicate distress. Those Latinos who are bicultural, or living in both Latino and Anglo cultures equally, seem to be significantly more strained by the caregiver role compared to those who are more traditional in their values (Calderon & Tennstedt, 1998). The pull between family duties and responsibilities and wanting to pursue one's own life and goals is frustrating to the bicultural caregiver. One study has supported the hypothesis that younger Latinos tend to be most depressed by caregiving because of the competing demands of family and the pursuit of autonomy (Cox & Monk, 1996). The younger, bicultural Latina may feel "stuck" between feeling angry at being designated the caregiver and feeling guilty for feeling angry in the first place (Valle, 1998).

In trying to address the problems associated with the care of a person with dementia, providers should first attempt to educate caregiver and families about the nature of dementia (Henderson & Gutierrez-Mayka, 1992). As stated earlier, many Latinos mistake dementia for a mental disorder, which is often viewed as a weakness in character. Telling the family that dementia is a medical illness characterized by increasing declines in memory and health alleviates the stigma associated with it. Education externalizes the blame for the patient's decline in health and helps remove guilt and blame from the caregiver. A caregiver and family may be then more amenable to assistance, which in turn will alleviate caregiver burden and perhaps facilitate early intervention.

The interested reader is referred to chapter 11 (this volume) for a detailed description of an effective caregiver education and intervention program called *El Portal* that was conducted in Los Angeles, CA for Latino caregivers. Also of relevance is chapter 6 (this volume) where a novel psychoeducational program for Latino caregivers is described that was successfully implemented in the San Francisco Bay area of northern CA.

IMPLICATIONS FOR SERVICE UTILIZATION AND THE DEVELOPMENT OF EFFECTIVE INTERVENTIONS

In our opinion, a primary barrier to service utilization is lack of knowledge about dementia. (Discussion of other barriers, as well as incentives for engagement in assessment and treatment programs, can be found in Árean & Gallagher-Thompson, 1996). As soon as a diagnosis is made or suspected, providers should begin to educate the family about dementia, clarifying that it is a medical disorder. Educating the caregiver and family on the importance of time off for the caregiver can ease the familial barriers a caregiver may face when trying to attend an intervention group. Furthermore, community gatekeepers (such as priests) need to be educated about the disorder so that they can educate the populace and promote the use of available services (Gallagher-Thompson et al., 1994).

A second barrier to service use is lack of time and resources. The mental health literature clearly shows that Latinos tend to use services on an as-needed basis, largely because they have little time to devote to regular appointments. Being flexible about time constraints is important for caregiver interventions to succeed. For instance, being available by phone or on an as-needed basis is more acceptable to many Latinos than is a fixed and regular schedule.

An additional barrier to use of services in the Latino community is the lack of culturally sensitive services. Most care is delivered through translators, and when a provider can speak Spanish, there is often a lack of understanding about how Latinos view health services. As much as possible, providers should educate themselves about clients' cultural and personal values, traditions, and beliefs. Without this awareness, interventions will not succeed. Providers should not be overly discouraged by the necessity for more than just good intentions, however, because a great deal of the necessary education can be achieved simply by asking caregivers and families about their cultures, how they view illness, and how they understand the use of supportive services.

JAPANESE AMERICAN CAREGIVING: GENERAL ISSUES OF OLDER ADULTS

Japanese American elders are a unique group of Asian Americans. They have a history of being targets of excessive racism and discrimination, culminating in the unconstitutional removal of their homes and property and incarceration in concentration camps during World War II (Itai & McRae, 1994; Kitano, 1982; Yamamoto & Wagatsuma, 1980). Following the war, former Japanese Americans internees found that their social, economic, and employment opportunities were extremely limited. An informal code of silence in which former internees refrained from discussing their internment experiences with family or friends (Loo, 1993;

Nagata, 1991) has been described, but few psychological studies have examined the long-term mental health sequelae of the internment in Japanese Americans, particularly its impact on aging.

Japanese Americans differ from other Asian American ethnic groups in how they treat the aging process. For example, they often have a *kanreki*, a celebration involving family and friends, on one's 60th birthday and additional birthday celebrations in subsequent years (Doi, 1991). These experiences and values are some of the characteristics that differentiate Japanese American seniors from other Asian American seniors, and they may have contributed to the development of risk factors and protections against distress that differ from those of other older adults.

A few mental health studies have specifically examined Japanese Americans (Furuta, 1981; Kuo, 1984; Nishio & Murase, 1983); however, older adults either were not included or were not the major focus of the study. In addition to the author's research, only one published study (Yamamoto et al., 1985) focused specifically on the mental health of Japanese American elders, though this study did not examine dementia as a category. Those researchers who have examined dementia prevalence found that adherence to a traditional Japanese lifestyle decreased the risk of cognitive decline (Graves et al., 1999). These authors suggest that lower cardiovascular disease and greater social support may play a protective role.

EXPLANATORY MODELS AND CULTURAL BELIEFS ABOUT DEMENTIA

Braun and Browne (1998a) reported that in traditional Japanese culture, psychological problems are perceived as stigmatizing, attributed either to genetics, bad karma, or poor family relations. They reported that the Japanese words used to describe dementia are *kichigai* (crazy, insane) and *bokeru* (senility or forgetful in old age). In addition, they reported that such difficulties are denied and kept within the family—often by hiding the individual who is experiencing problems. To discuss these problems with someone outside the family would result in losing face.

Caution is warranted in making such generalizations. Recent evidence suggests that there appears to be significant knowledge about Alzheimer's disease among this group, as well as interest and efforts to learn more about it. In the course of conducting research projects with Japanese American older adults, Iwamasa and colleagues have had many discussions regarding Alzheimer's disease. Contrary to what Braun and Browne's (1998a) assertions would predict, many of these discussions were unplanned and initiated by the older adults in informal conversation. Many participants in several research projects spoke of their own experience with friends, family, and loved ones who had dementia (Hilliard & Iwamasa, 1998a, 1998b; Iwamasa, 1998).

Traphagan (2000) discussed the difference between *chiho* (dementia) and *boke* among Japanese medical professionals as well as in the lay population of Japan. *Boke* is a less medical and at least partially controllable type of dementia, as compared to *chiho*, in which there is a definite assumption of a disease process. Traphagan contended that if an individual views himself or herself as experiencing boke, efforts are made to prevent or delay progression. He also argues that these efforts are seen as a moral imperative—that there is an obligation for an individual to be socially responsible by caring for his or her physical and mental health. Although it is clear that the value of being mentally and physically intact is held among Japanese American older adults, what is not clear is whether the concepts of chiho and boke are the same for Japanese American older adults as they are for those in Japan.

Rogers and Izutsu (1980) contend that Japanese older adults somaticize illness and deny emotional components to their illnesses. However, little empirical evidence has documented such claims. Indeed, in more recent research, Japanese American older adults included psychological and cognitive symptoms in their conceptualizations of depression and anxiety (Iwamasa & Hilliard, 1999; Iwamasa, Hilliard, & Osato, 1998). Furthermore, as many researchers and clinicians report, older adults are more sensitive to somatic complaints in general as they age. No study has examined whether or not Japanese American older adults differ from other ethnic groups in their level of somatization.

Braun and Browne (1998a) also discuss the concept of *shikata ganai*, meaning "one can't help it," in describing how dementia may be perceived by Japanese American older adults. Although this concept is common, many Japanese American older adults with whom Iwamasa and colleagues have worked commented on how they were engaging in interventions to prevent the onset of dementia. Examples include keeping physically active, learning something new every day, keeping one's mind alert, and getting out of the house and socializing (Iwamasa & Hilliard, 1999; Iwamasa, Hilliard, & Osato; 1998; Hilliard, Pai, & Iwamasa, 1998).

ATTITUDES TOWARD FAMILY CAREGIVING AMONG JAPANESE AMERICANS

In Japan, there is an emphasis on self-reliance and self-care, and welfare systems for older adults are perceived as Western, Christian-based systems. There continues to be an emphasis on home caregiving, with the Japanese government developing family training classes (*kazoku kaigosha*). However, many cities are beginning to offer day care, home helpers, and visiting nurses. Finally, although the ideal interpretation of filial piety focuses on the son, the daughter-in-law or adult daughter continues to bear the burden for caregiving in Japan (Jenike, 1997).

Braun and Browne (1998a) describe *amae*, the importance of interpersonal harmony and relationships. Filial piety (*oyakoko*) and obligation to one's family (*giri*) also affect caregiving of older adults, resulting in the expectation that the family is responsible for providing care for older adult family members and in resistance to obtaining outside help for caregiving (Braun & Browne, 1998b; Fujita, Ito, Abe, & Takeuchi, 1991).

However, in several studies, Iwamasa and colleagues have found that among Japanese American older adults in Los Angeles who attend the Seinan Senior Citizens' Center, most individuals live with their partners or alone (Iwamasa & Hilliard, 1999; Iwamasa, Hilliard, & Kost, 1998; Iwamasa, Hilliard, & Osato, 1998). Furthermore, the existence of Keiro Services, an agency that provides housing for Japanese American older adults, and other similar housing facilities has affected the emphasis on caregiving within the family. These agencies, however, are consistent with the Japanese cultural tradition of the importance of community. Many members of the administration and staff of these facilities are Japanese American or speak Japanese.

CARE RECIPIENT AND CAREGIVER ASSESSMENT ISSUES

Practitioners should be aware of the increasing diversity of Japanese American older adults. In addition to variations in age and language, generational differences among Japanese American older adults may result in differences in incarceration experiences, gender roles, education and socioeconomic status, acculturation, and perceptions of racism and discrimination, as well as perceptions of their own ethnic identities and those of other ethnic groups. Practitioners must be familiar with these within-group differences in the provision of care.

Cultural issues are also important in establishing rapport and communicating information. If there is a need for translation, it is important not to use family members. Such individuals typically are children or grandchildren of the care recipient. This change in roles from traditional family roles and behaviors is culturally insensitive and incongruent. Translators should be familiar with dementia and related health-care issues, as well as have experience and skills in working with Japanese American older adults.

IMPLICATIONS FOR CAREGIVERS

Depending on the personal characteristics of the individual who is experiencing cognitive decline, family members will confront a range of issues. Many later-generation older adults who have established stable social support networks outside their immediate families may desire to receive care from sources other than the family. When cognitive difficulties begin to occur, friends may provide references for specific health-care professionals whom they have heard positive things about. Additionally, those older adults who attend senior centers where dementia screenings and other health-care programs are available have increased access to health care for dementia. All of these factors lead to reductions in family responsibilities. However, this may also mean that families will have less information about the health care status of their loved ones.

Among families in which the older adult with dementia is living in a child's home, caregiving responsibilities are commonly left to a woman (typically the wife of the firstborn son, or the firstborn daughter if there is no son). This can lead to great stress and tension if the woman is also the primary caregiver for any children still in the home or if she works outside the home. It is particularly important for these burdened caregivers to be informed of any services they may be eligible for.

Nonverbal communication plays a primary role in Japanese American families (Trockman et al., 1997). Family members may have difficulty when the care recipient is no longer able to perceive such communication accurately and they also may misinterpret or personalize nonverbal signals from the individual with dementia.

Also of particular importance is the need for health care professionals to understand family values such as filial piety and responsibility for one's own care. The value of self-care may result in family members experiencing some difficulty in identifying whether the older adult is in need of assistance. Tempo and Saito (1996) provided a vignette describing a 75-year-old widow frequently visited by her family members. She always reassured them that she was fine and not to worry. The family did not realize that she needed assistance until she was found wandering about town, at which time formal caregiving activities were instituted.

IMPLICATIONS FOR SERVICE UTILIZATION AND DEVELOPMENT OF EFFECTIVE INTERVENTIONS

Given the decreasing stigma of Alzheimer's disease and the increasing interest in learning about it among Japanese Americans, many of the remaining barriers to services are the same ones commonly shared with other ethnic minority populations. Lack of knowledge of available services, prohibitive cost and location of services, language barriers, and ignorance of cultural issues on the part of health care providers are likely to impede the utilization of services (Braun & Browne, 1998a).

It is recommended that providers of care understand the specific communities and contexts in which Japanese American older adults live. Although knowledge of the history of Japanese Americans in the United States is important, it is not sufficient to provide appropriate services. In addition, collaborating with existing community agencies will increase the credibility of services and the likelihood that individuals will feel comfortable accessing them. Providing information to care recipients' family members so that they understand the course of dementia and have accurate expectations will also be helpful.

The development of culturally appropriate methods of assessment, conceptualizations of symptoms, and interventions will also increase the utilization of services. For example, instead of trying to "convince" the care recipient and family of the conventional Western concept of dementia, health care practitioners and caregivers should enter into clients' explanatory models of illness (Kleinman, Eisenberg, & Good, 1978) and explain why suggested interventions will be helpful. If health care providers' suggested interventions do not match the recipient's conceptualization of the problem, treatment compliance will likely be diminished (Kleinman et al., 1978).

Braun, Takamura, Forman, Sasaki, and Meininger (1995) recommend the following strategies for increasing service utilization among Japanese American dementia caregivers:

1. Culturally sensitive outreach materials should be written in the language of the targeted population and presented in the appropriate context.
2. Information should be disseminated through minority-oriented media.
3. Collaboration should be established with community groups and leaders who provide high-quality, highly regarded services.
4. Services should be evaluated for their accessibility and acceptability to the target population.

It is only by becoming knowledgeable about this culture and its values and incorporating them into research and service programs that new information will be generated regarding which kinds of programs are most effective, and for whom, to assist Japanese American caregivers' in their ever-changing and increasingly demanding roles.

CLOSING COMMENTS

One aim of this chapter was to increase the reader's "cultural competence" to some degree by providing a review and a synthesis of current information about dementia caregiving among three distinct ethnic and cultural groups. Development of cultural competence is becoming increasingly important to health care providers, and in fact several professional organizations have recently issued practice guidelines to aid their members in this task (cf. Hansen, Pepitone-Arreola-Rockwell, & Greene, 2000, whose work is oriented toward psychologists). As they note, "There is always a dialectical relationship between understanding people as individuals and understanding them as representatives of all the groups with which they identify. Multicultural competence is finding some reasonable, responsible, and ethical balance among these factors" (Hansen et al., 2000, p. 653). In the field of dementia-caregiving practice and research, the need is imperative. In our opinion, much work remains to be accomplished to sensitize health care providers to these issues, without relying on stereotypes or outmoded knowledge. Starting from the premise that we must respect the uniqueness of each client, professionals should embrace the challenge ahead and welcome the opportunities that are increasingly present to learn and grow oneself—and to respectfully assist others to do the same.

REFERENCES

Adams, B., Aranda, M. P., Kemp, R., & Takagi, K. (in press). Ethnic and gender differences in distress among Anglo-American, African-American, Japanese-American and Mexican-American spousal caregivers of persons with dementia. *Journal of Clinical Geropsychology.*

American Psychiatric Association. (1994). *Diagnostic and statistical manual of mental disorders* (4th ed.). Washington, DC: Author.

Árean, P., & Gallagher-Thompson, D. (1996). Issues and recommendations for the retention of older ethnic minority adults into clinical research. *Journal of Consulting and Clinical Psychology, 65,* 875–880.

Belgrave, L. L., Wykle, J. L., & Choi, J. M. (1993). Health, double jeopardy and culture: The use of institutionalization by African Americans. *Gerontologist, 33,* 379–385.

Braun, K. L., & Browne, C. V. (1998a). Perceptions of dementia, caregiving, and help seeking among Asian and Pacific Islander Americans. *Health and Social Work, 23,* 262–274.

Braun, K. L., & Browne, C. V. (1998b). Cultural values and caregiving patterns among Asian and Pacific Islander Americans. In D. Redburn & R. McNamara (Eds.), *Social gerontology* (pp. 155–182). New York: Greenwood Press.

Braun, K. L., Takamura, J. C., Forman, S. M., Sasaki, P. A., & Meininger, L. (1995). Developing and testing outreach materials on Alzheimer's disease for Asian and Pacific Island Americans. *Gerontologist, 35,* 122–126.

Brody, E. M. (1981). Women in the middle and family help to older people. *Gerontologist, 21,* 471–480.

Brody, E. M. (1985). Patient care as normative family stress. *Gerontologist, 25,* 19–29.

Butler, P. A. (1988). *Too poor to be sick.* Washington, DC: American Public Health Association.

Calderon, V., & Tennstedt, S. L. (1998). Ethnic differences in the expression of caregiver burden: Results of a qualitative study. *Journal of Gerontological Social Work, 30,* No. 1-2, 159–178.

Connell, C. M., & Gibson, G. D. (1997). Racial, ethnic and cultural differences in dementia caregiving: Review and analysis. *The Gerontological Society of America, 37,* 355C–364C.

Cool, L. E. (1987). The effects of social class and ethnicity on the aging process. In P. Silverman et al. (Eds.), *The elderly as modern pioneers* (pp. 263–282). Bloomington: Indiana University Press.

Cox, C., & Monk, A. (1990). Minority caregivers of dementia victims: A comparison of Black and Hispanic families. *Journal of Applied Gerontology, 9,* 340–354.

Cox, C., & Monk, A. (1993a). Black and Hispanic caregivers of dementia victims: Their needs and implications for services. In C. M. Barresi & D. E. Stull (Eds.), *Ethnic elderly and long-term care* (pp. 57–67). New York: Springer.

Cox, C., & Monk, A. (1993b). Hispanic culture and family care of Alzheimer's patients. *Health and Social Work, 18,* 92–100.

Cox, C., & Monk, A. (1996). Strain among caregivers: Comparing the experiences of African American and Hispanic caregivers of Alzheimer's patients. *International Journal of Aging and Human Development, 43,* 93–105.

Davis, K. (1985). *Access to health care: A matter of fairness.* Washington, DC: Center for National Policy.

Dilworth-Anderson, P., & Anderson, N. B. (1994). Dementia caregiving in Blacks: A contextual approach to research. In E. Light, N. Niederehe, & B. Lebowitz (Eds.), *Stress effects on family of Alzheimer's patients.* New York: Springer.

Doi, M. L. (1991). A transformation of ritual: The Nisei 60th birthday. *Journal of Cross-Cultural Gerontology, 6,* 153–163.

Elliott, K. S., Di Minno, M., Lam, D., & Tu, A. M. (1996). Working with Chinese families in the context of dementia. In G. Yeo & D. Gallagher-Thompson (Eds.), *Ethnicity and the dementias* (pp. 89–108). Washington, DC: Taylor & Francis.

Falcone, D., & Broyles, R. (1994). Access to long-term care: Race as a barrier. *Journal of Health Politics, Policy and Law, 19,* 583–596.

Folkman, S., & Lazarus, R. S. (1985). If it changes it must be a process: Study of emotion and coping during three stages of a college examination. *Journal of Personality and Social Psychology, 48,* 150–170.

Fox, K., Hinton, W. L., & Levkoff, S. (1999). Take up the caregiver's burden: Stories of care for urban African American elders with dementia. *Culture, Medicine and Psychiatry, 23,* 501–529.

Fredman, L., Daly, M., & Lazur, A. (1995). Burden among White and Black caregivers to elderly adults. *Journal of Gerontology, 50,* S110–S118.

Fujita, S., Ito, K. L., Abe, J., & Takeuchi, D. T. (1991). Japanese Americans. In N. Mokuau (Ed.), *Handbook of social services for Asian and Pacific Islanders* (pp. 61–78). New York: Greenwood Press.

Furuta, B. S. (1981). Ethnic identities of Japanese American families: Implications for counseling. In C. Getty & W. Humphreys (Eds.), *Understanding the family* (pp. 200–231). New York: Appleton Autumn.

Gaines, A. D. (2000). Alzheimer's disease in the context of Black (Southern) culture. *Journal of Gerontology: Social Sciences, 6,* 33–38.

Gallagher-Thompson, D., Árean, P., Coon, D. W., Menendez, A., Takagi, K., Haley, W., Argüelles, T., Rubert, M., Loewenstein, D., & Szapocznik, J. (2000). Development and implementation of intervention strategies for culturally diverse caregiving populations. In R. Schulz (Ed.), *Handbook on dementia caregiving* (pp. 151–185). New York: Springer.

Gallagher-Thompson, D., Árean, P., Rivera, P., & Thompson, L. W. (2001). Reducing distress in Hispanic family caregivers using a psychoeducational intervention. *Clinical Gerontologist, 23,* 17–32.

Gallagher-Thompson, D., Leary, M., Ossinalde, C., Romero, J. J., Wald, M. J., & Fernandez-Gamarra, E. (1997). Hispanic caregivers of older adults with dementia: Cultural issues in outreach and intervention. *Group: Journal of the Eastern Group Psychotherapy Association, 21,* 211–232.

Gallagher-Thompson, D., Moorehead, R., Polich, T., Argüello, D., Johnson, C., Rodriquez, V., & Meyer, M. (1994). Comparisons of outreach strategies for Hispanic caregivers of Alzheimer's victims. *Clinical Gerontologist, 15,* 57–63.

Gallagher-Thompson, D., Talamantes, M., Ramirez, R., & Valverde, I. (1996). Service delivery issues and recommendations for working with Mexican American family caregivers. In G. Yeo & D. Gallagher-Thompson (Eds.), *Ethnicity and the dementias* (pp. 137–152). Washington, DC: Taylor & Francis.

Geiger, H. J. (1996). Race and health care—An American dilemma? *New England Journal of Medicine, 335,* 815–816.

George, L. K. (1988). *Social participation in later life in the Black American elderly.* In J. Jackson (Ed.), New York: Springer.

Gibson, R. C. (1986). Blacks in an aging society. *Daedalus, 115,* 349–371.

Gibson, G. D., & Jackson, J. (1987). The health, physical functioning and informal supports of the Black elderly. *Millbank Memorial Fund Quarterly/Health and Society, 65,* 421–451.

Gonzales, E., Gitlin, L., & Lyons, K. (1995). Review of the literature of African American caregivers of individuals with dementia. *Journal of Cultural Diversity, 2,* 40–48.

Goode, W. J. (1960). A theory of role strain. *American Sociological Review, 25,* 483–496.

Graves, A. B., Rajaram, L., Bowen, J. D., McCormick, W. C., McCurry, S., & Larson, E. B. (1999). Cognitive decline and Japanese culture in a cohort of older Japanese Americans in King County, WA: The *Kame* Project. *Journal of Gerontology: Social Sciences, 54B,* S154–S161.

Haley, W. E., West, C., Wadley, V. G., Ford, G., White, F., Barrett, J., Harrell, L., & Roth, D. (1993). Psychological, social and health impact of caregiving: A comparison of Black and White dementia family caregivers and non-caregivers. *Psychology and Aging, 10,* 540–552.

Hansen, N. D., Pepitone-Arreola-Rockwell, F., & Greene, A. F. (2000). Multicultural competence: Criteria and case examples. *Professional Psychology: Research and Practice, 31,* 652–660.

Henderson, J. N., & Gutierrez-Mayka, M. (1992). Ethnocultural themes in caregiving to Alzheimer's disease patients in Hispanic families. *Clinical Gerontologist, 11,* 59–74.

Henderson, J. N., Gutierrez-Mayka, M., Garcia, J., & Boyd, S. (1993). A model for Alzheimer's disease support group development in African American and Hispanic populations. *Gerontologist, 33,* 409–414.

Hilliard, K. M., & Iwamasa, G. Y. (1998a). Conducting culturally appropriate survey research at a Japanese American senior center. Symposium (G. Iwamasa, chair) presented at the annual meeting of the Association for Advancement of Behavior Therapy, Washington, DC.

Hilliard, K. M., & Iwamasa, G. Y. (1998b). Are focus groups effective with Japanese American older adults? Poster session presented at the annual meeting of the Association for Advancement of Behavior Therapy, Washington, DC.

Hilliard, K. M., Pai, S. M., & Iwamasa, G. Y. (1998). Factors that influence healthy lifestyles among Japanese American older adults. Poster session presented at the annual meeting of the Asian American Psychological Association, San Francisco.

Hinrichsen, G. A., & Ramirez, M. (1992). Black and White dementia caregivers: A comparison of their adaptation, adjustment and service utilization. *Gerontologist, 32,* 375–381.

Hinton, W. L., Fox, K., & Levkoff, S. (1999). Exploring the relationships among aging, ethnicity, and family dementia caregiving. *Culture, Medicine and Psychiatry, 23*(4), 403–413.

Hinton, W. L., & Levkoff, S. (1999). Constructing Alzheimer's: Narratives of lost identities, confusion and loneliness in old age. *Culture, Medicine and Psychiatry, 23*(4), 453–475.

Horton, C. P., & Smith, J. C. (1990). *Statistical record of Black America.* Detroit, MI: Gale Press.

Itai, G., & McRae, C. (1994). Counseling older Japanese American clients: An overview and observations. *Journal of Counseling and Development, 72,* 373–377.

Iwamasa, G. Y. (November, 1998). *Conducting culturally appropriate research with Asian Americans: Methodological issues.* Chair of symposium panel presented at the annual meeting of the Association for Advancement of Behavior Therapy, Washington, DC.

Iwamasa, G. Y., & Hilliard, K. (1999). Depression and anxiety among Asian American elderly: A review of the literature. *Clinical Psychology Review, 19,* 343–358.

Iwamasa, G. Y., Hilliard, K., & Kost, C. (1998). The geriatric depression scale and Japanese American older adults. *Clinical Gerontologist, 19,* 13–24.

Iwamasa, G. Y., Hilliard, K., & Osato, S. (1998). Conceptualizing anxiety and depression: The Japanese American older adult perspective. *Clinical Gerontologist, 19,* 77–93.

Jenike, B. R. (1997). Gender and duty in Japan's aged society: The experience of family caregivers. In J. Sokolovsky (Ed.), *The cultural context of aging: Worldwide perspectives* (2nd ed., pp. 218–238). Westport, CT: Bergin & Garvey.

John, R., & McMillian, B. (1998). Exploring caregiver burden among Mexican Americans: Cultural prescriptions, family dilemmas. *Journal of Aging and Ethnicity, 1*(2), 93–111.

Kitano, H. H. (1982). Mental health in the Japanese-American community. In E. E. Jones & S. J. Korchin (Eds.), *Minority mental health* (pp. 149–164). New York: Praeger.

Kleinman, A. (1980). *Patients and healers in the context of culture: An exploration of the borderland between anthropology, medicine and psychiatry.* Berkeley: University of California Press.

Kleinman, A., Eisenberg, L., & Good, B. (1978). Culture, illness, and care: Clinical lessons from anthropologic and cross-cultural research. *Annals of Internal Medicine, 88,* 251–258.

Kramer, B. J., & Barker, J. C. (1994). Ethnicity in the elderly. *Journal of Cross-Cultural Gerontology, 9,* 403–417.

Kuo, W. H. (1984). Prevalence of depression among Asian Americans. *Journal of Nervous and Mental Disease, 172,* 449–457.

Lawton, M., Rajagopal, D., Brody, E., & Kleban, M. (1992). The dynamics of caregiving for a demented elder among Black and White families. *Journal of Gerontology B: Social Sciences, 47,* S156–S164.

Loo, C. (1993). An integrative-sequential treatment model for posttraumatic stress disorder: A case study of the Japanese American internment and redress. *Clinical Psychology Review, 13,* 89–117.

Morcyz, R. (1985). Caregiving strain and the desire to institutionalize family members with Alzheimer's disease. *Research on Aging, 7,* 329–361.

Morcyz, R., Malloy, J., Bozich, M., & Martz, P. (1987). Racial differences in family burden: Clinical implications for social work. *Journal of Gerontological Social Work, 4,* 107–125.

Mui, A. (1992). Caregiver strain among Black and White daughter caregivers: A role theory perspective. *Gerontologist, 32,* 203–212.

Nagata, D. K. (1991). Transgenerational impact of the Japanese American internment: Clinical issues in working with children of former internees. *Psychotherapy, 28,* 121–128.

National Alliance on Caregiving and the American Association of Retired Persons. (1997). *Family caregiving in the U.S.: Findings from a national survey.* Bethesda, MD.

Nishio, K., & Murase, K. (1983). Characteristics of psychotherapists and their clients in Japan and psychotherapists and their Japanese American clients in the U.S. Paper presented at the Conference of Japanese culture and mental health, East-West Center, Honolulu, HI.

Pearlin, L., Mullan, J., Semple, S., & Skaff, M. (1990). Caregiving and the stress process. *Gerontologist, 30,* 583–594.

Picot, S. J. (1995a). Rewards, costs, and coping of African American caregivers. *Nursing Research, 44,* 147–152.

Picot, S. J. (1995b). Family and cultural influences on illness. In W. J. Phipps, B. C. Long, & N. F. Woods (Eds.), *Medical-surgical nursing: Concepts and clinical practice* (5th ed.). St. Louis, MO: Mosby.

Rogers, T., & Izutsu, S. (1980). The Japanese. In J. F. McDermott, W. S. Tseng, & T. W. Maretzki (Eds.), *People and cultures of Hawaii: A psychocultural profile* (pp. 73–99). Honolulu: University Press of Hawaii.

Taylor, R. J. (1988). Aging and supportive relationships among Black Americans. In J. Jackson (Ed.), *The Black American elderly* (pp. 259–281). New York: Springer.

Taylor, R. J., & Chatters, L. M. (1991). Extended family networks of older Black adults. *Journal of Gerontology, 46,* S210–S217.

Tempo, P. M., & Saito, A. (1996). Techniques of working with Japanese American families. In G. Yeo & D. Gallagher-Thompson (Eds.), *Ethnicity and the dementias* (pp. 109–122). Washington, DC: Taylor & Francis.

Teng, E., Chui, H., & Sapevia, D. (1990). Senile dementia: Performance on a neuropsychological battery. *Recent Advances in Cardiovascular Disease, 11,* 27–43.

Terrell, F., & Terrell, S. L. (1981). An inventory to measure cultural mistrust among Blacks. *Western Journal of Black Studies, 5,* 180–184.

Traphagan, J. W. (2000). *Taming oblivion: Aging bodies and the fear of senility in Japan.* Albany: State University of New York Press.

Trockman, C., Murdaugh, C., Kadohiro, J. K., Petrovich, H., Curb, J. D., & White, L. (1997). Adapting instruments for caregiver research in elderly Japanese American women. *Journal of Cross-Cultural Gerontology, 12,* 109–120.

U.S. Bureau of the Census. (1992). *Sixty-five plus in America.* Washington, DC: U.S. Government Printing Office.

U.S. Department of Health and Human Services. (1991). *Health status of minorities and low-income groups: 3rd ed.* (DHHS Publication No. 271-848/40085). Washington, DC: U.S. Government Printing Office.

Valle, R. (1989). Cultural and ethnic issues in Alzheimer's disease family research. In E. Light & B. D. Lebowitz (Eds.), *Alzheimer's disease and family stress: Directions for research* (pp. 122–154). Rockville, MD: National Institute of Mental Health.

Valle, R. (1998). *Caregiving across cultures.* Washington, DC: Taylor & Francis.

Wenger, A. F. (1993). Cultural meaning of symptoms. *Holistic Nursing Practice, 7,* 22–35.

Whitfield, K. E., & Baker-Thomas, T. (1999). Individual differences in aging minorities. *International Journal of Aging and Human Development, 48*(1), 73–79.

Wood, J. B., & Parham, I. A. (1990). Coping with perceived burden: Ethnic and cultural issues in Alzheimer's caregiving. *Journal of Applied Gerontology, 9,* 325–339.

Yamamoto, J., Machizawa, S., Araki, F., Reece, S., Steinberg, A., Leung, J., & Cater, R. (1985). Mental health of elderly Asian Americans in Los Angeles. *The American Journal of Social Psychiatry, 1,* 37–46.

Yamamoto, J., & Wagatsuma, H. (1980). The Japanese and Japanese Americans. *Journal of Operational Psychiatry, 11,* 120–135.

Yee, B. W. K. (1990). Gender and family issues in minority groups. *Generations, 14*(3), 39–42.

Young, R. F., Edevie, S., Young, J. H., & Peters, J. (1996). Issues of recruitment and retention in Alzheimer's research among African and White Americans. *Journal of Aging and Ethnicity, 1,* 19–25.

2

Practical Interventions for the Reduction of Caregiver Distress: Experience From the Field

4

Specific Stressors of Spousal Caregivers: Difficult Behaviors, Loss of Sexual Intimacy, and Incontinence

Mary Mittelman, Antonette Zeiss, Helen Davies, and DeLois Guy

This chapter features three distinct programs, each of which focuses on a common stressful situation faced by spousal dementia caregivers whose husbands and wives still live at home. The first section details the program developed at New York University's Alzheimer's Disease (AD) Center to delay or prevent institutionalization. The second and third segments reflect the authors' clinical experience in helping spousal caregivers to cope with two common (but infrequently discussed) issues that arise in the later stages of dementing illness; namely, changes in sexual intimacy and management of urinary incontinence. In all three sections, numerous practical suggestions are provided for the use of clinicians whose clients are struggling with these concerns.

NEW YORK UNIVERSITY STUDY: SPOUSE-CAREGIVER INTERVENTION PROJECT

The goals of the NYU Spouse-Caregiver Intervention Project were to improve or maintain the well-being of caregivers and to make it possible for them to avoid premature nursing-home placement of their spouses. In this study, all primary caregivers were spouses of AD patients. The main focus of the intervention was on the caregiver, with secondary focus on other family members. The health and well-being of the patient were viewed as important primarily as they affected the spouse-caregiver and other family members. The goal of keeping the patient out of a nursing home was pursued only to the extent that it corresponded with the wishes of the spouse-caregiver without causing serious detriment to the patient.

This program was theoretically based in the stress process model proposed by Pearlin, Mullan, Semple, and Skaff (1990). This model suggests that caregiver well-being is affected not only by primary stressors originating directly from the illness and care of the patient, but also from secondary stressors such as lack of support from other family members. Psychosocial interventions can alter the secondary effects of the illness on caregivers by (a) increasing knowledge about dementia; (b) improving family support and reducing family conflict; (c) decreasing isolation; (d) directly providing assistance in the form of problem-focused strategies, practical solutions to common problems, and empathetic understanding; and (e) organizing appropriate formal supports.

The NYU Silberstein Aging and Dementia Research Center has been funded since 1987 to evaluate the benefits of this intervention. Over a 13-year period, 406 caregivers were enrolled in the study, the first cohort between 1987 and 1991 and the second cohort between 1991 and 1997. All caregivers were interviewed at regular intervals for as long as the patient lived, whether the patient was at home or in a nursing home, and for 2 years after the patient died.

Caregivers were randomly assigned to a treatment or a control group when they entered the study. The treatment consisted of three components: individual and family counseling sessions tailored to each caregiver's specific situation; weekly support group participation and continuous availability of counselors to help caregivers and families deal with crises and with the changing nature of the patient's symptoms; and provision of resource information and referrals for auxiliary help, financial planning, and management of patient behavior problems. Each caregiver in the treatment group received *all* the interventions, and each was provided with support for an unlimited time. Control caregivers received only routine services, that is, resource information and help upon request.

Results of the study in two key areas indicate its success. First, when we compared the rates of nursing home placement for the 206 caregivers in the first cohort, we found that the difference in the median time from enrollment to nursing home placement of AD patients was 329 days longer in the treatment group than in the control group (Mittelman, Ferris, Shulman, Steinberg, & Levin, 1996). The treatment had the greatest effect when patients were mildly or moderately demented, when nursing home placement is generally least appropriate. Second, the program improved depression in caregivers. At baseline, more than

40% of the caregivers in this study (50% of the females and 30% of the males) had high enough scores on the Geriatric Depression Scale (Yesavage, Brink, Rose, & Adey, 1983) to indicate possible clinical depression. An analysis of the first cohort of caregivers showed a steadily increasing difference between the treatment and control caregivers in the change from baseline in number of symptoms of depression (Mittelman et al., 1995). It is important to note that the effect on depression was not immediate in most cases and only became statistically significant 8 months after caregivers entered the study. The average difference in change in symptoms of depression between the treatment and control groups by the 12-month follow-up was almost 3 points (half of one standard deviation).

Treatment Program Components

Assessment of the Caregiver

This program began with a comprehensive assessment that helped the counselor to identify caregiving issues for intervention. It was also an opportunity to engage the caregiver in a therapeutic relationship, understand the dynamics of his or her particular situation, identify characteristics that facilitated or impeded coping and adjustment, and establish a baseline for future assessments.

The assessment included a battery of interview instruments with structured questions and coded choices for possible answers. It contained questions about demographic characteristics, including age, gender, religion, and ethnicity; and about culture, finances, and the marital and family relationships. These characteristics were important for understanding how the caregiver responded to the illness and the caregiving role. The counselor conducted the interview in such a way as to invite the caregiver to expand upon the answers to the structured questions and probed for further information. We have found that most AD caregivers want to tell their stories and they more readily identify problems and solutions when they have been active participants in the process.

The caregiver's emotional health was evaluated using a combination of mental-health rating scales and clinical observations. Because many studies have documented that caregivers of relatives with AD report a large number of depressive symptoms, we included a scale to measure depression specifically, as well as a general mental-health scale. Our clinical observations (while conducting the NYU study) suggest that family caregivers frequently report symptoms of anxiety as well, although this is not so well documented in the literature.

The caregiver's perceptions of how much this new role was weighing on him or her were also captured by scales designed to measure both stress and burden. A caregiver who scored high on these scales was usually in psychological distress. Because the counselor could not change the patient's condition or the progress of the disease, the realistic aim was to decrease the caregiver's perception of the negative aspects of the caregiver's role.

The assessment included a detailed evaluation of the quality of the social support structure, using a written checklist of quantity of support, satisfaction with support, and family conflict. The family is usually a vital part of a caregiver's support system and may be the key to success with coping and adjustment. During the assessment, the counselor tried to understand each family's unique culture, past history, and patterns of interaction.

A structured evaluation of the caregiver's personality was also included in order to design treatment strategies to maximize the effects of the caregiver's positive traits and to minimize the effects of difficult or dysfunctional ones. Some of the characteristics that indicate how well caregivers will cope and respond to treatment include how well they have handled previous hardships, how honest they can be about their own feelings, how optimistic they are, whether they can rely on a sense of humor, and how well they can "distance" themselves from the patient.

Finally, a checklist was developed to assess the appropriateness of the home to the needs and limitations of a person with AD. The home environment may pose safety risks for both patient and caregiver; these risks are only exacerbated as a patient's dementia becomes more severe. Throughout the disease, the counseling intervention advised taking preventive measures and making changes in the home as necessary to avert a crisis.

Counseling the Caregiver

Planning and carrying out a typical plan for treatment can be divided conceptually into five segments, with the information gained during assessment serving as a guide.

1. *Consider the caregiver's profile.* Take a moment to review your assessment. Are there special factors that need to be addressed? Some of a caregiver's characteristics will count more than others in affecting his or her capacity, motivation, and opportunity to provide long-term care.

2. *Identify problems and issues.* During assessment, the caregiver either expressed needs or exhibited behaviors that suggested the problems and issues for treatment.

3. *Set treatment goals and time frame.* Treatment goals should be clearly stated and relate directly to the problems. Goals may be immediate, short term, or long term. It is essential that the caregiver be clearly aware of, in agreement with, and committed to, attainment of these goals in order for the treatment plan to be realistic and effective. Treatment goals may include changes in a caregiver's behavior, cognition, or emotions; modifications of the environment; or changing

the psychosocial caregiving context. A treatment goal might be a call to a physician to schedule a check-up, learn how to hire a home health aide, or make out an application for Medicaid. A goal for a family member might be a weekly telephone call to provide support for the caregiver

4. *Design the intervention.* An intervention may be emotional support or instrumental action. It may be concrete or clinical, depending on the identified treatment goal. Usually an intervention will be a combination of services the counselor is to provide and specific steps the caregiver is to take. Some goals may require several actions if the treatment issue is complex.

5. *Evaluate treatment outcomes.* Both the counselor and the caregiver need to be able to measure their success. Counselors can expect that some goals, such as resolution of practical matters, may be easier to achieve than those that involve an attitudinal or emotional change. Allowing adequate time for a goal to be reached, coupled with the appropriate quality and quantity of intervention, will facilitate resolution of problems.

Common Caregiver Issues

No two caregivers are identical; nonetheless, experienced counselors have identified many common themes. Table 4.1 shows some of the most prevalent caregiving issues, accompanied by brief treatment suggestions. Many additional examples of helpful interventions can be found in *Guiding the Alzheimer's Caregiver: A Handbook for Counselors* by Mittelman, Bergman, Shulman, Steinberg, and Epstein (2000).

Helping Caregivers Manage Problem Behaviors

Many behaviors of the spouse with dementia frighten and upset caregivers, especially the first time they happen. Caregivers who learn to expect the unexpected can usually manage difficult behaviors more successfully, but all caregivers experience frustration and negative feelings about their ill family member. The counselor can help a caregiver remember even at those times that the spouse is a person with feelings and dignity, that the aberrant behavior is a symptom of the illness, and that there is a way to master the situation. Table 4.2 contains examples of behavioral techniques that have been shown to be effective with several common troublesome behaviors of demented persons, namely, agitation, wandering, sleep disturbances, and opposition to care.

Opposition to Care

As the disease progresses, AD patients lose their ability to manage the activities of daily living independently. Although many will accept the caregiver's help,

TABLE 4.1   Prevalent Caregiving Issues

Caregiver Issue	Unrealistic view of the disease or patient	Denial of the diagnosis	Experience of negative feelings
Suggestion 1	Provide information about the disease.	Accept the caregiver's need for denial.	Help the caregiver identify angry feelings.
Suggestion 2	Normalize the changes in the patient.	Explore and resolve the underlying reasons for denial.	Explore how they are projected, displaced, or repressed.
Suggestion 3	Dispel myths and false assumptions.	Focus on/optimize the patient's strengths.	Work toward resolution of feelings.

Caregiver Issue	Social isolation	Communication problems	Role change
Suggestion 1	Help caregiver to use existing social and familial networks.	Patient: Substitute reassurance and distraction for argument or reasoning.	Identify which roles or tasks are compatible with caregiver strengths.
Suggestion 2	Identify and use social resources for patient and caregiver.	Patient: Encourage nonverbal, emotional communication.	Seek alternative resources to fulfill undesired roles/tasks.
Suggestion 3	Refer caregiver to a support group.	Others: Learn to verbalize needs.	Teach new skills and behaviors for role.
Suggestion 4	Refer caregiver to a social service agency.	Others: Practice assertiveness.	Build self-efficacy to perform new role.

Caregiver Issue	Anticipatory grief	Financial insecurity	Caregiver self-neglect
Suggestion 1	Be alert to signs and symptoms of grief.	Prepare a viable plan for long-term care.	Equate self-care with care of the patient.
Suggestion 2	Allow caregiver to grieve over loss of companionship.	Assist caregiver with budgeting.	Monitor the caregiver's self-care.
Suggestion 3	Help caregiver pass through the stages of grief.	Refer caregiver to a lawyer for estate planning.	Assess abuse of alcohol or drugs.
Suggestion 4	Refer for therapy if caregiver has intense grief symptoms.	Obtain public services (entitlement) when relevant.	Assess for suicidality and treat/refer as necessary.

TABLE 4.2   Managing Common Problem Behaviors

Agitation	Wandering	Sleep Disturbances
Avoid precipitating the agitation: remain calm, speak simply, and use nonverbal cues.	Accompany the patient closely everywhere, especially in crowded areas like malls.	Activity: Keep patient as active as possible all day, especially physical activity.
Respond to the patient's feelings rather than to the behavior.	Maintain physical contact, such as holding hands or walking arm in arm.	Liquids: Have patient void before bed; reduce liquid intake late in the day.
Engage the patient in constructive activity.	If patient insists on going out, don't argue— follow along.	Ensure that the patient is warm and comfortable.
Reframe the behavior in positive ways.	Use distraction by offering an incentive to return home.	If patient wakes, calmly reassure and soothe patient.
If the patient is aggressive unto violence, walk away.	Register patient in a safe-return program.	If all else fails, consult a physician or hire a night attendant.

some patients resist or flatly refuse to be told what to do. In particular, persons with dementia often actively oppose the four specific tasks of bathing, dressing, eating, and going outside; suggestions for managing these are found in Table 4.3.

Proven Strategies and Techniques for Change

A variety of strategies for changing caregiver behavior were included in the NYU program. A brief description follows of several that were particularly effective (according to the caregivers themselves).

1. *Problem solving.* Continuous stress may undermine an AD caregiver's normal ability to solve problems. The counselor can lighten the burden and enable the caregiver to define and resolve daily stress with a step-by-step approach.
   (a) *Identify,* using probing techniques to articulate the problem.
   (b) *Clarify,* by reframing so that the problem belongs to the caregiver, not the patient, and can therefore be solved.
   (c) *Partialize,* by breaking down the problem into more understandable and more manageable parts.
   (d) *Identify* possible causes.

TABLE 4.3   Managing Personal Care Tasks

Bathing	Dressing	Eating	Going outside
Respect the patient's modesty and dignity. Establish a routine time to bathe (when patient is most cooperative). Bath: Fill tub beforehand. Shower: Use hand spray so patient can direct the water. Place patient away from faucets; provide distraction. Reward the patient after the bath. Use lotion or a warm towel to soothe the patient. Use a sponge bath or skip a day.	Wait a while and try again. Let someone else try; sometimes an aid has more luck than the caregiver. Help with buttons and fasteners; provide comfortable clothes with few or no fasteners. Don't push or rush; don't argue; provide incentives. Remove soiled clothing from view. Leave out only what you want patient to wear the next day. Give patient one item at a time.	Offer finger foods. Provide a model by eating with the patient. Puree foods for patients who have trouble swallowing. Supplement meals with snacks and liquids for balance. Hide food between meals. Put a lock on the refrigerator for compulsive eaters. Give the patient one thing to eat a time.	Offer distraction or clear directions. Provide incentives and constant reassurance. Do not ask the patient if s/he wants to go; do not argue about it. Allow enough time to avoid rushing or pressure. Take along another adult if needed. Bring familiar objects to help reorient patient. Always consider safety first.

(e) *Brainstorm,* by offering and listening to possible solutions.

(f) *Test alternative solutions,* by encouraging caregiver to find out what works best or what doesn't work at all.

(g) *Evaluate:* Is the caregiver satisfied? Move on to the next challenge. Not satisfied? Brainstorm again, select new alternatives, retest, and reevaluate until something works or the caregiver ceases to see this as a primary issue.

2. *Role play and modeling.* Reenacting a problematic caregiving scenario during a counseling session can *increase* the caregiver's self-awareness. In effect, the counselor becomes a mirror for the caregiver while simultaneously presenting a model for effective caregiving. During role play, the counselor and

the caregiver assume the roles of the patient, the caregiver, or another individual in a problem situation. The counselor guides the caregiver through a step-by-step reenactment of the situation. The caregiver then switches roles and they repeat the scene again. The counselor pays close attention to the caregiver's verbal as well as nonverbal communication. Once the scenario has been fully played out, additional options could be explored. As a homework assignment, the counselor could recommend that the caregiver keep a log of similar problematic episodes, listing those responses that work and those that do not.

3. *Cognitive restructuring.* Cognitive therapy tries to achieve emotional change by restructuring a person's belief system. The emotional distress and painful feelings—anger, anxiety, frustration, or depression—that caring for an AD spouse can generate may be exacerbated by mistaken beliefs. Frequently, these beliefs cause negative interactions between the caregiver and the spouse, which then evoke more debilitating emotions (like guilt) in the caregiver. Cognitive restructuring can help a caregiver become aware of these dysfunctional thinking patterns and then replace them by developing a new repertoire of assumptions, thoughts, perceptions, and coping mechanisms. Cognitive restructuring includes the following steps:
   (a) Identify the caregiver's nonproductive feeling or negative interaction with the patient.
   (b) Question what underlying assumptions or thoughts have precipitated the feeling or behavior.
   (c) Facilitate the caregiver's awareness of the link between the emotion and the thought.
   (d) Substitute a new assumption or thought for the unproductive one.
   (e) Help the caregiver identify a new feeling or behavior that came from modified cognition.

4. *Visualization and use of imagery.* The idea behind visualization is that if one can picture, or visualize, a new approach, one has a good chance of achieving it. Encourage the caregiver to use his or her imagination to find new ways of responding to difficult interactions with the patient or to rehearse new ways of coping. By visualizing these steps, the caregiver identifies a more functional approach to caring for the patient and is also better able to understand the need to modify his or her behavior to meet the patient's current needs.

5. *Use of humor.* Even the most tragic moments can be lightened with a sense of humor. At times, AD behaviors may be so peculiar that a caregiver will be torn between laughing and crying. Being able to laugh *with* an AD patient can relieve the patient's anxiety and diffuse a caregiver's sadness and despair. Be careful not to find humor where a caregiver or care recipient finds humiliation. Reassure the caregiver that laughing at a particular situation is

not the same as laughing at the patient.

6. *Stress management.* Caregiving is stressful both emotionally and physically. AD caregivers frequently feel frustrated, anxious, tense, and angry and may appear fatigued or exhausted. If undetected and unrelieved, stress can erode a caregiver's inner resources and may cause physical or mental illness. The caregiver can reduce stress through a variety of techniques such as finding periodic respite away from home, learning stress-management techniques, participating in physical exercise with or without the spouse, and using successful methods for relaxation; for instance, deep breathing, listening to soothing music, and prayer or other spiritual means of calming.

In summary, these interventions are highly effective in enabling caregivers to keep their spouses living at home in the early and intermediate stages of dementia. By decreasing caregivers' subjective feelings of burden and providing practical strategies for the management of concrete behavioral problems, appropriate intervention can allow a couple to continue a life together in love and caring, not simply in frustration and resentment. Only when this has been accomplished, when the fundamental issues of caregiver stress and effective patient care and management have been addressed, can other, more specific issues of the relationship come to the forefront. Sexual intimacy, so fundamental to many people's lives as loving, committed couples, is one of these issues. By first looking to the caregiver's satisfaction with providing in-home care, clinicians can set the stage for addressing such deeply meaningful, yet often overlooked, elements of spousal caregiving.

RESOLVING COUPLES' SEXUAL INTIMACY ISSUES

Most people who develop dementia have others who love them; very often this is a spouse or other long-term romantic partner. Much of the literature on dementia explores how the partner handles the challenges of providing personal care to the patient; the term "caregiver" captures this approach of representing the partner as someone whose essence becomes that of provider for the needs of a patient. Without disputing the importance of this approach, we have been especially interested in the impact of the dementia process on the relationship—the loving, committed, romantic, and sexual relationship of the couple who face dementia together, one as patient and one as partner and loving spouse, not just a caregiver.

In order to understand how couples face this process, and especially how the well partner experiences changes in intimacy and sexuality in the relationship, we (AZ and HD) conducted focus groups with spouses of patients with progressive dementias, at many stages of illness. Both male and female partners have taken part in these focus groups. They came from all socioeconomic levels, their relationships were of varying length, and there was ethnic diversity in the groups. Several major themes emerged as we heard their stories. We will review these themes and suggest how they can influence attempts to intervene with patients and their partners as they struggle with the loss of what is often the most valued relationship in their lives.

The Most Difficult Aspects of Change

Partners of patients with dementia reported five major areas in which they experienced change in the relationship with the patient:

1. Emotional intimacy—having someone to talk to and depend on emotionally
2. Helpmate—having someone to handle a share of day-to-day tasks and planning for major life decisions
3. Mental stimulation—having someone from whom they could learn things or who could raise interesting ideas
4. Recreational companionship—having someone who shares hobbies and interests
5. Physical intimacy—having someone to hug or snuggle with and to share sexual intimacy.

Our emphasis is on changes in sexual expression, but changes in the overall experience of intimacy in the relationship are inextricably connected to how sexual change is experienced, so we also briefly address the other areas to share some of the concerns that were described.

As we review the concerns, two basic and interrelated principles guide us. First, we believe that the onset of dementing illness does not erase sexuality, but rather alters the way in which love is given and received. Second, despite misleading writing in many caregiver manuals, inappropriate sexual behavior is a very infrequent problem in individuals with Alzheimer's disease, and it is usually brief, minor, and easily handled even when it occurs (e.g., Zeiss, Davies, & Tinklenberg, 1996). Ambiguous behaviors are more common, such as appearing in public incompletely dressed, which could suggest exhibitionism but more likely reflects self-care deficits. Misinterpretation of these events may be the source for some of the persistent lore regarding sexually disinhibited behavior in dementia. The other issue, however, is that when a patient with a dementing illness expresses sexual interest, some label it as inherently "inappropriate," displaying an underlying bias that dementia *should* erase sexuality. We believe that our sexuality is always with us, though it can take different forms over our lifetimes. Thus, our interest is not in guiding partners in how to quell expressions of sexual interest in the patient. Rather, we want to help well partners understand what they are willing to accept, given other changes in the relationship, and to help them guide the patient to the level of sexual expression comfortable in each situation.

Emotional Intimacy

Partners gave many poignant examples of changes in emotional intimacy. One partner said, "I speak to him less and less. It involves too much explanation." Another said, "I don't have the comfort of my husband. He was the one who made things right." One told a story about her memory of a time earlier in the marriage to illustrate the level of closeness there had been: "We were so close; when I was nursing one of our children, he asked to taste." Finally, one caregiver tearfully said, "My husband doesn't use his special nickname for me anymore. He has started using my proper name." Each tells of a loss at the core of the relationship—the sense that there is another person with whom one can share the most intimate details of one's life and receive love and support in return.

Helpmate

Partners made fewer comments about the loss of a partner who shared responsibility for everyday tasks. They did bemoan the loss of someone who could help with major life decisions: "When making decisions, there's no other person to review it with." "I miss being able to make plans with someone, to say, 'What do you think of a, b, or c?' "

Mental Stimulation

Well partners had many comments about the loss of someone who provided intellectual stimulation. Some specific comments included, "He was well-read; there was lots to talk about"; "She was a walking encyclopedia; now she reads some article in the paper twice"; "What's missing is conversation—meaningful conversation"; and, "My biggest loss is intellectual." All these partners saw linkages between the loss of an intellectually interesting partner and their own loss of interest in a sexual relationship with the patient.

Recreational Companionship

Well partners noted the loss of someone who shared recreational interests, making comments like, "He used to be so full of energy and busy; now he just sits all day"; "There's a lack of social life; we can't be with friends, travel, go to the theater"; and, "We used to travel constantly, had people over. Now that's all gone." More male partners expressed concerns about loss of social life; the female patient previously had responsibility for the couple's social life and as she lost ability to manage, the well partner did not take on the task. Often, shared recreational activities had set the stage for closeness and sexual intimacy, so this loss also reduced opportunities for sexual sharing.

Physical Intimacy

All of these relationship losses influence the way partners view physical intimacy in the relationship. Early in the dementia process, when the patient can still sustain some emotional intimacy, be a helpmate and recreational companion, and provide some intellectual stimulation, well partners usually express unchanged interest in sexual contact for the couple. They say, for example, "She's always coming up and giving me a hug or kiss; physical affection is unchanged." However, for these couples, if the demented partner is male, a common problem preventing continued sexual activity is his difficulty obtaining or maintaining an erection. This has been shown in research (Zeiss, Davies, Wood, & Tinklenberg, 1990) and was mentioned frequently in the focus groups, for example, "He couldn't get erections any more, starting when he was diagnosed 5 years ago." Such couples can be helped by easily available treatments for erectile dysfunction, including sildenafil (Viagra) or the use of a vacuum-constriction device. Referrals to a physician who is knowledgeable about treatment for sexual dysfunction is important in such cases; a psychologist or other provider of psychosocial care also can help the couple work on how to incorporate the medical treatment into their relationship without overwhelming demands on memory and adaptation for the patient.

As dementia progresses, it can be hard to sustain sexual interaction, even when the well partner remains interested, because of the complexity involved in a typical sexual interaction. As one partner described, "He's having trouble remembering if we are starting or ending sex." Orchestrating a successful sexual interaction involves knowing how to initiate sex; how long foreplay should last, what will be pleasurable, and how to tell when one's partner is ready to move to a next phase; how to manage penetration and find a comfortable position for intercourse; and how to pace intercourse so that each partner has a satisfying experience. Not surprisingly, as dementia progresses the patient is less and less able to handle each step, let alone manage the transitions from one step to another. And at least for the current cohort of older adults, the man is expected to be the primary orchestrator of the sexual interaction. Because there are far more couples where the patient is male and the well partner is female than the reverse, this cultural bias regarding the relative roles of each partner has major impact on the ability to continue satisfying sexual activity.

At this phase, we may try to help the female partner become comfortable taking more of a leadership role in guiding sexual interactions. She can use warmth, gentleness, and humor, so that the patient does not feel disrespected; her feeling empowered to express sexual interest and guide sexual activity can be rewarding for both. Alternatively, the partner can be guided in setting new, more realistic expectations of the patient. For example, sexual activity may be briefer and simpler than in the past, but still satisfying. Or sexual activity may be more focused on manual stimulation and not expected to progress to penetration and intercourse. Ann Davidson (1997) has described this process well: "I can acknowledge that I want lovemaking, despite Alzheimer's and all the changes in our lives. Then I must do what I need to do to make it happen. . . . We can put on a tape and play Baroque music. We can light a candle and caress. I can snuggle into his arms recalling lustier times. I can remember how much I have loved him and all that he has been in my life" (p. 180).

Usually, at some point in the progression of dementia, the well partner wishes to stop the couple's sexual activity; partners expressed such feelings as, "He tries to kiss me, and I don't feel like it—I see a little boy in him"; or, "I'm turned off; he's not the same person. I don't want this; it's just one more stress." In such cases, the well partner needs support and guidance in thinking about how to divert the patient's sexual overtures. In our experience, this is not usually difficult, if the partner can remain calm and matter-of-fact. Problems usually arise only if the well partner is emotionally upset about the patient's sexual interest and communicates disgust or rejection. Although dementia patients lose cognitive capacity, many remain extremely emotionally sensitive and can sense their partners' intense negative emotions. This can lead to a catastrophic response on the part of the patient. Thus, the well partner needs to be guided to accept the patient's longing for physical intimacy, accept his or her own right not to want to engage in physical intimacy, and find ways to gently and calmly distract the patient when he or she tries to initiate sex. In working with partners on this issue, it can be helpful to encourage them to separate the request from the nature of what is being requested. If this was some other activity that they would consider inappropriate or uncomfortable, would they do it? If not, would they be upset about saying no, or would they feel comfortable and calmly figure out how best to say no without punishing the patient?

When distraction is appropriate, it can take several forms. The goal may be to shift the patient's attention to some other, nonsexual interest. Or the partner can accept the patient's right to remain a sexual being and encourage the patient to be sexually active in a private context. Other partners may be able to accept the patient's desire for physical intimacy but turn that into a chance to give the patient a back rub or to sit on the couch together quietly without intense sexual stimulation. In order to find the solution that will work best, each partner needs to learn about the patient's ability to respond to different kinds of distraction and needs to be honest about his or her own ability to accept different levels of physical closeness.

When well partners do move to a level at which they no longer want sexual contact, they also need to adapt to their own sense of loss of a part of themselves. One caregiver put it well: "The sexual loss is very big; I'm missing the chance for me to be a sexual person." As partners make this transition, it is important to provide support and understanding regarding this loss. Partners tell us they almost never have a chance to discuss this topic, even when they have been involved in caregiver support groups or other helping services. Professionals can offer an opportunity to discuss this area; they also can provide permission for the well partner to remain sexual in whatever ways feel right. For example, one approach was suggested by a wife in a recent focus group: "It's one thing moving ahead to another relationship. My way is through a fantasy life, little mental excursions. I'm attracted to men who are like my husband was. I do a little mental wandering; it helps." Still others may feel ready to develop a new relationship after the patient is placed in a long-term care facility. We believe that adults have the right to wrestle with difficult decisions about when to start a new relationship. Some are committed to the specific wording of marriage vows: "Till death do us part." Others feel that they can honor the person they have loved and cared for while still moving on with some aspects of their lives. The role of the helping professional is to listen without judgment and allow each partner to find a solution that fits his or her own values and personal situation.

Recurring Comments

Overall, we heard three main recurring themes from caregiving partners. Though contradictory, many caregivers felt all three to be true simultaneously:

1. The well partner still feels in love—"We tell each other at least every day how much we love each other."
2. In many ways, the partner feels like a parent rather than a romantic partner—"It's like I'm his mother now."
3. The partner is in a difficult role for which there is no clear model—"I have one foot in married life and one foot in widowhood."

It varies how each person handles the complex mix of these three deeply felt realities of caring for a beloved but demanding life partner. But each caregiver needs to find a way to balance them, by both holding onto and letting go of the love, sexual attraction, and emotional intimacy that initially led to the bond with the patient who is demented. Professionals can provide help at different stages of the process. For some, problem-solving efforts to help the couple hold onto physical intimacy are most helpful. For others, guiding the well partner in ways to end sexual intimacy while still respecting the patent's right to have sexual feelings and interests is best. Finally, many partners mainly need someone who can help deal with the loss of sexual expression and suggest ways to fill this gap.

IN-HOME MANAGEMENT OF URINARY INCONTINENCE IN SPOUSES WHO ARE COGNITIVELY IMPAIRED

A common problem in later stages of dementia is urinary incontinence (UI), which, when it occurs in a spousal relationship, often causes considerable stress and embarrassment for both parties. UI is broadly defined as an involuntary loss of urine, with three types generally recognized: urge, stress, and combination or mix. *Urge incontinence* is the loss of urine in the presence of an urge to urinate and the inability to delay until one reaches an appropriate urinary receptacle. *Stress incontinence* is urine leakage when intra-abdominal pressure increases, as occurs with laughing, coughing, sneezing, or exertion. A person also may experience a *combination* of these two types. Sometimes, the loss of urine associated with an overdistended bladder is identified as a fourth type, *overflow incontinence* (Grimby, Milsom, Molander, Wiklund, & Ekelund, 1993; Rose, Baigis-Smith, Smith, & Newman, 1990).

The prevalence of UI is not clear at this time. The nature of the incontinence, location (community dwelling versus institutionalized), and degree of mobility or frailty are all important in characterizing and defining UI. Reported figures range from 13% to 53% for homebound elders (McDowell, Engberg, Rodriguez, Engberg, & Sereika, 1996); 11% to 90% for cognitively impaired persons (Skelly & Flint, 1995); 22% for community based/ambulatory persons, and as high as 84% for institutionalized persons (Skelly & Flint, 1995). An interaction of physiological, cognitive, mobility, and environmental factors is usually causative of UI. Inconsistencies in definition, method of assessment, coexisting diseases, and difficulty of obtaining data on such personal problem contribute to reporting discrepancies.

Impact

Urinary incontinence is burdensome for both the incontinent person and the caregiver. In spite of the difficulties it presents for researchers, UI is a major problem, with health, social, and financial consequences. It is estimated that billions of dollars are spent each year on UI products, special garments, and gadgets. In addition, treating the health problems caused by UI can easily become very expensive. Thus, it is a costly problem for the impaired person as well as the family.

Health problems such as urinary tract infection, cystitis, skin rashes, pressure sores, sleep disruption, falls, or depression may be related to UI. Furthermore, coexisting illnesses and their treatment can exaggerate incontinence; for example, by use of diuretics. Impaired mobility, muscular problems, and difficulty in hand maneuvers associated with arthritis or other musculoskeletal problems exaggerate incontinence and toileting difficulties. The resulting dependency only adds to feelings of inadequacy, frustration, anger, and conflict.

Caregiving is generally acknowledged as stressful (Schulz, O'Brien, Bookwala, & Fleissner, 1995). The care of a cognitively impaired person involves vigilance and responsibility for the care, safety, and overall well-being of the loved one; UI adds significantly to these burdens. The progressive nature of dementia means that tasks become more demanding and stressful as the patient deteriorates. Management of incontinence in a spouse who is cognitively impaired may begin with gentle verbal reminders, and progress over time to complete handling of the excretory function. The physical handling and moving of the care recipient, the unpleasantries of handling another person's bodily eliminations, and the increased responsibilities all add up to a significant increase in caregiver burden. Caregivers may view their tasks as tiring, difficult, and upsetting and may have concerns about the adequacy of their knowledge and abilities and their personal endurance, as well as fears about health threats and declines (Noelker, 1987).

People go to great lengths to deny and conceal UI, including reorganization of activities, restricted functioning, and hypervigilance. The caregiver engages in acts of hypervigilance for smell or wetness, protective concealment, and resource utilization (increased padding, towel use, frequent laundering). To ensure successful efforts, the caregiver engages in anticipatory as well as direct actions. All of this is done to reduce UI accidental episodes, with their consequences of loss of dignity, decline in self-confidence, embarrassment, shame, social isolation, anxiety, helplessness, loss of control, fearfulness, and sadness (Mitteness, 1987). Because of the time and energy involved in concealment regimens and routines as well as monetary cost, the caregiver may feel overwhelmed. As UI management proves progressively less successful or becomes too great a burden, the risk of institutionalization increases.

Chronic urinary incontinence often contributes to the decision to institutionalize one's spouse; in fact, UI is the second leading risk factor for institutionalization (McDowell, Burgio, Dombrowski, & Rodriguez, 1992). Frequency of accidents, inability of the caregiver to manage the clean-up process, cost, and concerns about skin problems may motivate a caregiver to consider placement.

The impact of incontinence and cognitive impairment is high for both members of the caregiving dyad. Thus, interactions between caregiver and care recipient are primed to become more conflictual, problematic, and strained. Anger, hostility, resentment, retaliation, and manipulation are just a few possible responses. The multiple negative psychological, social, health, and economic effects of urinary incontinence challenge health care professionals to design and implement effective treatment approaches.

Treatment Interventions

Medical-pharmacological approaches to UI generally use such drugs as anticholinergics and antispasmodics, or in some cases surgical intervention may be used to correct bladder position, remove tissue, correct weakened, pelvic muscles, or enlarge the bladder. On the other hand, behavioral treatment involves bladder-habit-training, pelvic-floor exercises, verbal or biofeedback, and environmental modifications (Rose et al., 1990). Bladder-habit-training consists of determining when the individual urinates and consistently assisting the individual to use the toilet or other urine receptacle at that time, thus establishing the habit of going at those times. Expressing praise for being dry or using the bathroom also engages reward principle. Scheduled toileting and prompted voiding are other techniques. (See Table 4.4 for highlights.)

Pelvic-floor, or Kegel, exercises may be used to strengthen the muscles around the urethra, vagina, and rectum, which are involved in the urinary process. However, individuals with dementia sometimes have trouble using the correct muscles. In such cases, biofeedback apparatus is used to remedy the problem.

Because mobility is integrally related to toileting, any mobility or functional impairments may constitute impediments to continence. Location, ease of use, and visibility are factors that are manipulated in environmental modification. Inaccessible toilets are adapted by clearing furniture from door pathways, elevating toilet seats, and installing grab bars, signs and pictures, and adequate lighting. The use of other types of urinary receptacles, such as portable commodes, urinals, bedpans, and special clothing and pads are other aids. The use of walkers, canes, and other mobility aids can enable an otherwise limited person to gain access to the toilet.

Clinical Example

Resources for Enhancing Alzheimer's Caregiver Health (REACH) was a recent multicenter experimental project designed to evaluate the effectiveness of supportive interventions for family caregivers of persons with dementia. (REACH is described in more detail in other chapters in this volume). One REACH site (at Birmingham, Alabama) utilized a skills-training intervention to minimize

TABLE 4.4   Strategies to Decrease/Manage UI

Increase toilet visibility and recognition	Decrease obstacles presented by clothing and diet	Communication techniques	Use of appliances, aids, and urinary collecting devices
Open bathroom door. Provide well-lit room and pathway. Clear pathway. Simple sign or picture. Locate toilet upon arriving anywhere. Limit or remove clutter; simplify room.	No, or easy-to-open, fasteners. Elastic-waist garments. Simple, few, or no undergarments. Initiate removal of undergarments. Limit afternoon and evening fluid intake. Reduce caffeine intake.	Use simple, one-command statements. Use calm, clear, unhurried voice. Use nonverbal cues and responses. Use positive statements and social pleasantries. Use verbal exchanges and feedback. Learn person's word or action for "urinate."	Use absorbent pads or alternate receptacle. Use walker, cane, or wheelchair. Install raised toilet seat. Install grab bar. Promptly remove wet or soiled pads, etc. Wash and dry soiled areas.

caregiver stress through management of behavioral problems. Family caregivers who were enrolled in the Skilled Training Condition (STC) were instructed to identify a significant care-recipient behavioral problem for which they desired assistance; UI was a very commonly reported problem. Using the "ABC" approach (identification of antecedents, behavior, and consequences), the assigned interventionist asked questions to pinpoint the specific nature of the caregiver-reported urinary incontinence. The antecedents and settings of incontinence episodes were identified, as were the reactions of caregiver and care recipient. A medication review for specific drugs that might influence urinary function was also completed. In addition, an in-home evaluation was done to determine factors such as bathroom location, bathroom pathway barriers, lighting, care recipient's mobility function, level of cooperation with toileting, cognitive function for toileting tasks, and visual and reading ability for simple sign reading.

The REACH team used data obtained from caregivers to isolate probable causes and design realistic, individualized interventions. Interventionists employed a simple, modified behavioral treatment approach, which considered the following UI management goals: medical evaluation, safety, comfort, problem management, dyad relationship issues, cost, and manageable burden. Caregiver-reported improvement, including reduction in frequency of UI episodes and improvements in the dyadic relationship, were key outcome measures.

Each caregiver program was individualized with special attention shown to risk-burden-benefit ratio for the respective dyad. For example, a caregiver would evaluate the burden, financial cost, and energy expenditure of scheduled toileting and clean-up of accidents versus simply using protective pads. Toileting regimens, prompted voiding, environmental modifications, simple behavioral techniques of praise and reward, and use of appliances and protective pads were the most common intervention strategies utilized. Strategies and sample programs are further outlined in Tables 4.4 and 4.5.

In general (based on anecdotal data and case notes), it can be stated that caregivers reported significant improvement in their ability to mange UI following participation in this program. Many of the strategies suggested by the interventionists had not previously been considered or tried; once they were, however, many positive changes were noted, including less stress in the dyadic relationship.

Spouses were appreciative of the very practical suggestions they were given and said that when they *remembered to use them*, fewer incidents occurred and/ or that they were easier to manage. Although REACH outcome results are not yet available, it seems likely to this author (DLG) that improved UI management will be associated with reduced caregiver burden and depression among these participants.

TABLE 4.5   Sample Programs for UI Management

Scheduled toileting (habitual toileting):	Assist person to use toilet; provide urinary receptacle every 2 hours.
	Allow time to use toilet/receptacle.
	Praise person for being dry; using toilet.
	Promote dignity, humanness, privacy.
Prompted voiding:	Remind person to use toilet.
As with scheduled voiding, allow sufficient time to use toilet/receptacle, praise the person for being dry/using toilet, and promote dignity, humanness, and privacy as much as possible.	Ask "Do you want/need to use toilet?"
	Check for dryness/wetness.
	Assist person to toilet/receptacle.
	Assist with using toilet/receptacle.
	Let person know when you will next toilet him/her.
	Initiate removal of undergarments.
	Give fluids.
Miscellaneous:	Make appropriate environmental modifications.
	Urinate before leaving home or starting an activity.

SUMMARY

In this chapter we have discussed a number of troublesome issues for spouse caregivers, along with concrete suggestions for managing or coping with them, based on the varied clinical and research experiences of the authors. Clearly, additional research and clinical work are needed to determine if the methods outlined here would be as effective with non-spouse caregivers, where different types of relationships and varying levels of closeness occur, as well as their acceptability to many ethnic, racial, and cultural groups that may not prefer the very direct, behaviorally based techniques that are included here.

REFERENCES

Davidson, A. (1997). *Alzheimer's: A love story*. Secaucus, NJ: Birch Lane Press.

Grimby, A., Milsom, I., Molander, U., Wiklund, I., & Ekelund, P. (1993). The influence of urinary incontinence on the quality of life of elderly women. *Age and Ageing, 22*, 82–89.

McDowell, B. J., Burgio, K. L., Dombrowski, M., & Rodriguez, E. (1992). An interdisciplinary approach to the assessment and behavioral treatment of urinary incontinence in geriatric outpatients. *Journal of the American Geriatric Society, 40*, 370–374.

McDowell, B. J., Engberg, S. J., Rodriguez, E., Engberg, R., & Sereika, S. (1996). Characteristics of urinary incontinence in homebound older adults. *Journal of the American Geriatric Society, 44*, 963–968.

Mittelman, M. S., Ferris, S. H., Shulman, E., Steinberg, G., Ambinder, A., Mackell, J., & Cohen, J. (1995). A comprehensive support program: Effect on depression in spouse-caregivers of AD patients. *Gerontologist, 35*, 792–802.

Mittelman, M. S., Ferris, S. H., Shulman, E., Steinberg, G., & Levin, B. (1996). A family intervention to delay nursing home placement of patients with Alzheimer's disease: A randomized controlled trial. *Journal of the American Medical Association, 276*, 1725–1731.

Mittelman, M. S., Bergman, H., Shulman, E., Steinberg, G., & Epstein, C. (2000). *Guiding the Alzheimer's caregiver: A handbook for counselors*. New York: New York University Medical School.

Mitteness, L. S. (1987). The management of urinary incontinence by community-living elderly. *Gerontologist, 27*, 185–193.

Noelker, L. S. (1987). Incontinence in elderly cared for by family. *Gerontologist, 27*, 194–200.

Pearlin, L. I., Mullan, J. T., Semple, S. J., & Skaff, M. M. (1990). Caregiving and the stress process: An overview of concepts and their measures. *Gerontologist, 30*(5), 583–594.

Rose, M. A., Baigis-Smith, J., Smith, D., & Newman, D. (1990). Behavioral management of urinary incontinence in homebound older adults. *Home Healthcare Nurse, 8*, 10–15.

Schulz, R., O'Brien, A. T., Bookwala, J., & Fleissner, K. (1995). Psychiatric and physical morbidity effects of dementia caregiving: Prevalence, correlates, and causes. *Gerontologist, 35,* 771–791.

Skelly, J., & Flint, A. J. (1995). Urinary incontinence associated with dementia. *Journal of the American Geriatric Society, 43,* 286–294.

Yesavage, J. A., Brink, T. L., Rose, T. L., & Adey, M. (1983). The geriatric depression rating scale: Comparison with other self-report and psychiatric rating scales. In T. Crook, S. H. Ferris, & R. Bartus (Eds.), *Assessment in geriatric psychopharmacology* (pp. 153–165). New Canaan, CT: Mark Powley Associates.

Zeiss, A. M., Davies, H. D., & Tinklenberg, J. R. (1996). An observational study of inappropriate sexual behavior in demented male patients. *Journals of Gerontology: Medical Sciences, 51A,* M325–M329.

Zeiss, A. M., Davies, H., Wood, M., & Tinklenberg, J. (1990). The incidence and correlates of male erectile dysfunction in Alzheimer's disease patients. *Archives of Sexual Behavior, 19,* 325–331.

5

Family Interventions to Address the Needs of the Caregiving System

Soledad Argüelles, Ellen J. Klausner, Trinidad Argüelles, and David W. Coon

Older adults with dementing disorders are cared for principally by their families (W. E. Haley, 1997). Increasing evidence has demonstrated that caregivers of such elder persons are at increased risk for depression, anxiety, and other medical problems (Bass, Noelker, & Rechlin, 1996; Cochrane, Goering, & Rogers, 1997; Collins & Jones, 1997; Fuller-Jonap & Haley, 1995; W. E. Haley et al., 1995; Jutras & Lavoie, 1995; Schulz et al., 1997; Schulz, O'Brien, Bookwala, & Fleissner, 1995). Given the expected rise in the numbers of older adults who will be diagnosed with dementing disorders, interventions directed at improving the health and quality of life of family caregivers will play an increasingly important role in the future. Although there is substantial literature about family caregiving in general and a growing number of well-conducted studies on interventions, the literature on interventions that are focused on the caregiving family as a whole is relatively limited (e.g., Bourgeois, Schulz, & Burgio, 1996; Kennet, Burgio, & Schulz, 2000; Knight, Lutzky, & Macofsky-Urban, 1993; Schulz et al., 1995). In recognition of the stress, burden, and changes experienced by the family system, it is imperative to continue developing, testing, and enhancing family interventions with the family system that is caring for the individual who is dementing. This chapter addresses a number of the issues

99

surrounding the development and implementation of family focused interventions by introducing key issues affecting the design and implementation of family-based interventions for caregivers; highlighting theoretical approaches to family therapy and reviewing recent work on family therapy with late-life families, including those providing care for loved ones who are memory impaired; describing a case example utilizing one current family-focused approach, Structural Ecosystems Therapy (SET); and recommending future directions for family therapy with caregivers of patients with dementia.

KEY ISSUES IN THE DEVELOPMENT OF FAMILY-BASED CAREGIVER INTERVENTIONS

In recent years clinical interest has grown in understanding the impact of caregiving on the family members of patients with Alzheimer's disease and associated dementing disorders. The efficacy of a wide range of treatment approaches aimed at enhancing the functioning of these caregivers has been examined, including psychoeducational programs, support groups, cognitive-behavioral techniques, self-help, respite care, skills-training, and individual and family therapy or counseling. Preliminary studies appeared to yield positive therapeutic results, yet as the number of empirical studies increased, evidence of potential benefit became less conclusive and were often contradictory (Bourgeois et al., 1996; Knight et al., 1993). The precise nature of the mechanisms specific to each intervention and their effects on the health and quality of life of caregivers of patients with dementia were not always well defined due to several important factors that had to be considered in the development, implementation, and evaluation of family therapy interventions for these caregivers.

For example, given the heterogeneity of both elders who are dementing and their caregivers, research studies are often complicated by selection factors. These may include differences in both the patient's characteristics (e.g., level of impairment or number of behavior problems) and the family caregiver characteristics (e.g., spouse versus adult child or in-home versus long-distance caregivers). There are also differences between the type of family or friend (e.g., extended family, stepfamily, family of choice, or gay or lesbian family) who provided care to the older adult, all of whom may display marked differences in roles as well as in their access to services and the perceived acceptability of services that are accessible (Gallagher-Thompson et al., 2000).

Moreover, wide variability exists in the definition of caregiving, depending upon the inclusion and exclusion criteria of the particular research study or service program offered (e.g., Gallagher-Thompson, Coon, Rivera, Powers, & Zeiss, 1998; Kramer & Kipnis, 1995), including definitions such as "providing special assistance (physical, financial or emotional)" (Scharlach, 1989, p. 229), or even "remaining ever vigilant" (Coon, Schulz, & Ory, 1999). Thus, caregivers might be described by more global definitions, such as "people who provide tangible, financial, emotional, or informational and coordination support to an impaired family member"; or by more narrow definitions such as the one used in SET (University of Miami, 1998) in this chapter's case study. The SET vignette utilizes the selection criteria of Resources for Enhancing Alzheimer's Caregiver Health (REACH), a multisite research project funded by the National Institute on Aging and the National Institute for Nursing Research (Coon et al., 1999; Wisniewski et al., 2001). The adult caregivers (at least 21 years of age) selected for this project were expected to live with a family member with dementia for at least 6 months, to provide at least 4 hours of direct care a day, and not to have a terminal illness. The project included entry criteria for the patient as well (e.g., the patient could not have a terminal illness). Because the Miami REACH site focused on family therapy, primary and secondary family caregivers were incorporated into the inclusion criteria, with the latter including any family members or friends directly or indirectly involved in the care of the patient on at least a biweekly basis. Secondary caregivers were usually identified by the primary caregiver, although sometimes they were actually instrumental in enrolling the family in the REACH project. Therefore, in order to conduct family therapy at the Miami site, the inclusion criteria required that more than one family caregiver participate.

Clinicians, program developers, and clinical researchers working with, and developing interventions for, late-life families must take into consideration the specific histories and current situations of older cohorts (Mangen, 1995). The author argues that "the area of aging and family requires greater flexibility on the part of researchers regarding the type of design" (Mangen, p. 150). The psychometric properties of the assessment tools, the household's definition of family, and response bias are just some of the issues that also need to be addressed with sensitivity and flexibility. Assessment and measurement issues associated with both patient and caregiver baseline and outcome levels of functioning also have the potential to influence or complicate intervention design and our understanding of the results, with early studies that use impressionistic case report data often compared to later studies that use more structured outcome measures. Some clinical results also may have been hampered by complex variables, including patient's length of illness and position along a continuum of care. In addition, because not all caregivers report their roles as stressful (McKinlay, Crawford, & Tennstedt, 1995; Tennstedt, Cafferata, & Sullivan, 1992), some studies may have underestimated the salutary effects of caregiving on family members (Kramer, 1997a, 1997b), with more recent work suggesting that this may vary across ethnic and racial groups (see Janevic & Connell, 2001, for a recent review). Most studies have not reported on the use of outcomes targeting the family system and its functioning as a whole. Finally, the relative importance of in-home versus traditional office assessment and treatment warrants additional consideration and investigation. Thus, marked differences in study methodology, target populations, measures, and outcomes have contributed to the difficulties in establishing the comparable clinical efficacy of various interventions to date. Despite these limitations, the utilization of diverse psychotherapeutic approaches, including individual counseling, family interventions, and support groups, have made significant contributions to furthering the goal of identifying promising interventions that reduce caregiver distress (Zarit, Davey, Edwards, Femia, & Jarrott, 1998).

FAMILY THERAPY AND OLDER ADULTS

Family therapy is a psychosocial approach aimed at treating emotional and behavioral difficulties within the family milieu. The goal of family therapy is the modification of family structure or functioning to reduce the stress of one or more family members (Qualls, 1996). Theoretical models that have served as the foundations of family therapy include (a) the *psychodynamic* approach (e.g., Boszormenyi-Nagy & Krasner, 1986), which focuses on the intrapsychic processes that take place between family members; (b) the *communication/strategic* approach (e.g., J. Haley, 1976), which attempts to strategize on how to solve problems in the here and now; (c) the *experiential/humanistic* approach (e.g., Whitaker, 1977), which uses the therapist's "person" to make changes in the family system and treats the family as always "becoming"; (d) the *Bowenian* approach (e.g., Bowen, 1978), which can be characterized as a bridge between the past and the present dealing with interlocking relationships; (e) the *behavioral* approach (e.g., Liberman, 1970), which is very pragmatic and works under the assumption that behaviors in the family need to be measured and operationalized; and (f) the *structural* approach, which aims to alter the transactions between family members and clarify boundaries (e.g., Minuchin, 1974). (The structural approach will be expanded upon as part of the Miami SET model described later in this chapter.)

As awareness of the important role that aging plays in the dynamics of families has increased, a number of family therapists have extended the use of these conventional models of treatment to *late-life families,* or families in which the aging process "provokes a shift in the family structure or function" (Qualls, 1996, p. 122). Key contributions have been made by Herr and Weakland (1979) whose seminal work utilized brief therapy with late-life families, Hargrave and Anderson (1992) who studied multigenerational families, and Neidhardt and Allen (1993) who applied a systems approach to family treatment. Moreover, Qualls (1995) and Zarit and Knight (1996) demonstrated how different family therapy theories and approaches could be applied to late-life families; and Davey, Murphy, and Price (2000) and Qualls (2000) explain why family therapy is the most appropriate treatment when dealing with older cohorts. They argue that due to the importance of the family in the lives of older individuals and the nature of many of the issues that older individuals face today, family interventions appear to be a promising and natural avenue that could enhance the quality of life of older individuals. Although controlled treatment trials investigating the application of family therapy techniques to late-life families are relatively few, this approach may prove to be beneficial in assisting families to cope with the deleterious effects of caregiving for patients with dementia. For instance, a recent study using cognitive-behavioral family therapy obtained satisfactory findings regarding symptom alleviation in a sample of Alzheimer's caregivers (Marriott, Donaldson, Tarrier, & Burns, 2000).

However, family therapy applied to late-life families will require careful modifications. Family therapists who treat older individuals must be especially sensitive to several important issues that are idiosyncratic to this cohort. For example, a thorough assessment of the older person's physical and mental health functioning is particularly crucial, especially in regard to the effective treatment of patients with Alzheimer's disease and related disorders and their families. In addition, therapists will have to be flexible in deciding which adults to include in therapy sessions, given the current definitions of what constitutes a late-life family. Qualls (1997, 1999a) identifies the importance of examining not only the individual historical patterns of behavior of the family members, but also the historical patterns of behavior of the relationships between family members. Furthermore, Qualls (1997, 1999a) discusses two issues that appear to be closely related to the multigenerational nature of families with a loved one who has dementia. These issues are: (a) the impact that the patient's loss of autonomy has on the family, and (b) value conflicts that are principally related to caregiving duties. Moreover, Qualls reports that many older client issues are indeed related to these family conflicts. Although the literature suggests that family therapy could be an effective intervention in working with older adults, many questions remain regarding which modalities are effective for older adults and their families and at which point in the course of the disease. In addition, there is very little literature on how best to conduct family therapy with systems that are struggling with dementia care, including which family members to include, where to conduct therapy, and what its focus and content should be, as well as issues regarding confidentiality and privacy (Coon et al., 1999; Thompson & Gallagher-Thompson, 1996).

FAMILY THERAPY FOR CAREGIVERS OF PATIENTS WITH DEMENTIA

When shifts within the social landscape—including increased rates of divorce, remarriage, geographical mobility, and two-career families—are coupled with increased life expectancy and increased years of caregiving, family resources shrink. The result is a sharp decrease in the number of adults and family members available to care for the needs of older adults. Thus, when faced with crises, families and caregivers are likely to experience increasing levels of distress, along with the reawakening of old family conflicts (Qualls, 1996). When the familiar coping styles and strategies that served older family members well in prior years are no longer effective in managing the stressors of late life, subsequent distress may occur, not only in the caregiver but across the entire family unit as well.

Family interventions can help these families and caregivers abandon their repetitive, nonproductive approaches in favor of exploring new and productive methods to solve problems and address feelings related to these problems. Zarit et al. (1998) and Zarit (1996) identified family therapy, support groups, and family meetings as the three major interventions often utilized in the treatment of caregiver distress. The authors further explain that each of these treatment modalities can offer different yet very helpful strategies to ameliorate caregiver distress, and that a combination of these treatment modalities is often times the treatment of choice. For instance, Mittelman and her colleagues (Mittelman et al., 1995; Mittelman et al., 1996) obtained positive results with a comprehensive support program for the spousal caregivers of Alzheimer's patients. This successful psychosocial treatment consisted of individual therapy for the primary caregiver, family counseling, accessibility to additional counseling as needed, and support group participation. Caregivers in this study reported fewer distressing symptoms and received increased aid from their families, which resulted in a marked reduction in patient institutionalization. Similarly, Whitlatch, Zarit, and von Eye (1991) tested a caregiving intervention that included individual sessions for the caregiver combined with a family meeting that also yielded positive results. However, Zarit and Edwards (1996) explain that clinicians should distinguish between family *therapy* and family *meetings* when dealing with caregiving families. Family meetings are behaviorally driven, focusing on the development of realistic plans that determine how family members can best assist the primary caregiver. Furthermore, these meetings avoid clinician engagement in historical family problems and family members' tendency to quantify the assistance being provided (i.e., competition between how much assistance each member should provide), and instead support each person's specific plan to do their share. Family therapy, as discussed before, purports not only to increase caregiver assistance, but also attempts to alter interactions between family members; therefore, it is more comprehensive, longer lasting, and addresses deeper problems.

Finally, medical and technological advances have resulted in individuals living longer with chronic illness, and more contemporary families are separated by geographic distances, so more older adults are living alone (U.S. Census Bureau, 2001). As a result, family therapists need to learn how to utilize technological techniques to bridge these family distances as well as more effective ways to incorporate the extrafamilial systems relied on by many of today's elderly. Extrafamilial systems are those informal or formal support systems that assist primary caregivers with the care of the Alzheimer's patient (e.g., neighbors, Alzheimer's Association personnel). The need to access the extrafamilial systems becomes more a reality as American families "shrink," that is, when the number of blood relatives living nearby who could help with caregiving tasks substantially diminishes (U.S. Census Bureau, 2001). The Miami REACH site is currently investigating the efficacy of the innovative family therapy intervention called Structural Ecosystems Therapy (SET) in combination with computer technology, to help alleviate the distress and enhance the well-being of family caregivers of patients with dementia.

THEORETICAL BACKGROUND OF STRUCTURAL ECOSYSTEMS THERAPY

Structural Ecosystems Therapy operates under the basic assumption that the family reinforces undesirable behaviors. Szapocznik and colleagues developed this therapy modality as a result of direct experience working with Hispanic and African American families of troubled teenagers, and based on his early work with Cuban elders (e.g., Szapocznik, Santisteban, Hervis, Spencer, & Kurtines, 1982). Keeping the contextual framework of his work, the developers did not seek to change the individual or his or her social context, but instead to work within it by changing the person's interactions (also known as transactions) with the environment (Szapocznik et al., 1997). SET focuses on the process among interactions, not the content.

SET as described in Szapocznik et al. (1997) is an integration and cultural adaptation of two key models of family research: structural family therapy (Minuchin & Fishman, 1981) and the social ecological approach or ecosystemic approach of the world (Bronfenbrenner, 1977, 1979, 1986). These are used in conjunction with the practical application of clinical research completed at the Center for Family Studies at the University of Miami with diverse populations in the last two decades (e.g., Nelson, Mitrani, & Szapocznik, 2000; Szapocznik et al., 1982). Because of the geographical and cultural context in which SET is implemented, its developers culturally tailored the intervention for the Latino (especially Cuban) and African American populations. For example, in their exploration of family psychology and cultural diversity, Szapocznik and Kurtines (1993) emphasize the importance of studying families within the contexts in which they exist in order to "help bridge the gap between the literatures on family and culture." These authors also explore the significant implications of *nesting*, where the individual is seen as nested within the family and the family within the culture, especially in the context of the Hispanic American culture. This nesting becomes even more of an issue in the context of an illness such as Alzheimer's disease and related disorders (ADRD), where, culturally speaking, the family may have misconceptions about ADRD (Árean & Gallagher-Thompson, 1996; Gallagher-Thompson et al., 2000) as well as ineffective ways to handle it. Moreover, the concept of *familism* is embedded in the strong value placed on family by Hispanics (Sabogal, Marin, G., Otero-Sabogal, Marin, B., & Pérez-Stable, 1987), and Cuban families have been found to hold value orientations consistent with other Hispanic groups (Szapocznik, Scopetta, Aranalde, & Kurtines, 1978).

Through the concept of familism, Szapocznik and colleagues developed the structural family therapy known as SET, and in a series of pilot studies (Scopetta et al., 1977; Szapocznik et al., 1997) found SET not only effective, but also culturally sensitive. In sum, the value orientation of the clients (e.g., family oriented, hoping to someday return to their country of origin) and the present-oriented approach of the therapist in particular are very important within this therapeutic approach (Szapocznik et al., 1997, p. 168). When implemented with REACH caregivers, for instance, the goals of the therapy consist of reducing the distress of managing and living with a dementing illness, while at the same time maintaining and enhancing family functioning (University of Miami, 1998).

The ecological model considers the fact that caregivers develop, live in, and are thus influenced by, multiple social contexts. Bronfenbrenner (1977, 1979, 1986) labeled these contexts microsystems, mesosystems, exosystems, and macrosystems. (SET therapists are not expected to emphasize changes in the macrosystems.) *Microsystems* refer to those influences that caregivers have immediate contact with. These include family members, friends, neighbors, religious institutions, workplace, and formal services (e.g., nursing home services, respite care services) (University of Miami, 1998). *Mesosystems* refer to the interactions among the microsystems, such as the relationship between caregivers and their family members or between the patient with Alzheimer's and day-care staff. *Exosystems* include settings in which caregivers do not play an active role but are influenced by them. Examples might be the workplaces of family members that might provide flexible work schedules and legislature that could provide additional funding for respite care. *Macrosystems* refer to societal values, ideologies, laws, and customs of a particular culture, such as the respect a particular society shows toward an individual with dementia.

THERAPIST ACTIVITIES USED IN SET

The three basic therapist activities used in the Structural Ecosystemic Therapy are joining, diagnosing, and restructuring (Minuchin & Fishman, 1981; Szapocznik &

Kurtines, 1989; University of Miami, 1998). Although these three activities take place throughout therapy, emphasis on one versus another depends on the length of time the family has been in treatment. Joining and diagnosing are more prevalent from the outset of treatment, as in the following example:

1. *Joining:* This activity is the blending of the therapist with the family system. The building of this therapeutic alliance with all the parties involved in treatment is crucial for altering the interactions between systems. The SET therapist joins with the family using three techniques: Maintenance, tracking, and mimesis.
   a. Maintenance: The therapist respects the family's structure and rules. An example of maintenance is when the adult children are in charge of the patient's health care decisions, so the therapist consults with them on the issue rather than forcing the primary caregiver to gain control of this issue.
   b. Tracking: The therapist joins with the family system by identifying with the family's history and idiosyncrasies. An example of tracking is when the therapist asks a sister who is not involved in the caregiving of a patient with dementia how her brother's illness has affected her life. This technique invites the sister to participate in a discussion related to caregiving.
   c. Mimesis: The therapist blends with the family system by adopting their style and language. An example of mimesis is when a family system deals with the hardships of caregiving by using humor and the therapist begins to use humor as well.
2. *Diagnosis:* The second activity SET therapists engage in is diagnosing the family system (Szapocznik & Kurtines, 1989; Szapocznik et al., 1991; University of Miami, 1998). Here the SET therapist identifies the interactional patterns that prevent the family system from reaching its desired goals. This activity is rather complex and it encompasses six diagnostic dimensions: flexibility, structure, resonance, developmental stage, identified patienthood, and conflict resolution. For a complete discussion of these dimensions, we refer the reader to the University of Miami's *REACH Manual of Operations* (1998). An example of diagnosing the family's flexibility is assessing the family's capability to accept or change new roles that the patient used to fill (e.g., head of the household) or that have been brought about due to the demental illness (e.g., caregiver). An example of a pattern of denial in conflict resolution arises when relatives see nothing atypical about the patient with Alzheimer's giving away his money.
3. *Restructuring:* Once the therapist has joined with the family and diagnosed its problematic interactions, restructuring may then occur. To change interaction patterns the therapist uses techniques such as working in the present, refram-

ing, shifting boundaries and alliances, and redirecting communications. For example, REACH families are redirected to focus on current conflictual interactions regarding caregiving, not on conflicts that took place 20 years ago.

LOGISTICAL COMPONENTS IN SET

Although the efficacy of SET is still being investigated as part of the national REACH project, the logistical aspects such as the setting and dosage appear to have been adequate. The techniques discussed in the preceding section are used for intervening in both the familial and extrafamilial interactional patterns. Moreover, SET does not exclude any family members, friends, or neighbors who might be potential sources of support and assistance to the caregivers. The inclusion of other systems is one of the strengths of SET, especially in Latino families who are more likely to have extrafamilial ties. The flexibility of SET allows therapists to hold sessions in any setting that would be appropriate and therapeutic. Many of the sessions were conducted at the caregivers' or other family members' homes. This has facilitated the therapeutic process because the natural environment enhances the joining, diagnosing, and restructuring of problematic interactions. SET therapists have intervened with other caregiver systems such as visiting nursing homes with caregivers, assisting in the funeral arrangements of an Alzheimer's patient, and including the patient's physician in sessions. The SET therapist meets with the familial or extrafamilial systems for approximately 1-hour sessions. During the first 4 months of treatment, the sessions are held weekly; during the next 2 months biweekly, and monthly for the last 6 months.

USE OF A COMPUTER TELEPHONE INTEGRATION SYSTEM (CTIS) TO AUGMENT SET

The use of the SET model in its present form has been augmented at the Miami REACH site by the use of the CTIS system. This customized system involves an integration of computers and a screen phone having both text and voice. As described in Argüelles & von Simson (1999), the screen phones are installed in the caregiver's home, with training and installation conducted by the family's therapist. The CTIS system augments SET by adding the CTIS phone as a communication tool that augments linkages not only among the network of family members, but also to outside systems such as the Alzheimer's Association and other community services. This expansion of the caregiver's communication channels is made possible by features that facilitate conference calling to other family members and caregivers and help caregivers participate in on-line discussion and support groups. The telephone also provides linkages to the therapist and it has a respite feature where messages could be recorded for the patient (e.g., a greeting from a grandson who lives in another country could be recorded and replayed for the patient to enjoy). Because this system facilitates linkages both within and outside the family system, it is very beneficial to the nesting process necessary to successfully implement SET. Indeed, the CTIS may augment SET's efficacy by increasing the networks the caregiver can access with the assistance of a simple telephone call. In fact, as Argüelles and von Simson (1999) discuss, the system may also provide additional benefits such as "a leisure experience" for caregivers.

CHALLENGES OF SET AND CTIS IMPLEMENTATION

SET posed three main challenges. The first was the training. All therapists held at least a master's degree in clinical psychology, counseling psychology, or social work. Two of the therapists held doctoral degrees in clinical psychology. Therapists underwent comprehensive training in geriatrics, SET techniques, and the CTIS. The preliminary training took approximately 2 months. The number of hours varied depending on the therapist's expertise on SET and geriatrics. An inexperienced SET therapist required approximately 200 hours of training. Because the CTIS was a new modality, and the therapists in turn needed to train the caregivers, all therapists had to be trained how to use it. The comprehensive SET therapy training encompassed not only an introduction and thorough review of the SET, but also pairing with a senior therapist and working with a pilot family. Weekly supervision sessions took place by a seasoned therapist and clinical supervisor until all the families had terminated the intervention.

A second challenge was encouraging therapists to use the CTIS to conduct on-the-phone sessions. Although the families with the CTIS also had in-person therapy, sometimes having phone therapy sessions incorporated relatives, friends, and systems that were unable to meet in person due to practical problems or distance (e.g., residing in another state). Due to the "nontraditional" therapy augmentation (on the phone), it was sometimes difficult for therapists to break the old pattern of conducting most therapy sessions in person.

The final major challenge of SET relates to the therapist's ability to customize treatment to different cultural groups or other groups of caregiving families. In our case, SET was successfully tailored to meet the specific needs of White non-Hispanic and Cuban-American families of patients with dementia. Examples of tailoring differences included allotting a little more time for social graces at the home of Cuban American families.

CASE SAMPLE OF THE USE OF SET
AUGMENTED BY CTIS

The following vignette illustrates how the use of SET augmented by CTIS mobilized both familial and extrafamilial resources to alleviate the caregiver's stress and improve her well-being.

Mrs. Martha Gómez is a 49-year-old Cuban woman who is the primary caretaker of her 85-year-old father-in-law (Pedro) who is demented. In addition to his Alzheimer's disease of 3 years, Pedro's eyesight was poor due to his cataracts. When the therapist met the family, Martha was very distressed due to both her caregiving role and her own diabetes. Although Martha's husband, Juan, was supportive of her, he felt trapped between his wife and his father. On the one hand, Juan was experiencing guilt about the possibility of placing his father in a nursing home. On the other hand, he was cognizant of how Martha's health was becoming increasingly compromised by the difficulties of caregiving. Juan held a full-time job that kept him away from home most of the day. Martha, in contrast, was caring for her father-in-law at home on a full-time basis. Martha and Juan have a son (Luis) and two small grandchildren who live nearby. However, the only help the family had was a nurse assistant who came to the home 5 days a week to assist with the grooming of Pedro.

Martha was open to therapy, but other family members were hesitant, excusing themselves with the fact that they were too busy working. The therapist then decided that perhaps while she was directly joining with Martha and indirectly joining with Juan and Luis, Martha could benefit from an expansion of her extrafamilial interactions. Due to the duties of caregiving, Martha's involvement in the church had decreased significantly. In response, the therapist encouraged her to not only participate in church services, but to attend Bible courses. Martha and the therapist worked together trying to assess Martha's wishes as well as how her spirituality would help her in the caregiving role. Being at the caregiver's home facilitated making the necessary phone calls to the Archdiocese and to her church. Martha's church involvement not only provided spiritual comfort, but it also provided her with a respite time in which she would leave the house. Emphasizing the benefits of taking care of her health also proved beneficial.

Martha also had the screen phone installed in her home. Another aspect of her extrafamilial systems that was worked on was her involvement in on-line discussion groups. By participating in these support groups, Martha was able to speak to other caregivers. The group interactions provided both emotional support and information about services for ADRD caregivers and patients, specifically, and about Alzheimer's disease and caregiving in general.

Much of the information that Martha and Juan subsequently used to place Pedro in a nursing home was gathered from the support group participants. Martha learned to reach out to old friends who also provided her with information regarding nursing homes. And finally, another extrafamilial service that Martha accessed using the CTIS was the Alzheimer's Association, which she frequently contacted regarding pertinent caregiving issues and services.

By this time, Martha's family was already becoming familiar, through Martha's efforts, of the type of work that Martha and the therapist were doing. The son, Luis, finally agreed to participate in an on-the-phone therapy session. This first session was productive and focused on joining with him and reframing Martha's "nagging" as her wish to talk with her son and share her feelings. A home-based session subsequently took place in which the son provided a good deal of support and practical ideas regarding nursing home placement for his grandfather. Similar to Luis, a session took place including Martha's husband. This session focused on facilitating enactments around the couple's concern for each other. Moreover, the therapist facilitated a working alliance among them that led to a conjoint decision dealing with the potential institutionalization of Pedro.

Martha and Juan went together to several nursing homes to decide which one was more convenient. The flexibility of SET allowed the therapist to accompany Martha to one of the nursing home visits. In order to facilitate the visiting process, questions to be asked and things to look for were brainstormed prior to the visits. By the end of treatment Martha was feeling less anxious and Pedro was placed in a nursing home. Also, Martha felt the support from her family members, and her guilt around the decision to place Pedro had decreased. She now had more time for social and church activities, and by experiencing less anxiety she could take better care of herself. Overall, everyone in the Gómez family were experiencing less distress and they all contributed to the decision of placing Pedro.

CONCLUSIONS ABOUT SET AUGMENTED BY CTIS

The novel integration of these two systems (SET and CTIS) is currently being evaluated for its treatment efficacy and dosage as part of the REACH program. Data demonstrating the effects of the interventions on important caregiver areas such as depression and burden appear promising, but they are not yet available. However, preliminary results and case reports suggest that the integration of both systems appears to be helpful to the families. For example, caregivers treated through SET and CTIS appear better able to build intergenerational bonds with their children, some of whom may have been previously alienated or live far away. Another advantage of CTIS is that family members may feel "safer" talking about issues such as funeral arrangements on the phone. However, in the absence of visual cues or gestures, family members need to be reminded that their verbal communication needs to be more precise. For additional comments, interested readers are referred to Mitrani and Czaja (2000) who discuss the intervention and its effectiveness through a clinical case presentation.

FUTURE DIRECTIONS IN FAMILY THERAPY

A wide array of psychosocial interventions has been developed for caregivers of patients with dementia, evolving from early support and psychoeducational programs to the emergence of a range of interventions tailored for specific caregiver needs. The theoretical paradigms guiding both the content and the process of these interventions are also many and varied. Even though there is a paucity of research on the effect of family therapy on families caring for a loved one with dementia, family therapy appears to be a promising approach that can benefit family caregivers as well as the patients themselves. As a treatment approach, family therapy may fit well into the fabric of daily life that characterizes the families of older adults. Not only can this modality assist the entire family's adaptation to aging, it could prove particularly effective for the family's stress associated with negotiating the elaborate health and social service systems that are integral parts of late-life.

With increased life expectancy, the numbers of older persons diagnosed with severe cognitive impairment is expected to rise in the coming decades. As a result, interest continues to grow in the development and utilization of psychosocial treatments targeted toward families of patients with dementia. The literature on family interventions designed to address the needs of these family systems suggests several themes for clinicians, clinical researchers, and program developers to consider.

First, it is imperative that we gain additional understanding of the complex relationship between patients with dementia and family caregivers through additional research so that effective family interventions can be developed, empirically tested, and disseminated to service providers. Moreover, the interventions' central ingredients or mechanisms of change that drive desired outcomes must also be identified to help program developers with limited budgets effectively integrate these interventions into existing pathways of care or within programs in development. Thus, additional clinical research trials using family interventions (both family therapy and family meetings) are needed to provide evidence of the efficacy and generalizability of specific family approaches. The development and study of these interventions, appropriately targeted to problems related to caregiving for patients with dementia, could improve the care of patients with dementia as well as the quality of life for both patient and family.

Second, working with caregivers of patients with dementia can bring about new approaches to family therapy with late-life families. To date, only a few of the theoretical approaches examined in traditional family therapy have been incorporated and examined in these particular caregiving families. Therefore, future work needs to consider the utility of different theoretical approaches as well as the development and use of novel therapeutic techniques into family interventions. Because family caregivers may need to discuss or focus attention on their history with the patient who has dementia but some patients are unable to participate in many aspects of family sessions, *cuento*, reminiscence, validation, and pet therapies, among others, might prove helpful to the caregiving system. For example, cuento therapy, even though it is often used with Spanish-speaking children (Constantino, Malgady, & Rogler, 1986) allows the family to draw from old memories and would perhaps permit patients to participate, especially in the mild to moderate stages of the illness. Similarly, a variation of reminiscence therapy (Scogin & McElreath, 1994), which has been used with older persons in a support group setting, might be adapted to a family modality. Other venues to explore in future research related to family therapy and caregiving systems include pet therapy and horticultural therapies. These therapies might even be used in conjunction with SET plus CTIS, described in this chapter, especially if implemented at home or sanctioned within the family's community. Future modifications of family therapy also might make use of the Internet and videoconferencing technology to expand family therapy interventions to include family members located at great distances from both patient and caregiver. Czaja, Eisdorfer, and Schulz (2000) and Czaja (in press) address the fact that technology can indeed assist caregivers not only with informal support, but also with sorely needed formal care services.

Finally, family interventionists need to keep in mind the diversity of today's caregiving families. The identification of effective family interventions for tightly controlled clinical trials needs to be balanced with interventions that can be effectively tailored or adapted to meet the needs of ethnically and racially diverse families. For instance, although SET and CTIS was conducted with both White non-Hispanic and Cuban-American caregivers in Miami and these families perceived it as helpful, this approach, like other family therapy approaches, probably will need thoughtful modifications to effectively serve other ethnic or racial groups in other geographic locations. Thus, the need to advance the study of family therapy and family meetings with diverse caregiving families is imperative, especially when one considers not only ethnic and racial diversity, but also differences in terms of acculturation level, sexual orientation, geographic proximity, living situation, geographic region or area, employment status, and caregivers providing care to elders with dementia and other comorbid conditions. Moreover, both within and across these groups, family treatment requires a better understanding of what "members" constitute the late-life family to be included in treatment and where therapy should take place, particularly when these families are geographically dispersed. Although it is oftentimes assumed that home-based family therapy is more promising due to the need of the caregiver to stay home, this approach versus others has not been investigated thoroughly. When taken together, these themes suggest that clinicians, clinical researchers, and program developers all can play important roles in the ongoing development of innovative family interventions that are designed to help families meet the challenges of caregiving for a patient with dementia while improving the quality of life of caregivers, patients, and other family members.

Readers can get additional information regarding caregiver needs by contacting the following organizations:

Alzheimer's Association (800) 272-3900. www.alz.org

National Family Caregivers Association (800) 896-3650. www.nfcacares.org

American Association of Retired Persons (800) 424-3410. www.aarp.org

Alliance for Aging, Inc. (800) 963-5337

Some of these organizations also have local chapters.

REFERENCES

Árean, P. A., & Gallagher-Thompson, D. (1996). Issues and recommendations for the recruitment and retention of older ethnic minority adults into clinical research. *Journal of Consulting and Clinical Psychology, 64,* 875–880.

Argüelles, S., & von Simson, A. (1999). Innovative family and technological interventions for encouraging leisure activities in caregivers of persons with Alzheimer's disease. *Activities, Adaptation, and Aging, 24*(2), 83–99.

Bass, D. M., Noelker, L. S., & Rechlin, L. R. (1996). The moderating influence of service use on negative caregiving consequences. *Journal of Gerontology: Social Sciences, 51B,* S121–S131.

Boszormenyi-Nagy, I., & Krasner, B. (1986). *Between give and take: A clinical guide to contextual therapy.* New York: Brunner/Mazel.

Bourgeois, M. S., Schulz, R., & Burgio, L. (1996). Intervention for caregivers of patients with Alzheimer's disease: A review and analysis of content, process, and outcomes. *International Journal of Human Development, 43,* 35–92.

Bowen, M. (1978). *Family therapy in clinical practice.* New York: Aronson.

Bronfenbrenner, U. (1977). Toward an experimental ecology of human development. *American Psychologist, 32,* 513–531.

Bronfenbrenner, U. (1979). *The ecology of human development.* Cambridge, MA: Harvard University Press.

Bronfenbrenner, U. (1986). Ecology of the family as a context for human development: Research perspectives. *Developmental Psychology, 22,* 723–742.

Cochrane, J. J., Goering, P. N., & Rogers, J. M. (1997). The mental health of informal caregivers in Ontario: An epidemiological survey. *American Journal of Public Health, 87,* 2002–2007.

Collins, C., & Jones, R. (1997). Emotional distress and morbidity in dementia carers: A matched comparison of husbands and wives. *International Journal of Geriatric Psychiatry, 12,* 1168–1173.

Constantino, G., Malgady, R. G., & Rogler, L. H. (1986). Cuento therapy: A culturally sensitive modality for Puerto Rican children. *Journal of Consulting and Clinical Psychology, 54,* 639–645.

Coon, D., Schulz. R., & Ory, M. (1999). Innovative intervention approaches for Alzheimer's disease caregivers. In D. E. Biegel & A. Blum (Eds.), *Innovations in practice and service delivery across the lifespan* (pp. 295–325). New York: Oxford University Press.

Czaja, S. J. (in press). Telecommunications technology as an aid to family caregivers. In W. A. Rogers & A. D. Fisk (Eds.), *Human factors interventions for the health care of older adults.* Hillsdale, NJ: Erlbaum.

Czaja, S. J., Eisdorfer, C., & Schulz, R. (2000). Future directions in caregiving: Implications for interventions. In R. Schulz (Ed.), *Handbook on dementia caregiving* (pp. 283–319). New York: Springer.

Davey, A., Murphy, M., & Price, S. (2000). Aging and the family: Dynamics and therapeutic interventions. In W. C. Nichols, M. A. Pace-Nichols, et al. (Eds.), *Handbook of family development and intervention* (pp. 235–252). New York: Wiley & Sons.

Fuller-Jonap, F., & Haley, W. E. (1995). Mental and physical health of male caregivers of a spouse with Alzheimer's disease. *Journal of Aging and Health, 7,* 99–118.

Gallagher-Thompson, D., Árean, P., Coon, D. W., Menéndez, A., Takagi, K., Haley, W. E., Argüelles, T., Rubert, M., Loewenstein, D., & Szapocznik, J. (2000). Development and implementation of intervention strategies for culturally diverse caregiving populations. In R. Schulz (Ed.), *Handbook on dementia caregiving* (pp. 151–185). New York: Springer.

Gallagher-Thompson, D., Coon, D. W., Rivera, P., Powers, D., & Zeiss, A. M. (1998). Family caregiving: Stress, coping, and intervention. In M. Hersen & V. B. Hasselt (Eds.), *Handbook of clinical geropsychology* (pp. 469–493). New York: Plenum Press.

Haley, J. (1976). *Problem-solving therapy.* San Francisco: Jossey-Bass.

Haley, W. E. (1997). The family caregiver's role in Alzheimer's disease. *Neurology, 48,* S25–S29.

Haley, W. E., West, C. A. C., Wadley, V. G., Ford, G. R., White, F. A., Barrett, J. J., Harrell, L. E., & Roth, D. L. (1995). Psychological, social, and health impact of caregiving: A comparison of Black and White dementia family caregivers and noncaregivers. *Psychology and Aging, 10,* 540–552.

Hargrave, T. D., & Anderson,W. T. (1992). *Finishing well: Aging and reparation in the intergenerational family.* New York: Brunner/Mazel.

Herr, J. J., & Weakland, J. H. (1979). *Counseling elders and their families.* New York: Springer.

Janevic, M. R., & Connell, C. M. (2001). Racial, ethnic and cultural differences in the dementia caregiving experience: Recent findings. *Gerontologist, 41,* 334–347.

Jutras, S., & Lavoie, J. P. (1995). Living with an impaired elderly person: The informal caregiver's physical and mental health. *Journal of Aging and Health, 7,* 46–73.

Kennet, J., Burgio, L., & Schulz, R. (2000). Interventions for in-home caregivers: A review of research 1990 to present. In R. Schulz (Ed.), *Handbook on dementia caregiving* (pp. 61–125). New York: Springer.

Knight, B. G., Lutzky, S., & Macofsky-Urban, F. (1993). A meta-analytic review of interventions for caregiver distress: Recommendations for future research. *Gerontologist, 33,* 240–248.

Kramer, B. J. (1997a). Gain in the caregiving experience: Where are we? What next? *Gerontologist, 37,* 218–232.

Kramer, B. J. (1997b). Differential predictors of strain and gain among husbands caring for wives with dementia. *Gerontologist, 37,* 239–249.

Kramer, B. J., & Kipnis, S. (1995). Eldercare and work-role conflict: Toward an understanding of gender differences in caregiver burden. *Gerontologist, 35,* 340–348.

Liberman, R. P. (1970). Behavioral approaches to family and couple therapy. *American Journal of Orthopsychiatry, 40,* 106–118.

Mangen, D. J. (1995). Methods and analysis of family data. In R. Blieszner & V. H. Bedford (Eds.), *Handbook of aging and the family* (pp. 148–177). Westport, CT: Greenwood Press/Greenwood Publishing.

Marriott, A., Donaldson, C., Tarrier, N., & Burns, A. (2000). Effectiveness of cognitive-behavioural family intervention in reducing the burden of care in carers of patients with Alzheimer's disease. *British Journal of Psychiatry, 176,* 557–562.

McKinlay, J. B., Crawford, S. L., & Tennstedt, S. L. (1995). The everyday impacts of providing informal care to dependent elders and their consequences for the care recipients. *Journal of Aging and Health, 7,* 497–528.

Minuchin, S. (1974). *Families and family therapy.* Cambridge, MA: Harvard University Press.

Minuchin, S., & Fishman, H. C. (1981). *Family therapy techniques.* Cambridge, MA: Harvard University Press.

Mitrani, V. B., & Czaja, S. (2000). Family-based therapy for family caregivers: Clinical observations. *Aging and Mental Health, 4,* 200–209.

Mittelman, M., Ferris, S. H., Shulman, E., Steinberg, G., Ambinder, A., Mackell, J. A., & Cohen, J. (1995). A comprehensive support program: Effect on depression in spouse-caregivers of AD patients. *Gerontologist, 35,* 792–802.

Mittelman, M. S., Ferris, S. H., Shulman, E., Steinberg, G., & Levin, B. (1996). A family intervention to delay nursing home placement of patients with Alzheimer disease: A randomized controlled trial. *Journal of the American Medical Association, 276,* 1725–1731.

Neidhardt, E. R., & Allen, J. A. (1993). *Family therapy with the elderly.* Newbury Park, CA: Sage.

Nelson, R. H., Mitrani, V. B., & Szapocznik, J. (2000). Applying a family-ecosystemic model to reunite a family separated due to child abuse: A case study. *Contemporary Family Therapy, 22,* 125–146.

Qualls, S. H. (1995). Clinical interventions with later-life families. In R. Blieszner & V. H. Bedford (Eds.), *Handbook of aging and the family* (pp. 474–487). Westport, CT: Greenwood Press/Greenwood Publishing.

Qualls, S. H. (1996). Family therapy with aging families. In S. H. Zarit & B. G. Knight (Eds.), *A guide to psychotherapy and aging* (pp. 121–137). Washington, DC: American Psychological Association.

Qualls, S. H. (1997). Transitions in autonomy: The essential caregiving challenge. An essay for practitioners. *Family Relations, 46,* 41–45.

Qualls, S. H. (1999a). Family therapy with older adult clients. *Psychotherapy in Practice, 55,* 977–990.

Qualls, S. H. (1999b). Realizing power in intergenerational family hierarchies: Family reorganization when older adults decline. In M. Duffy (Ed.), *Handbook of counseling and psychotherapy with older adults* (pp. 228–241). New York: Wiley & Sons.

Qualls, S. H. (2000). Therapy with aging families: Rationale, opportunities and challenges. *Aging and Mental Health, 4,* 191–199.

Sabogal, F., Marin, G., Otero-Sabogal, R., Marin, B., & Pérez-Stable, E. J. (1987). Hispanic familism and acculturation: What changes and what doesn't? *Hispanic Journal of Behavioral Sciences, 11,* 136–147.

Schulz, R., Newson, J., Mittelmark, M., Burton, L., Hirsch, C., & Jackson, S. (1997). Health effects of caregiving: The caregiver health effects study, an ancillary study of the cardiovascular health study. *Annals of Behavioral Medicine, 19,* 110–116.

Schulz, R., O'Brien, A. T., Bookwala, J., & Fleissner, K. (1995). Psychiatric and physical morbidity effects of dementia caregiving: Prevalence, correlates, and causes. *Gerontologist, 35,* 771–791.

Scharlach, A. E. (1989). A comparison of employed caregivers of cognitively impaired and physically impaired persons. *Research on Aging, 11,* 225–243.

Scogin, F., & McElreath, L. (1994). Efficacy of psychosocial treatments for geriatric depression: A quantitative review. *Journal of Consulting and Clinical Psychology, 62,* 69–74.

Scopetta, M. A., Szapocznik, J., King, O. E., Ladner, R., Alegre, C., & Tillman, M. S. (1977). *Final Report: The Spanish drug rehabilitation research project (NIDA Grant #HB1 DA01696).* Miami, FL: University of Miami, Spanish Family Guidance Center.

Szapocznik, J., & Kurtines, W. M. (1989). *Breakthroughs in family therapy with drug abusing and problem youth.* New York: Springer.

Szapocznik, J., & Kurtines, W. M. (1993). Family psychology and cultural diversity: Opportunities for theory, research and application. *American Psychologist, 48,* 400–407.

Szapocznik, J., Kurtines, W. M., Santisteban, D. A., Pantin, H., Scopetta, M., Mancilla, Y., Aisenberg, S., McIntosh, S., Pérez-Vidal, A., & Coatsworth, J. D. (1997). The evolution of structural ecosystemic theory for working with Latino families. In J. G. García & M. C. Zea (Eds.), *Psychological interventions and research with Latino populations* (pp. 166–190). Boston: Allen and Bacon.

Szapocznik, J., Rio, A. T., Hervis, O. E., Mitrani, V. B., Kurtines, W. M., & Faraci, A. M. (1991). Assessing change in family functioning as a result of treatment: The Structural Family Systems Rating Scale (SFSR). *Journal of Marital and Family Therapy, 17,* 295–310.

Szapocznik, J., Santisteban, D., Hervis, O., Spencer, F., & Kurtines, W. M. (1982). Life enhancement counseling and the treatment of depressed Cuban American elders. *Hispanic Journal of Behavioral Sciences, 4,* 487–502.

Szapocznik, J., Scopetta, M., Aranalde, M. A., & Kurtines,W. (1978). Cuban value structure: Clinical implications. *Journal of Consulting and Clinical Psychology, 46,* 961–970.

Tennstedt, S. L., Cafferata, G. L., & Sullivan, L. (1992). Depression among caregivers of impaired elders. *Journal of Aging and Health, 4,* 58–76.

Thompson, L. W., & Gallagher-Thompson, D. (1996). Practical issues related to maintenance of mental health and positive well-being in family caregivers. In L. Cartensen, B. Edelstein, & L. Dornbrand (Eds.), *The practical handbook of clinical gerontology* (pp. 129–150). Thousand Oaks, CA: Sage.

University of Miami. (1998). *Manual of operations for Resources for Enhancing Alzheimer's Caregivers Health.* Miami, FL: Author. Unpublished manuscript.

U.S. Census Bureau. (2001). America's families and living arrangements. Population Characteristics, P20–537. Washington, DC: U.S. Department of Commerce.

Whitaker, C. A. (1977). Process techniques of family therapy. *Interaction, 1,* 4–19.

Whitlatch, C., Zarit, S. H., & von Eye, A. (1991). Efficacy of interventions with caregivers: A reanalysis. *Gerontologist, 31,* 9–14.

Wisniewski, S. R., Belle, S. H., Coon, D. W., Marcus, S., Ory, M. G., & Schulz, R. (2001). The Resources for Enhancing Alzheimer's Caregiver Health (REACH) project design and methods. (Manuscript submitted for publication.)

Zarit, S. H. (1996). Interventions with family caregivers. In S. H. Zarit & B. G. Knight (Eds.), *A guide to psychotherapy and aging* (pp. 139–159). Washington, DC: American Psychological Association.

Zarit, S. H., Davey, A., Edwards, A., Femia, E. E., & Jarrott, S. E. (1998). Family caregiving: Research findings and clinical implications. In A. S. Bellack & M. Hersen (Series Eds.) & B. Edelstein (Vol. Ed.), *Comprehensive clinical psychology* (pp. 429–523). New York: Pergamon Press.

Zarit, S. H., & Edwards, A. (1996). Family caregiving: Research and clinical intervention. In R. T. Woods (Ed.), *Handbook of the clinical psychology of ageing* (pp. 333–368). New York: Wiley & Sons.

Zarit, S. H., & Knight, B. G. (1996). *A guide to psychotherapy and aging: Effective clinical interventions in a life-stage context.* Washington, DC: American Psychological Association.

6

Skill-Building: Psychoeducational Strategies

Louis D. Burgio, Nancy Solano, Susan E. Fisher, Alan Stevens, and Dolores Gallagher-Thompson

Numerous studies have documented the stressful nature of caregiving for a family member with a progressive dementing illness (Anthony-Bergstone, Zarit, & Gatz, 1988; Gallagher, Rose, Rivera, Lovett, & Thompson, 1989; Schulz, Visintainer, & Williamson, 1990). Caregivers of patients with dementia report experiencing more symptoms of psychological distress and receive more psychiatric diagnoses compared to either the general population or caregivers of nondementia patients (Schulz et al., 1990). Reviews of the caregiving literature correlate caregiver burden with a range of psychological problems such as depression, anxiety, hostility, and poor self-reported physical health (Bourgeouis, Schulz, & Burgio, 1996; Schulz, O'Brien, Bookwala, & Fleissner, 1995).

In response to the growing body of literature documenting caregiver burden, a broad variety of programs and services to address these concerns have been developed. Several skill-based interventions for caregivers have been described in the literature and found to be a useful approach for caregivers (Bourgeois et al., 1996; Gallagher-Thompson & DeVries, 1994; Gallagher-Thompson, Lovett, et al., 2000). Skill-based interventions fall within a continuum ranging from psychoeducational to specific problem-focused approaches. For example, inter-

119

ventions may range from increasing knowledge of dementia to developing skills to manage care recipient behavioral problems. These interventions can be used in any of the phases of caregiving, with the content aimed at the specific challenges associated with that particular phase.

This chapter is organized into three parts. First, we will briefly describe the theoretical framework used to explain caregiver stress and briefly review the efficacy of psychoeducational and skills-training interventions for family caregivers. This section will be subdivided based on whether the intervention was conducted using an individual, group, or comprehensive multicomponent format. Second, we will discuss how skill-based interventions were employed in the REACH project (Resources for Enhancing Alzheimer's Caregiver Health) and how these interventions were modified for ethnic minority caregivers. Last, we will provide practical suggestions for clinicians who are interested in providing skills-based interventions for caregivers.

MODELS OF CAREGIVING AND IMPLICATIONS FOR INTERVENTION

Several theoretical models of stress provide a convenient framework for conceptualizing the caregiving experience (Cohler, Groves, Borden, & Lazarus, 1989; Haley, Levine, Brown, & Bartolucci, 1987). Schulz, Gallagher-Thompson, Haley, and Czaja (2000) developed a theoretical/conceptual framework for intervention approaches using a stress-based model that describes the content, process, and goals of an intervention. The framework focuses on four relatively independent dimensions that must be considered when implementing an intervention: (a) the primary entity being targeted by the intervention (caregiver, care-recipient, or the social and physical environment); (b) the primary domain being targeted (cognitive skills, knowledge, behavior, or affect); (c) the intensity of the intervention (individual, group, or family; frequency and duration of sessions); and (d) personalization (extent to which intervention is tailored to the individual needs of the participant). According to Schulz and colleagues (2000), interventions that are high on all four dimensions (i.e., high intensity, highly personalized, targeting multiple domains and targets) will be more effective than interventions low on these dimensions.

REVIEW OF THE SKILLS-TRAINING LITERATURE

Skill-based interventions have been implemented in a variety of formats including individual, group, and comprehensive multicomponent programs. Several studies have been conducted to determine the efficacy of skill-based interventions using each of these formats. Unfortunately, few published accounts provide information on the specific skills taught (Bourgeois et al., 1996; Kennet, Burgio, & Schulz, 2000).

Individual Format

Although individual therapy is more costly and less time efficient, clinicians may consider this the best treatment modality for some caregivers. For example, individual therapy may be most appropriate with more complex cases involving severe depression, suicidal ideations, substance abuse, situations in which confidentiality may be an issue such as elder abuse, or when the caregiver has sensory deficits. Moreover, some individuals may not feel comfortable in a group and prefer individual therapy.

A small body of empirical studies has shown that individual behavioral-skills-training is a useful modality for caregivers. Two of these reports are case studies. Kaplan and Gallagher-Thompson (1995) provided cognitive-behavioral treatment to a 72-year-old wife caregiver who was clinically depressed. Through the use of standardized depression measures, the authors reported full remission of major depression at the completion of treatment. In another case study, Gwyther (1990) assisted a 68-year-old female caregiver to reappraise her situation, use formal and informal caregiver services, and develop behavior-management skills. The author reports that after intervention, the caregiver experienced unspecified improvements in feelings of conflict.

A few studies have compared different modalities of individual therapy. For example, Schmidt, Bonjean, Widem, and Schefft (1988) compared two forms of brief individual psychotherapy for caregivers: problem solving with emotional expression, and problem solving alone. Results suggest that problem solving plus emotional expression resulted in reduced caregiver psychiatric symptoms and improved caregiver/care-recipient relationships. In another comparison study, Gallagher-Thompson and Steffen (1994) compared depressed caregivers who received either individual cognitive-behavioral therapy or individual psychodynamic therapy. The authors reported successful resolution of depression in 71% of caregivers; however, no differences were found between the two treatment groups. When length of caregiving was considered, results showed that caregivers who had provided care for greater than 3.5 years benefited more from cognitive-behavioral treatment than caregivers who had provided care for briefer periods of time. The results from this study suggest that teaching specific coping skills instilled hope in long-term caregivers by showing them that there were still techniques they could use to reduce their negative responses to caregiving.

Individual approaches have also focused on teaching caregivers specific problem-solving skills to address symptoms commonly associated with dementia. For example, Pinkston and colleagues examined the utility of training caregivers to effectively manage the behavior problems of impaired elderly care-recipients (Pinkston & Linsk, 1984; Pinkston, Linsk, & Young, 1988). The behavior-management skills-training resulted in improvements in 73% of all behaviors targeted, 78% of which were maintained for 6 months posttreatment. Caregivers reported improvements in their ability to change care-recipient's behavior, improvements in perceived relationship with care-recipients, reduced embarrassment, and less strain during interactions with care-recipients.

In a study by Bourgeois, Burgio, Schulz, Beach, and Palmer (1997), seven caregivers were taught to use prosthetic memory aids to decrease care-recipient repetitive verbalizations. The prosthetic memory aids involved the use of simple statements written on cue cards or erasable tablets that were intended to cue care-recipients' memory for everyday events (e.g., "Carol gets home from work at 6 p.m."). Compared to seven matched controls, care-recipients in the treatment group showed reductions in repetitive verbalizations that maintained up to 6 months posttreatment.

Group Format

Although the skill-based interventions have been used in an individual format, (Gallagher-Thompson, Árean, et al., 2000), there are several advantages to group approaches for caregivers. First, groups provide the potential for a sense of belonging and affiliation that help counter the social isolation and loneliness often experienced by caregivers. Second, group participation offers an opportunity for caregivers to have their experiences validated and affirmed. Third, groups provide opportunities for interpersonal learning by providing multiple sources of feedback, a range of alternative perspectives, creative ideas, new insights, and help with the various phases of caregiving (e.g., placement and bereavement).

Gallagher-Thompson and various colleagues have developed several group psychoeducational interventions for caregivers. These interventions have integrated cognitive theory (Beck, Rush, Shaw, & Emery, 1979) and behavioral theory (Lewinsohn, Muñoz, Youngren, & Zeiss, 1986) with the stress-based model described earlier in this chapter (Schulz et al., 2000). These interventions include (a) a life satisfaction class (Thompson, Gallagher, & Lovett, 1992) that targets depressive symptoms by teaching participants several skills to increase their level of engagement in pleasant activities; (b) a problem-solving class (Gallagher, Thompson, Silven, & Priddy, 1985) that teaches caregivers systematic approaches to resolving problems associated with caregiving; and (c) a coping with frustration class (Gallagher-Thompson & DeVries, 1994; Gallagher-Thompson et al., 1992) that teaches caregivers to manage negative feelings towards caregiving. Currently, work is being done to develop and evaluate the effectiveness of group CBT interventions with ethnic minority caregivers (Gallagher-Thompson et al., 2000). (Treatment manuals for these psychoeducational classes are available upon request from Dr. Gallagher-Thompson; note that versions are available in Spanish and English for several of these classes.)

The interventions developed by Gallagher-Thompson and several colleagues have been shown to be effective at decreasing distress among caregivers. For example, Lovett and Gallagher (1988) compared a life-satisfaction (e.g., increasing pleasant activities) group to a problem-solving-skills group. Results showed that participants in both groups experienced reduced stress, depression, and increased morale compared to the control group. Similarly, Gallagher-Thompson, Lovett, et al. (2000) found decreased depression scores among participants in the life satisfaction intervention compared to either problem-solving or wait-list control.

In a study by Bourgeois, Schulz, Burgio, and Beach (2000), the relative effects of two skills-training programs for caregivers were evaluated on a variety of care-recipient and caregiver outcomes. Caregivers were assigned to one of three conditions: behavior management training, affective self-management training, or friendly-visit control. Compared with controls, reductions in the mean frequency of observed problem behavior were found in the behavior-management skills-training group. Caregivers in the affective self-management group significantly improved their mood ratings compared to controls. These effects also maintained at both follow-up assessments.

Individual Versus Group Format

Additional studies have compared the effectiveness of individual and group interventions for reducing caregiver distress. For example, Toseland, Rossiter, Peak, and Smith (1990) compared the effects of individual and group counseling. Overall, both groups experienced significant improvements in coping with caregiver stress. Additional outcomes varied according to whether the participant received individual versus group treatment. Specifically, caregivers who received individual therapy reported greater improvements in psychological functioning and well-being than those in the group intervention. However, group therapy participants reported expanded social support networks at the completion of treatment.

Zarit, Anthony, and Boutselis (1987) compared individual therapy and group approaches of stress-management training with a wait-list control. All three interventions produced improvements on measures of burden and psychiatric symptomatology. Improvements were maintained for the first year of follow-up. Steffan, Futterman, and Gallagher-Thompson (1998) compared the outcomes between depressed caregivers who participated in either individual or group therapy. The individual therapy participants received either psychodynamic or cognitive-behavioral therapy. Caregivers in the group therapy condition received psychoeducational classes focused on reducing depression through either increasing pleasant events or through learning problem-solving skills. Although there were no differences between groups on Beck Depression Inventory scores (time differences were found), caregivers in group therapy were significantly less likely to meet diagnostic criteria for major depressive disorder than caregivers in individual therapy.

In summary, both group and individual psychoeducational and skills-based interventions with skills-training components appear to be beneficial for family caregivers. Unfortunately, most of the reviewed studies fail to describe adequately treatment implementation and caregiver characteristics. Moreover, the studies failed to consider the differences in individual caregiver goals and needs, factors that are known to moderate treatment effect.

COMPREHENSIVE, MULTICOMPONENT INTERVENTIONS

Given the lack of consensus on the superiority of one intervention over another, comprehensive, multicomponent intervention programs offering a wide range of services have been developed. These interventions combine several focused approaches, such as individual counseling, peer support, home-based support, and family therapy, designed to address a broad range of issues. The studies included in this section will highlight the unique applications to implementing this approach.

Numerous barriers may prevent caregivers from utilizing support services. Changes in technology have expanded the possibilities for providing interventions to a wide range of caregivers. For example, use of psychoeducational videos is an innovative method for increasing access to caregivers who lack transportation or live in rural areas. In a study by Chang (1999), caregivers were randomized to a cognitive-behavioral (CB) intervention or an attention only (AO) placebo. The 8-week CB intervention consisted of videotapes (to be viewed in the home) that taught behavior-management skills and strategies for increasing pleasant events. Caregivers in both groups reported significant increases in caregiver satisfaction and decreases in emotion-focused coping. Several other research groups will likely be evaluating the use of innovative technological strategies for caregivers. For example, two of the REACH interventions (in Miami and Boston) are evaluating technology-based interventions. The results of these studies are eagerly awaited and will undoubtedly provide further direction for the future development of innovative interventions.

Interventions that integrate family communication skills into existing programs have also showed promising results. Ostwald, Hepburn, Caron, Burns, and Mantell

(1999) assigned 94 caregivers to either an immediate or delayed treatment group receiving the same intervention. Training consisted of information about dementia, problem-solving skills, and improving family communication and cooperation. The intervention was successful in reducing caregivers' negative reactions to disruptive behaviors and in reducing caregiver burden over time. Promising results were also obtained by Marriott, Donaldson, Tarrier, and Burns (2000) who conducted a prospective single-blind randomized controlled trial of a cognitive-behavioral family intervention. Caregivers were assigned to either a family-based intervention or a control group. Results showed a significant reduction in distress, depression, and problem behaviors in the intervention group compared with the control groups at posttreatment and at a 3-month follow-up assessment.

Researchers have also investigated the efficacy of interventions that provide treatment for both the care-recipient and caregiver. Quayhagen and Quayhagen (1989) assigned dyads to a family-based cognitive stimulation program. Home-based training sessions focused on communication skills, memory-provoking exercises, and problem-solving techniques. Results showed that care-recipients in the treatment group maintained cognitive and behavioral functioning and improved emotionally over time. Caregivers maintained mental health status and burden over time and enhanced their coping resources.

Another useful multicomponent intervention that is more time-intensive but highly effective is individualized care-planning for caregivers. In a study by Buckwalter et al. (1999), 245 caregivers were randomized to either a psychoeducational nursing intervention group or an attention-control group. Individualized care plans were developed for caregivers in the intervention group that focused on the management of behavior problems. Compared with the attention-control group, the intervention group showed significant improvement at both 6- and 12-month assessments in depression, tension-anxiety, anger-hostility, fatigue-inertia, and confusion-bewilderment.

In sum, although these multicomponent studies generally yield favorable results, it is difficult to evaluate the effectiveness of specific features of each program. Thus, clinicians may need to include all components in order to achieve the best outcomes in practice.

REACH SKILLS-TRAINING INTERVENTION

REACH is a cooperative agreement funded by the National Institutes of Health (NIH) to examine interventions for alleviating the burdens associated with family caregiving (Coon, Schulz, & Ory, 1999). There are six REACH intervention sites, yielding a multisite collaborative effort that utilizes multidisciplinary staff to deliver a variety of interventions culturally tailored to meet the needs of a range of ethnic populations (e.g., African Americans were a key focus at Birmingham,

Hispanics at Palo Alto). The overall goal of the REACH program was to characterize and test the most promising home- and community-based interventions for enhancing family caregiving, particularly with minority families. REACH psychoeducational and skill-based training approaches involved either training the caregiver in care-recipient behavioral-management strategies or teaching the caregiver effective coping strategies. For a more detailed description of the REACH project see Coon et al. (1999). Formal results of the REACH project are not yet available, but will be published in the near future.

The sites and interventions that will be discussed in this chapter are Alabama's skills-training approach used with African Americans and Anglos, and California's psychoeducational approach used with Hispanic and Anglos. Although these interventions were delivered in a research context, it is our experience that they can be generalized to a variety of settings including private practice, senior centers, and community organizations such as the Alzheimer's Association.

THE ALABAMA REACH PROJECT

The intervention of the Alabama REACH project was influenced strongly by Haley's Stress Process Model. Haley, Brown, and Levine's (1987) stress process model focuses on stress as a relationship between the caregiver and the environment. This model includes stressors, appraisal, coping responses, social support, and adaptational outcomes. Haley and colleagues propose that each component of the model be assessed independently for a clear conceptual understanding of the relationship between stressors and caregivers (see Figure 6.1).

Stressors are described consistently as environmental and psychological influences that are problematic for the caregiver. How the caregiver appraises the stressors, copes with the stressors, and uses available resources combine to form the conceptual description of mediators. Variability in caregiver outcomes is believed to be influenced by the differing mediators used by, and available to, each individual caregiver. The physical and psychological well-being of the caregiver and care-recipient are also conceptualized as outcomes. The skills-training intervention of the Alabama REACH project combined treatment components that target stressors (problem behaviors) and mediators (behavior management and problem-solving skills) within a single intervention protocol.

The Alabama REACH project was designed to assist caregivers of Alzheimer's care-recipients by providing resources in the form of education, support and, most important, active skills training. The caregiver/care-recipient dyads were recruited from various medical settings, including the Visiting Nurses Association of the Birmingham Area (VNA), University of Alabama Alzheimer's Disease Center (ADC), and the UAB Geriatric Primary Care Clinic, as well as from numerous community agencies serving the Alzheimer's disease (AD) population.

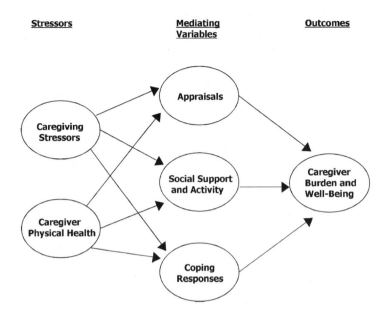

FIGURE 6.1   Stress process model for caregiver intervention.

Caregiver/care-recipient dyads were randomized into one of two conditions: skills-training condition (STC) or minimal support condition (MSC). For the purposes of this chapter, we will be describing only the STC.

Skills-Training Condition

The skills-training intervention combined care-recipient-focused behavior-management skills training and caregiver-focused problem-solving skills training into a single treatment package. Bourgeois and colleagues (2000) examined behavior management and caregiver-focused problem solving in separate groups and found that each offered some benefit with spousal caregivers of persons with dementia.

Behavior management skills training focused on ameliorating problem behaviors exhibited by the person with dementia. Behavior-management techniques are perhaps the most frequently prescribed treatments to address challenging behaviors. The skills-training approach, as conceived in the Alabama REACH intervention, required caregivers to receive both a basic education in behavior management techniques as well as instruction and support in the technical application of specific behavioral and environmental treatments. To emphasize the importance of environmental influences on human behavior, caregivers were taught to identify environmental antecedents and consequences surrounding a specific behavior of interest (i.e., the ABCs of behavior management). Behaviors were defined in objective, concrete terms (e.g., repeating the same question 10 times within 10 minutes). This process provided caregivers with a simple yet effective tool to identify potential causes and reactions to problem behaviors exhibited by care-recipients. The identification of contextual influences on care-recipient behavior led to the creation of specific behavioral-environmental interventions to change the antecedents and consequences.

Antecedent intervention strategies were used to prevent the occurrence of problem behaviors. Although a diverse set of behavioral strategies were taught to caregivers, commonly used strategies included communication skills, prosthetic memory aids, and positive reinforcement. Nonverbal and verbal communication skills assisted the caregivers in communicating accurately and effectively with care-recipients. Recommended communication techniques included physical gestures, compassionate touching, one-step instructions, and statements to communicate gratitude and affection. Prosthetic memory aids such as labels, cue cards, and memory boards were used to facilitate both orientation and memory of factual information (e.g., time of next meal, names of grandchildren). Caregivers were also taught to encourage positive care-recipient behaviors such as independence in activities of daily living and constructive engagement in activities.

Interventions employed after the problem behavior occurred focused on a caregiver's response to a problem behavior exhibited by a care-recipient. Distraction and diversion techniques were frequently prescribed as a way to end a challenging behavior without rationalizing or reasoning with the care-recipient. Factual appraisal of problem behaviors was also encouraged (e.g., repetitive questions are related to memory problems and not intentional behaviors).

The second component of the Alabama REACH intervention provided caregivers with skills training in the use of problem-solving techniques. Caregivers were given specific instruction in the application of problem-solving skills for achieving personal goals, such as increasing caregiver pleasant events and positive health behaviors. The identification and achievement of personal goals often elude caregivers due to the overwhelming duties associated with caring for a loved one with dementia. Careful attention was given to motivating caregivers to use problem-solving skills to address their own personal goals. Caregivers were taught to conceive of strategies to cope with difficult and novel life events, called "problems." A "solution" then was described as a situation-specific response developed to cope with the problem. After completing the process of devising solutions to problems, caregivers were encourage to proceed to solution implementation, which involved actual application of solutions in the context of their caregiving roles.

Behavior management and problem-solving skills training for caregivers enrolled in the STC were conducted via a one-time group workshop followed by 16 individualized treatment contacts. The 3-hour group workshop initiated the skills-training activities for caregivers. Caregivers attended the workshops in groups of three to eight. Workshops were taught jointly by a psychologist and a doctoral-level nurse. The fundamental goal of the workshop was to establish a similar knowledge base in behavior management and problem solving across all caregivers enrolled in the STC. Interactive instructional activities were used to encourage sharing among caregivers and between caregivers and workshop leaders. For example, caregivers and workshop leaders applied each of the six steps of problem solving to the case of an adult-child caregiver with the goal of obtaining respite two evenings per week. The caregiver planned to spend the respite time having meals with her husband and two children. The goal of obtaining respite was not without barriers for the caregiver. The relevant barriers were identified and defined as problems to be addressed with the problem-solving techniques. Each of the following problem-solving steps were discussed: (a) naming the problem, (b) naming all possible solutions, (c) naming and evaluating the pros and cons of each possible solution, (d) selecting and trying one solution, (e) evaluating whether it worked or not, and (f) using this information to solve other problems in the future. Caregivers were encouraged to offer solutions and to assist in the identification of pros and cons related to each of the possible solutions. To supplement the didactic activities, caregivers were also provided with a skill-training notebook and with videotapes that demonstrated critical behavior-management and problem-solving techniques.

At structured intervals after the workshop, caregivers were visited by one of the REACH interventionists, who assisted them in the use of behavior-management skills, formulation of a personal goal, and application of problem solving to barriers associated with goal obtainment. Caregivers received four weekly home visits during the first month of the intervention and two more visits during the second month. During the next 10 months, home visits were alternated monthly with therapeutic phone calls, during both of which behavior management and problem-solving skills were refined. The primary therapeutic method during all contacts following the workshop included the application and generalization of behavior management and problem-solving skills to the creation of written, multistep behavioral programs and goal statements.

Individualized behavioral programs, or "behavioral prescriptions," were written by project staff and provided to caregivers. Behavioral programs targeted a single, objectively defined challenging behavior exhibited by the care-recipient (e.g., repeated questions). Behavioral programs provided the caregiver with concrete suggestions for changing antecedents and consequences thought to be related to the targeted behavior. Interventionists and caregivers worked continuously and jointly to implement, evaluate, and modify behavioral programs until the problem behavior was managed.

Goal statements (e.g., returning to work 1 day per week) summarized a specific personal goal identified by the caregiver and targeted for achievement using problem-solving skills. More specifically, problem-solving techniques were applied to barriers or "problems" associated with goal obtainment. As a result of this process, the interventionist and caregiver identified specific tasks to be completed by the caregiver (e.g., investigate the cost and availability of adult day care) in order to achieve some success in the goal. Goal statements and resulting problem-solving exercises were highly individualized. A large proportion of caregivers used problem-solving skills in order to obtain or organize social support services, allowing the caregiver time to achieve personal goals. When a behavior problem came under control, or if a caregiver-focused goal was completed, new target behaviors and caregiver-focused goals were established.

THE CALIFORNIA REACH PROJECT

The intervention of the California REACH project was based on a cognitive-behavioral approach to treatment. Cognitive-behavioral therapy (CBT) is a well-established treatment modality that employs both cognitive and behavioral techniques in the design of interventions. Although it is beyond the scope of this chapter to describe CBT in detail, it is important to understand the assumptions that are common to all cognitive-behavioral approaches to treatment, whether in individual or group format. (For a more detailed description of one CB approach, see Coon, Rider, Gallagher-Thompson, & Thompson, 1999; Dick, Gallagher-Thompson, Coon, Powers, & Thompson, 1996; Thompson, 1996.)

First, CBT assumes a relationship between thoughts or beliefs, emotions, and behavior (see Figure 6.2). The beliefs individuals have about an event or experience will impact how they feel and behave in that situation. Likewise, the activities and behaviors that one engages in will affect mood and thoughts. Thus, a depressed caregiver may be caught in a downward spiral of negative thoughts that lead to more depressed feelings and disengagement from pleasant and meaningful activities.

A second assumption is that changing behaviors and thoughts will result in changes in mood. By identifying and altering negative or dysfunctional thoughts and by participating in meaningful activities, the depressed caregiver will experience improvement in mood. Therefore, much of the work of CBT is aimed at teaching the skills needed to change the dysfunctional thinking and behaviors that contribute to negative mood. The consequence of teaching these skills is an increase in the individual's sense of self-efficacy, competency, and coping abilities. As caregivers learn to recognize the contribution of their own unhelpful

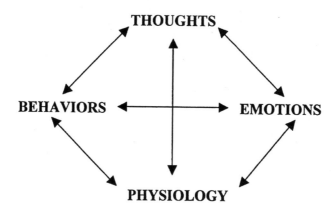

FIGURE 6.2   Cognitive-behavioral model.

thinking patterns on their negative mood, they feel empowered and are able to change negative mood more effectively.

Finally, all CBT approaches utilize a set of common techniques to help clients learn the skills for managing and changing negative mood. These techniques include monitoring of mood and target behavior, monitoring of dysfunctional thoughts, challenging dysfunctional thoughts, developing skills for altering dysfunctional thoughts or problem behavior, and practicing new skills.

The Palo Alto REACH project was designed to investigate the relative effectiveness of three psychologically based approaches for Hispanic and Anglo female caregivers. The caregivers were recruited from the VA Palo Alto Health Care System and local community agencies such as the Alzheimer's Association, community-based senior programs, Alzheimer's day care centers, and health care network programs. Caregivers were randomized into one of three conditions: coping with caregiving (CWC), enhanced support group (ESG), or a minimal support condition (MSC). For the purposes of this chapter, we will be describing only the CWC.

Coping With Caregiving

This class was designed to teach a limited number of mood-management skills to ameliorate the stress of caregiving and alleviate caregiver distress. Two key approaches were actively used to achieve these goals: (a) emphasis on reducing negative affect by learning how to relax in stressful situations, by appraising the care-receivers behavior more realistically, and by communicating assertively;

and (b) emphasis on increasing positive mood and the contingency between mood and activities, developing strategies to do more small, everyday pleasant activities, and learning to set self-change goals and reward oneself for accomplishments along the way.

The intervention consisted of 10 weekly sessions that met in small, interactive classes. The intervention taught caregivers cognitive-behavioral skills to manage their stress. The participants were encouraged to practice these skills both in and outside class to reinforce learning and receive valuable feedback. The term "class" was chosen in lieu of "group therapy" to reduce the stigma associated with seeking services (Gallagher-Thompson & DeVries, 1994). Participants were provided with a manual that contained all the material and work sheets that were reviewed in class. CWC classes for the REACH Hispanic caregivers were offered in English or Spanish by bilingual and bicultural staff. At the completion of the 10 meetings, participants met once a month thereafter for a total of eight booster sessions.

Phases of the Intervention

There were four phases of the CWC (see Table 6.1). In the first phase (classes 1 to 4), the class focused on an overview of dementia, the nature of caregiver stress, and relaxation techniques. Moreover, the relationship between thoughts, behaviors, and emotions were discussed and illustrated (see Figure 6.2). Participants were taught to identify the antecedents, beliefs, and consequences (the ABC model). Homework assignments at this initial phase included a relaxation log, monitoring of mood and behaviors during the week, and daily thought records. This homework task teaches caregivers to record their mood on a daily basis, to record situations or events associated with the mood, and to track changes during the day or week. Caregivers monitored their moods using a daily mood-rating form, which asked participants to rate their moods each day. Caregivers brought these forms to each session and shared them with one another. This helped them become aware of the relationship between mood changes and pleasurable and nonpleasurable activities.

After group members learned how to monitor their moods, they were taught specific CB techniques such as keeping a record of dysfunctional thoughts (class 3 and 4). Caregivers completed a form called the daily record of unhelpful thoughts (DRUT). This form consists of several columns that record the situation (the event that led to unpleasant emotions), the automatic unhelpful thoughts (the negative thoughts that accompanied the event), the feelings, and some possible challenges to the unhelpful thoughts (more helpful alternative thoughts). Participants were assigned DRUT during class and for homework. During class, group members helped one another identify unhelpful thinking patterns and develop challenges to these thought patterns. As caregivers practiced this process through

TABLE 6.1   Coping With Caregiving (CWC) Course Outline and Program

	Goals	Homework
Initial Phase		
Class 1	Overview of dementia, understanding frustration, practicing to relax	Daily relaxation diary
Class 2–4	Identifying unhelpful thoughts about caregiving, changing unhelpful thoughts into adaptive thoughts and linking to behaviors, identifying danger signals and stop signs	Relaxation diary, daily thought record
Second Phase		
Class 5–6	Understanding types of communication and practicing how to be more assertive in caregiving situations and with family members	Practice assertive communication
Third Phase		
Class 6–9	Identifying pleasant events and activities, understanding and overcoming personal barriers to increasing pleasant events.	Daily mood rating, pleasant events tracking form
Class 10	Review of major skills that were taught	
Fourth Phase		
8 boosters	Maintain skill base and fine-tune skills.	Apply skills in everyday situations

frequent repetition, they were able to detect and challenge automatic thoughts before the thoughts contributed to negative emotions.

In the second phase (classes 5 and 6), communication patterns were discussed and caregivers were encouraged to practice being more assertive in caregiving situations and with family members. The various types of communication were reviewed, including passive, aggressive, and assertive communication and the messages each of these patterns conveys to others. The class emphasized the differences between effective and assertive communication approaches. During the class, caregivers role-played with other group members who pretended to be a family member, a friend, or a health care professional with whom they were having difficulty expressing their needs. For homework, group members were instructed to pick a situation where they normally had difficulty and mentally plan how they were going to be assertive (not passive or aggressive), and they were asked to put their plan into action when the opportunity presented itself.

In the third phase (classes 7 to 10), the relationship between mood and participation in pleasant events was presented. Caregivers were taught the importance of engaging in pleasurable activities and how to identify and schedule pleasurable activities in their daily lives. Participants also learned how to overcome personal barriers to increasing pleasant events. For homework, the caregivers developed a list of pleasant events they enjoyed and were later asked to graph their mood along with the number of times they engaged in the pleasant event over the week. The goal of this exercise was to emphasize the relationship between mood changes and participation in pleasurable activities. During the 10th and final session, the skills taught in the class were reviewed and caregivers were asked to list problem areas where they thought they could use their skills in the future.

The final phase (8 booster sessions) focused on helping caregivers maintain the skill they obtained over the course of the intervention. Moreover, given the unpredictable nature of illness, the caregivers had the opportunity to learn how to apply their skills to new stressors that developed.

Tailoring the CWC for Hispanic Caregivers

Extensive pilot work was conducted to develop a treatment manual that was culturally relevant and appropriately translated. The manual was conceptually translated to ensure the inclusion of culturally relevant content and process material while maintaining the integrity of the interventions' theoretical framework. A key component of piloting the manual was consulting with key community leaders who suggested that an educational approach (rather than one labeled as group psychotherapy) would be culturally consistent and viewed as nonstigmatizing to Hispanic caregivers (Árean & Gallagher-Thompson, 1996). Moreover, the manuals were streamlined, the reading level and homework forms were simplified, and more culturally relevant examples were included.

In the process of tailoring *CWC* for the Hispanic caregivers, developers of the class incorporated key values from the Latino culture. For example, we integrated the Latino value of *personalismo* (the importance of proper interpersonal relations and social interactions) through the use of *platicar*, the exchange of pleasantries or "whatever comes to mind" at the beginning of each session. This process served as a bridge to intervention material and facilitated interventionists' becoming viewed as a part of the participants' regular, trusted support system. Similarly, we integrated the value of *familismo* by inviting family members to attend sessions along with the primary caregiver. Family invitations were accepted to a greater degree among Latinas compared to their Caucasian counterparts.

Improving access to services for ethnic minority caregivers is crucial. The growth in the member of Latino elders is expected to be significant in the future, and the demands on the few existing resources by this community will only increase. Providing skill-based interventions in the languages that reflect the diversity of caregivers is greatly needed.

PRACTICAL SUGGESTIONS

The following steps are intended to serve as a guide for clinicians and other health care professionals who are in the process of designing and implementing a skill-based intervention.

1. Begin by surveying the field for materials that will help guide the intervention. Several manuals have been designed and found effective for a variety of target complaints. Some manuals have been translated into other languages for work with an ethnic minority group. Moreover, there are several valuable resources on the Internet. The best place to begin is the Alzheimer's Association Web site *www.alz.org* or call the help line at 1-800-660-1993.

2. Determine whether the intervention will be offered as an individual, group, or comprehensive, multicomponent format.

3. Other factors to consider are the location of the intervention, confidentiality issues, and whether the intervention will be time-limited versus open-ended.

4. Determine the desired outcome of the intervention and identify instruments that will allow you to assess whether the intervention was effective.

5. Typically, insurance companies do not reimburse for psychoeducational groups. Thus, working on a contract basis for a community agency or choosing a modest fee that would permit people to pay out-of-pocket would be the best options.

6. Nontraditional methods of delivery such as video or on-line support may also be an innovative method of improving access to a wider range of caregivers such as those who lack transportation, have mobility problems, or live in rural areas.

In conclusion, numerous skill-based interventions have been designed for caregivers within the community; however, these programs often end when the research protocol is completed. Intervention manuals that can easily be used and translated into practice with diverse groups of caregivers are necessary to meet the needs of future caregivers.

REFERENCES

Anthony-Bergstone, C. R., Zarit, S. H., & Gatz, M. (1988). Symptoms of psychological distress among caregivers of dementia patients. *Psychology and Aging, 3,* 245–248.

Árean, P., & Gallagher-Thompson, D. (1996). Issues and recommendations for the recruitment and retention of older ethnic minority adults into clinical research. *Journal of Consulting and Clinical Psychology, 64,* 875–880.

Beck, A. T., Rush, J., Shaw, B., & Emery, G. (1979). *Cognitive therapy of depression.* New York: Guilford Press.

Bourgeois, M. S. (1992). Evaluating memory wallets in conversations with persons with dementia. *Journal of Speech and Hearing Research, 35,* 1344–1357.

Bourgeois, M., Burgio, L., Schulz, R., Beach, S., & Palmer, B. (1997). Modifying repetitive verbalization of community dwelling patients with AD. *Gerontologist, 37,* 343–349.

Bourgeois, M. S., Schulz, R., & Burgio, L. (1996). Interventions for caregivers of patients with Alzheimer's disease: A review and analysis of content, process, and outcomes. In R. K. Kastenbaum & J. Hendricks (Eds.), *The International Journal of Aging and Human Development.* Amityville, NY: Baywood.

Bourgeois, M. S., Schulz, R., Burgio, L. D., & Beach, S. (2000). Skills training for spouses of patients with Alzheimer's disease: Outcomes of an intervention study. *Journal of Clinical Geropsychology, 8,* 53–73.

Buckwalter, K. C., Gerdner, L., Kohout, F., Hall, G. R., Kelly, A., Richards, B., & Sime, M. (1999). A nursing intervention to decrease depression in family caregivers of persons with dementia. *Archives of Psychiatric Nursing, 13,* 80–88.

Chang, B. L. (1999). Cognitive-behavioral intervention for homebound caregivers of persons with dementia. *Nursing Research, 48,* 173–182.

Cohler, B., Groves, L., Borden, W., & Lazarus, L. (1989). Caring for family members with Alzheimer's disease. In E. Light & B. Lebowitz (Eds.), *Alzheimer's disease treatment and family stress: Directions for research* (pp. 50–105). Washington, DC: National Institute of Mental Health.

Coon, D. W., Rider, K., Gallagher-Thompson, D., & Thompson, L. (1999). Cognitive-behavioral therapy for treatment of late-life distress. In M. Duffy (Ed.), *Handbook of counseling and psychotherapy with older adults* (pp. 487–510). New York: Wiley & Sons.

Coon, D. W., Schulz, R., & Ory, M. (1999). Innovative intervention approaches with Alzheimer's caregivers. In D. Biegel & A. Blum (Eds.), *Innovations in practice service and delivery across the lifespan.* New York: Oxford University Press.

Dick, L., Gallagher-Thompson, D., Coon, D., Powers, D., & Thompson, L. W. (1996). *Cognitive-behavioral therapy for late-life depression: A patient's manual.* Stanford, CA: VA Palo Alto Health Care System and Stanford University.

Gallagher, D., Rose, J., Rivera, P., Lovett, S., & Thompson, L. W. (1989). Prevalence of depression in family caregivers. *Gerontologist, 29,* 449–456.

Gallagher, D., Thompson, L. W., Silven, D., & Priddy, M. (1985). *Problem solving for caregivers: Class leaders' manual.* Palo Alto, CA: VA Palo Alto Health Care System and Stanford University School of Medicine.

Gallagher-Thompson, D., Árean, P., Coon, D., Menendez, A., Takagi, K., Haley, W. E., Argüelles, T., Rupert, M., Loewenstein, D., & Szapocznik, J. (2000). Development and implementation of intervention strategies for culturally diverse caregiving populations. In R. Shulz (Ed.), *Handbook on dementia caregiving populations* (pp. 151–185). New York: Springer.

Gallagher-Thompson, D., & DeVries, H. M. (1994). Coping with frustration classes: Development and preliminary outcomes with women who care for relatives with dementia. *Gerontologist, 34,* 548–552.

Gallagher-Thompson, D., Lovett, S., Rose, J., McKibbin, C., Coon, D., Futterman, A., & Thompson, L. W. (2000). Impact of psychoeducational interventions on distressed family caregivers. *Journal of Clinical Geropsychology, 6,* 91–110.

Gallagher-Thompson, D., Rose, J., Florsheim, M., Jacome, P., DelMaestro, S., Peters, L., Gantz, F., Arguello, D., Johnson, C., Moorehead, R. S., Polich, T. M., Chesney, M., & Thompson, L. W. (1992). *Controlling your frustration: A class for caregivers.* Palo Alto, CA: Veterans Affairs Palo Alto Health Care System.

Gallagher-Thompson, D., & Steffen, A. M. (1994). Comparative effects of cognitive/ behavioral and brief psychodynamic psychotherapies for the treatment of depression in family caregivers. *Journal of Consulting and Clinical Psychology, 62,* 543–549.

Gwyther, L. (1990). Letting go: Separation-individuation in a wife of an Alzheimer's patient. In R. J. Kastenbaum & J. Hendricks (Eds.), *The international journal of aging and human development.* Amityville, NY: Baywood.

Haley, W. E., Brown, S. L., & Levine, E. G. (1987). Experimental evaluation of the effectiveness of group intervention for dementia caregivers. *Gerontologist, 27,* 376–382.

Haley, W. E., Levine, E. G., Brown, S. L., & Bartolucci, A. A. (1987). Stress, appraisal, coping, and social support as predictors of adaptational outcomes among dementia caregivers. *Psychology and Aging, 2,* 323–330.

Kaplan, C. P., & Gallagher-Thompson, D. (1995). The treatment of clinical depression in caregivers of spouses with dementia. *Journal of Cognitive Psychotherapy, 9,* 35–44.

Kennet, J., Burgio, L. D., & Schulz, R. (2000). Interventions for in-home caregivers: A review of research 1990 to present. In R. Schulz et al. (Eds.), *Handbook of dementia caregiving intervention research.* New York: Oxford University Press.

Lewinsohn, P., Muñoz, R., Youngren, M., & Zeiss, A. (1986). *Control your depression.* Englewood Cliffs, NJ: Prentice-Hall.

Lovett, S., & Gallagher, D. (1988). Psychoeducational interventions for family caregivers: Preliminary efficacy data. *Behavior Therapy, 19,* 321–330.

Marriott, A., Donaldson, C., Tarrier, N., & Burns, A. (2000). Effectiveness of cognitive-behavioural family intervention in reducing the burden of care in carers of patients with Alzheimer's disease. *British Journal of Psychiatry, 176,* 557–562.

Ostwald, S. K., Hepburn, K. W., Caron, W., Burns, T., & Mantell, R. (1999). Reducing caregiver burden: A randomized psychoeducational intervention for caregivers of persons with dementia. *Gerontologist, 39,* 299–309.

Pinkston, E. M., & Linsk, N. L. (1984). Behavioral family intervention with the impaired elderly. *Gerontologist, 24,* 576–583.

Pinkston, E. M., Linsk, N. L., & Young, R. N. (1988). Home-based behavioral family treatment of the impaired elderly. *Behavior Therapy, 19,* 331–334.

Quayhagen, M. P., & Quayhagen, M. (1989). Differential effects of family-based strategies on Alzheimer's disease. *Gerontologist, 29,* 150–155.

Schmidt, G. L., Bonjean, M. J., Widem, A. C., & Schefft, B. K. (1988). Brief psychotherapy for caregivers of demented relatives: Comparison of two therapeutic strategies. *Clinical Gerontologist, 7,* 109–125.

Schulz, R., Gallagher-Thompson, D., Haley, W., & Czaja, S. (2000). Understanding the interventions process: A theoretical/conceptual framework for intervention approaches to caregiving. In R. Schulz (Ed.), *Handbook on dementia caregiving* (pp. 33–60). New York: Springer.

Schulz, R., O'Brien, A., Bookwala, J., & Fleissner, K. (1995). Psychiatric and physical morbidity effects of dementia caregiving: Prevalence, correlates and causes. *Gerontologist, 35,* 771–791.

Schulz, R., Visintainer, P., & Williamson, G. M. (1990). Psychiatric and physical morbidity effects of caregiving. *Journals of Gerontology: Psychological Sciences, 45,* 181–191.

Steffen, A. M., Futterman, A., & Gallagher-Thompson, D. (1998). Depressed caregivers: Comparative outcomes of two interventions. *Clinical Gerontologist, 19,* 3–15.

Thompson, L. W. (1996). Cognitive-behavioral therapy and treatment for late-life depression. *Journal of Clinical Psychology, 57*(Suppl. 5), 29–37.

Thompson, L. W., Gallagher, D., & Lovett, S. (1992). *Increasing life satisfaction class leaders' and participant manuals.* Palo Alto, CA: VA Palo Alto Health Care System and Stanford University School of Medicine.

Toseland, R. W., Rossiter, C. M., Peak, T., & Smith, G. C. (1990). Comparative effectiveness of individual and group interventions to support family caregivers. *Social Work, 35,* 209–217.

Zarit, S., Anthony, C., & Boutselis, M. (1987). Interventions with caregivers of dementia patients: Comparison of two approaches. *Psychology and Aging, 2,* 225–232.

7

In-Home Interventions: Helping Caregivers Where They Live

Laura N. Gitlin and Lisa P. Gwyther

Most persons with dementia or other debilitating conditions are cared for at home by one or more family members (Haley & Bailey, 1999). Family caregivers frequently become the hidden patients who experience dramatic negative consequences. These consequences have been documented to include emotional distress, depression, poor health, fatigue, financial burdens, and higher rates of mortality compared to noncaregivers (Ory, Yee, Tennstedt, & Schulz, 2000; Schulz & Beach, 1999; Schulz, O'Brien, Bookwala, & Fleissner, 1995). Accordingly, family caregivers experience a wide range of service needs that change and evolve over time as caregiving responsibilities increase. The home, as the natural life space and context of caregiving, is an ideal setting in which to provide services to families that are designed to support their efforts to enable older adults to age in place. Nonetheless, although services delivered in the home have become a routine component of long-term care for older patients, families rarely receive formal services in that setting that address their specific requirements.

Why offer services to families in their homes? National health care trends suggest that homes and communities increasingly will serve as the primary setting for delivering a vast array of health and human services to patients and their family caregivers (Spitzer, 1998). For this reason, it is important to understand the benefits and unique challenges of providing in-home help to family members and the delivery characteristics of these types of services. At present, there is no empirical evidence to suggest that providing an intervention to families in their own homes is more effective or beneficial than providing the same program in a formal care setting (Wallace et al., 1998). That is, we do not know if the home setting affords greater benefit than a formal care setting to persons receiving an intervention. Yet research does show that home visits by health professionals yield more knowledge of care difficulties and result in greater compliance to care recommendations and that patients improve more quickly in their own homes (Ramsdell, Swart, Jackson, & Renvall, 1989). Adult learning theory also supports the practice of providing services to families in their own homes; it suggests that adults learn most effectively when new skills are taught in the context in which they are actually used. Moreover, adult learners may benefit from repeated opportunities to practice new skills in real-life situations.

The purpose of this chapter is to describe the basic characteristics and common challenges of in-home interventions for families. Two different interventions are described, each targeting families of persons with dementia, to provide an in-depth examination of the service delivery characteristics and challenges of in-home care. One intervention involves family caregiver education in the context of service provision. The other involves skill training in the use of home environmental modifications. Most in-home interventions for families have not been described in sufficient detail to enable replication. The next step in providing home services to family caregivers is not only to demonstrate efficacy, but also to specify clearly the components of treatment and best practices. The two interventions described in this chapter illustrate the commonalties and differences in the types of services that can be provided at home, the way in which each intervention overcomes common challenges, and the specific strategies that can be offered to support family caregivers of persons with dementia. These interventions also highlight the roles of different health and human service professionals (social workers, occupational therapists, and physical therapists) and their unique contributions in assisting families at home.

CHARACTERISTICS OF HOME-BASED INTERVENTIONS FOR FAMILIES

A range of services may be provided to family caregivers in their homes. These services may include psychoeducational counseling, home environmental modification, skills training, education, care management, telephone support, friendly visitor services, chore services, back injury prevention, respite, family therapy, and other services. Each of these interventions differs in its objectives and the specific caregiver concern or psychological, physical, or social need that is targeted. For example, a psychotherapeutic or counseling intervention primarily targets the affective well-being of caregivers and an educational intervention primarily seeks to expand the understanding or knowledge base of caregivers, whereas a skill-training intervention primarily focuses on modifying behavioral actions and improving management skills of caregivers. Home interventions also differ in their basic service delivery characteristics. For example, home interventions may vary in the level of intensity (frequency and duration), method of contact (group or one on one), method of delivery (e.g., video, educational materials, role-play, demonstration), and level and type of expertise required to deliver the service (level of professional training).

Although interventions delivered in the home may differ along these dimensions, they do share an important characteristic. For the most part, a home-based approach tends to be tailored to address specific concerns and individualized needs of families. This is in contrast to prescriptive interventions that are based on the premise that a standard approach or set of strategies meets the needs of those who are served. Because the progression of dementia and physical frailty as well as the resources and needs of families vary considerably, customization is an important feature of in-home interventions. It is feasible to customize services in the home, because providers are able to obtain an in-depth understanding of daily care issues and the real-life context in which families are caregiving. Families may be more receptive to recommendations from service providers that directly correspond or relate to their particular values, beliefs, lifestyle, and personal caregiving needs.

Another shared characteristic of in-home interventions is the use of validation as a supportive, therapeutic technique. Validation involves providing feedback to families about the value of their efforts, confirming that their approach is effective and appropriate, and labeling the techniques that are used. Observing a family member caregiving or listening to how a caregiver describes their efforts enables a formal provider to supply meaningful feedback and confirmation. In striving to provide the best care possible, families often seek validation that their decisions and actions are effective and appropriate. Verbal confirmation by a formal provider that the care being provided is effective, safe, and appropriate can enhance a family member's personal sense of mastery and confidence in being a caregiver and may reduce the level of upset experienced.

BENEFITS OF PROVIDING SERVICES
IN THE HOME TO FAMILY CAREGIVERS

Providing services in homes affords multiple benefits to both caregivers and health professionals (Toth-Cohen et al., 2001). Chief among the benefits to family caregivers is the convenience of meeting with health professionals at mutually determined dates and times without having to arrange for the safety and well-being of an elder who is frail. This saves a caregiver time and mental and physical energy. This is particularly important for families caring for persons at the moderate to severe stages of dementia when constant supervision of the person who is impaired is often required. Another benefit for some caregivers is that they often have more control over the encounter with health professionals, who become invited guests. Typically, interactions in the home are guided by caregivers who may find it easier in that setting to express their personal concerns and obtain the level and type of services and information they wish to receive or are ready to handle.

For the provider, the benefits of providing services in the home include the opportunity to gain a more in-depth perspective of the multiple issues that caregivers confront and the unique situations of households. This enables service providers to derive recommendations that are tailored or customized to the specific concerns and contexts of care provision. Another important benefit for service providers is the opportunity to observe directly both the caregiver and family member who is impaired in the natural context in which caregiving, personal care tasks, and interactions occur.

COMMON CHALLENGES

Providing services in the home presents challenges that are distinct to that setting. Formal care settings enforce regimented and predictable procedures, timelines, interactions, and routines that structure or guide the delivery of supportive services to family caregivers. In these settings, the families are "clients" or "patients" who must follow the procedural rules and behaviors that such contexts impose. Homes, in contrast, represent unpredictable, unique, and variable contexts. Unexpected events such as the presence or participation of other family members, household emergencies, telephone calls, or visitors are common occurrences that may impact the intervention process adversely or positively and may not be foreseen or controlled by service providers. As a "guest" in the home, a provider must follow the lead of the family member who directs the interactions, including such practicalities as to where to sit, how long to stay, what topics to address, or what areas of the home are available for observation. Nevertheless, the provider is still confronted with the challenges that occur in the office, such as establishing a positive relationship or rapport, systematically identifying the specific concerns of the family caregiver, and minimizing the demand characteristics of the intervention.

Building Rapport

Although building rapport is an important part of patient-provider interactions in any care setting, it becomes particularly critical in home care. The family member as primary caretaker has intimate knowledge of the care situation, including which techniques may work and those that do not. Also, families develop their own style of care based on the meaning of caregiving and their personal beliefs about what constitutes appropriate care of a person who is impaired. A family caregiver's meanings, beliefs, and approaches to care may differ from those of the service. For example, a service provider may emphasize the safety of a patient and base recommendations on an underlying concern of risk. The goal of a caregiver, however, may be to preserve the biographical integrity of the care receiver and to take risks that achieve that goal. For an intervention to be useful and acceptable to a family, a provider must be able to recognize value differences, respect the family's perspective, and develop strategies that match their world view.

Empathetic and active listening, probing, and using the language of the caregiver (e.g., avoiding medical terminology) are basic techniques that help build rapport and demonstrate respect for the family. Conversely, prescriptive, judgmental tones and providing too much information may overwhelm the caregiver and threaten the delicate relationship between family and provider.

Identifying Caregiver Needs

There are no published, standardized assessments that can be used uniformly by service providers to elicit caregiver needs systematically. Also, more than one session may be necessary to obtain the family's perspective and most intimate concerns. Establishing rapport through demonstration of mutual respect and trust facilitates uncovering the real concerns of families. It is also important to record systematically the perspective of the provider and to examine areas of agreement and discordance with the family's self-identified needs.

One approach is to begin the assessment process by asking open-ended questions that allow caregivers to tell their own stories. As in the tradition of enthnography, this meaning-oriented form of interviewing elicits information through open-ended probes like the following: "Tell me about a typical day." "What is a good day or bad day like?" "How is it now compared to before?" "What do you think works and does not work?" This interviewing approach provides caregivers with a forum in which to describe their experiences and emphasize the aspects of caregiving that are going well and those areas for which they seek help. From this discussion, the provider may be able to identify the immediate problem or one that the caregiver perceives as most pressing to begin the intervention process. As the intervention unfolds, assessment of other caregiver needs and concerns often emerge.

Demand Characteristics of Home Interventions

Despite the convenience of in-home interventions, such programs may be demanding because they require active involvement and behavioral change on the part of the caregiver. For example, it entails mental energy and a behavioral commitment for interventions involving introspection of family psychodynamics or learning new communication techniques and other skills to manage task performance. This can be overwhelming for some families, particularly caregivers who are clinically depressed or easily overwhelmed (Gitlin, Corcoran, Winter, Boyce, & Marcus, 1999). Consequently, it is important for a service provider to recognize the level of behavioral demand that an intervention may place on a caregiver and to develop strategies to minimize this potential burden. In this case, one approach for the overwhelmed caregiver may be to proceed slowly and offer only one new strategy at a session to ensure that it can be effectively utilized and incorporated into daily routines. Another approach is to increase progressively the level and depth of information and skills that are provided, based on the stage of caregiving and expressed need of the family member.

HOME ENVIRONMENTAL SKILL-BUILDING PROGRAM

One promising intervention for families caring for persons with dementia, particularly individuals at the moderate stage, is an environmental approach (Corcoran & Gitlin, 2001; Gitlin, Corcoran, Winter, Boyce, & Hauck, 2001). This approach provides caregivers with knowledge about the disease process and problem-solving skills by which to identify and modify aspects of the physical and social environment that may contribute to troublesome behaviors or serve as barriers to providing care effectively. It is a multicomponent, tailored intervention that is delivered by an occupational therapist. Dr. Gitlin and Dr. Corcoran have developed this approach into a systematic program called the Environmental Skill-building Program (ESP). ESP is currently being tested using a randomized controlled study with 255 families as part of a National Institutes of Health multisite cooperative research program called REACH (Resources for Enhancing Alzheimer's Caregiver Health). Described here is the supportive evidence for an environmental approach and the basic characteristics of ESP, including its underlying theoretical base, approach to assessment, and the range of strategies offered to family caregivers.

Support for a Home Environmental Intervention

The use of environmental strategies is being offered increasingly by health- and human-service providers to enhance safety and reduce behavioral and functional difficulties associated with dementia (Corcoran & Gitlin, 1992). In clinical practice, environmental recommendations for home safety have become routine in hospital and home care (Alzheimer's Association, 1997). Nevertheless, only a few studies have systematically evaluated this approach, and more research is required to substantiate its apparent multiple benefits. Early exploratory studies showed that family caregivers accept and utilize environmental strategies and perceive them as helpful in addressing specific dementia-related behaviors. These studies, however, used single-case and panel designs, and the outcomes were limited to utilization rates of environmental strategies and self-reported benefits. In a pilot study of 12 family caregivers, Pynoos and Ohta (1991) found that 66% of recommended environmental strategies were reported by caregivers as initially effective in managing specific problems, and of those, 89% remained in use at study follow-up. Consistent with this study, Gitlin and Corcoran (1993) found that among 17 spouse caregivers, 92% of environmental strategies offered by occupational therapists to improve bathing routines were subsequently implemented by caregivers and were reported helpful in reducing resistance to bathing. For managing incontinence, caregivers used 53% of the recommendations that were offered. More recently Corcoran and Gitlin (2001) found that in a study of 100 caregivers participating in an in-home intervention, 81% of strategies recommended by an occupational therapist were subsequently used independently in the home.

These studies suggest that caregivers are selective in which environmental strategies to use, but those that are acceptable tend to be implemented and incorporated into the daily routines of caregivers. Other studies have also shown that caregivers, independent of a formal service provider and through trial and error, adjust the physical home environment in response to safety concerns, wandering, or a decline in self-care (Olsen, Ehrenkrantz, & Hutchings, 1993). A more recent study using a randomized control-group design, showed that a 3-month occupational therapy home-environmental intervention had a modest positive effect for both caregivers and care recipients (Gitlin et al., 2001). In that study of 202 caregivers of patients with dementia, intervention caregivers reported fewer declines in patients' instrumental activities of daily living and showed a trend toward less decline in self-care and fewer behavior problems in patients at 3-months posttest, when compared to controls. Also, intervention spouses reported reduced upset; women reported enhanced self-efficacy in managing behaviors; and women and African Americans reported enhanced self-efficacy in managing functional dependency.

Theoretical Framework

The rationale for using the environment of the home as a therapeutic modality is based in several related theories and conceptual frameworks, including a competence-environmental press framework and recent advances in control theory. A competence-environmental press framework suggests that as competency

declines, an unchanging physical and social environment poses significant demands—or press—on an individual that may result in negative behavioral and
functional outcomes (Lawton & Nahemow, 1973). Applied to the context of
dementia, the framework suggests that as the disease progresses, a person may
have increasing difficulty navigating the physical and social components of the
home environment. The person may ignore or misinterpret cues and environmental
information that would otherwise support adaptive behavior. Troublesome behaviors that are typically associated with dementia, such as agitation, resistance to
assistance with daily care, wandering or incontinence, may be attenuated by the
demands of the physical and social environment of the home. Thus, adjusting
and simplifying dimensions of the environment to match reduced competency may
minimize excess disability or dysfunctional behaviors. For example, removing
unnecessary objects from a room minimizes the demands of that environment
such that orientation may be enhanced and confusion and agitation reduced.

To understand the multiple dimensions of the home environment, a model
offered by Barris, Kielhofner, Levine, and Neville (1985) and extended by Corcoran and Gitlin (1991) is useful, particularly in dementia care. In this model, the
environment is conceptualized as four hierarchically arranged and interacting
layers: *objects* (physical tools or items in the home); *tasks* that compose daily
life routines (such as dressing, bathing, and toileting); *social groups and their
organizations* (household composition and other social resources); and *culture*
(values and beliefs that shape the provision of care in the home). Each layer may
be modified to balance the demands of the environment with the individual's level
of competency or abilities. In the ESP described here, strategies are introduced that
target three layers of the environment: objects, tasks, and social groups. At
the object layer, recommendations may include assistive devices for bathing or
toileting, reducing clutter, or posting reminders and brief instructional lists. At
the task layer, recommendations may include simplifying activities, using tactile
or verbal cueing, or learning effective communication techniques. Social group
modifications consist of strategies for expanding or supporting the network of
paid and unpaid helpers, such as helping the caregiver obtain respite breaks or
effectively coordinate an array of helpers.

The fourth layer of the environmental model, *culture,* is not directly manipulated or targeted for change in the intervention. Rather, culture informs the process
of delivering this intervention and developing environmental strategies that fit
the household context. Applied to the context of caregiving, research shows that
caregivers develop their own preferred ways of carrying out routines that reflect
values and beliefs about what is appropriate or best for their family member
(Corcoran, 1992; Hasselkus, 1988). This framework suggests that environmental
strategies must fit the culture of the home, that is, the rules, values, and beliefs
that guide caregiving. The cultural layer of the environment informs the service

provider about ways of working effectively with a caregiver and tailoring strategies to fit the perspective of the family.

The theory of personal control is another important perspective underlying ESP that provides a rationale for why an environmental approach may benefit caregivers. According to recent advances in personal control theory, maintaining control is a universal imperative that is achieved by using primary mechanisms such as changing the immediate environment (e.g., people, objects), secondary mechanisms such as changing cognition or emotions, or a combination thereof (Schulz & Heckhausen, 1999). The unsuccessful application of these mechanisms to achieve control may result in negative affective consequences such as emotional upset and lowered self-efficacy. Applied to the caregiving context, family members may be motivated to use an environmental strategy—a primary mechanism—as a part of their repertoire of coping strategies to achieve personal control over overwhelming and unpredictable situations. Maintaining personal control may in turn reduce upset and enhance self-efficacy beliefs among caregivers.

Goals and Activities of ESP

The overall goal of the Environmental Skill-Building Program is to enable family caregivers to build skills for effective utilization of the physical and social environment in order to manage daily problems associated with dementia care. Specifically, ESP strives to enhance knowledge about caregiver-identified problems and the role of the environment, enable caregivers to problem solve and develop an effective approach to manage these problems, enable caregivers to implement specific strategies, and then generalize these approaches and strategies to emerging problem areas over time. Figure 7.1 illustrates the multiple components and associated activities of ESP. ESP is standardized in that each caregiver receives all of these components. However, each component is tailored to the particular difficulties identified as part of the initial and ongoing assessment of a caregiver's concerns. The intervention targets 12 potential problem areas: caregiver-centered concerns (e.g., fatigue, feelings of guilt, concern for the future, body aches and pains), assisting the patient in bathing, assisting in dressing, meal preparation, home safety, mobility, communication, engagement in leisure, the patient's wandering, toileting, incontinence, or other. Education about dementia may involve helping caregivers understand that manifest behaviors are related to the disease process rather than a reflection of purposeful negative or hostile behaviors. Skill-building involves helping caregivers name and frame problem areas, identify actions that are effective and those that are not effective, and recognize factors in the physical and social environment that may contribute to the problem area. A range of modifications may be introduced, including but

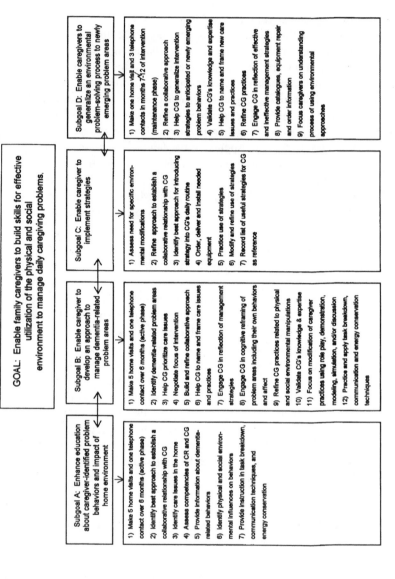

FIGURE 7.1 Task analysis of the Philadelphia Home Environmental Skill-Building Program.

not limited to installing grab bars and a tub bench and then instructing caregivers in their use to promote safe transfer while bathing the patient; placing the patient's clothing in the order in which they are worn to facilitate initiation and sequence in dressing; developing daily routines that provide rest breaks for both caregiver and care recipient. Other modifications include teaching energy conservation and breaking down tasks into components. Modifications are designed to simplify task performance by minimizing differences between personal capabilities and environmental demands.

Another component of ESP is the involvement of a physical therapist to address specific caregiver concerns such as fear of the care recipient falling, difficulties helping care recipient transfer or recover from a fall, or personal body aches and pains from the strain of caregiving. The occupational therapist evaluates the need for a visit by a physical therapist in the first two home visits using five criteria:

1. if the caregiver has experienced back pain within the past 3 months while physically helping or transferring the care recipient
2. if the caregiver is concerned about hurting his or her back while physically helping or transferring the care recipient
3. if the caregiver is concerned that one or both of the family members will be hurt while physically helping or transferring the care recipient
4. if the caregiver or care recipient has musculoskeletal problems or balance problems that represent a risk to either while physically helping or transferring the care recipient
5. if any other health risks exist that indicate a need for physical therapy services.

Caregivers who fit one or more of these criteria receive a visit from a physical therapist. The physical therapist (PT) instructs caregivers in fall-recovery techniques, proper body mechanics, and balance and strength exercises. Most important, the PT helps the caregiver practice new techniques to integrate into daily routines (Cornman-Levy, Gitlin, Corcoran, & Schinfeld, 2001).

Yet another component of ESP is ongoing consultation with a social worker. There are numerous issues for which the occupational therapist may require additional information and knowledge such as community resources, financial considerations, or formal respite opportunities.

Delivery Characteristics

ESP primarily involves direct one-on-one contact with the primary caregiver at home. The care recipient is included in sessions when feasible and acceptable to the caregiver and when appropriate for the target problem area that is addressed. The occupational therapist uses a variety of mechanisms to provide education and skill building such as written materials, role-play, and demonstration. Role-play is particularly important because it enables the caregiver to practice the use of a new technique, such as verbal cueing with the interventionist, and obtain immediate feedback.

As noted earlier, ESP is a 12-month intervention with two phases: active and maintenance. The active phase occurs over 6 months and involves five home visits and one telephone contact. Rapport building and assessment of caregiver needs are ongoing but are the particular focus of the first two visits. Discussion, direct observation, or simulation of a caregiver's approach follows identification of specific problems experienced by the caregivers. The interventionist introduces specific strategies and education as early as the first visit if appropriate. Also, equipment is ordered and installed in this phase. It is particularly helpful to develop a contractual relationship with an agency that has the capability to coordinate the purchase, installation, and quality control of equipment orders. This is an important aspect of the intervention because there are few resources from which caregivers can independently obtain needed equipment such as handrails, grab bars, locks, and raised toilet seats.

The maintenance phase occurs over the next 6 months and involves one home visit and three telephone contacts. During each contact, the interventionist reviews techniques and skills and explores ways of using these learned skills to manage newly emerging problem areas. Though validation is a critical technique used in each intervention contact, it is particularly salient in the maintenance phase to empower caregivers and help them generalize from one situation to the next.

The number, length and type of contact (home visit or telephone) are fixed features of the ESP protocol, although the caregiver and interventionist can determine the spacing of visits. Also, the ESP protocol requires customization such that interventionists in collaboration with caregivers determine the specific focus or problem areas of the intervention. Family caregivers can modify the intervention and choose which strategies to accept and use. However, the 12 intervention domains are fixed. That is, the intervention targets up to 12 specific areas of concern as described earlier. Therefore, areas of difficulty such as clinical depression or marital discord are not addressed in the ESP, and caregivers who need such help are referred to an appropriate agency.

Characteristics of Interventionists

Providing ESP requires the expertise of a skilled occupational therapist and physical therapist. This intervention builds on the knowledge base and traditional practices of OT and PT and requires about 25 hours of training in the ESP protocol. Specifically, therapists with experience in home care and working with older people provide the necessary depth from which to learn the ESP protocol. Of particular importance is expertise in evaluating person-environment transactions, developing innovative strategies that modify this dynamic relationship, and being capable of forming a partnership or working collaboratively with a caregiver.

Challenges of the ESP

There are a number of challenges specific to implementing this type of intervention. Chief among them is the need for sensitivity in rearranging objects in people's homes. It is important for interventionists to understand the symbolic value of object placement and environmental setup to families (Gitlin, 2000). Also, rearranging or minimizing objects in the environment to enhance orientation and awareness may be beneficial for the person with dementia, but it may detract from the comfort, novelty, and utility of rooms in the home for other family members. Therefore, obtaining the right balance between the environmental needs of all household members may be challenging for interventionists. Furthermore, some modifications to the environment are perceived as stigmatizing. For example, installing grab bars or a stair glide may be objectionable to some families. Again, obtaining the right balance between the safety needs of family members and personal values, and tailoring strategies to fit the culture of the household, present as a clinical challenge.

ESP is a client-centered intervention in that the problem areas targeted reflect the primary concerns of caregivers. This can be challenging for an interventionist who may identify needs and issues other than those raised by the caregiver. Interventionists must learn how to raise their concerns and professional perspective while maintaining the primary focus of intervention on the caregiver's self-identified needs. An important aspect of ESP is providing an opportunity for interventionists to express their concerns and perspectives with other interventionists and health professionals. This is accomplished by holding monthly debriefing meetings in which interventionists formally present case material and obtain feedback from peers. This debriefing mechanism facilitates clinical reasoning and enables interventionists to move away from a procedural, prescriptive approach to serving families.

Assessment Forms

Each aspect of the ESP intervention is documented using forms developed by the investigators and tailored to the particularities of this approach. Each assessment form serves a different purpose: to assess the delivery components of the intervention (frequency, duration), to identify caregiver areas of difficulty and the relative importance of their modification, or to record strategies introduced in the intervention and their acceptance and subsequent use or nonuse by caregivers. These forms facilitate clinical reflection as well as enable the investigative team to formally evaluate treatment fidelity and empirically analyze the intervention process. Forms used with the ESP protocol can be obtained by contacting the author (LNG).

THE INDIVIDUALIZED FAMILY EDUCATION INTERVENTION

Another promising approach is the individualized family education intervention. IFEI is based on research conducted at the Duke University Center for the Study of Aging on interventions to overcome identified barriers to service use among family caregivers of persons with dementia (Gwyther, Ballard, & Hinman-Smith, 1990). The findings from early studies of support group strategies, in-home respite care, and individualized care management were integrated within a theoretical framework that explains service use in the context of markers in caregiving careers (Montgomery, Marquis, & Klaus, 2000).

Background of the Intervention

Seven themes emerged from the early Duke studies of Alzheimer's family caregiver interventions. The first is the notion that diversity in caregiver roles and tasks is not random. There are consistent patterns to the type, intensity, and duration of care tasks performed related to the sex, generation, socioeconomic status, and ethnicity or culture of the caregiver. Caregiving is a dynamic process that unfolds over time and it can be likened to a career of variable length. Although there is great individual variation in the trajectory of caregiving careers, there is some uniformity based on whether or not the caregiver is a spouse or an adult child.

A second theme from early Duke studies of Alzheimer's care suggests reluctance, delay, and inappropriate use or even nonuse of formal and informal support services relative to "identified need" (Gwyther, 1994).

Different patterns of service emerge as a third theme. Because they may assess needs differently, spouses tend to use different services and to a different degree than do adult children.

Variation based on socioeconomic and ethnic differences is another theme. In the Duke in-home respite study, respite users were more likely to be African American with lower levels of income and education than Alzheimer's family caregivers who did not use respite services but did participate in Alzheimer's

Association support groups. There was a preference among respite users for teaching and information provided in the context of provision of a service from trusted respite workers. Group educational approaches about the value and availability of in-home respite reached too few families in need, too late and with too little personally relevant information. New respite service users often received only 6 hours of in-home respite a week, despite an average preference for 15 hours per week. Moreover, 25% of respite users received in-home respite service for only 1 month, of a potential subsidized service window of 2 years before placement or death of the person with Alzheimer's.

The fifth theme to emerge from all the Duke studies of Alzheimer's family caregiver interventions is that targeting, timing of interventions, and the lag time over which impact is observed is critical (George & Gold, 1990). Duke's in-home respite study documented the advantages of targeting timely information through trusted sources using individualized modes of communication. Its study of individualized care management found that families were not receptive to information about respite options until they became aware that the care recipient could not be left alone. Although it is assumed that family caregiver education is often delivered too late, it is equally likely that specific family caregiver education about respite may be more effective if delayed until later in the caregiving career.

The sixth theme relates to the fifth. Research findings suggest that dosage and intensity of intervention, even educational intervention, is critical. Too much information at one time or at the wrong time may have a negative impact. More information is not always better in helping family caregivers make care decisions. Information and recommendations need to be timed and dosed so as not to overwhelm family caregivers. Furthermore, caregivers are more satisfied with individually tailored recommendations. The Duke study of individualized care management found that greater numbers of recommendations for changes in care reduce overall compliance with professional recommendations (George & Gold, 1990).

The final theme to emerge from the university's first studies of Alzheimer's family care in the community, which found that knowledge of service availability, need for help, and even the availability of a service were not sufficient to ensure appropriate and timely use of services. Some families seemed to cope adequately just by being reassured of service availability. These studies also documented that specific aspects of the information and how it is delivered are important determinants of service use (Gwyther & Ballard, 1988).

Families seeking information are different from those seeking services. Service seekers are disproportionately at risk in terms of income, social support, education, minority status, and isolation and also tend to be caring for persons later in the course of the illness. Families who seek information only are more likely to be caring for persons with mild to moderate Alzheimer's disease.

A Pilot Study of IFEI

A pilot study at Duke's Bryan Alzheimer's Disease Research Center Clinic tested the feasibility and acceptability of IFEI. The intervention was based on a list of common questions that families had asked Duke social workers over the course of caring for family members with a progressive dementia. At the first clinic visit, family members were asked to check which of 16 such questions were of immediate interest to him or her *at the present time*. A social worker then packaged customized information from Duke Family Support Program files based on the question, the presumed reading level, and a brief assessment of the family care context. The social worker mailed the information to the family caregiver within 5 days of the patient's first clinic visit.

Two weeks after the package of customized responses to the self-identified questions was mailed, the social worker telephoned the family caregiver to confirm receipt. Immediately checking with the family in this manner provided an opportunity to ask about the relevance and adequacy of the materials relative to family caregiver expectations. The telephone call also provided an opportunity to remind the family caregiver that his or her questions would change over the course of the illness.

Findings from this pilot study provided support for the hypothesis that identifying common questions in advance of self-identified need could be helpful for families. Simply suggesting such questions in a routine way normalizes and universalizes family caregiver experience while triggering family members to think ahead about issues that they may not consider spontaneously.

Prompt and convenient delivery of specific educational information in response to a caregiver's self-selected "need-to-know-more" questions encouraged families to call back as needs changed. Having a good experience with provision of targeted customized information builds trust over time and encourages appropriate use of professional guidance. The low cost of this educational strategy, primarily by telephone and mail, suggested its potential generalizability beyond a clinical context.

It was hypothesized that this intervention would be especially appropriate for traditionally underserved and isolated, low-income rural family caregivers. These "hard to sell" families were successfully reached under the auspices of federal and state Alzheimer's demonstration programs. An advantage of the IFEI for demonstration sites was that nonspecialist service providers or paraprofessionals could provide it once the question list and a range of materials addressing each question were provided by Alzheimer's center education specialists.

The earlier experience of Duke social workers' training rural service providers confirmed the value of offering initial training for more than one person from each rural site. Ongoing technical assistance can then be available to these local providers as they provide education or support to local families.

The Individualized Family Education Intervention and its relationship to markers in caregiving careers was then systematically studied, with Alzheimer's Association funding, in the more real-world context of the federal and state Alzheimer's Demonstration programs in Michigan, Maine, Oregon, and South Carolina.

The goal of the four-state study was to assess the impact of a low-cost, individualized educational intervention on a culturally and geographically diverse group of family caregivers of persons with dementia. Objectives included assessing the impact of dosage and intensity of educational materials and an innovative delivery system on caregiver's utilization of support services and ultimately on caregiver outcomes of burden, distress and duration of family care. The families in this four-state intervention were at a point in their caregiving careers at which they were seeking in-home evaluation, respite or care management.

Delivery Model

The IFEI is a technical assistance model, not one of train-the-trainer. Duke social workers provide the materials and backup technical assistance to geographically dispersed service providers. The local service providers in turn provide customized support and education for their regular clients in the context of service provision. This intervention model is, in essence, an enrichment service with potential for broad dissemination.

The IFEI is sufficiently flexible to be used in a variety of settings and by all levels of providers. Furthermore, the question-based approach to caregiver education addresses issues of caregiver diversity as well as consistent patterns of change in caregiving over time. The IFEI highlights the importance of timing and dosing information to assist caregiver coping. Finally, this strategy acknowledges the necessity of delivering services in a culturally appropriate and nonthreatening manner. The flexibility to adapt the educational materials for each question enhances its viability for a broad range of caregiver contexts.

Intervention Context

The IFEI was tested in 4 of 14 federal and state Alzheimer's demonstration programs. The Alzheimer's demonstration programs were uniquely successful in targeting and reaching rural and underserved low-income and minority populations who had not responded to traditional Alzheimer's Association support group and educational programs. Program administrators and service providers from Michigan, Oregon, South Carolina, and Maine met with Duke staff to refine the list of common questions, offer suggestions for materials appropriate to their population, and review the goals and methods of IFEI.

Case managers received a package of educational materials that addressed 13 questions. In addition, each case manager received a form to record specific recommendations for each family caregiver. The form had room for three categories of recommendations: formal or paid services, informal or unpaid help from family or volunteers, and personal coping strategies. The local service providers were encouraged to be specific with written recommendations. For example, if a day respite program was recommended, the form had room to include the cost, sources of help with payment, hours, available transportation, and contact person, including the best times to reach the contact. Case managers were also encouraged to reinforce service or coping strategies that were obviously effective and to limit new suggestions at each 4-month recommendation interval.

The IFEI begins with a request for service or information from a demonstration site. After initial intake information and linkage to the requested service, family caregivers are given or mailed the list of questions with directions to check the ones that are immediately relevant to his or her current situation. When the caregiver completes the question form, the local service provider uses the intake information to assess the reading level and appropriateness of materials available within the question packages the family selected. The local provider determines how much of the information within each question will be given or mailed to the family caregiver. If the question is about local service options, local information is sent or delivered in the context of a home visit. At the same time, the service plan or recommendation sheet is filled out and one copy is left with or mailed to the family. A telephone call 5 days after delivery of the question responses and service plan confirms receipt and reminds families that the personal relevance of various questions changes over the course of the illness. At this later telephone check-in with the family caregiver, the care manager asks open-ended questions to determine if the information in response to the questions was adequate, understandable, and enough. The care manager asks specifically about information the family caregiver may have expected that is missing. The care manager then calls the family again at 4-month intervals to see if recommendations were implemented, the nature of barriers to use of the recommendations, and if the educational materials were helpful. The care manager may revise the recommendations at these 4-month intervals and ideally reminds the family caregiver to call whenever questions change or additional suggestions are needed. If the recommendations are revised, the revised sheet is prepared and delivered to the family in person or by mail. This is, in essence, a family consultation service model.

Key Elements of IFEI

The IFEI is similar to Web-based FAQs (frequently asked questions) models. This customized or individualized education strategy is not the same as a psychoeducational intervention. Trusted local service providers offer culturally competent information for specific family caregivers from a range of materials packaged by Alzheimer's education specialists. Local service staff are backed up by toll-free telephone access to technical assistance from a centralized Alzheimer's disease center education core. There is no attempt to train the care manager to "train family caregivers." It is assumed that local care managers are local experts and only technical assistance is offered to expand the range of information available to geographically dispersed family caregivers.

The IFEI is based on an assumption that one size fits one person for now. It encourages the timing of education and recommendations to teachable moments in a family caregiver's "career." Families are reminded regularly to expect changes in care needs and issues. Dosing of information is based on the author's clinical experience. Overwhelmed family caregivers seem to appreciate brevity and bulleted information.

The IFEI service providers learned to reinforce successful caregiver use of services and coping strategies. This validation of family caregiver expertise in problem solving often breaks down some resistance to modest professional guidance.

Another key element of the IFEI is its reliance on the telephone as a method of delivering information, correcting misconceptions, and reinforcing positive coping among home-based family caregivers. The telephone is familiar technology, uniquely acceptable to older family caregivers. It offers a preview and a reminder of the care manager's continuing availability, expertise, and concern. It addresses the time and energy constraints of overwhelmed family caregivers and agency staff and offers the potential for continuity, repetition, and privacy. Finally, regular telephone contact establishes trust over time. The mailed information that follows up the telephone call is an opportunity for concrete giving to caregivers who often feel that they are doing all the giving and missing opportunities to be a care receiver.

The IFEI is designed for low-cost and low-tech delivery of educational information by telephone and mail to Alzheimer's family caregivers in the context of in-home services. The local nonspecialist-based intervention builds on trust established between local providers and family caregivers who may have more in common with each other than they would with outside experts. Local care managers often have many responsibilities in addition to work with Alzheimer's families. These service providers vary in education, qualifications, and experience with Alzheimer's care. The consistent information provided in the question packets offers a consistent level of current expertise that cannot be expected from general staff.

The toll-free direct access to technical assistance from Duke's Family Support Program was used sparingly but appropriately by local staff. In addition to this technical assistance by phone, regular updated packages of family and provider education materials were mailed directly to local service providers by Duke staff. These updated "care packages" served as reminders to the care managers in much the same way that the care managers' follow-up calls reminded families of inevitable changes.

Finally, face-to-face technical assistance was offered to care managers through annual site visits by Duke and state program administrators to the individual sites in all four states. These visits were scheduled at the convenience of local care managers to insure maximum benefit. Care managers were told that this was not a compliance check, but an opportunity for direct contact, consultation, and feedback. If requested, Duke staff offered community education or professional in-service presentations in conjunction with site visits to reinforce the value of caregiver education. Forms, screening questionnaires, and other information about IFEI can be obtained by contacting the author (LPG).

SUMMARY

In conclusion, the concept of the home as the primary context of providing services to caregivers unfortunately has received little attention. Only recently has the home been recognized as an important treatment delivery setting due to the confluence of national health care trends, an increase in the number of families providing care, and recent research on the multiple negative consequences of long-term caregiving. The two interventions described here highlight the diverse approaches that may benefit families, particularly those caring for individuals with dementia. These interventions differ with regard to their primary mode of delivery (in-home visit versus telephone), interventionist (occupational therapist versus case manager, social worker), and target domain (skills training versus knowledge building). Yet they also share common characteristics such as customization of information and skill-building, flexibility in dose and intensity, and provision of services that are caregiver-directed. Both interventions represent promising new directions in family care that are currently being systematically tested.

REFERENCES

Alzheimer's Association. (1997). *Key elements of dementia care.* Chicago: Alzheimer's Association.

Barris, R., Kielhofner, G., Levine, R. E., & Neville, A. (1985). Occupation as interaction with the environment. In G. Kielhofner (Ed.), *A model for human occupation.* Baltimore: Williams & Wilkins.

Corcoran, M. A. (1992). Gender differences in dementia management plans of spousal caregivers: Implications for occupational therapy. *American Journal of Occupational Therapy, 46,* 1006–1012.

Corcoran, M. A., & Gitlin, L. N. (1991). Environmental influences on behavior of elderly with dementia: Principles for intervention in the home. *Physical and Occupational Therapy in Geriatrics, 9*(3–4), 5–22.

Corcoran, M. A., & Gitlin, L. N. (1992). Dementia management: An occupational therapy home-based intervention for caregivers. *American Journal of Occupational Therapy, 46,* 801–808.

Corcoran, M., & Gitlin, L. N. (2001). Family caregiver acceptance and use of environmental strategies in occupational therapy intervention. *Physical and Occupational Therapy in Geriatrics, 19*(1), 1–15.

Cornman-Levy, D., Gitlin, L. N., Corcoran, M., & Schinfeld, S. (2001). Caregiver aches and pains: The role of physical therapy in helping families provide daily care. *Alzheimer's Care Quarterly, 2,* 47–55.

George, L. K., & Gold, D. T. (1990). Easing caregiver burden: An intervention to overcome barriers to service utilization. Durham, NC: Final report to the AARP Andrus Foundation from the Duke Center for the Study of Aging.

Gitlin, L. N. (2000). Adjusting "person-environment systems": Helping older people live the "good life" at home. In R. Rubenstein, M. Moss, & M. Kleban (Eds.), *The many faces of aging: Essays in honor of M. P. Lawton* (pp. 41–54). New York: Springer.

Gitlin, L. N., & Corcoran, M. A. (1993). Expanding caregiver ability to use environmental solutions for problems of bathing and incontinence in the elderly with dementia. *Technology and Disability, 2,* 12–21.

Gitlin, L. N., Corcoran, M. A., Winter, L., Boyce, A., & Hauck, W. W. (2001). A randomized, controlled trial of a home environmental intervention to enhance self-efficacy and reduce upset in family caregivers of persons with dementia. *Gerontologist, 41,* 15–30.

Gitlin, L. N., Corcoran, M. A., Winter, L., Boyce, A., & Marcus, S. (1999). Predicting participation and adherence to a home environmental intervention among family caregivers of persons with dementia. *Family Relations, 48,* 363–372.

Gwyther, L. P. (1994). Service delivery and utilization: Research directions and clinical implications. In E. Light, G. Niederehe, & B. Lebowitz (Eds.), *Stress effects on family caregivers of Alzheimer's patients* (p. 56). New York: Springer.

Gwyther, L. P., & Ballard, E. L. (1988). *In-home respite care: Guidelines for programs serving family caregivers for memory-impaired adults.* Durham, NC: Duke University Center for the Study of Aging.

Gwyther, L. P., Ballard, E. L., & Hinman-Smith, E. A. (1990). *Overcoming barriers to appropriate service use: Effective individualized strategies for Alzheimer's care.* Durham, NC: Duke University Center for the Study of Aging.

Haley, W. E., & Bailey, S. (1999). Research on family caregiving in Alzheimer's disease: Implications for practice and policy. In B. Vellas & J. L. Fitten (Eds.), *Research and practice in Alzheimer's disease: Vol. 2* (pp. 321–332). Paris: Serdi.

Hasselkus, B. R. (1988). Rehabilitation: The family caregiver's view. *Topics in Geriatric Rehabilitation, 4*(1), 60–70.

Lawton, M. P., & Nahemow, L. E. (1973). Ecology and the aging process. In C. Eisdorfer & M. P. Lawton (Eds.), *The psychology of adult development and aging* (pp. 619–674). Washington, DC: American Psychological Association.

Montgomery, R. J. V., Marquis, J., & Klaus, S. (2000, November). Profiles of respite service use [Special Issue 1]. *Gerontologist, 40,* 336. Abstract of presentation at the Gerontological Society of America Annual Meeting, Washington, DC.

Olsen, R. V., Ehrenkrantz, E., & Hutchings, B. (1993). Creating supporting environments for people with dementia and their caregivers through home modifications. *Technology and Disability, 2,* 47–57.

Ory, M. G., Yee, J. L., Tennstedt, S. L., & Schulz, R. (2000). The extent and impact of dementia care: Unique challenges experienced by family caregivers. In R. Schulz (Ed.), *Handbook on dementia caregiving: Evidence-based interventions for family caregivers* (pp. 1–32). New York: Springer.

Pynoos, J., & Ohta, R. J. (1991). In-home interventions for persons with Alzheimer's disease and their caregivers. *Occupational Therapy and Physical Therapy in Geriatrics, 9,* 83–92.

Ramsdell, J. W., Swart, J., Jackson, E., & Renvall, M. (1989). The yield of a home visit in the assessment of geriatric patients. *Journal of the American Geriatrics Society, 13,* 17–24.

Schulz, R., & Beach, S. D. (1999). Caregiving as a risk factor for mortality: The caregiver health effects study. *Journal of the American Medical Association, 282,* 2215–2219.

Schulz, R., Gallagher-Thompson, D., Haley, W., & Czaja, S. (1999). Understanding the intervention process: A theoretical/conceptual framework for intervention approaches to caregiving. In R. Schulz (Ed.), *Handbook on dementia caregiving: Evidence-based interventions for family caregivers* (pp. 33–60). New York: Springer.

Schulz, R., & Heckhausen, J. (1999). Aging, culture and control: Setting a new research agenda. *Journal of Gerontology: Psychological Sciences, 54B,* 139–145.

Schulz, R., O'Brien, A. T., Bookwala, J., & Fleissner, K. (1995). Psychiatric and physical morbidity effects of dementia caregiving: Prevalence, correlates, and causes. *Gerontologist, 35,* 771–791.

Spitzer, A. (1998). Nursing in the health care system of the postmodern world: Crossroads, paradoxes and complexity. *Journal of Advanced Nursing, 28,* 164–171.

Toth-Cohen, S., Gitlin, L. N., Corcoran, M., Eckhardt, S., Johns, P., & Lipsett, R. (2001). Providing services to family caregivers at home: Challenges and recommendations for health and human service professions. *Alzheimer's Care Quarterly, 2,* 23–32.

Wallace, J. I., Buchner, D. M., Grothaus, L., Leveille, S., Tyll, L., LaCroix, A. Z., & Wagner, E. H. (1998). Implementation and effectiveness of a community-based health promotion program for older adults. *Journal of Gerontology: Medical Sciences, 33A,* 301–306.

8

Primary Care: Partnering With Health Care Providers

Robert Burns, Linda Nichols, Jennifer Martindale-Adams, David W. Coon, Katie Maslow, and John Selstad

PRIMARY CARE AND FAMILY CAREGIVING

A primary-care provider, often the family physician, is usually the first health care professional to whom Alzheimer's patients and caregivers turn. However, the roles of physicians and primary care in the treatment of patients with Alzheimer's disease and related dementias (ADRD) are not always clear. In the past 3 years, at least nine separate consensus statements and practice guidelines have emphasized the importance of physicians in the treatment of ADRD patients. Consensus statements and practice guidelines have been issued by several medical associations and consensus groups, including the American Medical Association ([AMA], 1999), the U.S. Department of Veterans Affairs (1997), the Alzheimer's Disease Managed Care Advisory Council (Fillit, Knopman, Cummings, & Appel, 1999a, 1999b), and the American Association for Geriatric Psychiatry, the Alzheimer's Association, and the American Geriatrics Society (Small et al., 1997). The primary focus of these statements and guidelines ranges from diagnosis to management, but all documents also include the importance of the family caregiver. In addition, the American Medical Association has stressed the link between family caregivers, the patient, and the primary care physician across time and health care settings (AMA, 1993). Despite these official endorsements of the role of physicians in working with caregivers, there is a dearth of physician-based or primary-care-based interventions for caregivers of any kind, including ADRD caregivers.

This lack of physician- and primary-care-based assistance for caregivers is, in many ways, a function of the health care system and the role of the physician in dementia management. Physicians are typically involved with dementia in the diagnostic phase. In fact, medical literature consists mainly of assessment techniques that might assist the physician in correctly diagnosing dementia. Other published studies consist of evaluative techniques that assess behavioral problems and psychiatric syndromes, including depression and anxiety, and clinical studies involving drug trials. Unfortunately, published accounts are rare of using practical, research-driven advice in providing supportive, behaviorally based care for patients and caregivers in noninstitutional, primary-care settings.

To a large extent, physicians have developed a biomedical model for care of the patient and for the caregiver dyad. Although there are advantages to medicalizing ADRD (primarily, increased awareness of the diseases and a research emphasis for treatment), medicalization has created significant negative effects for patients and caregivers, as well as for physicians and other primary care staff. Physicians who are oriented in the medical model utilize diagnostic and evaluative energies in the work-up of cognitive impairment; after reaching a diagnosis, they are often uncertain or do not know what to do for the patient and family (Brotman & Yaffe, 1994; Fortinsky, Leighton, & Wasson, 1995). For many physicians, even the diagnosis of dementia remains problematic, with studies suggesting that fewer than 50% of dementia cases are diagnosed by physicians (Callahan, Hendrie, & Tierney, 1995; Wind, Van Staveren, Jonker, & Van Eijk, 1994). Boise and colleagues (1999) studied 78 primary care physicians—(rural and urban, from Oregon and Ohio, the majority of whom had been in practice for more than 10 years—to determine how dementia was diagnosed and what barriers existed to diagnosis. Two important barriers were time and reimbursement. Confronted by patients' multiple medical problems, physicians were less likely to spend time on cognitive problems, especially those that appear to be "untreatable," even though families want the involvement and assistance of their physicians (Haley, Clair, & Saulsberry, 1992; Silliman, 1989).

In the study by Boise and colleagues (Boise, Camicioli, Morgan, Rose, & Congleton, 1999), many physicians did not recognize dementia symptoms, particularly early ones, unless directed to them by a family member or by an adverse event, such as an accident or lack of adherence to treatment. Even though physicians are generally aware of assessment techniques, these techniques are not always used (Boise, Camicioli, et al., 1999; Fortinsky & Wasson, 1997). Family members complain that some physicians do not recognize dementia and that those who do still may choose not to chart its diagnosis. Families also report that even physician entry of the diagnosis in the patient chart does not necessarily mean the patient and family were informed of the diagnosis. Furthermore, families complain that they were informed in an abrupt and dismissive manner that implied nothing could be done for either patient or family (Beisecker, Chrisman, & Wright, 1997; Boise, Camicioli, et al., 1999; Boise, Morgan, Kaye, & Camicioli, 1999; Connell & Gallant, 1996; Glasser, Rubin, & Dickover, 1989; Haley et al., 1992; Knopman, Donohue, & Gutterman, 2000). Despite families' needs, physicians remain unsure if families or patients want a diagnosis and often do not provide one (Boise et al., 1999), although the availability of cognition-enhancing drugs argues for early diagnosis. In addition, for many areas of the health and social service system, such as home health care, a formal diagnosis may even be a requirement for entry.

The failure of primary-care physicians to provide the needed family-caregiver support forces the caregiver to seek assistance outside the formal medical care system. Other health care professionals, such as psychologists, therapists, and social workers, are most often involved in caregiver/care-recipient interventions. These interventions, such as family therapy, behavioral management, support groups, and day care, have generally targeted psychosocial functioning. However, integration of family caregiving into the formal medical and health care system is an important clinical and policy issue. Most people have contact with the formal medical care system, because it serves as the portal into other formal and informal systems.

THE ROLE OF MANAGED CARE IN FAMILY CAREGIVING

One response to real or perceived gaps in traditional fee-for-service primary care has been the rise of managed care. During this time of rapid change and upheaval in the health care industry, patients with ADRD and their family caregivers are among the hundreds of thousands of Medicare beneficiaries who have chosen to join Medicare HMOs and other managed care organizations (MCOs). Although the 1997 Balanced Budget Act created additional options for Medicare managed care and integrated delivery systems, neither the government nor managed care has developed coordinated efforts to improve managed care for ADRD patients and their families. Problems also remain concerning awareness, accessibility, and appropriateness with regard to ADRD patients and their families (Maslow & Selstad, 2001). Sorely needed programs and services are not available in all geographic communities, and even when services are available, many families remain unaware of those available to assist them. In addition, the majority of programs and services are not culturally tailored to meet the needs of many ethnic or racial minority groups. Patient and family needs vary, not only over the course of the disease, but also in response to life changes unrelated to dementia; information and services useful at one point may not be helpful at another, and this too adds another layer of complexity (e.g., Aneshensel, Pearlin,

Mullan, Zarit, & Whitlatch, 1995; Bourgeois, Schulz, & Burgio, 1996; Coon, Schulz, & Ory, 1999; Cotrell, 1996; Cox, 1999; Gallagher-Thompson et al., 2000; Gallagher-Thompson, Solano, Coon, & Árean, in press; Hamilton, Braun, Kerber, Thurlow, & Schwieterman, 1996; Webber, Fox, & Burnette, 1994). Finally, the fragmentation and complexities of the service environment combined with lack of public funding can substantially hinder access as well. Even so, many communities have taken steps in the right direction to create programs and services that make a difference for people with dementia and their families (Maslow & Selstad, 2001). Much less progress has been made regarding ADRD programs and services in the primary and acute medical care arenas, and even less has been accomplished with regard to the integration of health care and supportive services.

EXPECTATIONS OF CAREGIVERS AND PROVIDERS IN PRIMARY CARE

Even when physicians and caregivers interact, there are mismatched expectations around dementia (Miller, Glasser, & Rubin, 1992). Caregivers and physicians have different perspectives on what is important. Caregivers want more concrete and practical information and assistance than physicians now offer (specifically about the nature of the disease, medications, guidance, and training to manage behavioral symptoms) as well as specific referrals to community agencies (Boise, Camicioli, et al., 1999; Boise, Morgan, et al., 1999; Cohen, 1991; Connell & Gallant, 1996; Fortinsky & Hathaway, 1990; Glasser et al., 1989; Haley et al., 1992; Levine & Zuckerman, 1999). Caregivers also want more emotional support and attention, including recognition of their own anxiety (Fortinsky & Hathaway, 1990; Levine & Zuckerman, 1999) than physicians may be able to offer (Brotman & Yaffe, 1994). Physicians are often frustrated by the expectations of families, the inadequacy of what the medical system has to offer patients, and their ability to manage dementia patients (Miller et al., 1992; Boise, Camicioli, et al., 1999). The mismatch of expectations can lead families to perceive physicians as indifferent to their needs after the dementia diagnosis is made (Miller et al., 1992), and this perception undoubtedly reflects the physician's lack of information about how to manage dementia. Physicians have reported being uncomfortable giving advice about behavioral symptoms (Miller et al., 1992; Boise, Camicioli, et al., 1999). Given the lack of practical information for physicians on behavioral management and the importance of the community and other health care professionals in the management of dementia, "nonmanagement" by the physician may be the current alternative of choice (Fillit et al., 1999a). Families report that physicians frequently do not provide them with information about the condition, the medications available, or community-based organizations that could be useful for information, referral, support, or intervention, including the Alzheimer's Association (Beisecker et al., 1997; Boise, Camicioli, et al., 1999; Boise, Morgan, et al., 1999; Connell & Gallant, 1996; Glasser et al., 1989; Haley et al., 1992; Knopman et al., 2000). As a result, too many ADRD patients and families "feel abandoned, and find their way belatedly, if at all, to information, programs, and services that could help them" (Maslow & Selstad, 2001, p. 34).

This chapter presents two innovative approaches based in primary care and managed care systems for helping families care for relatives with dementia: the Providers and Alzheimer's Caregivers Together (PACT) project, and the Chronic Care Networks for Alzheimer's Disease (CCN/AD), formed by the Alzheimer's Association and the National Chronic Care Consortium (NCCC). These projects take different approaches to integrating family caregiving into the primary care setting, although both work to expand the network of assistance for caregivers.

PROVIDERS AND ALZHEIMER'S CAREGIVERS TOGETHER

Incorporating caregiver assistance into the primary care practice agenda was the goal of PACT, one of six intervention sites funded by NIA-NINR as part of the REACH project (Resources for Alzheimer's Caregivers Health). The focus of the study was to provide information and training for caregivers in managing their own stress as well as behavioral problems of the loved one with dementia.

PACT Theoretical Framework

From the literature, it is clear that caregivers have a need for information, particularly for managing troubling behaviors and their own stress, and that physicians are not always aware of the resources or information caregivers need and are not prepared to meet caregivers' expectations. To meet the needs of caregivers and physicians in a primary care, physician-oriented setting, our knowledge-based intervention was grounded in the following practice and theory concepts:

1. Information and education for ADRD caregivers improves their ability to manage care recipient behaviors and cope with their own stress.
2. As the primary care provider is an important point of contact (often the first and frequently the only contact), the formal care system (provider) and informal care system (caregiver) must share responsibility for dementia care.
3. A theoretical model of stress and coping that focuses on the interaction between individual and environment provides an excellent framework for interventions that target behavior and stress.

Component 1. Information and Education

Knowledge about the disease and information on the management of behavioral symptoms are areas of concern and need for AD caregivers (Wykle, 1996; Wykle & Segall, 1991). One Alzheimer disease diagnosis and treatment consensus statement (generated by the American Association for Geriatric Psychiatry, the Alzheimer's Association, and the American Geriatrics Society) suggests that educational materials can be important interventions that "reduce the risk of caregiver depression and improve tolerance and the capacity to care for patients in the home" (Small et al., 1997, p. 1369). Patients, especially older individuals, want patient education and health information material, and they save and read the material. However, most do not normally request material and thus need encouragement and permission to ask for it (Shank, Murphy, & Schulte-Mowry, 1991). The same study showed that, in general, patients have no clear preference for the material's form or from whom they would like to receive it; however, materials that are easier to understand and written at an appropriate reading level should be better received.

Knowledge about dementia and its management is a well-accepted outcome in dementia research, particularly for support groups (Zarit & Teri, 1991). Knowledgeable caregivers are more likely to have realistic expectations concerning their care-recipient's capabilities and are more likely to feel competent and confident of their caregiving (Graham, Ballard, & Sham, 1997). Feelings of competency, self-esteem, and mastery are related to lowered levels of depression and other negative affective states (Dunkin & Anderson-Hanley, 1998; Schulz, O'Brien, Bookwala, & Fleissner, 1995). However, Coen and colleagues (1999) found that group education alone, while increasing knowledge, did not improve caregivers' quality of life or burden, or decrease care-recipient behavioral disturbances and suggest that group education is not as effective as intensive, individually tailored caregiver education (Coen, O'Boyle, Coakley, & Lawlor, 1999).

Component 2. Shared Caregiving—The Formal and Informal Systems

Families alone cannot meet the multiple needs (multiple chronic illnesses and functional impairments) of older family members who are frail. Caregiving responsibilities must be shared by family and professionals, combining formal and informal services (Barrett, Haley, & Powers, 1996; Bass, Noelker, & Rechlin, 1996; McGovern & Koss, 1994). The formal and informal care systems can be and should be complementary. However, the foci of the two systems are often not in alignment, as shown by the mismatch of care expectations and perspectives held by caregivers and physicians (Bogardus, Bradley, & Tinetti, 1998; Boise, Camicioli, et al., 1999; Boise, Morgan, et al., 1999; Levine & Zuckerman, 1999).

For example, formal systems provide expert knowledge (Stone, Cafferata, & Sangl, 1982), but they are not always user-friendly, nor do they always provide the information needed by caregivers (Fortinsky, 1998; Fortinsky et al., 1995; Haley et al., 1992). The formal professional system cannot easily meet the humanistic needs of the caregiver, because it must be cost effective. Thus, service is generalized rather than personalized and turnover in personnel may damage the therapeutic relationship.

Despite these constraints, the two systems must work together to provide adequate care. The primary care setting is an ideal place to develop interventions that are specifically designed to decrease family caregivers' burdens. The primary care setting combines the formal and informal systems of providers and caregivers in a real-life scenario, and it is the first and continuing access point in the health care system for the patient and caregiver.

Component 3. Stress and Caregiving

Our knowledge and skill-building intervention fits Lazarus and Launier's (1978) action-oriented, environment-focused stress and coping model. This model of stress conceptualizes stress and coping in terms of both person and environment, and it is also amenable to low-cost educational interventions aimed at specific caregiver problems. Lazarus and Launier's model is similar to several others that have been applied to caregiving, including the Cohen, Kessler, and Gordon (1995) model adapted by the REACH investigators (Schulz, Gallagher-Thompson, Haley, & Czaja, 2000) that links environment stressors to health outcomes. Goode and colleagues have stressed the need for clinical interventions to strengthen psychosocial resources, such as coping, social support, and stressfulness appraisals, and thereby to improve long-term mental and physical health outcomes for caregivers (Goode, Haley, Roth, & Ford, 1998).

Lazarus and Launier define stress as an interaction between individual and environment. A situation is evaluated as stressful when individuals feel that the demands confronting them tax or exceed their resources. Thus, there are two components of stress; stress is "located" in the environment (e.g., the presence of a person with dementia who needs continuous help and supervision) and in the stressed individual (e.g., a caregiver's perception of burden, emotional responses, etc.). Coping with stress can include both action-oriented management of environmental demands and intrapersonal efforts to manage internal responses (both cognitive and emotional) to these environmental demands (Lazarus & Launier, 1978).

Action-oriented coping depends in part upon information directed toward diminishing, tolerating, or mastering situational demands. For our intervention—in order to fit the model's action-oriented, environment-focused coping strategies and further reinforce and supplement the traditional provider/patient/

caregiver dialogue (Shank et al., 1991)—information is given to each caregiver in the form of skill building and written materials that focus on the specific problems the individual reports encountering in caring for the care recipient. Increasing caregiver ability to manage problem behaviors should increase competency and confidence and thereby decrease depression (Dunkin & Anderson-Hanley, 1998; Graham et al., 1997; Schulz et al., 1995). In turn, positive health outcomes should occur (Goode et al., 1998). These findings were borne out in a study by Teri and colleagues, where caregivers who learned to manage behavior problems had significant decreases in depressive symptoms (Teri, Lodgson, & Yesavage, 1997).

The second component of stress, internal to the stressed individual, is also targeted in this knowledge and skill-building intervention. Caregivers receive materials that help them learn assertiveness, relaxation techniques, how to recognize and change negative thoughts, and other intrapersonal coping strategies. Intrapersonal efforts change how a person thinks or feels and can reduce emotional distress in situations where the course of events cannot be changed. A crucial aspect of this theory is the notion that the perceptions of demands and coping are very individualized, and interventions must be tailored to the problems identified by the caregiver. Because behavioral problems may be a result of environmental factors, such as family dynamics and conflict (Vitaliano, Young, Russo, Romano, & Magana-Amato, 1993), teaching caregivers to manage these dynamics and conflict may be beneficial for both care recipients and caregivers.

PACT Interventions

The PACT interventions are conducted in a primary care setting and are designed to aid caregivers in management of patients at home, through assistance of the primary provider network. These interventions are simple and are offered in a setting where ADRD patients and ADRD caregivers are found—the primary care setting. In standard geriatrics practice, ADRD patients are seen approximately four to six times per year, although in primary care practice the number of visits is often lower. PACT interventions occur at each visit. Phone calls between visits sustain intervention effects while decreasing transportation and care difficulties.

During the regularly scheduled primary care visit for the patient, a health interventionist provides training to the caregivers in behavior management of the recipient and in management of their own stress. The interventionist and caregiver work together to assess the caregiver's current knowledge and identify areas of concern about the patient's or their own functioning. After problem identification, the interventionist and caregiver (a) discuss actions that could be taken; (b) arrive at the most feasible solutions to individual issues; and (c) identify, modify, and reinforce resources that can assist the caregiver in managing behaviors in the home and reduce the caregiver's own stress. Thus, caregiver and interventionist develop a specific plan of action. The caregiver also receives behavior-specific or coping-skill-specific educational materials that are tied to problems identified in the in-person session. Intervention contacts are approximately 20 to 45 minutes.

The rationale for a primary-care-based, caregiver-support model is strong. Caregivers do use the health care system but may not be able to use time-intensive services such as support groups, due to factors such as transportation, time constraints, and language or cultural barriers. The PACT interventions are natural adjuncts to care in a primary setting and are based on lessons learned from health-promotion research activities. For example, for smoking cessation in primary care, factors that predict success include using multiple means of motivating behavior change, involving both physicians and nonphysicians in an individualized, face-to-face effort, and repeating the motivational message on multiple occasions over the longest possible time period (Kottke, Battista, DeFriese, & Brekke, 1988). Treatments that are simple, repetitive, and presented in different and interesting ways are much more likely to be adopted than intensive, nonrepetitive treatments (Kottke et al. 1988). Thus, the goal of patient and caregiver education is more than giving information; the intent is empowerment, to provide support, control, and knowledge in managing self-care deficits more effectively (Hiromoto & Dungan, 1991). Moreover, when patients and caregivers are encouraged to participate in care, knowledge increases and anxiety decreases (Dodd, 1988).

Content and Materials

There are two different sets of content for the caregiver interventions: education sessions on dementia behavior-management of the person with dementia and stress and coping behavior management for the caregiver.

Behavioral Issues

This component focuses on behaviors exhibited by the person with dementia, such as ADL tasks, as well as on specific behaviors identified by the caregiver as problematic, such as aggressive behavior or wandering. Targeted education on how to manage dementia behaviors is designed to empower the caregiver to better cope with stressful situations. Several sources have been used to develop the educational materials that focus on behavioral management practices: nursing and psychology theory and practice in dementia care management; the work of dementia-focused groups and organizations, such as the national Alzheimer's Disease and Related Disorders Association; and the Office of Geriatrics and Extended Care, Veterans Health Administration, Department of Veterans Affairs. These best practices have been adapted for family caregivers with care recipients in either home or institutional settings. These references range from easily accessible materials for family caregivers, such as *The 36-Hour Day* (Mace & Rabins, 1999) and *There's Still a Person in There: The Complete Guide to Treating and Coping with Alzheimer's* (Castleman, Gallagher-Thompson, & Naythons, 1999), to tapes and materials designed primarily for institutional caregivers (Teri, 1994; Teri et al., 1992), as well as scholarly articles (Algase, 1992; Beck, Baldwin, Modlin, & Lewis, 1990; Beck, Modlin, Heithoff, & Shue, 1992; Kolanowski, Hurwitz, Taylor, Evans, & Strumpf, 1994; Rossby, Beck, & Heacock, 1992; Strumpf, 1994) that may be of interest to some clinicians and caregivers.

Comprehensive pamphlets written at a fifth-grade reading level are provided to address PACT caregiver issues and concerns. Each pamphlet contains suggestions that are categorized and numbered. This documentation enables the interventionist to determine which suggestions caregivers tried, which were most helpful, and which do not work for certain problems and certain care recipients. The 25 behavior modification pamphlets focus on dementia behaviors ranging from bathing, combativeness, confusion and hallucinations, to medications, nutrition, sexuality and wandering.

Caregiver Coping

The stress and coping management component includes cognitive strategies (such as identifying perfectionism, pessimism, and all-or-none thinking), coping with highly emotional situations, obtaining support from significant others, assertiveness, relaxation, stimulus control, short-term goal setting, small-step and attainable goals, and coping with negative thoughts and feelings. Targeted education that extends behavior management to include instruction and education in intrapersonal efforts to change how the caregiver thinks or feels may be particularly useful in reducing emotional distress in situations where the course of events cannot be changed. The stress management and coping content and materials draw upon many of the same resources as the dementia-behavior-management component, with the addition of communication, problem solving (Gottman, Notorius, Gonso, & Markman, 1976), and stress reduction and relaxation (Davis, Eshelman, & McKay, 1980) resources. The 13 stress modification pamphlets cover a variety of topics including adult day care, assertiveness, grief, problem solving, and healthy lifestyle.

CHRONIC CARE NETWORKS
FOR ALZHEIMER'S DISEASE

In response to the lack of ADRD identification, diagnostic assessment, and care management activities presented earlier, the Alzheimer's Association and the

National Chronic Care Consortium (NCCC) joined forces in 1996 to develop, execute, and evaluate a new model of comprehensive coordinated care for ADRD patients and their families. This unique national partnership subsequently spawned the Chronic Care Networks for Alzheimer's Disease (CCN/AD) initiative—a consortium of seven promising community-level partnerships consisting of Alzheimer's Association chapters, comprehensive medical and community-based provider networks, and managed care organizations (MCOs). These local partnerships were chosen from applicants across the country to implement and evaluate similar project goals and objectives formulated by the CCN/AD advisory and working groups. When taken together, these national sites represent the majority of MCO settings currently in existence, including staff models, group and IPA models, modified fee-for-service, partial capitation, and full risk. The CCN/AD brings together these providers of managed care, community-based care, and consumer education and advocacy in unprecedented local partnerships to improve the care of persons with ADRD and their family caregivers in managed care plans.

The CCN/AD's intervention focuses on the implementation of guidelines, protocols, and pathways that create timely, comprehensive, appropriate, and effective systems of care that address the unique needs of patients with dementia and their caregivers. The CCN/AD is designed to improve the identification and early diagnosis of dementia within primary care by implementing state-of-the-art tools and comprehensive care guidelines; and also to plan and manage care and support for patient and family caregiver over time and across the continuum of services by establishing strong linkages between primary care and the range of community services that address dementia. These systems are to be developed in a manner that results in improved health outcomes and greater customer satisfaction and that can be sustained under risk-based financing. Therefore, the thrust of the model requires managed care to expand its administrative and contracting roles to encompass a more patient- and family-centered approach, incorporating the full range of care needed by people with ADRD and their families.

Finally, the CCN/AD initiative pays particular attention to changing the internal systems of the partners (e.g., training and education, information systems, care management model, clinic procedures) in ways that will sustain this "new standard of care" when the funded project period and its evaluation are completed.

CCN/AD Model

Several advisory groups composed of health care professionals and Alzheimer's Association chapter staff from the various project sites were formed to develop the framework, guidelines, strategies, and tools that make up the CCN/AD model. To aid in the model's development, these advisory groups relied on both available research findings (e.g., Beisecker et al., 1997; Boise, Camicioli, et al., 1999; Connell & Gallant, 1996; Glasser et al., 1989; Haley et al., 1992) as well as on their own clinical expertise and extensive experience in working with ADRD patients and families. They sought to develop a model that would not only address the needs of the whole person (not just the dementia) and support the family across all stages of the person's illness, but would also prove feasible in the real world of health care. Thus, the model intends to incorporate knowledge and services developed over the years to care for ADRD people and their families, so that these families are effectively connected to, and integrated with, exiting information, programs, and services whenever they need them. This approach was deliberately taken rather than one that began with the creation of new sources of information, referrals, and services with unknown utility.

As shown in Table 8.1, the first three components of the model (identification, diagnostic assessment, and medical care management) are intended to ameliorate problems associated with lack of ADRD recognition and diagnosis as well as

TABLE 8.1   The Chronic Care Networks for Alzheimer's Disease Model

---

• *Identification of People with Possible Dementia.* A two-step process to identify people who may have dementia and should receive a diagnostic assessment:

  1. triggers to identify people who may have dementia.
  2. a brief family questionnaire to identify people who may have dementia.

• *Diagnostic Assessment.* Conducted on individuals identified in the preceding process. Includes medical and other histories, physical examinations, mental status tests, laboratory tests, imaging, and other procedures. Divided into three categories: those conducted for everyone, those for everyone unless a good reason exists to not do them, and those not to be done unless a good reason exists to do them.

• *Care Management.* Care management blueprints were developed to guide ongoing medical and nonmedical care management protocols at each site. Blueprints identify desired outcomes, areas for assessment and goal-formation, as well as possible interventions in six domains (e.g., medical treatment, nutrition, and advance directives) for three time periods: initial identification, longitudinal monitoring and treatment, and end of life.

• *Family Caregiver Information and Support.* Uses a conceptual framework that defines phases of caregiving based on the tasks and challenges faced by family caregivers. Identifies specific objectives for family caregivers in all six phases: (1) prediagnostic; (2) diagnostic; (3) role change; (4) chronic caregiving, (5) transition to alternative care, and (6) end of life. Uses grids listing the objectives to identify information, programs, and services needed to achieve the objectives and to specify partners responsible for them (e.g., Alzheimer's Association chapter or National Chronic Care Consortium member organization).

---

lack of ongoing medical management for ADRD patients. As a result, the CCN/ AD model does not rely solely on physicians, but rather affords opportunities for nurses, social workers and other health care professionals, local Alzheimer's Association staff, and other partner staff to play central roles. Determining how to take what has been learned (albeit primarily in nonmedical settings) and incorporate it into day-to-day health care practice has been and continues to be a major CCN/AD task. Provider education and training about the model, its tools, guidelines, strategies, and procedures is one cornerstone of the CCN/AD's efforts to implement coordinated systems of care. Given the variation in available staff, practice patterns, and other characteristics of partners, the CCN/AD expects considerable tailoring of the model to meet the needs of these individual partnerships, including addressing any differences in the background and disciplines of the providers who are trained to implement the model's components and the particular strategies and modes used to train those providers (e.g., one-to-one informal meetings, small group discussions, large lectures, videotapes). The family is another cornerstone in the CCN/AD's foundation, and the remainder of this presentation focuses on the CCN/AD's involvement and support of the family caregiver. Additional details on the CCN/AD as a whole, its tools and innovations, is available on the NCCC Web site at www.nccconline.org/about/alzheimers.htm and in the literature (Maslow & Selstad, 2001).

Involving and Supporting Family Caregiving

A central objective of the CCN/AD is to involve and support family caregivers across the course of the illness. Therefore, a key first step in developing the model was to gain a thorough understanding of family caregivers' perspectives, needs, and strengths. Subsequently, each part of the model (Table 8.1) has features that are designed to achieve family involvement and support. A variety of approaches intentionally infused into the model help the CCN/AD to meet this objective, including innovative methods of involving family caregivers in the identification of possible dementia and initial assessment activities, as well as ongoing medical and nonmedical care management.

Identification of People with Possible Dementia

The CCN/AD uses a two-step process to identify individuals with possible dementia who warrant a diagnostic assessment. The activities of this model component (i.e., the triggers and the family questionnaire) directly involve family caregivers, honoring the fact that family members are often the first to notice dementia-related changes in their loved ones (Boise, Camicioli, et al., 1999; Boise, Morgan, et al., 1999; Costa et al., 1996; Haley et al., 1992; Knopman et al., 2000; Small et al., 1997). The CCN/AD triggers are defined as tools that describe the signs and symptoms of possible dementia. The first step in identification uses three sets of triggers: (a) six triggers recommended by an expert panel to the U.S. Agency for Health Care Policy and Research (Costa et al., 1996); (b) the Alzheimer's Association's Ten Warning Signs of Alzheimer's Disease (Alzheimer's Disease and Related Disorders Association [ADRD], 1999); and (c) seven triggers developed by the CCN/AD to include signs and symptoms particularly likely to be noticed by health care providers and office staff. Although the triggers are used to train providers, they also appear on posters and pamphlets placed in participating provider offices and in newsletters and on educational material mailed to patients in the participating managed care plans. Poster, pamphlet, and newsletter applications of the triggers are intended to stimulate family caregivers to consider possible signs and symptoms of dementia in their family member or friend and to encourage them to discuss their observations with health care providers. The second identification step is a brief questionnaire that asks the family member if the patient has problems with the following: (a) repeating or asking the same thing over and over; (b) remembering appointments, family occasions, and holidays; (c) writing checks, paying bills, and balancing the checkbook; (d) deciding what groceries or clothes to buy; and (e) taking medications according to instructions. Early observational data suggest family member responses are consistent with existing diagnoses for dementia; but more important, the scores are alerting providers to unrecognized cases (Maslow & Selstad, 2001). Because all provider staff participating in the CCN/AD are trained with the triggers, it is possible that staff will identify most of the new cases of dementia identified through the project. However, the family questionnaire and family responses to triggers are not only important in helping identify patients with possible dementia, but also communicate the CCN/AD philosophy that family perspectives are valued and families play a critical role in dementia care.

Diagnostic Assessment

The second part of the CCN/AD model recommends assessment procedures for patients with possible dementia, including medical and other histories, physical examinations, mental status tests, laboratory tests, and imaging procedures. The procedures are grouped into three categories: those that need to be done for every person evaluated, those done for every person unless a good reason exists not to do them, and those that should not be completed unless good reasons exist to do them. Family history is one of the key procedures to complete for every person, and information obtained from the person with possible dementia is to be corroborated with the family whenever there is one. These procedures include two family caregiver assessments to be completed when the patient is not present: family caregiver strain, and family caregiver perceptions of the cognitive and behavioral symptoms of the patient. The latter can provide valuable information that otherwise might be overlooked in busy primary care. Caregiver responses to these two questionnaires can help health care and chapter partners recognize the differences among caregivers and begin to individualize care plans that include the family caregiver. In addition, the use of these assessment tools effectively communicates to caregivers not only that family perspectives are valued and that families play critical care roles, but also that their own health and emotional well-being are important. Once identified, CCN/AD families consent to have their names released via a fax referral system to the local Alzheimer's Association chapter so that the chapter can identify educational material, programs, and services that may be helpful for the patient and the family; and so that the chapter can begin to establish an ongoing relationship that assists in the care management of the patient and family across the course of the disease. A recent study found that when families are left to identify and contact the Alzheimer's Association themselves, those families who did eventually get in touch with the chapter waited an average of more than 2 years (29 months) between a dementia diagnosis and their initial contact (Bass, McCarthy, Eckert, & Bichler, 1994). The CCN/AD fax referral system is an attempt to reduce that lag time to within a couple of weeks.

Care Management

The CCN/AD leadership created and added blueprints to the model to help guide the partner sites with their own protocol development across three time periods: initial identification, longitudinal monitoring and treatment, and end-of-life. These blueprints delineate desired outcomes, areas for assessment and goal formation, and possible interventions in six domains: client function, medical care, psychosocial function, client nutrition, advance directives planning, and caregiver support. Still, care management protocols must be tailored to meet the unique structure, staffing, and practices of the partnerships at each site. The protocols will change over time as partners identify problems with their own protocols and generate new ideas or integrate promising solutions that have been implemented at other sites. The blueprints for five of the six domains involve family caregivers by incorporating their values and goals in the desired outcomes, soliciting their observations and concerns to help guide the assessment of domain-related issues, and considering their preferences in the selection of appropriate interventions. The blueprint entitled "Domain 2—Caregiver Support" (see Table 8.2) focuses specifically on desired outcomes, areas for assessment and goal formation, and possible interventions to support family caregivers. Thus, the care management blueprints strongly emphasize family caregiver involvement and support, with the sites facing the formidable task of determining how to step off these blueprints and into truly coordinated care. For example, one site uses a common care plan that encompasses all the domains and is e-mailed between partners who are

TABLE 8.2 Domain 2—Caregiver Support

	Initial Identification Phase	Longitudinal Monitoring and Treatment Phase	End-of-Life Phase
Pathway Outcome	Caregiver(s) are identified and given information and support in accordance with their needs and wishes.	Caregiver(s) are supported to enable them to maximize their caregiving role(s) while maintaining appropriate balance in their personal lives.	Caregiver(s) achieve maximum satisfaction with their role(s).
Assessment	• Identify current and potential caregivers. • Record contact information in patient chart. • Assess caregiver concerns, agenda, needs, and availability. • Assess caregiver knowledge. • Assess caregiver role in ADLs and IADLs. • Assess caregiver's perception of patient's living environment (appropriateness and safety).	• Update caregiver information. • Follow up on status of previous caregiver concerns and needs. • Assess for new issues and burdens. • Assess caregiver's role in ADLs and IADLs. • Assess caregiver's perception of patient's living environment for appropriateness and safety.	• Assess caregiver comfort and concerns with end-of-life issues. • Assess burden of caregiver tasks and need for respite. • Evaluate caregiver's perception of patient's environment regarding appropriateness for meeting end-of-life needs.
Goal Formation	• Provide caregiver with information, referrals, and resource materials. • Establish caregiver role(s) as appropriate in conjunction with patient/caregiver.	• Review and revise caregiver roles as appropriate according to changing needs in conjunction with patient and caregiver. • Provide caregiver support to maximize ability to fulfill role with appropriate balance and satisfaction.	• Adjust caregiver roles by providing additional support services as needed to achieve maximum caregiver satisfaction.

(continued)

TABLE 8.2 *(continued)*

	Initial Identification Phase	Longitudinal Monitoring and Treatment Phase	End-of-Life Phase
Interventions	Refer to Alzheimer's Association and consider: • educational materials • counseling referral • social work referral • support group • respite and aide services • family meeting • other community referrals • home nursing referrals • PT, OT, and SLP referrals • chaplaincy referrals	Refer to Alzheimer's Association and consider: • previous interventions • chaplaincy referral	Refer to Alzheimer's Association and consider: • previous interventions • hospice referral
Response	• Assess goal attainment. • Adjust goals or strategies if goals not met.	• Assess goal attainment • Adjust goals or strategies if goals not met.	• Assess goal attainment. • Adjust goals or strategies if goals not met.

Supporting documents might include information from Alzheimer's Association Chapter, community services, and educational materials. (Community resource grid is attached.)

Note: ©1998 National Chronic Care Consortium and the Alzheimer's Association. Revised April 1999. Reprinted with permission.

assisting ADRD families. Partner staff enter information about the action steps taken to resolve issues within each domain as well as next steps and unmet needs of the patient and family. This site adaptation of the protocol creates a synergistic pathway of care that bridges partnering organizations by working back and forth together to meet patient and caregiver needs through a coordinated system.

Family Caregiver Information and Support

The final part of the model uses a conceptual framework and related tools to help the partner site identify and organize the available information, programs, and services available to support the family caregiver in the partnership service area. The advisory group selected a framework developed by Caron and his colleagues at the University of Minnesota that is based on phases of caregiving rather than stages of ADRD. This framework defines caregiving in terms of tasks and challenges faced by the family across each of six phases: prediagnostic, diagnostic, role changes, chronic caregiver, transition to alternative care, and end of life. This framework helped the CCN/AD leadership to develop yet another project tool—a grid that lists objectives for each caregiving phase and cells to specify information, programs, and services available to partners to achieve those objectives. Sites use the grids to identify resources in their communities and to determine which partner organization (e.g., the managed care partner or Alzheimer's Association chapter) will either supply appropriate referrals or actually provide the service. Empty cells in the grid identify information, programs, and services that partnerships need in their area. Encouraging staff from the different partnering organizations to complete the grid together has increased their awareness of one another's services and reduced duplication of material and services. This component of the model places primary emphasis on family caregiving tasks and challenges, thereby increasing the likelihood that information and services provided actually meet the caregiver's needs, versus providing "whatever the organization has 'on the shelf' " (Maslow & Selstad, 2001, p. 42).

In sum, CCN/AD is an exciting endeavor designed to respond to the challenges faced by primary health care providers with ADRD patients, and developed to address the concerns patients and families have expressed. Effective implementation of the CCN/AD requires extensive changes in existing health care practices and systems and maintaining strong working partnerships at each site. An extensive evaluation of the project is currently in progress. More specifically, the partners are evaluating the impact of tools, protocols, and pathways on service use, costs, provider attitudes, partner systems, and patient and caregiver outcomes in order to determine if a coordinated range of services for patients with dementia is an effective care strategy, and whether or not that strategy should be included in a Medicare HMO benefit plan. Clearly, the hope is that these improvements will result in increased patient and family satisfaction with medical care and better quality-of-life outcomes, but project outcomes, including key outcomes for family caregivers, will not be known until late 2002.

CHALLENGES TO IMPLEMENTING PRIMARY CARE INTERVENTIONS

There are multiple challenges to implementing any primary care intervention, including

TABLE 8.3 Programs and Materials for People with Alzheimer's Disease and Related Disorders—Diagnostic Phase

Objective	Program(s)*	Provided by	Appropriate Materials
1. Obtain an accurate diagnosis. Know how to get a second opinion if necessary.			
2. Understand how the diagnosis was made.			
3. Know how to approach the patient with the news.			
4. Know about possible treatments.			
5. Experience a caregiving partnership with physician, health plan, and community agencies.			
6. Begin to accept the diagnosis and the patient's limitations.			
7. Understand the need for proactive planning, including financial, legal, and care plans.			
8. Seek out supportive services as needed (early-stage support groups, education sessions, etc.).			

*All programs and materials should be adapted to meet the needs of families with different ethnic, cultural, and economic backgrounds and different primary languages.

©1998 National Chronic Care Consortium and the Alzheimer's Association. Revised April 1999. Reprinted with permission.

- the low level of knowledge about dementia by primary care providers
- limited visits by patient with dementia to the primary care setting
- the small amount of time available in the primary care setting for visits
- the lack of Medicare or insurance reimbursement for family caregiver interventions

- limited staffing for teaching intervention
- the lack of experience in partnering from primary care to the community

As can be seen from the studies cited previously, there is a lack of knowledge about dementia and dementia caregiving among primary care physicians, and there is little information targeted to help primary care physicians with this. Another impediment to implementing training about dementia in the primary care setting is the number of visits made by the care recipient during the year. Although good clinical care for older persons who are frail would suggest at least three to six visits per year for an ADRD patient, this number, in fact, is often less. For example, without the PACT protocol, the majority of ADRD patients would have been scheduled for follow-up visits every 6 to 12 months. Though the patient's health status may be relatively stable over this period of time, behavioral problems and caregiver stress are not likely to remain constant. Annual or biannual visits may not be sufficient to address ongoing or emerging problems.

The most important challenges to implementing interventions for dementia caregivers in the primary care setting are physician time and reimbursement. Reimbursement for each visit must cover all overhead expenses, including the physician's salary and salaries of all office personnel, including any individuals who would provide training for the caregiver, rent, utilities, and administrative and patient-care-related supplies. Primary care, whether in a managed care or fee-for-service setting, is based on an average visit length of 15 to 20 minutes. Reimbursement for primary care, as opposed to specialty care reimbursement, does not adequately account for the time needed to evaluate and manage these older, typically more complex patients.

Reimbursement for patient visits is based on coding patient encounters. Seven components are used in describing patient encounters to determine the CPT code to be used for billing and reimbursement. The most important determinant of level of service is complexity of medical decision making, which is based on (a) risk assessment (type and number of diagnoses, risk of complications, morbidity or mortality between now and next encounter); (b) amount and complexity of data (tests, interaction with other physicians, additional data from others); and (c) number of diagnoses and management options (number of new problems, workups required). However, for many ADRD patients, office visits are not for new medical problems but for behavioral exacerbations, and the amount of time reimbursed ranges from less than 5 minutes to a maximum of 10 minutes. Even with higher levels of complexity, reimbursement still may not cover the time spent educating the caregiver. Other types of services or visits (by the physician or other providers) that could be used for caregiver training are either not reimbursable or are reimbursed at a lower rate, or the patient must be present, which can be difficult for patients who are frail and their caregivers.

One way to address these issues of reimbursement is by the partnering of primary care and community resources. However, effective implementation of partnerships or networks like the CCN/AD requires extensive changes in existing health care practices and systems and the maintenance of strong working partnerships. Any successful partnership will require the development of tools, protocols, and pathways to assist primary care providers in diagnosis and in determining how, when, and with whom to refer or link ADRD patients and families. Even though these partnerships may offer numerous benefits, initial costs, provider attitudes, and existing administrative and clinical systems still may impede the establishment of successful networks.

STRATEGIES FOR SUCCESS

For many primary care providers, the option of educating the caregiver is not financially feasible and would threaten the economic viability of their practices. There are other options being explored that may assist primary care providers. One option is self-education of caregivers, with guidance from the primary care provider (Fillit et al., 1999a, 1999b). The framework proposed by the Alzheimer's Disease Managed Care Advisory Council (Fillit et al., 1999a, 1999b) incorporates the dissemination of materials and education through health-plan hot lines, case managers, and member newsletters, as well as self-referral to supportive community services such as day care. For many caregivers, educational materials can be overwhelming and therefore need to be limited to applicable problems and to come in small doses. The PACT pamphlets, which are problem-focused, written at a fifth-grade reading level, and printed in large type, could be used by providers to target specific problems mentioned by caregivers.

Yet another option is home care with information delivered by home care nurses on managing behavioral symptoms of dementia and reducing stress. The home environment is the perfect natural laboratory for hands-on teaching and role-playing. However, the advent in 2000 of prospective payment for home care, which provides payment per patient diagnosis instead of by visit, has strained the financial capabilities of many home care agencies and may limit their ability to provide this type of service.

Another option is team care or partnerships, that is, education delivered by various members of the health care team. Though this model may or may not be feasible in primary care (based on reimbursement issues), the health care team can be expanded by linking directly from primary care to supportive community services. The Chronic Care Networks for Alzheimer's Disease has identified four important lessons for organizations that are interested in implementing the CCN/AD partnership model within their own partnerships.

- *Stay flexible* enough to tailor the model in such a way that it will survive the rapidly changing health care environment. The model can and should be tailored to meet the needs of individual systems.
- *Size up partner resources* to determine effectively how much of the model is reasonable to do at any one time. The whole model, one tool, or several components?
- *Develop strong partnerships, identify existing infrastructures, and rally a core group of champions* before beginning to implement model components. The CCN/AD sites had already established partnerships. However even with these strong partnerships, changing health care environments often taxed the systems or changed participating partners in ways that hindered or stalled implementation. Those with existing infrastructures and champions across system levels appear to fare better.
- *Sell the benefits of enrollment* during provider education and training, as well as with patients and families. This often required partners to learn and implement basic social marketing principles. The benefits have to be clear, the process simplified for providers, and patients and families sometimes have to be given time to adjust to a diagnosis before they are willing to be plugged into a pathway that shares the information across partners, even when that pathway appears very helpful to them. We also have to recognize and appreciate family diversity, in terms of the acceptability of help-seeking and health care practices regarding dementia and family caregiving. One size clearly does not fit all. This requires ongoing staff training and consultation to meet the needs of our multicultural society effectively.

Clearly, the strategies and tools designed to implement the CCN/AD may prove useful to other individuals, groups, and systems that are trying to coordinate appropriate care for people with dementia and their family caregivers. For that reason, the project leadership charged itself with the goal of developing and quickly circulating user-friendly products, materials, tools, program descriptions and other innovations to other professionals, and disseminating project findings to managed care organizations, dementia advocates, policy makers, and health- and long-term-care providers. (Duplication of the CCN/AD tools for clinical and education purposes is authorized without prior written approval if users acknowledge the National Chronic Care Consortium and the Alzheimer's Association as the source.) CCN/AD tools and project information are available through the National Chronic Care Consortium or can be downloaded at www. ncconline.org/about/alzheimers.htm (contact information appears at the end of this chapter).

FUTURE DIRECTIONS

All these options can be subsumed under the model of disease management. Given the increased costs and greater service usage for the organization (Gutterman, Markowitz, Lewis, & Fillit, 1999; Taylor & Sloan, 2000; Weiner, Powe, Weller, Shaffer, & Anderson, 1998) and poorer quality of life for patient and caregivers, the development of a plan to manage dementia is imperative for managed care organizations (Fillit et al., 1999a). However, the management of dementia to maximize the effective use of relatively scarce and expensive resources is also critical from a community- and systems-based perspective.

The Alzheimer's Disease Managed Care Advisory Council has recently suggested a paradigm for the management of dementia by physicians or in primary care settings: chronic disease management. Disease management for chronic diseases is a comprehensive management strategy designed to reduce the effects of exacerbation of the disease and to provide a continuum of care for the disease. This model recognizes both the need for all disciplines and professionals involved to participate in caregiver care and the importance of the continuum of care. Though primary care providers may be the first person that caregivers and patients turn to, they should not be the last nor the only resource for assistance in dementia management. The chronic disease management model for dementia incorporates clinical practice guidelines for the identification, evaluation, diagnosis, and treatment of dementia, but expands these areas. The four major issues for effective medical management of dementia (Fillit et al., 1999b) include (a) recognition and diagnosis, (b) drug treatments, (c) nonpharmacological management of medical comorbidity, and (d) care of the caregiver. Although focus is on the person with dementia, there is also understanding that patient and caregiver form a unit that must be treated.

> The importance of education and support for the AD caregiver cannot be underestimated. As AD patients require more and more assistance in performing their activities of daily living, their caregivers will also require more support in handling the increased demands on their time, their possible financial problems, and their emotional strain. (Fillit et al., 1999b, p. 322)

Clearly, primary-care-based interventions must have three targets: the person with dementia, the caregiver, and the physician or primary-care provider. Families alone have difficulty meeting the multiple needs of frail elders, particularly those with dementia; rather, this responsibility must be shared by both family and professionals.

Readers can get additional information regarding caregiver needs by contacting the following organizations:

Alzheimer's Association: (800) 272-3900, www.alz.org

American Medical Association: Caregiver Health Assessment, www.ama-assn. org/ama/pub/category/4642.htm

National Family Caregivers Association: (800) 896-3650, www.nfcacares.org

National Chronic Care Consortium: 8100 26th Avenue South, Suite 120, Bloomington, MN 55425; www.nccconline.org/about/alzheimers.htm

REFERENCES

Algase, D. L. (1992). A century of progress: Today's strategies for responding to wandering behavior. *Journal of Gerontological Nursing, 18*(11), 28–34.

Alzheimer's Disease and Related Disorders Association. (1999). *Is it Alzheimer's? Warning signs you should know.* Chicago: Author.

American Medical Association. (1993). Physicians and family caregivers: A model for partnership. *Journal of the American Medical Association, 269,* 1282–1284.

American Medical Association. (1999). *Diagnosis, management and treatment of dementia.* Chicago: Author.

Aneshensel, C. S., Pearlin, L. I., Mullan, J. T., Zarit, S. H., & Whitlatch, C. J. (1995). *Profiles in caregiving: The unexpected career.* San Diego, CA: Academic Press.

Barrett, J. J., Haley, W. E., & Powers, R. E. (1996). Alzheimer's disease patients and their caregivers: Medical care issues for the primary care physician. *Southern Medical Journal, 89*(1), 1–9.

Bass, D., McCarthy, C., Eckert, S., & Bichler, J. (1994). Differences in service attitudes and experiences among families using three types of support services. *American Journal of Alzheimer's Care and Related Disorders and Research,* 28–38.

Bass, M., Noelker, L. S., & Rechlin, L. R. (1996). The moderating influence of service use on negative caregiving consequences. *Journals of Gerontology, 51,* S121–S131.

Beck, C., Baldwin, B., Modlin, T., & Lewis, S. (1990). Caregivers' perception of aggressive behavior in cognitively impaired nursing home residents. *Journal of Neuroscience Nursing, 22,* 169–172.

Beck, C., Modlin, T., Heithoff, K., & Shue, V. (1992). Exercise as an intervention for behavior problems. *Geriatric Nursing, 13,* 273–275.

Biegel, D. E., Bass, D. M., Schulz, R., & Morycz, R. (1993). Predictors of in-home and out-of-home service use by family caregivers of Alzheimer's disease patients. *Journal of Aging and Health, 5,* 419–438.

Beisecker, A. F., Chrisman, S. K., & Wright, L. J. (1997). Perceptions of family caregivers of persons with Alzheimer's disease: Communication with physicians. *American Journal of Alzheimer's Disease, 12,* 73–83.

Boise, L., Camicioli, R., Morgan, D. L., Rose, J. H., & Congleton, L. (1999). Diagnosing dementia: Perspectives of primary care physicians. *Gerontologist, 39,* 457–464.

Boise, L., Morgan, D. L., Kaye, J., & Camicioli, R. (1999). Delays in the diagnosis of dementia: Perspectives of family caregivers. *American Journal of Alzheimer's Disease, 14,* 20–26.

Bogardus, S. T., Bradley, E. H., & Tinetti, M. E. (1998). A taxonomy for goal setting in the care of persons with dementia. *Journal of General Internal Medicine, 13*, 675–680.

Bourgeois, M. S., Schulz, R., & Burgio, L. (1996). Interventions for caregivers of patients with Alzheimer's disease: A review and analysis of content, process and outcomes. *International Journal of Aging and Human Development, 43*, 35–92.

Brotman, S. L., & Yaffe, M. J. (1994). Are physicians meeting the needs of family caregivers of the frail elderly? *Canadian Family Physician, 40*, 679–685.

Callahan, C. M., Hendrie, H. C., & Tierney, W. M. (1995). Documentation and evaluation of cognitive impairment in elderly primary care patients. *Annals of Internal Medicine, 122*, 422–429.

Caron, W., Pattee, J., & Otteson, O. (2000). *Alzheimer's disease: The family journey.* Plymouth, MN: North Ridge Press.

Castleman, M., Gallagher-Thompson, D., & Naythons, M. (1999). *There's still a person in there: The complete guide to treating and coping with Alzheimer's.* New York: Putnam.

Coen, R. F., O'Boyle, C. A., Coakley, D., & Lawlor, B. A. (1999). Dementia carer education and patient behaviour disturbance. *International Journal of Geriatric Psychiatry, 14*, 302–306.

Cohen, D. (1991, May/June). The subjective experience of Alzheimer's disease. *American Journal of Alzheimer's Care and Related Disorders and Research*, 6–11.

Cohen, S., Kessler, R. C., & Gordon, L. U. (1995). *Measuring stress.* New York: Oxford University Press.

Connell, C. M., & Gallant, M. P. (1996). Spouse caregivers' attitudes toward obtaining a diagnosis of a dementing illness. *Journal of American Geriatric Society, 44*, 1003–1009.

Coon, D. W., Schulz, R., & Ory, M. G. (1999). Innovative intervention approaches with Alzheimer's disease caregivers. In D. Biegel & A. Blum (Eds.), *Innovations in practice and service delivery across the lifespan* (pp. 295–325). New York: Oxford University Press.

Costa, P. T., Williams, T. F., Somerfield, M., et al. (1996). *Recognition and initial assessment of Alzheimer's disease and related dementias: Clinical practice guideline.* Rockville, MD: U.S. Department of Health and Human Services, Public Health Service, Agency for Health Care Policy and Research. AHCPR Publication No. 97-0702. November 1996.

Cotrell, V. (1996). Respite use by dementia caregivers: Preferences and reasons for initial use. *Journal of Gerontological Social Work, 26*, 35–55.

Cox, C. (1999). Service needs and use: A further look at the experiences of African American and White caregivers seeking Alzheimer's assistance. *American Journal of Alzheimer's Disease, 14*, 93–101.

Davis, M., Eshelman, E. R., & McKay, M. (1980). *The relaxation and stress reduction workbook.* Richmond, CA: New Harbinger.

Dodd, M. J. (1988). Efficacy of proactive information on self-care in chemotherapy patients. *Patient Education Counseling, 11*, 215–225.

Dunkin, J. J., & Anderson-Hanley, C. (1998). Dementia caregiver burden: A review of the literature and guidelines for assessment and intervention. *Neurology, 511*(Suppl. 1), S53–S60.

Fillit, H., Knopman, D., Cummings, J., & Appel, F. (1999). Opportunities for improving managed care for individuals with dementia: Part 1—The issues. *American Journal of Managed Care, 5*, 309–315.

Fillit, H., Knopman, D., Cummings, J., & Appel, F. (1999). Opportunities for improving managed care for individuals with dementia: Part 2—A framework for care. *American Journal of Managed Care, 5,* 317–324.

Fortinsky, R. H. (1998). How linked are physicians to community support services for their patients with dementia. *Journal of Applied Gerontology, 17,* 480–498.

Fortinsky, R. H., & Hathaway, T. J. (1990). Information and service needs among active and former family caregivers of persons with Alzheimer's disease. *Gerontologist, 30,* 604–609.

Fortinsky, R. H., Leighton, A., & Wasson, J. H. (1995). Primary care physicians' diagnosis, management, and referral practices for older persons and families affected by dementia. *Research on Aging, 17,* 124–148.

Fortinsky, R. H., & Wasson, J. H. (1997). How do physicians diagnose dementia? *American Journal of Alzheimer's Disease, 12*(2), 51–61.

Gallagher-Thompson, D., Solano, N., Coon, D., & Árean, P. (in press). Recruitment and retention of Latina dementia family caregivers in intervention research: Issues to face, lessons to learn. *Gerontologist.*

Glasser, M., Rubin, S., & Dickover, M. (1989). Caregiver views of help from the physician. *American Journal of Alzheimer Care and Related Disorders, 4,* 4–11.

Goode, K. T., Haley, W. E., Roth, D. L., & Ford, G. R. (1998). Predicting longitudinal changes in caregiver physical and mental health: A stress process model. *Health Psychology, 17,* 190–198.

Gottman, J., Notorius, C., Gonso, J., & Markman, H. (1976). *A couple's guide to communication.* Champaign, IL: Research Press.

Graham, C., Ballard, C., & Sham, P. (1997). Carers' knowledge of dementia, their coping strategies and morbidity. *International Journal of Geriatric Psychiatry, 12,* 931–936.

Gutterman, E. M., Markowitz, J. S., Lewis, B., & Fillit, H. (1999). Cost of Alzheimer's disease and related dementia in managed-Medicare. *Journal of the American Geriatric Society, 47,* 1065–1071.

Haley, W. E., Clair, J. M., & Saulsberry, K. (1992). Family caregiver satisfaction with medical care of their demented relatives. *Gerontologist, 32,* 219–226.

Hamilton, E. M., Braun, J. W., Kerber, P., Thurlow, C., & Schwieterman, I. (1996). Factors associated with family caregivers' choice not to use services. *American Journal of Alzheimer's Disease, 11,* 29–38.

Hiromoto, B. M., & Dungan, J. (1991). Contract learning for self-care activities. A protocol study among chemotherapy outpatients. *Cancer Nursing, 14,* 148–154.

Knopman, D., Donohue, J. A., & Gutterman, E. M. (2000). Patterns of care in the early stages of Alzheimer's disease: Impediments to timely diagnosis. *Journal of the American Geriatric Society, 48,* 300–304.

Kolanowski, A., Hurwitz, S., Taylor, L. A., Evans, L., & Strumpf, N. (1994). Contextual factors associated with disturbing behaviors in institutionalized elders. *Nursing Research, 43*(2), 73–79.

Kottke, T. E., Battista, R. N., DeFriese, G. H., & Brekke, M. L. (1988). Attributes of successful smoking cessation interventions in medical practice: A meta-analysis of 39 controlled trials. *Journal of the American Medical Association, 259,* 2883–2889.

Lazarus, E. B., & Launier, R. (1978). Stress-related transactions between persons and environment. In L. Pervin & M. Lewis (Eds.), *Perspectives in international psychology* (pp. 287–325). New York: Plenum Press.

Levine, C., & Zuckerman, C. (1999). The trouble with families: Toward an ethic of accommodation. *Annals of Internal Medicine, 130*, 148–152.

Mace, N., & Rabins, P. (1999). *The 36-hour day—A family guide to caring for persons with Alzheimer's disease, related dementing illnesses, and memory loss in later life* (3rd ed.). Baltimore: Johns Hopkins Press.

Maslow, K., & Selstad, J. (2001). Chronic Care Networks for Alzheimer's Disease: Approaches for involving and supporting family caregivers in an innovative model of dementia care. *Alzheimer's Care Quarterly, 2*, 33–46.

McGovern, R. J., & Koss, E. (1994). The use of behavior modification with Alzheimer patients: Values and limitations. *Alzheimer's Disease Associated Disorders, 8*(Suppl. 3), 82–91.

Miller, B., Glasser, M. L., & Rubin, S. M. (1992). A paradox of medicalization. *Journal of Aging Studies, 6*, 135–148.

Rossby, L., Beck, C., & Heacock, P. (1992). Disruptive behaviors of a cognitively impaired nursing home resident. *Archives of Psychiatric Nursing, 6*(2), 98–107.

Schulz, R., Gallagher-Thompson, D., Haley, W., & Czaja, S. (2000). Understanding the interventions process: A theoretical/conceptual framework for intervention approaches to caregiving. In R. Schulz (Ed.), *Handbook on dementia caregiving: Evidence-based interventions for family caregivers* (pp. 33–60). New York: Springer.

Schulz, R., O'Brien, A. T., Bookwala, J., & Fleissner, K. (1995). Psychiatric and physical morbidity effects of dementia caregiving: Prevalence, correlates, and causes. *Gerontologist, 35*, 771–791.

Shank, C. J., Murphy, M., & Schulte-Mowry, L. (1991). Patient preferences regarding educational pamphlets in family practice center. *Journal of Family Practice, 23*, 429–432.

Silliman, R. A. (1989). Caring for the frail older patient: The doctor-patient-family caregiver relationship. *Journal of.General Internal Medicine, 4*, 237–241.

Small, G. W., Rabins, P. V., Barry, P. P., Buckholtz, N. S., DeKosky, S. T., Ferris, S. H., Finkel, S. I., Gwyther, L. P., Khachaturian, Z. S., Lebowitz, B. D., McRae, T. D., Morris, J. C., Oakley, F., Schneider, L. S., Streim, J. E., Sunderland, T., Teri, L. A., & Tune, L. E. (1997). Diagnosis and treatment of Alzheimer's disease and related disorders: Consensus statement of the American Association for Geriatric Psychiatry, the Alzheimer's Association, and the American Geriatrics Society. *Journal of the American Medical Association, 278*, 1363–1371.

Stone, R., Cafferata, G. L., & Sangl, J. (1982). Caregivers of the frail elderly: A national profile. *Gerontologist, 27*, 616–626.

Strumpf, N. E. (1994). Innovative gerontological practices as models for health care delivery. *Nursing Health Care, 15*, 522–527.

Taylor, D. H., & Sloan, F. A. (2000). How much do persons with Alzheimer's disease cost Medicare? *Journal of the American Geriatric Society, 48*, 639–646.

Teri, L. (1994). Behavioral treatment of depression in patients with dementia. *Alzheimer's Disease Associated Disorders, 8*(Suppl. 3), 66–74.

Teri, L., Logsdon, R., & Yesavage, J. (1997). Measuring behavior, mood, and psychiatric symptoms in Alzheimer disease. *Alzheimer Disease and Associated Disorder, 11*(Suppl. 6), 50–59.

Teri, L., Truax, P., Logsdon, R., Uomoto, J., Zarit, S., & Vitaliano, P. P. (1992). Assessment of behavioral problems in dementia: The revised memory and behavior problems checklist. *Psychology of Aging, 7,* 622–631.

U.S. Dept of Veterans Affairs. (1997). *Dementia identification and assessment: Guidelines for primary care practitioners.* Oak Brook, IL: University Health System Consortium.

Vitaliano, P. P., Young, H. M., Russo, J., Romano, J., & Magana-Amato, A. (1993). Does expressed emotion in spouses predict subsequent problems among care recipients with Alzheimer's disease? *Journals of Gerontology, 48,* 202–209.

Webber, P. A., Fox, P., & Burnette, D. (1994). Living alone with Alzheimer's disease: Effects on health and social service utilization patterns. *Gerontologist, 34,* 8–14.

Weiner, M., Powe, N. R., Weller, W. E., Shaffer, T. J., & Anderson, G. F. (1998). Alzheimer's disease under managed care: Implications from Medicare utilization and expenditure patterns. *Journal of the American Geriatric Society, 46,* 762–770.

Wind, A. W., Van Staveren, G., Jonker, C., & Van Eijk, J. T. M. (1994). The validity of the judgement of general practitioners on dementia. *Journal of Geriatric Psychiatry, 9,* 543–549.

Wykle, M. L. (1996). Interventions for family management of patients with Alzheimer's disease. *International Psychogeriatrics, 8*(Suppl. 1), 109–111.

Wykle, M. L., & Segall, M. (1991). A comparison of Black and White family caregivers experience with dementia. *Journal of National Black Nurses Association, 5,* 29–41.

Zarit, S., & Teri, L. (1991). Interventions and services for family caregivers. In K. W. Schaie (Ed.), *Annual review of gerontology and geriatrics* (pp. 241–265). New York: Springer.

9

Capitalizing on Technological Advances

Ann Steffen, Diane Feeney Mahoney, and Kathleen Kelly

The following challenges may appear familiar to those who work with family caregivers of patients with dementia:

• Iris, aged 59, cares for her 85-year-old mother in a rural community. Although Iris likes the idea of attending educational and support programs for dementia caregivers, she lives an hour away from the nearest caregiver support group. Because Iris finds it difficult to arrange for someone to be with her mother and doesn't like traveling when the weather is bad, she attends caregiver programs only rarely.

• John, 62, is employed and rushes home at lunchtime every day to check on his wife who is in the early stages of Alzheimer's. He knows that he should be learning more about the disease and making plans, but his evenings and weekends involve being with his wife and taking care of basic household tasks. He also feels guilty leaving his wife alone in the evening to attend educational programs, since they spend so much time away from each other during the day. He wishes there were easier ways to access information and support without having to leave his home.

• Wilma, who is 79, cares for her husband who was diagnosed with Alzheimer's disease 5 years ago. Her daughter lives nearby and helps with things like shopping and doctor's visits, but Wilma worries about asking her to help out more because her daughter also works full-time and has her own family. Wilma doesn't drive any more, and doesn't take public transportation at night because she feels unsafe in her part of the city.

The situations experienced by Iris, John, and Wilma are quite common among caregivers. Many families cannot participate in the traditional approach to caregiver support services (i.e., where the caregiver needs to be physically present to obtain information, consult with professionals, or attend a support group). For families living in rural areas, distance can compound already difficult transportation needs and add to the caregiver's sense of isolation (Buckwalter, Russell, & Hall, 1994). Mental health services for caregivers are unavailable in most rural communities, and rural caregivers are also less likely to have the financial and insurance resources to afford the services that do exist. Others caregivers, including those from urban areas, lack transportation or patient respite care. For caregivers who are juggling demands at work and in the home, research has shown that less flexibility, control, and support at work are associated with caregiving-related role strain (Fredriksen & Scharlach, 1997). This chapter considers how recent technological advances can be used to provide services to family caregivers of patients with dementia. We first present a very brief introduction to technology use by middle-aged and older adults and dementia caregivers in particular. Three examples of technology-based services are explored in depth: REACH for TLC (Telephone-Linked Care); Link2Care Internet-based information and referral; and Coping With Frustration, a psychoeducational intervention that uses video, bibliotherapy, and telephone sessions. We conclude this chapter with recommendations for providing technology-based services for caregivers and suggest priorities for future research in this area.

TECHNOLOGY USE BY OLDER ADULTS

As the 1990s witnessed a period of rapid development and deployment of computer technology, concerns were raised about the digital divide—the lack of access to, affordability of, and use of technology by underserved populations including older adults (U.S. Department of Commerce, 1995). However, there is evidence that many middle-aged and older adults are quite receptive to at least some forms of modern technology (Czaja, 1997; Kelly, 1997; Zimmer & Chappell, 1999). Research on interest in the use of technology by middle-aged and older adults has led to a proposed field of *gerontechnology*, defined as "the study of technology and aging for the improvement of the daily functioning of the elderly" (Bouma, 1993, p. 1). This interest is upheld by recent usage statistics. For example, compared to 18- to 24-year-olds, middle-aged computer users are likely to spend an average of 6.3 more days per month on the Internet and stay logged on 235 minutes longer (Media Metrix, 2000).

Few technology-based services for dementia caregivers have been described in the research literature. Nursing home studies conducted through the Veterans Administration have demonstrated marked reduction in residents' Alzheimer-related behavioral problems when their attention was distracted by a "pseudo-conversation" (Camberg & Volicer, 1994). A conversation with a family member is taped and played through a stereo headset placed on the resident when he or she becomes agitated. This concept of playing a pseudo-conversation to reduce agitation was transformed into an automated distraction telephone conversation as part of the Telephone-Linked Care project described later in this chapter. In the early 90s, only one federally funded technology project, known as ComputerLink, had been designed for, and evaluated with, dementia caregivers (Brennan, Moore, & Smyth, 1991). It offered the user decision support, an electronic encyclopedia on AD, and an e-mail communication component that became the most frequently used option (Brennan, Moore, & Smyth, 1995). Access to a computer network resulted in higher levels of perceived support for Alzheimer's caregivers (Gallienne, Moore, & Brennan, 1993). Interestingly, when comparisons were made between the use of the Computerlink by Alzheimer caregivers and caregivers for persons with AIDS, AD caregivers reported that they could spend less time on the system (Brennan & Ripich, 1994). Smyth and Harris (1993) offered a more practice-oriented description of this telecomputing-based service.

REACH FOR TLC (TELEPHONE-LINKED CARE)

An Alzheimer's nurse specialist once mentioned how her answering machine frequently recorded messages between 2 a.m. and 4 a.m. from family caregivers. She quoted one as saying, "I know that you are not there but I just need to vent right now!" Like other professionals working with dementia caregivers, this nurse wished that there were programs for caregivers during the night, on weekends, or at other times when direct contact is not possible. Her wish, the research of others, and the request from the National Institute on Aging for innovative technological applications for Alzheimer's disease caregivers (National Institutes of Health, 1994) became the genesis for a telephone-based intervention system.

REACH for TLC is an automated telephone-communication system designed to help family caregivers of people with Alzheimer's disease who display disruptive behaviors. The telephone system offers several features: (a) advice to caregivers on ways to manage troublesome behaviors frequently associated with Alzheimer's disease, (b) an automated but personalized conversation for the person with AD to distract them from a disruptive episode, and (c) voice-mail connection to a caregiver support group and a panel of experts in geriatric care.

BACKGROUND AND PROJECT DEVELOPMENT

A decade of prior research has resulted in the development of automated telephone calls for patients in monitoring hypertension, dietary intake, and health care behaviors. Two randomized clinical trials demonstrated positive outcomes with this approach (Friedman, Stollerman, Mahoney, & Rozenblyum, 1997). Although the content varies among the applications, the general structure of the conversation is to greet the patient who calls in, request them to enter their password, conduct the core conversation, and then offer closing remarks. REACH for TLC, however, is the first application developed to support caregivers rather than patients, to offer a variety and range of conversations from 1 minute to 10 minutes, and to remain active for a 12-month period. TLC also extended the capacity of the monitoring system to include the voice-mail applications and a respite call.

The content for an advice component was developed from multiple sources, including information on strategies to manage disruptive behaviors (Hall, 1988; Hall & Buckwalter, 1987), environmental adaptations (Stolley & Buckwalter, 1992), and resource materials from the National Alzheimer's Association and the Alzheimer's Disease Education and Referral Center (ADEAR) sponsored by the National Institute on Aging. Advice about caregiver issues and strategies for managing disruptive behaviors were gleaned from a caregivers' Web site (Mahoney, 1998). Two traditional focus groups were held locally with Alzheimer's disease caregivers to obtain feedback on the design features and intervention components. The overall system design and the advice content were critiqued by a multidisciplinary advisory board of experts from the fields of nursing, pharmacy, medicine, psychology, neurology, nutrition, and behavioral medicine.

Target Audience of REACH for TLC

To be eligible for the project, caregivers had to report that they were (a) a current primary caregiver of a family member with Alzheimer's disease, (b) caregiving for at least 6 months, (c) providing a minimum of 4 hours of care per day, (d) capable of using a telephone and had telephone access, (e) planning to remain in the area for at least 6 months, and (f) caring for a patient displaying at least one distressing behavior. Caregivers were excluded if they did not live with the care recipient, had a terminal illness, were undergoing cancer therapy, had three or more hospitalizations in the past year, or were involved in another caregiver intervention study.

DESCRIPTION OF THE PROGRAM

The REACH for TLC system is a telephone-linked computerized system that gives caregivers access to a four-part intervention through their regular home telephone using ordinary telephone lines. The four modules are as follows:

1. *Caregiver Monitoring and Counseling Module.* Once a week, participating caregivers call into REACH for TLC and it queries caregivers about problematic behaviors exhibited by the care recipient. If none are detected, the caregiver is reminded about the other system options and given a choice to switch to them or end the conversation. If problematic behaviors are detected, the program branches to offer information about strategies to reduce them. If over a 2-week period, the caregiver reports increasing stress or care-recipient behavioral problems, a computer-generated alert will be sent to the provider previously identified by the caregiver. If the situation continues in week 3, the system triage nurse is alerted to make a follow-up call to the provider's office to ensure awareness.

2. *Caregiver Voice-Mail Bulletin Board.* Designed to be an in-home support group, any participating caregiver can anonymously ask all participating TLC caregivers a question about caregiving issues or offer advice in response to questions by other caregivers. They can also send and receive personal messages to others on the system through their individual mailbox.

3. *Ask-the-Expert Module.* Caregivers can call into the triage nurse's voice-mail and leave a question for the nurse or the experts. The nurse specialist will monitor this line and either respond directly or triage the call to the appropriate expert on our advisory board and ensure that the questions are answered in a timely manner.

4. *Activity/Distraction Module.* This is an 18-minute conversation intended to engage the person with AD in a simple nondemanding conversation designed to distract the person from disruptive behavior. The conversation is individualized and uses the care recipient's name and fosters the recollection of favorite memories such as favorite activities, people, flowers, foods, and holidays. The system starts when the caregiver calls in and tells the care recipient that the telephone call is for him or her and presses 1 on the touch-tone telephone keypad. The conversation is designed to proceed even if the care recipient does not verbalize any responses. For nonverbal users, strategically placed pauses allow the conversation to continue by holding their attention. For verbal users, as soon as they

respond the system proceeds to the next conversation point. The system will also adapt if a verbal user then changes to a nonverbal one; a paused timing feature is automatically implemented to continue the conversation.

DESCRIPTION OF THE TECHNICAL SYSTEM

The system is activated when a caregiver dials in and enters her or his system password. The call is then routed through the telecommunications department telephone network at the host site, using a PBX mechanism. The caregiver is offered a choice of menu items using the module numbering described previously. If the caregiver chooses the voice mail options (2 and 3), which rely exclusively on the telephone network, then the telephone network remains the interface between the caller and those modules. When the caregiver selects the caregiver counseling (option 1) or the care recipient's distraction module (option 4), the call is transferred to the interactive voice response (IVR) computer network. The IVR subsystem contains digitizing voice hardware to decode telephone touch-tone data and to process prerecorded human voice messages. The system asks questions that the participant answers by pressing the corresponding number on the telephone keypad (e.g., 1 for yes, 2 for no). This information is stored and then compared against existing data; if there are any discrepancies or if preset parameters are exceeded, alert reports are generated. The database is updated every 24 hours to ensure that accurate and current information is available for the next conversation. Details on the specification of the TLC system architecture are available (Friedman et al., 1997; Mahoney, Tarlow, & Sandaire, 1998).

CHALLENGES TO IMPLEMENTATION

When implementing innovative systems, technical problems are always to be expected. However, field problems are more likely to be unique. We contacted numerous providers and found some who were reluctant to refer caregivers to the project. These professionals expressed concerns about the use of computers and believed that we were trying inappropriately to substitute technology for their humanistic care. Also, competition for family caregivers was high, with more than 15 other research teams in our area simultaneously recruiting Alzheimer's family caregivers or their care recipients for other projects. We found less interest among caregivers who had previously had to hide the telephone due to the care recipient's inappropriate verbalizations or frustrations in attempting to use it; these caregivers worried about misuse by the care recipient. Details on recruitment and technical implementation issues, along with a discussion about strategies used to address them, can be found in the literature (Mahoney, 2000; Tarlow & Mahoney, 2000).

INTEGRATION INTO PRACTICE AND FUTURE USES

The system was designed to complement social and medical providers who serve AD caregivers. Other TLC systems have gained the interest of managed care programs because they can monitor large groups of individuals who are at-risk and signal alerts to the providers only when needed. In our project, we monitored a small group ($N = 49$). This meant that we had few but meaningful alerts. For example, stress patterns for two caregivers increased significantly and triggered the system's alert notice. When the system triage nurse called the providers to ensure that the faxed message was received, she was informed that one of the caregivers was known to be having problems, but they had not heard from her during the Christmas period. Her mother was beginning to have mild but frequent paranoid delusions that were resulting in anger outbursts. As a result of the alert and subsequent discussion with the caregiver, the physician started the caregiver's mother on a new course of treatment, which improved her condition. In the other situation, the provider called in to tell our triage nurse how appreciative she was for the alert. The caregiver and care recipient had received a home visit the month before, and there had been no indications that more was needed before the next routine 3-month follow-up. The TLC system, however, recorded a recent onset of hitting behaviors by the care recipient and related increased distress by the caregiver. The team's geriatric nurse practitioner made an immediate home visit, verified the problem, and therapeutic and resource supports were implemented that day. The caregiver felt safe telling the system about the problem but had been uncomfortable about making a call "to complain." Without the monitoring, there would have been another 2 months of unnecessary stress and probably escalating abuse for the caregiver before the situation was discovered.

PRELIMINARY RESULTS

Our major outcome results (as supported by the National Institute on Aging) will be reported as part of the forthcoming REACH multisite study findings (Gitlin et al., in press). However, at this time we are able to report findings from our site-specific analyses on the adoption of technology. We found strong support for our hypothesis that there would be differential adoption of the various components that comprise the TLC technology according to users preferences and needs. We had believed that caregiving needs and related intervention tools change over the course of AD family caregiving and one intervention would not fit everyone's needs. Our qualitative and quantitative evaluation supported this premise. The caregiver-monitoring and the care-recipient distraction telephone conversation were most utilized. Whereas differential adoption did occur as expected, the characteristics of the adopters were unexpected. Contrary to our hypothesis regarding the influence of user characteristics, we did find evidence that those with greater perceived management of the situation adopted the intervention. We had believed that those with greater resources and perceived abilities would be less likely to need and use another form of support. In fact, it is plausible that because these caregivers do avail themselves of new opportunities, they are more likely to find support that meets their needs. Finally, use of the intervention was also related to being older, having more years of education and, most important, receiving a proficiency rating following the user training. Being male approached significance. Prior technology experience, caregiver relationship, perceived stress, and sources and types of counseling exerted no influence on usage (Mahoney, Tarlow, & Jones, 2001).

Technology is evolving so quickly that by the time a system is fully developed, implemented, and tested, the current system is obsolete. Many of the technical compatibility problems we experienced during our 5-year development period are now being resolved, and future applications should be less difficult to implement. As wireless technology improves, a stand-alone respite-distraction telephone programmed specifically for the care recipient would overcome the reluctance to share the family telephone.

LINK2CARE

Link2Care is a computer-based service demonstration project that uses a secure Website to provide information, services, and support to caregivers of adults with dementia. Funded by the California Endowment, Link2Care brings together three innovative programs: Family Caregiver Alliance's (FCA) successful service model, information clearinghouse, and Web site; the University of Wisconsin's Comprehensive Health Enhancement Support System (CHESS); and the California Caregiver Resource Centers (CRC) to provide a groundbreaking service for caregivers of adults with dementia.

BACKGROUND AND PROJECT DEVELOPMENT

Family Caregiver Alliance is a nationally recognized nonprofit organization known for serving families and caregivers of cognitively impaired adults through education, advocacy, services, and research. Family Caregiver Alliance has been operating an open Web site at www.caregiver.org since 1996; this site primarily serves informal caregivers who are dealing with the long-term-care needs of their family member. The Web site features several sections: in-depth information about cognitive impairments; care planning and management; public policy; research updates; topical interviews with experts in health care, social services, advocacy and policy; and information specific to a San Francisco Bay Area audience (i.e., a local service directory of respite and support group resources and an events calendar of educational programs, conferences, and workshops). FCA began offering an on-line group in 1998; this group offered insight into the needs of isolated caregivers who were using the Internet as a means of communication, information gathering, and support. The following excerpts are typical of the comments made by on-line caregivers: "Hi, I just found the caregiver support group. I am so glad to find an online group, as it's very hard for me to go anywhere anymore. My mother has lived with my husband and me for 12 years and has started to decline rapidly this last year. She has trouble remembering what day or year this is—I am only 40 and have not been able to have a real life of my own . . . I guess I just need someone else to talk to besides my husband"; and "My computer and this list [FCA on-line group members] are my lifeline." In addition to the comments from the online group members, FCA receives and responds to e-mail requests from caregivers across the United States.

Target Audience of Link2Care

The target population for Link2Care is (a) adults aged 18 or older who (b) define themselves as a primary caregiver (either a relative, friend, or partner) for an adult with (c) dementia (from Alzheimer's, frontotemporal dementia, Lewy-body dementia, stroke, Parkinson's, Huntington's disease, or other related dementia). These caregivers also need to (d) live in the 40-county catchment area of the five participating Caregiver Resource Centers, (e) be a client of a participating Caregiver Resource Center (have completed an intake and client assessment process by a CRC family consultant), and (f) have access to a computer or Internet appliance and to the Internet.

DESCRIPTION OF THE PROGRAM

The overall goal of Link2Care is to increase caregiver well-being and coping skills through convenient access to information, connections to other caregivers, and services provided in the home via electronic delivery. Link2Care was built upon the consumer health information system CHESS (Comprehensive Health Enhancement Support System), developed by the Department of Industrial Engineering and Preventive Medicine at the University of Wisconsin-Madison. In other health modules developed for consumers such as the one for HIV-positive patients, researchers found that those users of CHESS could improve their quality of life and promote more efficient use of the health care system by using a computerized system that provided information, decision support, connections to health professionals, and peer support (Gustafson et al., 1999). The primary objectives of Link2Care are to (a) decrease caregivers' perceptions of isolation through connections to other caregivers and the CRC family consultants, (b) increase access to information and advice on issues related to caregiving, and (c) increase caregivers' coping and planning skills. The secondary goals are to develop, implement, and evaluate an effective Internet-based service delivery system that is capable of wider replication and to explore and document the impact on clinical staff (e.g., training needs, change in professional-client interaction, etc.).

Link2Care is used to complement services delivered by the CRCs; it is meant to provide an enriched information and support environment that is readily available and convenient to the caregiver. In order to use Link2Care, family caregivers must complete the intake process (usually by telephone) and an in-home assessment, culminating with the development of a care plan by a CRC family consultant. The care plan may call for a caregiver to receive a mix of services provided either by the CRC or through referral to other community service programs. It is at the point of assessment that the caregiver is referred to Link2Care and can register to participate online. Link2Care is a password-secured Internet site that provides a number of features. There are six main sections to the site:

1. *Decision and Planning Guides* ("Decisions, Decisions—Your Planning Guide"; "Ask an Expert"). The decision and planning guides component contains a self-paced decision support program focusing on the issues of facility placement. The program uses three steps: (a) it identifies if the caregiver is in a situation that may limit his or her options or lead more rapidly to a decision to place, (b) it provides a framework to examine the relative importance of a variety of considerations influencing placement decisions, and (c) it provides suggestions on how best to use that information and what additional resources may be helpful. The next interactive program in this section is a self-paced action plan. First, a caregiver identifies an area for change, such as stress reduction or using community services. Next, the program leads the user through a number of issues related to making changes in their caregiving situation. Based on the responses, the user receives a "chance of success rating" with strengths and areas of improvement identified. Users can return and modify any variable to reevaluate their action plan and work through the program on any caregiving issue.

"Ask an Expert" provides the caregiver with access to technical expertise in the areas of medicine, law, and social services. Caregivers may post a question on any topic to be forwarded to the panel. The experts for the Link2Care program are drawn from the Caregiver Resource Centers and can handle questions about care planning, family issues, basic resource information, care management, and related social support concerns. The legal experts are drawn from attorneys who specialize in elder law and have worked with caregivers on issues of estate planning, conservatorships, durable powers of attorney, and other related issues. Medical experts cover the specialties of neurology, geriatrics, pharmacology, psychology, and nursing and answer questions concerning diagnosis, treatment, medications, physical care management, behavioral problems, and related medical issues. Basic memoranda of understanding have been executed between Family Caregiver Alliance (as the Link2Care project administrator) and the Caregiver Resource Centers, the Alzheimer's Research Centers in northern California, and the law firm of Kato & Feder to provide technical answers on a pro bono basis during the life of the project.

2. *Taking Care of Yourself* (assessments; journaling; tips). This section of the site focuses on caregiver self-care needs. There is a quick screening for depression, with resulting recommendations for services in the community and within the Link2Care site. An easy-to-use journaling section allows caregivers to write about their experiences; this information can then be saved and viewed only by the user. The journaling section has entry pages that have some identifying information such as what mood the caregiver was in that day and what the high and low points were for the day. The journaling section also has exercises to aid in writing an entry. And finally, the journal section can be searched by words in the journal entries or by moods, allowing the user to go back to identify trends. The last subsection of Taking Care of Yourself contains self-care tips for the caregiver on a wide variety of topics.

3. *Caregiver Connections* (personal stories; caregiver discussion groups). The first feature in this section involves personal stories that reflect individual accounts of caregiving; the user can click on highlighted topics to get additional information. For example, a story about a grandfather with Alzheimer's disease may have a subtopic about how families with young children can cope with dementia. In this Caregiver Connections section, there are also two discussion groups using different formats. First, there is a bulletin board format for an open discussion group moderated by a peer support group leader. The second group is facilitated by CRC staff and runs on a *listserv* (e-mail) format. These groups center on specific topics such as depression, anger management, using community services, placement, and other related caregiving issues.

4. *Reading Room* (overview of dementia; questions and answers; instant library; Web links). The Reading Room contains in-depth information about diagnoses. Caregivers can obtain quick references in the overview of dementia section and can then get more information in the questions and answers section. The instant library contains a wide range of articles on these topics; articles are used with authors' permission. The Web links section provides live links to

reviewed and qualified sites, covering topics such as general health, assistive technologies, elder abuse, and others.

5. *Community Resources* (resource directory; consumer guide; events calendar; Caregiver Resource Centers). The Community Resources section allows caregivers to search the CRC database of 40 northern and central California counties for service information. The database is maintained by each CRC for their geographical area and combined at the site level. The consumer guide contains information for caregivers deciding to use services (e.g., tips for what to look for in a day care program). An events calendar lists conferences, special groups, workshops, videoconferences, and other programs for the entire catchment area. Finally, this section also includes in-depth information about the Caregiver Resource Center services and staff.

6. *Beginners Guide* (basic Web skills; About Link2Care). This section is available for those caregivers who are new to using the Internet and need some basic tips. Information about all the partners involved in Link2Care is also provided.

DESCRIPTION OF THE TECHNICAL SYSTEM

Clients of a Caregiver Resource Center can participate in Link2Care by on-line registration through Family Caregiver Alliance's Web site. There are three steps to the registration process. First, users are asked to read and acknowledge the waiver form; this provides background information about Link2Care and the assessment data used for evaluation of the project. Next, users are asked to complete the registration form, including selection of a code name and password. After the code name and password is sent to FCA, verification of client status with a Caregiver Resource Center is completed and an e-mail confirmation of registration is sent. After the registration process is completed, Link2Care participants are free to use the site. Although the site is self-explanatory, users may ask for a participant manual and technical assistance from FCA via an 800 number.

CHALLENGES TO IMPLEMENTATION

The challenges to implementation have been twofold. First, there were technical challenges to merging several distinct sections and programs from existing Web sites. Cross-platform compatibility issues needed to be worked out as well as a protocol for updating site information. The second challenge was to train CRC staff who were participating in the Link2Care project on how to market the service, understand the components of the site, and how to work with clients using electronic means. On the issue of marketing, CRC staff spoke directly with clients about the Link2Care program, had computers with Internet access for demonstrating Link2Care at public events, sent direct mailings to clients and community service providers, placed articles in their newsletters, and disseminated press releases to the local media about the project.

INTEGRATION INTO PRACTICE AND FUTURE USES

With the majority of U.S. households having access to the Internet and the increase in the numbers of baby boomers facing long-term-care decisions for themselves and their older relatives, Internet-based applications are attractive for professionals and families alike. However, there are not yet empirical data supporting the use of these services for family caregivers. The area has not been studied in a methodologically rigorous way, and there is a clear need to controlled outcome studies. This idea-rich, data-poor status is changing rapidly as the funding community becomes comfortable with technology projects and as federally funded projects come to fruition. The current estimates of one in four families facing long-term-care issues make the Internet a particularly attractive and cost-effective platform for a variety of services (e.g., communicating with caregivers, providing training on care issues, monitoring high-risk health situations in the home, and supporting caregivers in the provision of long-term-care services).

COPING WITH FRUSTRATION

This program is a combined video, telephone, and bibliotherapy format that was developed to provide dementia caregivers with a psychoeducational intervention for anger and frustration. There is a growing literature on the use of telephone-based physical (Guy, 1995) and mental health services for older adults (Evans, Smith, Werkhoven, Fox, & Pritzl, 1986). A small preliminary study has explored the usefulness of an anger management intervention that relies on video, written, and telephone-based coaching and that can be offered in group settings or in caregivers' homes (Poth & Steffen, 2000; Steffen, 2000).

BACKGROUND AND PROJECT DEVELOPMENT

Gallagher-Thompson and DeVries (1994) have described a cognitive-behavioral group treatment for anger in family caregivers. This psychoeducational intervention teaches relaxation, cognitive restructuring, and assertion skills in a class format using an accompanying workbook (Gallagher-Thompson et al., 1992a,

1992b). By targeting a number of common situations (e.g., behavioral problems of the dementia patient, lack of assistance from family members, etc.), the intervention helps participants apply these skills to their ever-changing caregiving environment. Preliminary data from the Coping with Frustration classes indicated that the anger management program reduced hostility and improved caregivers' level of confidence in their ability to provide quality care. This intervention was originally developed to be offered in small group settings in the community; the treatment package was then turned into an 8-week videotaped series with accompanying workbook so that it could be tested for use with homebound dementia caregivers.

Target Audience of Coping With Frustration

This project involved family caregivers who volunteered to participate in a research study for stress-management intervention. Criteria for inclusion were as follows: participant must (a) self-report to be providing at least 5 hours per week of face-to-face direct care for a cognitively impaired older relative diagnosed with Alzheimer's Disease, multiinfarct dementia, or some other dementing illness; (b) be able to describe at least one patient behavior or caregiving situation in the past 2 weeks that was upsetting or stressful for the caregiver; (c) have access to a working television and VCR weekly for 8 weeks; (d) exhibit no evidence of psychosis, cognitive impairment, alcoholism, immediate suicidal risk, or bipolar disorder; (e) not be concurrently in psychotherapy; (f) if receiving psychotropic medication, be stabilized on same dose for at least 12 weeks; (g) be willing to accept random assignment to conditions; and the patient (h) had to be living in the community (i.e., not in a nursing home or assisted-living facility).

DESCRIPTION OF THE PROJECT

The 8-week video and workbook program includes instruction and homework assignments on awareness training, tension-reduction strategies (i.e., relaxation training, thought-stopping and distraction techniques), cognitive-change strategies (i.e., cognitive restructuring and self-instructional training), and assertion training. Each weekly video segment lasts 30 minutes; the series includes use of a primary presenter, guest presenters for specific components, brief interviews with a confederate "caregiver," and an enacted role-play of assertion skills. All examples use caregiving-specific situations to describe and model cognitive-behavioral strategies for anger management. The actual viewing of each weekly video segment includes approximately 10 minutes of didactics, 5 minutes of caregiving-relevant examples, 10 minutes of guiding participants through self-monitoring assignments and worksheets, and 5 minutes of imagery-based relaxation practice. In each weekly segment, participants are instructed several times to pause the video, turn to specific pages in their workbook, and complete specific worksheets.

An accompanying workbook (Gallagher-Thompson et al., 1992b) provides reading material and worksheets. For each session, several pages of related reading materials are provided (e.g., session 1 covers a review of the various stressors associated with providing care; session 2 reading provides information about anger and the role of relaxation, etc.). This didactic material was written specifically for the workbook and was designed to be easily understood (i.e., sixth-grade reading level, frequent use of subheadings and summaries). The workbook also includes worksheets that correspond to specific self-monitoring assignments discussed in the video (i.e., examining unhelpful thinking patterns, recognizing anger-eliciting situations and signs of anger, practicing relaxation). Blank pages are included in the workbook so that participants can take notes while watching the video. Together, the video series and accompanying workbook were developed with older adults in mind and use several modifications of treatment strategies to accommodate differences between younger and older adults. These modifications include a slower pacing of material, repetition, and multimodal presentation of material (Zeiss & Steffen, 1996).

Home-based viewers receive all eight video segments and the workbook at the time of their first assessment and are instructed to watch one segment each week for 8 weeks. Trained staff make weekly phone calls to monitor progress and problem-solve any difficulties with viewing the videos or completing the weekly assignments. Weekly monitoring sheets are completed at the time of each staff telephone contact with participants in the home-viewing condition. Staff indicate the date that each segment was viewed, whether the participant watched the video more than once, and any problems with the video or work sheets. Staff also note participants' responses to questions about the reading, self-monitoring assignments, and relaxation practice in order to monitor homework compliance. In the class-based viewing condition, participants meet weekly for 8 weeks for 90 minutes in small groups (4 or 5 caregivers per group) with a trained facilitator present at each meeting. In this setting, each video segment is viewed, new information is reviewed verbally, and caregivers are asked to provide examples and discuss the homework assignment from the previous week. Participants in this condition do not have contact with the facilitator or any project staff between group meetings.

Challenges to Implementation

Of the three projects described in this chapter, the Coping With Frustration video intervention is the least technologically complex. This means that there are few technical challenges associated with the project. For example, even the low-income caregivers who contacted us about the project had VCRs and were able to participate in the intervention; none of the caregivers who requested information on this "stress management program" were ineligible for not having a VCR. (We did have one caregiver whose VCR broke in the middle of the intervention and had to problem-solve with her regarding repair decisions.) Review of staff monitoring forms indicated that home-based participants watched the segments as instructed and had a high rate of compliance with homework assignments.

The biggest challenge in implementing this intervention is its apparent simplicity in the eyes of caregivers. Individuals who are familiar with educational videos and offerings on television expect the series to be primarily informational, rather than focused on cognitive and behavioral change strategies. This means that many caregivers have to be oriented to the differences between educational or informational videos and the present intervention that focused on active behavior change. For example, caregivers have to be coached and encouraged to watch only the targeted video segment for each week, rather than peeking ahead to see what the next video is about. Similarly, participants need to understand and really believe that watching the video is only the first step of each weekly intervention—that they cannot expect to benefit from the program unless they also read the accompanying workbook and complete the weekly behavioral assignments (e.g., relaxation practice, thought records, assertion practice). In other words, professionals and caregivers alike need to understand that the combined program as a whole is involved in stress reduction, and that the video per se is not likely to be the primary mechanism for change. For these same reasons, it is not recommended that videos and workbooks be offered without the scheduled weekly telephone sessions that are used to coach the caregiver through the details of the intervention.

PRELIMINARY RESULTS

Research with a small sample ($N = 33$) of caregivers provides initial support for this mechanism to deliver psychoeducational interventions for caregivers (Steffen, 2000). The results of this preliminary study suggest that family caregivers may benefit from innovative anger management interventions based on cognitive-behavioral principles and techniques. The Coping With Frustration video and bibliotherapy intervention resulted in family caregivers feeling less depressed and angry and more confident of their ability to handle caregiving challenges (Steffen, McKibbin, Zeiss, Gallagher-Thompson, & Bandura, 2002) than caregivers who didn't receive the intervention. Both the home-based and class-based formats showed advantages over a wait-list control condition for most outcome measures.

INTEGRATION INTO PRACTICE AND FUTURE USES

For professionals who may be interested in group-based applications of the project, more information is needed to compare the in-home versus group mechanisms for cost-effectiveness. Staff-participant contact time can easily be estimated for the home and class-viewing conditions, but other information is also germane to a cost/benefit analysis. Per participant, more staff time was spent in phone calls to home-viewers than in class with group-viewers. However, the logistics of arranging class sites and scheduling classes also required an additional effort. These nuances of intervention provision will be important for clinicians who are deciding on an optimal treatment format.

Additional research is currently under way to test a revised video and workbook series that includes a greater focus on management of dementia patients' behavior problems (Steffen et al., 2001). The distance-learning features of the program (i.e., no face-to-face contact) also allow us to examine differences in the responses of rural and urban caregivers across nine midwestern and central states.

DISCUSSION

In our introduction to this chapter, we suggested that many middle-aged and older adults are already frequent and avid users of technology, including computer-based services. This is likely to expand dramatically over the coming 10 to 20 years. As the next cohort of caregivers age, advanced telephone and computer technologies will be viewed increasingly as assets. Social and health care providers in the future are also likely to understand the benefits of technology-assisted programs, rather than fearing them as cumbersome or dehumanizing. In addition, access to the Internet is expected to be easier and more affordable, leading to the development of more Internet-based applications for caregivers.

Most professionals are well aware of the challenges associated with the dynamic nature of dementia care; caregiving situations can be quite heterogeneous. In addition, the progressive nature of the dementias means that families have to revise old coping strategies and continually adapt to new demands. The research literature suggests that older adults are more receptive to technology if they perceive it to be useful (Czaja, Guerrier, Nair, & Landauer, 1993). This highlights the importance of flexibility in technology-based interventions for dementia caregivers. In caregiving situations, families value interventions that can be adapted to their unique situation (Mahoney & Shippee-Rice, 1994; Mahoney, Shippee-Rice, & Pillemer, 1988). Interventions for family caregivers, whether they are more tradition- or technology-based and whether they use telephone or the Internet, need to include mechanisms for tailoring the intervention to the specific needs of participants.

Research examining the effectiveness of technology-based services for dementia caregivers is still in its infancy. However, the few available studies offer preliminary results that are quite promising. Bass, McClendon, Brennan, and McCarthy (1998) found that participation in a computer support network reduced strain in some caregivers. Mahoney (1998) has reported that caregivers who are early technology adopters are likely to value highly an Internet-based support group. This is meaningful information, because Mahoney's caregivers' represent a wide geographical range, and many were users who did not want the intimacy or bother of arranging face-to-face contacts. Thus, the Internet offers a new means of offering services to those whose needs are not met by traditional services. As research in this area expands, we will draw a better understanding of how to effectively package and target these technologies for specific audiences and how to develop programs for caregivers with limited resources. Research suggests that education and income are related to awareness and adoption of new technologies (Zeithaml & Gilly, 1987). For example, Festervand and Wylde (1988) identified two groups of older adults who are more likely than others to use new technology: (a) younger, more affluent older adults with prior experience with technology, and (b) socially active seniors. By contrast, Mahoney and colleagues, as described earlier, found no effect from prior experience with technology, and their users tended to be older rather than younger (Mahoney et al., 2001). Their key finding to TLC intervention adoption was successful training. The approach to training took into consideration geriatric teaching and learning principles with a successful user return demonstration a key component of the orientation session. Clearly, the field is still in the early stages of discovery per each new intervention. As more attention is paid to the evaluation aspects and the similarities and differences in outcomes and user characteristics, we will be better able to develop clinically useful and efficacious interventions.

The field of informatics primarily targets business users and younger adults as its prime audience. Technological developments specifically targeted to older adults are still rare, and user evaluation of standard features even rarer. We hope that the systems described here will help stimulate the design of more caregiving systems with rigorous user evaluations so that we can continue to learn about the best means to enhance family caregiving through technology.

Professionals in the field of aging and long-term care will need to incorporate the use of technology into their own individual practices and in their communication with clients. When applying new technologies in conjunction with traditional sources of support such as counseling, case management, education, and so on, agency staff will need to be trained in the use of the technology. This training should be provided within the context of an organizational culture that supports its use with equipment and technical support. Any staff reluctance to change the way business is done has to be overcome by providing training opportunities and creating buy-in for change. Services provided by use of technology applications have to be seen as a complement to their role and as a way to provide more tailored, on-demand support and communication to clients. Technology-based applications are here to stay. Now is the time for professionals to shape how this technology will be used in new and creative ways to benefit caregivers.

ACKNOWLEDGMENT

Research discussed in this chapter was supported by the National Institute of Aging (AG13255, D. Mahoney, Principal Investigator), The National Institute of Mental Health (MH61956, A. Steffen, Principal Investigator), and the Missouri Alzheimer's Research Program (A. Steffen, Principal Investigator).

REFERENCES

Bass, D. M., McClendon, M. J., Brennan, P. F., & McCarthy, C. (1998). The buffering effect of a computer support network on caregiver strain. *Journal of Aging and Health, 10,* 20–43.

Bouma, H. (1993). Gerontechnology: A framework on technology and aging. In H. Bouma & J. A. Graafmans (Eds.), *Gerontechnology* (pp. 1–6). Amsterdam: ISO Press.

Brennan, P., Moore, S., & Smyth, K. (1991). Computerlink: Electronic support for the home caregiver. *Advances in Nursing Science, 13,* 14–27.

Brennan, P., Moore, S., & Smyth, K. (1995). The effects of a special computer network on caregivers of persons with Alzheimer's disease. *Nursing Research, 44,* 166–172.

Brennan, P. F., & Ripich, S. (1994). The use of a home care network by persons with AIDS. *International Journal of Technology Assessment in Health Care, 10,* 258–272.

Buckwalter, K. C., Russell, D., & Hall, G. (1994). Needs, resources, and responses of rural caregivers of persons with Alzheimer's disease. In E. Light, G. Niederehe, & B. D. Lebowitz (Eds.), *Stress effects on family caregivers of Alzheimer's patients* (pp. 301–315). New York: Springer.

Camberg, L., & Volicer, L. (1994). Selected memories to manage problem behaviors in Alzheimer's disease. [Monograph]. Health Services Research and Development Program, Brockton-West Roxbury Veterans Administration Medical Center.

Czaja, S. J. (1997). Using technologies to aid the performance of home tasks. In A. D. Fisk & W. A. Rogers (Eds.), *Handbook of human factors and the older adult*. San Diego, CA: Academic Press.

Czaja, S. J., Guerrier, J. H., Nair, S. N., & Landauer, T. K. (1993). Computer communication as an aid to independence for older adults. *Behavior and Information Technology, 12,* 197–207.

Evans, R. L., Smith, K. M., Werkhoven, W. S., Fox, H. R., & Pritzl, D. O. (1986). Cognitive telephone group therapy with physically disabled elderly persons. *Gerontologist, 26,* 8–11.

Festervand, T. A., & Wylde, M. A. (1988). The marketing of technology to older adults. *International Journal of Aging and Technology, 1,* 156–162.

Fredriksen, K. I., & Scharlach, A. E. (1997). Caregiving and employment: The impact of workplace characteristics on role strain. *Journal of Gerontological Social Work, 28,* 3–22.

Friedman, R., Stollerman, J., Mahoney, D. F., & Rozenblyum, L. (1997). The virtual visit: Using telecommunications technology to take care of patients. *Journal of the American Medical Informatics Association, 4,* 413–425.

Gallagher-Thompson, D., & DeVries, H. M. (1994). "Coping with frustration" classes: Development and preliminary outcomes with women who care for relatives with dementia. *Gerontologist, 34,* 548–552.

Gallagher-Thompson, D., Rose, J., Florsheim, M., Gantz, F., Jacome, P., Del Maestro, S., Peters, L., Argüello, D., Johnson, C., Moorehead, R. S., Polich, T. M., Chesney, M., & Thompson, L. W. (1992a). *Controlling your frustration: A class for caregivers: Leaders manual.* Palo Alto, CA: Department of Veterans Affairs Medical Center.

Gallagher-Thompson, D., Rose, J., Florsheim, M., Gantz, F., Jacome, P., Del Maestro, S., Peters, L., Argüello, D., Johnson, C., Moorehead, R. S., Polich, T. M., Chesney, M., & Thompson, L. W. (1992b). *Controlling your frustration: A class for caregivers: Participant workbook.* Palo Alto, CA: Department of Veterans Affairs Medical Center.

Gallienne, R. L., Moore, S. M., & Brennan, P. F. (1993). Alzheimer's caregivers: Psychosocial support via computer networks. *Journal of Gerontological Nursing, 19,* 15–22.

Gitlin, L. N., Burgio, L., Czaja, S., Mahoney, D., Gallagher-Thompson, D., Burns, R., Hauck, W. W., Belle, S. H., Schulz, R., & Ory, M. G. (in press). Effect of multi-component interventions on caregiver burden and depression: The REACH multi-site initiative at six months follow-up. *Psychology and Aging.*

Gustafson, D. H., Hawkins, R., Boberg, E., Pingree, S., Serlin, R., Graziano, F., & Chan, C. L. (1999). Impact of a patient-centered, computer-based health information/support system. *American Journal of Preventive Medicine,16,* 1–9.

Guy, D. H. (1995). Telephone care for elders: Physical, psychosocial and legal aspects. *Journal of Gerontological Nursing, 21,* 27–34.

Hall, G. R. (1988). Care of the patient with Alzheimer's disease living at home. *Nursing Clinics of North America, 23,* 31–46.

Hall, G. R., & Buckwalter, K. (1987). Progressively lowered stress threshold: A conceptual model for care of adults with Alzheimer's disease. *Archives of Psychiatric Nursing, 1,* 399–406.

Kelly, K. (1997). Building aging programs with online information technology. *Generations, 21,* 15–18.

Mahoney, D. F. (1998). A content analysis of an Alzheimer family caregivers virtual focus group. *American Journal of Alzheimer's Disease, 13,* 309–316.

Mahoney, D. F. (2000). Developing technology applications for intervention research: A case study. *Computers in Nursing, 18,* 260–264.

Mahoney, D. F., & Shippee-Rice, R. (1994). Training family caregivers of older adults: A program model for community health nurses. *Journal of Community Health Nursing, 11,* 71–78.

Mahoney, D. F., Shippee-Rice, R., & Pillemer, K. (1988). *Training family caregivers: A manual for group leaders.* Manchester, NH: University of New Hampshire Press.

Mahoney, D. F., Tarlow, B., & Jones, R. N. (2001). Factors affecting the use of a telephone-based intervention for caregivers of people with Alzheimer's disease. *Journal of Telemedicine and Telecare, 7,* 139–148.

Mahoney, D. F., Tarlow, B., & Sandaire, M. S. (1998). A computer-mediated intervention for Alzheimer's caregivers. *Computers in Nursing, 16,* 208–215.

Media Metrix. (2000). Media metrix Web report: January 1999—December 1999. [Online]. Retrieved February 5, 2001. Available: www.mediametrix.com

National Institutes of Health. (1994, August 12). Enhancing family caregiving for Alzheimer's disease and related disorders. RFA AG-94-003. *NIH Guide, 33*(30).

Poth, T., & Steffen, A. M. (2000). Anger management in dementia caregivers: A case study. *Clinical Gerontologist, 22,* 83–87.

Smyth, K. A., & Harris, P. B. (1993). Using telecomputing to provide information and support to caregivers of persons with dementia. *Gerontologist, 33,* 123–127.

Steffen, A. M. (2000). Anger management for dementia caregivers: A preliminary study using video and telephone interventions. *Behavior Therapy, 31,* 281–299.

Steffen, A. M., Gant, J. R., Coon, R. W., Gallagher-Thompson, D., Thompson, L., Burgio, L., & Stevens, A. (2001). *The dementia caregiving skills program: Reducing stress and enjoying time with your family member.* St. Louis: University of Missouri.

Steffen, A. M., McKibbin, C., Zeiss, A. M., Gallagher-Thompson, D., & Bandura, A. (2002). The revised scale for caregiving self-efficacy: Reliability and validity studies. *Journal of Gerontology: Psychological Sciences, 57B,* P74–P86.

Stolley, J., & Buckwalter, K. (1992). Confusion management. In G. Bulechek & J. McCloskey (Eds.), *Nursing interventions* (pp. 120–134). Philadelphia: W. B. Saunders.

Tarlow, B., & Mahoney, D. F. (2000). The cost of recruiting Alzheimer's disease caregivers for research. *Journal of Aging and Health, 12,* 450–510.

U.S. Department of Commerce, National Telecommunications and Information Administration. (1995). Falling through the net: A survey of the "have nots" in rural and urban America [electronic file]. Washington, DC: NTIA. Available: gopher://ntiaunix2.ntia.doc.gov as urb-rur.txt [text only].

Zeiss, A. M., & Steffen, A. M. (1996). Treatment issues with elderly clients. *Cognitive and Behavioral Practice, 3,* 371–389.

Zeithaml, V. A., & Gilly, M. C. (1987). Characteristics affecting the acceptance of retailing technologies: A comparison of elderly and nonelderly consumers. *Journal of Retailing, 63,* 49–68.

Zimmer, Z., & Chappell, N. L. (1999). Receptivity to new technology among older adults. *Disability and Rehabilitation, 21,* 222–230.

10

Anticipatory Grief and Loss: Implications for Intervention

Julia Kasl-Godley

Dementia, and the concomitant changes in cognitive, interpersonal, and psychological functioning, are a source of chronic stress for individuals afflicted with the disease (LaBarge & Trtanj, 1995) and for family members involved in their care (e.g., Pearlin, Mullan, Semple, & Skaff, 1990). These changes often are experienced as losses for both the person with dementia and the caregiver, particularly within the context of the caregiver/care-recipient relationship. The experience of loss is itself a source of distress (Farran, Keane-Hagerty, Salloway, Kupferer, & Wilken, 1991; Gonyea, 1989). The manner in which caregivers experience and manage their grief reactions to these pre-death losses can influence not only caregiving outcomes but also subsequent adjustment to bereavement once the care recipient has died. This interdependence between pre-death grief and post-death adaptation suggests that caregiving and bereavement be viewed on a continuum, as part of a single chronic stressful situation (Bass, Bowman, & Noelker, 1991). This viewpoint argues for greater convergence among caregiving and bereavement interventions (Schulz, Newsom, Fleissner, Decamp, & Nieboer, 1997). However, with few exceptions, interventions for caregivers do not reflect this need. Rarely is management of the caregiver's changing relations with the individual who is demented and the associated losses a specific target of intervention. This chapter will explore issues of pre-death grief and loss in caregivers of patients with dementia and the implications for caregiver intervention.

EXPERIENCE OF LOSS

Caregivers of those with dementia experience an accumulation of losses. Many of these losses are interpersonal in nature, affecting the caregiver's relationship with the care recipient, family members, and the larger social network. These losses include loss of social and recreational activities, loss of family unity, loss of a way of life, loss of control, loss of roles, and a loss of the person with dementia through progressive declines in the person's cognitive, psychological, social, and physical functioning and ultimately, through death (Bull 1998; Loos & Bowd, 1997).

One area in which these losses are felt the most is the relationship between the caregiver and person with dementia. Caregivers describe changes in communication and interaction (Williamson & Schulz, 1993), disrupted roles and identity as a partner and companion (Gwyther, 1990; Rudd, Viney, & Preston, 1999), diminished intimacy and emotional closeness (Morris, Morris, & Britton, 1988; Mullan, 1992; Wright, 1991), and lost reciprocity (Bledin, MacCarthy, Kuipers, & Woods, 1990; Gallagher-Thompson, DalCanto, Jacob, & Thompson, 2001). These changes can produce chronic stress on the relationship and negatively affect the caregiver. For example, a worsening of the quality of the relationship between the caregiver and care recipient is associated with increased caregiver burden (Draper, Poulos, Poulos, & Ehrlich, 1995). Lack of emotional closeness and intimacy between the caregiver and care recipient has been found to be associated with increased caregiver resentment (Williamson & Schulz, 1990), anger, and difficulty performing the caregiving role (Morris et al., 1988).

Some caregivers effectively cope with these losses. They report doing so by staying involved in family and social activities, accommodating role changes, finding ways to sustain their relationship with the person with dementia (Bull, 1998), maintaining a sense of importance and meaning in the caregiving role (Collins, Liken, King, & Kokinakis, 1993), and coming to terms with the diagnosis, through a process of acceptance, adjustment, letting go (Morgan & Laing, 1991). Other caregivers have a much more difficult time managing their losses. In this chapter, we argue that the degree to which caregivers are able to cope effectively and adapt to relationship and role changes and losses is determined, to a large extent, by how caregivers manage their grief around these losses.

PRE-DEATH GRIEF REACTIONS

Traditionally, pre-death grief has been defined as anticipatory grief, or the cognitive and emotional reactions to losses other than death associated with caring for someone with a terminal illness. Anticipatory grief seems to be triggered by an individual's growing awareness of the impending loss of a loved one and the associated losses in the past, present, and future (Rando, 1986). It is characterized by guilt, depression, sorrow, anger, hostility, anxiety, mourning the absence of the ill person in the future, feelings of loss, and decreased ability to function at usual tasks. Anticipatory grief can occur at the time of diagnosis of the terminal disease and then at each exacerbation of the disease, with each subsequent loss potentially triggering reactions from previous losses and anticipation of future losses. Anticipatory grief is thought to serve several functions, which include (a) resolving unfinished business or difficult aspects of the interpersonal relationship; (b) decreasing attachment to the terminally ill person; and (c) redirecting energy into other relationships (Fulton & Gottesman, 1980). The assumption is that this process prepares individuals for the death of the terminally ill person and facilitates adaptation to bereavement.

Several quantitative and qualitative investigations of caregivers for people with dementia have found anticipatory grief—particularly from loss of companionship with the care recipient and the care recipient's loss of functional abilities—to be a common and relatively constant occurrence (Jones & Martinson, 1992; Lindgren, Connelly, & Gaspar, 1999; Theut, Jordan, Ross, & Deutch, 1991). The type of anticipatory grief reaction experienced is associated with particular mental and physical health consequences (Walker & Pomeroy, 1997). For example, caregivers experiencing anger and guilt in response to loss are more distressed and have more acute physical health problems than caregivers who are accepting of losses (Walker & Pomeroy, 1997). In addition to anticipatory reactions, caregivers show a variety of grief behaviors that may assist them in preparing for the death of the care recipient, including discussing with someone the possibility that the care recipient would die, thinking about what the future will be like without the care recipient, and discussing death with the care recipient (Ponder & Pomeroy, 1996).

FACTORS THAT INFLUENCE PRE-DEATH GRIEF REACTIONS

One might ask why some caregivers experience anger or guilt whereas other caregivers experience acceptance. One factor likely to influence the type of grief reaction experienced is the caregiver's appraisal or perception of the meaning of the loss. For example, a caregiver who attributes the care recipient's diminished abilities, such as forgetting to write down a phone message, to laziness or disrespect may experience anger whereas a caregiver who attributes the behavior to the disease process may experience acceptance. Caregivers' appraisal of, and reaction to, dementia-related changes may be determined in part by cultural norms and expectations of caregiving such as caregiving ideology (Haley et al.,

1996; Lawton, Rajagopal, Brody, & Kleban, 1992) and quality of the caregiver/ care-recipient relationship prior to the onset of the disease.

Studies of ethnic differences in caregiving have found that in comparison to Caucasians, African American caregivers experience greater caregiving mastery and satisfaction, less subjective burden, and less sense of intrusion on their lives (Lawton et al., 1992). It has been speculated that these differences may be due to African Americans' more readily incorporating the impaired person into their daily lives and family systems (Dilworth-Anderson & Anderson, 1994) and more strongly holding a traditional caregiver ideology (Lawton et al., 1992). Unfortunately, none of the existing studies on grief in caregivers of patients with dementia examined the influence of ethnicity and cultural norms on expressions and experience of grief and associated caregiving impact.

The quality of the relationship prior to the illness has been found to influence both the initial reaction to the diagnosis and response over time. In comparison to caregivers with a good prior relationship, caregivers with a poor prior relationship experience less empathy and more conflict with the care recipient, have a harder time accepting the disease and letting go, and are more distressed (Morgan & Laing, 1991). Additionally, in comparison to caregivers with an affectionate prior relationship, caregivers with less affectionate prior relationships show greater negative aspects of grief (anger, hostility, depersonalization, and social isolation) (Lindgren et al., 1999). The nature of the premorbid relationship and the care recipient's ability to respond to caring and affectionate behaviors influence the process of maintaining connection and letting go (Jones & Martinson, 1992), which is an important focus for grief interventions.

Another factor that may influence the type of grief reaction experienced is the intensity of caregiving demands. The intensity of demands of caregiving may make it difficult to process losses and may preclude detachment and redirection of energy to other relationships (Collins et al., 1993) or into grieving. In fact, caregivers of patients with dementia report difficulty with acceptance of dementia and associated losses regardless of length of time caregiving (Ponder & Pomeroy, 1996), which suggests that it may be difficult to move beyond anger and guilt (or at least make room for other grief reactions). A final factor that may impact the grief process is the reduced cognitive capacity of the person with dementia. This impairment limits the caregiver's and care recipient's ability to address unfinished business, though this limitation will vary with the care recipient's degree of impairment. Unfinished business may be particularly problematic if the caregiver/care-recipient relationship is characterized by ambivalence and conflict.

Collectively, particular factors are likely to influence caregivers' grief reactions to dementia-related losses other than death; these grief reactions are likely to impact caregivers' adjustment to loss and to coping with caregiving. This coping response, in turn, is likely to influence adaptation to bereavement. Thus, interventions that target these factors pre-death likely will assist caregivers both in coping with dementia-associated losses and subsequent adaptation to bereavement.

ASSOCIATION BETWEEN PRE-DEATH AND POST-DEATH GRIEF REACTIONS

The association between pre-death grief reactions and post-death adaptation has been documented in a few prospective studies of grief and bereavement in caregivers for community-dwelling and institutionalized persons with dementia. These studies have found that characteristics of the caregiving experience prior to the death of the care recipient influence caregivers' functioning after the death of the care recipient (bereavement). These characteristics include depression and guilt, caregiving role overload and strain, a diminished sense of personal mastery, ambivalence and guilt about nursing home placement, relationship complications (past conflict, guilt, and regret specific to the caregiver/care-recipient relationship), and feelings of loss of intimacy and separation from the care recipient (Aneshensel, Pearlin, Mullan, Zarit, & Whitlatch, 1995; Bass & Bowman, 1990; Mullan, 1992; Pruchno, Moss, Burant, & Schinfeld, 1995). Interestingly, loss of intimacy with the care recipient pre-death has been found to be associated with lower distress and depression and a greater sense of mastery at bereavement. Experiencing a sense of loss suggests that the caregivers have processed their grief over the loss, which is a goal of grief interventions.

These findings suggest that particular characteristics of, or reactions to, caregiving are associated with poor adaptation to bereavement. This association likely results when caregiving erodes the caregiver's social and psychological resources (e.g., mastery), which are the very resources that the caregiver must call upon to cope with bereavement (e.g., Bass & Bowman, 1990; Mullan, 1992). For example, the association between pre-death grief and post-death adaptation appears to be influenced by the degree of social support received (social resource), with the relationship holding with high but not low levels of support from family and friends both during caregiving and after the death of the care recipient (Collins et al., 1993).

One could conceptualize anticipatory grief reactions using this same model; that is, anticipatory grief reactions to dementia-associated interpersonal losses may mitigate or exacerbate caregiving stress, which in turn influences post-bereavement adaptation. For example, grief reactions during caregiving could impact role and relationship strains. Acceptance of loss and letting go could reduce strain and promote a sense of mastery or competence whereas anger or guilt could create further strain, diminishing the caregiver's sense of competence and increasing distress. This diminished sense of mastery may make it harder to adjust to the role changes that accompany bereavement (e.g., negotiating new relationships) and may lead to continued rumination about caregiving even when the caregiver is bereaved. Ruminative guilt has been found to be associated with persistence of depressive symptoms, greater perceived stress, and greater social isolation during bereavement (Bodnar & Kiecolt-Glaser, 1994). Taken together, it seems likely that the caregiver's ability to identify, express, tolerate, and manage negative grief reactions and to increase healthy grief behaviors would reduce caregiving role and relationship strain, which may in turn reduce distress and promote mastery.

BEREAVEMENT INTERVENTIONS

Despite the evidence that pre-death grief affects post-death adaptation, caregiver interventions have not systematically addressed pre-death grief. The limited consideration of the continuity between pre-death and post-death experiences may explain in part the limited effectiveness of interventions for the bereaved (none of which target or are limited to dementia caregivers). A recent review of this literature found in general that bereavement interventions show relatively weak effect sizes (Kato & Mann, 1999), though the authors caution that many of the studies were atheoretical and methodologically flawed.

A PILOT PROGRAM

By way of example, we highlight an 8-week pilot group designed to assist caregivers in managing grief reactions. The group was advertised for caregivers wanting help "dealing with grief, sadness, anger and guilt due to loss through death or placement of the person with dementia." Eligible participants were either caring for someone in the moderate to late stages of dementia or were bereaved. We included both current and bereaved caregivers under the assumption that the grief process and strategies to promote adaptation to loss are similar in both continuing and bereaved caregivers. This assumption is supported by findings among caregivers of cancer patients but remains an empirical question in dementia caregivers.

At present, we have completed two rounds of the group, with a total of 13 caregivers participating. All participants were women, the majority of whom were Caucasian and adult daughters caring for institutionalized parents. During the first round, the groups met weekly for 1 1/2 hours for 6 weeks. Based on feedback from the first round, the second round was lengthened; the group met weekly for 2 hours for 8 weeks. The group consisted of supportive discussion, psychoeducation, cognitive restructuring, art therapy, and resource dissemination. Supportive discussion allowed participants to share current concerns in a supportive atmosphere. Psychoeducation served to educate participants about grief and loss and to normalize reactions. Art therapy was used to access difficult or painful emotional reactions and to process them in a contained manner, the assumption being that inherent in the creation of art objects is a distancing and objectification of feelings that may make strong or difficult emotions easier to discuss. Cognitive restructuring was used to illustrate the ways in which beliefs or attributions influence feelings and how modifying beliefs can alter feelings and make them more manageable. Depressive symptoms and grief reactions were assessed, respectively, using the short form of the Geriatric Depression Scale and the present feelings towards loss section of the Texas Revised Inventory of Grief (TRIG). Assessments were conducted before the group started (pretest), at the end of the group (posttest), and then at 3-month follow-up.

Based on our experience with this group, we found a combination of supportive discussion or psychoeducation, art therapy, and cognitive restructuring to be beneficial in assisting caregivers in managing their grief and reducing distress. All group members demonstrated substantial declines in depressive symptomology. Reductions of unresolved feelings of grief also were observed in many participants. Although the assessment results are considered tentative given the small sample size and lack of a comparison group, they were consistent with the participants' reports on a measure evaluating the group. Comments included "A real necessity for families dealing with a dementia relative"; "I wish that it was continuing"; "Your effort has made a world of difference for me. Please, please don't stop helping people—you have so much to give."

CONCLUDING REMARKS

Caregivers experience grief in response to dementia-associated interpersonal losses. The type of grief reaction experienced can mitigate or exacerbate caregiving stressors and further diminish or bolster psychological and interpersonal resources, which in turn influence bereavement adaptation. Thus, in order to maximize coping with losses in caregiving and the likelihood of adaptation of bereavement, caregivers should be helped to identify and experience their reactions to loss while finding meaning in the caregiving role and continued, albeit altered, connection with the person with dementia. To date, however, caregiving interventions have not specifically addressed pre-death grief as a factor that influences caregiving outcomes, nor have they attempted to modify its impact on caregiving as a way to facilitate adaptation to bereavement.

Interventions are needed that explore interpersonal losses and remaining connections, facilitate identification and expression of grief reactions, teach distress tolerance and skill development (e.g., accessing and creating support, management of roles), and generally promote adaptive aspects of pre-death grief and reduce maladaptive aspects. Interventions should consider appraisals or perception of loss, expressions of loss and the associated sociocultural influences, history of loss, type of grief reactions and behaviors, level of care-recipient impairment, intensity of caregiving demands, and relationship history and quality. Available resources, some of which are specific to dementia caregiving, include Worden's (1991) grief counseling approach, Rando and colleagues' work on anticipatory grief (e.g., Rando, 1986); Gallagher-Thompson and associates' psychoeducational approach to affect regulation (Gallagher-Thompson et al., 1992a, 1992b; Gallagher-Thompson, Ossinalde, & Thompson, 1996); and nursing guidelines for managing grief and loss in dementia caregivers (Cutillo-Schmitter, 1996; Liken & Collins, 1993; Walker, Pomeroy, McNeil, & Franklin, 1994a, 1994b).

REFERENCES

Aneshensel, C. S., Pearlin, L. I., Mullan, J. T., Zarit, S. H., & Whitlatch, C. J. (1995). *Profiles in caregiving: The unexpected career.* San Diego, CA: Academic Press.

Bass, D. M., & Bowman, K. (1990). The transition from caregiving to bereavement: The relationship of care-related strain and adjustment to death. *Gerontologist, 30,* 35–42.

Bass, D. M., Bowman, K., & Noelker, L. S. (1991). The influence of caregiving and bereavement support on adjusting to an older relative's death. *Gerontologist, 31,* 32–42.

Bledin, K. D., MacCarthy, B., Kuipers, L., & Woods, R. T. (1990). Daughters of people with dementia. Expressed emotion, strain and coping. *British Journal of Psychiatry, 157,* 221–227.

Bodnar, J. C., & Kiecolt-Glaser, J. K. (1994). Caregiver depression after bereavement: Chronic stress isn't over when it's over. *Psychology and Aging, 9,* 372–380.

Bull, M. A. (1998). Losses in families affected by dementia: Coping strategies and service issues. *Journal of Family Studies, 4,* 187–199.

Collins, C., Liken, M., King, S., & Kokinakis, C. (1993). Loss and grief among family caregivers of relatives with dementia. *Qualitative Health Research, 3,* 236–253.

Cutillo-Schmitter, T. A. (1996). Managing ambiguous loss in dementia and terminal illness. *Journal of Gerontological Nursing, 22,* 32–39.

Dilworth-Anderson, P., & Anderson, N. B. (1994). Dementia caregiving in Blacks: A contextual approach to research. In B. Lebowitz, E. Light, & G. Niederehe (Eds.), *Stress effects on family caregivers of Alzheimer's patients* (pp. 385–409). New York: Springer.

Farran, C. J., Keane-Hagerty, E., Salloway, S., Kupferer, S., & Wilken, C. S. (1991). Finding meaning: An alternative paradigm for Alzheimer's disease family caregivers. *Gerontologist, 31,* 483–489.

Fulton, R., & Gottesman, D. J. (1980). Anticipatory grief: A psychosocial concept reconsidered. *British Journal of Psychiatry, 137,* 45–54.

Gallagher-Thompson, D., Rose, J., Florsheim, M., Jacome, P., DelMaestro, S., Peters, L., Gantz, F., Argüello, D., Johnson, C., Moorehead, R. S., Polich, T. M., Chesney, M., & Thompson, L. W. (1992a). *Controlling your frustration: A class for caregivers: Leaders manual.* Palo Alto, CA: VA Palo Alto Health Care System.

Gallagher-Thompson, D., Rose, J., Florsheim, M., Jacome, P., DelMaestro, S., Peters, L., Gantz, F., Argüello, D., Johnson, C., Moorehead, R. S., Polich, T. M., Chesney, M., & Thompson, L. W. (1992b). *Controlling your frustration: A class for caregivers: Participant workbook.* Palo Alto, CA: VA Palo Alto Health Care System.

Gallagher-Thompson, D., Ossinalde, C., & Thompson, L. W. (1996). *Coping with caregiving: A class for family caregivers.* Palo Alto, CA: VA Palo Alto Health Care System.

Gallagher-Thompson, D., Dal Canto, P. G., Jacob, T., & Thompson, L. W. (2001). A comparison of marital interaction patterns between couples in which the husband does or does not have Alzheimer's disease. *Journal of Gerontology: Psychological Sciences, 56,* 140–150.

Gonyea, J. G. (1989). Alzheimer's disease support groups: An analysis of their structure, format and perceived benefits. *Social Work in Health Care, 14*(1), 61–72.

Gwyther, L. P. (1990). Letting go: Separation-individuation in a wife of an Alzheimer patient. *Gerontologist, 30,* 698–702.

Haley, W. E., Roth, D. L., Coleton, M. I., Ford, G. R., West, C. A. C., Collins, R. P., & Isobe, T. L. (1996). Appraisal, coping, and social support as mediators of well-being in Black and White family caregivers of patients with Alzheimer's disease. *Journal of Consulting and Clinical Psychology, 64,* 121–129.

Jones, P. S., & Martinson, I. M. (1992). The experience of bereavement in caregivers of family members with Alzheimer's Disease. *IMAGE: Journal of Nursing Scholarship, 24,* 172–176.

Kato, P. M., & Mann, T. (1999). A synthesis of psychological interventions for the bereaved. *Clinical Psychology Review, 19,* 275–296.

LaBarge, E., & Trtanj, F. (1995). A support group for people in the early stages of dementia of the Alzheimer's type. *Journal of Applied Gerontology, 14,* 289–301.

Lawton, M. P., Rajagopal, D., Brody, E., & Kleban, M. H. (1992). The dynamics of caregiving for a demented elder among Black and White families. *Journal of Gerontology: Social Sciences, 47,* S156–S164.

Liken, M. A., & Collins, C. E. (1993). Grieving: Facilitating the process for dementia caregivers. *Journal of Psychosocial Nursing and Mental Health Services, 31,* 21–26.

Lindgren, C. L., Connelly, C. T., & Gaspar, H. L. (1999). Grief in spouse and children caregivers of dementia patients. *Western Journal of Nursing Research, 21,* 521–537.

Loos, C., & Bowd, A. (1997). Caregivers of persons with Alzheimer's disease: Some neglected implications of the experience of personal loss and grief. *Death Studies, 21,* 501–514.

Morgan, D. G., & Laing, G. P. (1991). The diagnosis of Alzheimer's disease: Spouse's perspectives. *Qualitative Health Research, 1,* 370–387.

Morris, R. G., Morris, L. W., & Britton, P. G. (1988). The relationship between marital intimacy, perceived strain and depression in spouse caregivers of dementia sufferers. *British Journal of Medical Psychology, 61,* 231–236.

Mullan, J. T. (1992). The bereaved caregiver: A prospective study of changes in well-being. *Gerontologist, 32,* 673–683.

Pearlin, L. I., Mullan, J. T., Semple, S. J., & Skaff, M. M. (1990). Caregiving and the stress process: An overview of concepts and their measures. *Gerontologist, 30,* 583–594.

Ponder, R. J., & Pomeroy, E. C. (1996). The grief of caregivers: How pervasive is it? *Journal of Gerontological Social Work, 27,* 3–21.

Pruchno, R. A., Moss, M. S., Burant, C. J., & Schinfeld, S. (1995). Death of an institutionalized parent: Predictors of bereavement. *Omega, 31*(2), 99–119.

Rando, T. A. (1986). *Loss and anticipatory grief.* Lexington, MA: Lexington Books.

Rudd, M. G., Viney, L. L., & Preston, C. A. (1999). The grief experienced by spousal caregivers of dementia patients: The role of place of care of patient and gender of caregiver. *International Journal of Aging and Human Development, 48,* 217–240.

Schulz, R., Newsom, J. T., Fleissner, K., Decamp, A. R., & Nieboer, A. P. (1997). The effects of bereavement after family caregiving. *Aging and Mental Health, 1,* 269–282.

Theut, S. K., Jordan, L., Ross, L. A., & Deutsch, S. I. (1991). Caregiver's anticipatory grief in dementia: A pilot study. *International Journal of Aging and Human Development, 33,* 113–118.

Walker, R. J., Pomeroy, E. C., McNeil, J. S., & Franklin, C. (1994a). Anticipatory grief and Alzheimer's disease: Strategies for intervention. *Journal of Gerontological Social Work, 22*(3/4), 21–39.

Walker, R. J., Pomeroy, E. C., McNeil, J. S., & Franklin, C. (1994b). A psychoeducational model for caregivers of patients with Alzheimer's disease. *Journal of Gerontological Social Work, 22*(1/2), 75–91.

Walker, R. J., & Pomeroy, E. C. (1997). The impact of anticipatory grief on caregivers of persons with Alzheimer's disease. *Home Health Care Services Quarterly, 16,* 55–76.

Williamson, G. M., & Schulz, R. (1993). Coping with specific stressors in Alzheimer's Disease caregiving. *Gerontologist, 33,* 747–755.

Williamson, G. M., & Schulz, R. (1990). Relationship orientation, quality of prior relationship, and distress among caregivers of Alzheimer's patients. *Psychology and Aging, 5,* 502–509.

Worden, J. W. (1991). *Grief counseling and grief therapy: A handbook for the mental health practitioner* (2nd ed.). New York: Springer.

Wright, L. K. (1991). The impact of Alzheimer's disease on the marital relationship. *Gerontologist, 31,* 225–237.

3

Case Examples of Interventions Tailored to Specific Caregiving Groups

11

Ethnic Minority Caregivers

Elizabeth Edgerly, Lisa Montes, Edith Yau, Sandy Chen Stokes, and Darlyne Redd

Over the past decade health care providers have become increasingly aware of the unique needs of culturally diverse patients and families. Across the United States, organizations and providers have been working to develop culturally competent and sensitive services for AD patients and caregivers. Based on the authors' experience it appears that for every successful program, there have been at least two unsuccessful attempts at developing new programs. Our goal in this chapter is to describe four programs that attain the goal of reaching four of the largest ethnic and cultural groups in the United States: the Latino, Japanese, Chinese, and African American communities. We intend to highlight key factors contributing to the desirable outcome of the projects that can be replicated in other geographic and cultural communities. The programs selected use different strategies to address the topic of dementia and issues of concern to caregivers. This selection was made purposefully to illustrate some alternative approaches to reaching this population in diverse cultural groups.

Research suggests that there are several general factors that are important for successful outreach programs:

1. *Building relationships, confidence, and trust within the community over time.* This is especially important if the providers are attempting to reach out to an ethnic group of which they are not a member (Valle, 1981). It also applies, however, to persons from within the cultural community who are not well known to the key agencies, families, and professionals involved (Elliott, Di Minno, Lam, & Tu, 1996).

2. *Learning about the ethnic culture and how the community views dementia before attempting to work within the community* (Valle, 1989). This includes clarifying the myths associated with dementia, recognizing the social stigma associated with memory loss, and understanding the way that important terms such as "dementia" are defined when translated from English.

3. *Identifying key leaders within the community who serve as gatekeepers.* For those who provide care to persons with dementia, this may be trusted health care workers, church leaders, or staff at neighborhood centers. Success is often contingent on "buy in" from these individuals (Brownlee, 1978; Green, 1982; Valle, 1989).

4. *Allowing time to develop friendly social relationships with individuals within the community before attempting to provide services* (Elliott et al., 1996). This may take a few weeks, months, or even years to accomplish and is critically important if an organization or individual is to be trusted within the ethnic community. By developing these relationships, providers can get a foot in the door to groups that they otherwise would not reach.

These general strategies are necessary but not sufficient in the development of dementia services for ethnically diverse caregivers. The descriptions to follow will look at how agencies and action groups, working with the four diverse groups mentioned, have incorporated these principles and other program components to facilitate the development of useful community interventions. The program descriptions include (a) an overview of the development of the project, including review of needs assessment, staffing patterns, and target population; (b) goals of the program; (c) outcomes to date; (d) challenges to overcome in implementing this type of program; (e) case examples of one or more families served; and (f) ideas on how this program might be tailored to other groups.

MODEL PROJECT FOR LATINO CAREGIVERS

Overview of the Program

The Alzheimer's Association of Los Angeles's El Portal is a dementia-specific outreach and service program that targets Latino family members and individuals affected by dementia in Los Angeles County. The target area has an estimated 3,000 persons with dementia who are of Latino origin, representing U.S.-born citizens and 22 Spanish-speaking countries. Though all persons in the service area speak Spanish, they embody different racial groups, cultures, and generations. The many services of the program include case management, support groups, dementia day services, legal assistance, transportation, counseling, and linkages to diagnostic services. A Spanish-language help line, respite subsidies for in-home and day respite, scholarships for Safe Return Wanderers' Registry, and a variety of educational programs assist families further with their caregiving needs. El Portal also provides translation, advocacy, and assistance with service coordination through *servidores comunitarios* (care advocates). Bilingual and bicultural, care advocates conduct community outreach, lead support groups, conduct family education programs, and serve as an access point for the community (J. Hilgert & R. Ramirez, personal communication, June 2000).

Goals of the Program

The idea for El Portal, emerged in the early 1990s at a meeting of Los Angeles County's Dementia Care Network. The Alzheimer's Association of Los Angeles was a leading agency in this venture. The network proposed five major goals for a Latino Alzheimer's demonstration project to address the issue of isolation among Latino dementia-caregivers and the limited culturally appropriate and dementia-specific services in Los Angeles County.

- community outreach, networking, and awareness
- coordination of services and service delivery
- program expansion and development
- material evaluation, development, and dissemination
- evaluation of intervention and strategies

Outcomes to Date

Over the course of 8 years, El Portal has served more than 1,000 families and is believed to have achieved the most complete record of Latino dementia-caregivers nationwide. The project also has established three Latino dementia day-service programs and seven Latino-specific support groups in an area where there was previously only one. The success of El Portal's programs and resources, such as their care advocates, is well recognized both nationally and internationally. The program's continued success is due in part to their well-established partnerships with local community organizations whose staff and dedication maintain the life of their programs (J. Hilgert & R. Ramirez, personal communication, February 2001).

Challenges

El Portal did not achieve its current success without addressing numerous challenges. Finding culturally competent staff, conducting community outreach, building partnerships with existing community agencies, and securing funding were necessary to develop the strong network of services it offers today.

Cultural Diversity in the Community

The local Latino community within El Portal's service area is ripe with diversity, encompassing a variety of backgrounds and beliefs. Because of that, El Portal faced the challenge of developing culturally appropriate services for their community. A needs assessment involving Latino caregivers and existing service organizations proved crucial in helping to uncover the demographic and cultural makeup of the local Latino population. Focus groups, caregiver workshops, public surveys, and caregiver feedback were among the many methods El Portal used to gather information. These efforts also helped to instill a sense of ownership in the services the community members helped to create and built a foundation of trust that resulted in increased customer satisfaction and service utilization.

Organizational Challenges

The founders of El Portal knew that it was critical to have services and staffing in place to avoid promising services that could not be rendered. With this in mind, they engaged in a rigorous process of carefully recruiting bilingual, biliterate, and bicultural individuals from the greater Latino community. Basic organizational skills, a working knowledge of the service area, and sensitivity to the Latino community were minimum skills required for all staff positions as well as *corazon* (heart). A background in geriatrics or dementia was not required. El Portal then partnered with existing Latino community organizations to participate in training, mentorship, and ongoing professional development throughout their years of service to provide updated dementia knowledge and skills. Figure 11.1 depicts a graphic that was used on various outreach materials and that was well-received in the Latino community.

Educating Caregivers and Dispelling Preconceived Beliefs

To connect with members of the Latino community, El Portal's outreach workers visited local community centers, churches, laundromats, and other casual environments where the community typically gathered. They distributed colorful, bilingual postcards with El Portal's phone number and spoke with people in a friendly, nonthreatening manner. This helped to increase El Portal's visibility in the community and the community's knowledge of Alzheimer's. During their outreach, El Portal's staff found that many of the people they encountered were uninformed about Alzheimer's disease, dementia, or the services in their area. The challenge was not only to meet the needs of the growing dementia-affected, elderly popula-

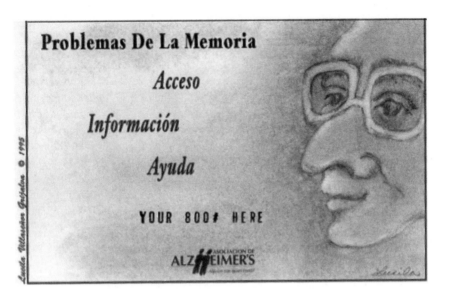

FIGURE 11.1 Example of culturally sensitive outreach material used at the El Portal program, Los Angeles, CA.

tion in their area, but to do so while maintaining sensitivity to the varying cultural and health beliefs of the Latinos they hoped to serve.

Funding Challenges

The Alzheimer's Association of Los Angeles received a Federal Health Resources and Services Administration (HRSA) grant from the State of California for their proposed Alzheimer's demonstration project. This provided the association with $500,000 per year over the course of 3 years. This was later matched up to 50% by in-kind contributions from community partner agencies. Further support was provided for an additional 4 years by HRSA, the Administration on Aging (AOA), and local private foundations. This program has proven to be highly attractive to funding sources and has been self-sustaining for the past 5 years.

Case Example

El Portal's programs have been key in dispelling the sense of isolation and despair that many dementia caregivers feel. Mrs. Y., an adult child, serves as primary caregiver to her mother who has Alzheimer's. Before being "found" by El Portal's care advocates, Mrs. Y. was disconnected from any supportive services and lacked specific knowledge about her mother's condition. "I was feeling so overwhelmed and alone. I was sure no one understood what was happening to my family. Just to know that you understand and can understand why I get so angry and frustrated with her when she can't understand. I was afraid to tell anyone and just kept it bottled up inside. I was afraid that I just had to deal with this all alone and I just didn't think I could. I was losing hope until I found you." A care advocate assisted Mrs. Y. by connecting her with a Spanish-language support group and coordinating legal and respite services for her family. The care advocate also made it possible for Mrs. Y. and her family to receive Spanish-language literature about Alzheimer's disease and to learn coping strategies that will help her and the family adapt to the changes seen in the mother.

How This Program Might Be Tailored to Other Groups

El Portal is successful because it uses a community-organizing/partnership model to encourage capacity building and the strengthening of resources among community-based organizations. Here are some suggestions on how to apply these methods in your local community (J. Hilgert & R. Ramirez, personal communication, June 2000):

1. Begin with a small service area and learn about the cultural and demographic makeup of that population. Completing a needs assessment can assist in this process.
2. If you decide to use focus groups during your needs assessment, try to include both family members and members of the community who demonstrate leadership and trust, such as local leaders of faith groups.
3. Find and educate care advocates who are bicultural, bilingual, and familiar with the community, which will no doubt prove fruitful.
4. Establish and nurture relationships with community partners; together you can plan an effective marketing campaign.
5. Take time to make programs meaningful to the community at large and work collaboratively with an established agency.

For additional information about the El Portal Latino Alzheimer's project, contact the Alzheimer's Association of Los Angeles, 5900 Wilshire Blvd. Suite 1700, Los Angeles, CA 90036; (323) 938-3379.

SERVICES FOR JAPANESE AMERICAN CAREGIVERS

Development of the Programs

Thirty years ago a few Sansei (third-generation Japanese Americans) recognized that the Issei (first-generation Japanese Americans) were unable to utilize mainstream services available to older persons in the San Francisco area because of cultural and language barriers. The Sansei began a program of assistance to help elders complete social security forms and to provide nighttime escort services in San Francisco's Japantown. From these efforts, a nonprofit organization called Kimochi, Inc. was started, and over the years this organization has developed into a prominent senior service organization, which provides culturally sensitive care for the elderly in the Japanese American community of San Francisco. This includes the Kimochi Home, which provides licensed residential care, respite care, and a day care program for frail elders.

This organization has served as an effective focal point for the coordination and integration of various intervention programs that are useful to Japanese caregivers. Its success within the community laid the groundwork for the development of the Japanese American Skilled Nursing Home Project. A committee of interested community leaders conducted a survey to assess the long-term health care needs of Japanese Americans in the Bay Area. The majority wished to remain at home for as long as possible when faced with chronic illness or long-term-care needs. This led to the publication of materials specifically for Japanese American seniors and their families, which provide information on how to access services and resources that can aid in caring for a family member at home.

This desire to remain independent at home led to the creation of In-Home Supportive Services (IHSS), which is offered as part of the Kimochi mission. Through this new IHSS contract, Kimochi provided case management and supervision. Older Japanese viewed these in-home services as nonthreatening, in part because the programs addressed physical needs and because the people were familiar with and trusted Kimochi. Through this new program, participants developed trust in their case manager and slowly revealed their concerns about memory loss or other health problems. To address the needs of those elders who were not eligible for IHSS, Kimochi also created a home-care registry. The purpose of the registry was to refer monolingual Japanese and Asian seniors to trained home-care workers who could provide culturally sensitive care, such as prepare Asian-style meals and follow other customs and traditions of an Asian home.

Prior to these community efforts, the needs of older persons and issues around caregiving were not discussed overtly. Dementia or memory impairment in particular were taboo topics. In Japanese culture, it is common for an older person to hide memory problems by withdrawing from social activities out of embarrassment and shame. Japanese families feel a strong sense of obligation to care for their elders without complaint. As emphasized in our introduction, understanding these widely held beliefs and values is essential in creating an effective outreach program.

Kimochi considered developing support groups to provide an opportunity for participants and family members to gather and share. They conducted a needs assessment and determined that people in the community were very uncomfortable sharing personal information outside the family. Educational programs, however, were highly desirable. Accordingly, Kimochi developed KEIRO, an educational group that provided a speaker on a different topic at each meeting. Offering topics gave families a framework for their discussions, which was more comfortable and culturally acceptable.

Goals of the Program

In keeping with the spirit of *kimochi*—appreciation for the sacrifices and hardships of the Issei and Nisei (second generation)—Kimochi, Inc. continues to express respect, gratitude, and love for the elders through services that enable them to age with dignity, pride, support, and friendship. As the Japanese American community ages, there are many families dealing with caregiving issues and witnessing friends and family members who experience memory and functional impairment. Kimochi has been focused on providing culturally sensitive care for those that have dementia despite the stigma associated with it.

Outcomes to Date

After nearly 30 years of established trust, Kimochi serves hundreds of elders each day 7 days a week. They have expanded their catchment area to extend outside Japantown and include at least two other districts where Japanese American elders reside.

Challenges

The biggest obstacle in the community is the obligation that families feel in caring for their parents. Respect and filial piety are so ingrained in the culture that families feel a sense of guilt if they seek help or services. Kimochi's philosophy is to emphasize that they are an extension of the family and that the family members do in fact continue to provide care and support. Other challenges include the following:

1. Addressing the growing demands from the community to help increasingly greater numbers of seniors to be as independent as possible.

2. With changes in the economy and a low unemployment rate, it becomes difficult to recruit essential staff to maintain and increase services.

3. Funding is constantly a challenge as with any nonprofit organization. The majority of the funding is dependent on San Francisco's Commission on the Aging. Funds are also generated through fund-raisers, fee-for-service programs, private donations, and foundation grants.

4. Recognizing and overcoming organizational limitations with regard to diversification of the participants in the program. Kimochi's target population is Japanese Americans but as the community changes and as needs increase, the question then becomes, How do you stay true to your mission without its becoming more costly?

5. Identifying ways to provide information about dementia and dementia care services in a nonthreatening way. The community continues to be uncomfortable with discussing dementia openly, which places some limitations to the types of programs that can be implemented.

Case Example

Mrs. H.'s parents moved from New York to Hawaii once her dad retired. After Dad's death, Mother was showing symptoms of forgetfulness and was diagnosed with Alzheimer's disease. She soon moved to San Francisco to live with Mrs. H. Other family members in San Francisco also participated in caring for Mrs. H.'s mother. Mrs. H.'s aunt, her mother's sister, volunteered at Kimochi's nutrition center for many years. She began to bring her sister along with her each week. Over time the mother developed friendships there. Two years ago, she began going to Kimochi Home's adult social day program once a week. Gradually, she started going 3 days and then 5 days a week. The family also began using Kimochi's respite program when they went on vacation.

Mrs. H. says she feels like her mother's condition hasn't worsened. She attributes this in part to Kimochi's involvement. Although dementia is a difficult topic to discuss in the community at large, it was relatively open in this family partly because Mrs. H.'s sister works in the medical field. It was she who began noticing changes in the mother's behavior and memory that prompted getting a diagnosis. Mrs. H. says when she tells friends her mother has Alzheimer's disease it often initiates discussion about their concern for their own parents' future as they age. But she thinks that dementia is still an uncomfortable topic for the community.

Mrs. H. says, "Kimochi has made a difference in my life, it represents an important place for my mother." She feels her mother would be less at ease at other centers or adult day programs because her mother has a certain level of comfort the moment she is at Kimochi. She knows the people there, they speak Japanese, the food is familiar, but more important, they share some same life experiences. "My mother is really happy being at Kimochi and I don't have to worry about her. Kimochi has given me a break, and it is such a relief to know she is being well taken care of." Mrs. H. emphasized that she has no worries about her mother at Kimochi because she sees the cheerfulness and affection the staff has around her mother. Mrs. H. has her mother helping at the family business when she is not at Kimochi.

For more information on Kimochi, Inc. visit their Web site at www. Kimochi-inc.org

A PROGRAM FOR CHINESE SENIORS WITH ALZHEIMER'S DISEASE

Overview of the Program

The John XXIII Multiservice Center is a program of the Catholic Charities organization, which provides a comprehensive range of psychosocial and medical services in downtown San Jose, California. For example, a needs assessment in the center's catchment area showed a much higher incidence of depression in the Chinese elders than had been found among American elders. Although the clients who completed the assessment asked many questions about other medical problems, they never asked for help with mental health issues. The clients often reported how afraid they were of getting Alzheimer's disease, but few attended presentations about the disease that were offered at the senior center. Seniors attending the presentations stated they were there for a friend or were there purely out of curiosity. It appeared that there was social stigma associated with Alzheimer's disease and other mental health disorders. However, many attendees at these public education forums later requested additional information about getting a diagnosis for memory problems.

Based on this experience, the need was identified for education and services pertaining to Alzheimer's Disease and related dementias in the Chinese community. The John XXIII center partnered with the Greater San Francisco Bay Area Alzheimer's Association Chapter to help develop and implement several programs in the Chinese community of Santa Clara County.

Goals of the Program

The goals for this new collaboration between John XXIII Multiservice Senior Center and the Alzheimer's Association of the Greater San Francisco Bay Area were as follows:

- community outreach, networking, and awareness
- early identification of persons with dementia through facilitating diagnostic workups
- coordination of services and service delivery
- program expansion and development
- material evaluation, development, and dissemination
- evaluation of intervention and strategies

Outcomes to Date

More than 250 Chinese elders and adult children have participated in Alzheimer's-related educational and support programs at the center since its inception in 1998.

Marketing efforts have resulted in two television, several radio, and four newspaper interviews in Chinese-language media sources. Each of these interviews has resulted in numerous calls from concerned individuals.

Implementation of the Program

This program was implemented in four phases: a public-awareness campaign; identification of persons with memory loss and dementia and their caregivers; identification of linguistically and culturally appropriate resources; and development and implementation of new dementia supportive services.

Phase I: Public-Awareness Campaign

A major focus of this initial phase was to address the social stigma associated with dementia. Early in the development of this program we learned that the Chinese in Taiwan often use three characters to refer to Alzheimer's disease: the first means "stupid," the second "catatonic," and the third "disease." After years of hard work on the part of health professionals in Taiwan, the proper name, Alzheimer's disease, has finally been accepted by the general public in Taiwan, but people who immigrated to the United States 20 years ago continue to use the old name for Alzheimer's disease. We addressed this stigma through a media outreach campaign on Chinese television, radio stations, and in newspapers. In this way, information was made available not only to local Chinese residents, but also to viewers, listeners, and readers living as far away as Nevada, Oregon, and Washington.

A second strategy for increasing public awareness was to offer free informational workshops about dementia. "Alzheimer's Beginning to Cope" (ABC) programs were provided by staff of the Alzheimer's Association of the Greater San Francisco Bay Area and were translated into Mandarin by staff of the John XXIII Multiservice Center. The ABC presentations covered topics such as normal aging and dementia, diagnosing dementia, how family and friends can help persons with Alzheimer's disease, and community resources available to those who have the disease and to their caregivers as well.

Phase II: Identification of Persons with Dementia and Caregivers

In an effort to identify persons with dementia and their families in the Chinese community, workshops were conducted in Mandarin on topics such as normal memory loss, reversible and irreversible memory loss, communication between caregiver and patient, coping with difficult behavior, and research and new treatment options. The average number of participants in the training sessions was 40. Through these efforts approximately 15 to 20 individuals were identified who were in need of additional services.

Phase III: Identifying Community Resources

Community outreach and collaboration with other organizations was stepped up in order to offer additional services for patients and their families. Staff who were working on the project gathered data about local day care centers and other community agencies in order to identify those who were both dementia- and culturally competent.

Phase IV: Program Expansion and Development

Based on a needs assessment conducted at John XXIII, a Chinese caregiver support group was formed, facilitated by two Mandarin-speaking volunteers. The group was attended by an average of 6 people per month, all Chinese-speaking but serving in variety of caregiving roles. The caregiver support group met on weekends to accommodate the schedules of working family members.

In the next 3 years, the joint John XXIII/Alzheimer's Association project will provide the following bilingual and bicultural services: translation of English materials into Chinese, development of information and referral services, production of video and audio tapes in Chinese, and creation of a Chinese Alzheimer's

Web site. Center presentations, community outreach, and media education will continue. Through a grant from the Administration on Aging, bilingual care advocates will be hired to work with the Chinese community to provide care coordination, consulting, in-services, and family support. These new staff positions will focus on early identification of families, coordination of services, and care coordination.

Challenges

There have been many challenges to overcome in implementing the program. One formidable barrier remains—that of language. There continue to be few paid care-providers of services in the San Jose area that serve monolingual Chinese speakers. Often families resort to hiring non-Chinese-speaking caregivers out of desperation. For the person with dementia this can compound their confusion and frustration. Additionally, the needs assessment showed that caregivers had difficulty finding accurate information about the disease, accessing treatment, getting a reliable diagnosis and prognosis, and understanding end-of-life issues, financial issues, and legal issues.

Case Example

Mr. C., who developed dementia a few years ago, emigrated from Taiwan to California with his wife 8 months ago. They moved in with their son, daughter-in-law, and two grandchildren. Soon after, the father's symptoms began to worsen. He would wander away and get lost, pace up and down during the night, could no longer follow a conversation, and became very withdrawn. His wife responded by becoming depressed, anxious, angry, and guilty. The family didn't know what to do. When Mr. C.'s son read a newspaper article about the center's caregiver support group, he called the author (SS) and was invited to one of the training sessions, where he learned how to cope with his father's difficult behavior. The son passed on what he had learned to his mom. The son agreed to have his father complete a series of memory tests given by the Alzheimer's Diagnostic Center at the VA Palo Alto/Stanford University School of Medicine in order to discover how advanced his father's dementia was and what type of dementia they were dealing with. He also joined his first caregiver support group.

Mr. C. continues to live with his family and receives most of his care from his wife. His wife reports that she has been less depressed and less anxious since they were helped by the program. Both Mrs. C. and her son say the program has helped them accept and deal with Mr. C.'s behavior changes.

"Now that I know my father's behavior is related to the disease," the son says, *"I can treat him like a patient, not as a father. That has made all the difference in the world."*

Where to go for more information: John XXIII Multiservice Center, 195 East San Fernando Road, San Jose, CA 95112; (408) 282-8669.

How This Program Might Be Tailored to Other Groups

The philosophy of both Kimochi and John XXIII in caring for the whole person is crucial to care for all groups and all people. It requires taking into consideration the history and experiences of each generation, language, culture, and traditions. Depending on who the population is, here are some suggestions:

1. Learn the cultural experience of the people you are serving.
2. Provide staff or volunteers who represent the community.
3. Offer food that is familiar to that group.
4. Discover the individual regardless of any group you are working with.

INTERVENTIONS FOR AFRICAN AMERICAN CAREGIVERS

Overview of the Program

The Minority Recruitment Satellite (MRS) at the University Alzheimer's Center of University Hospitals of Cleveland/Case Western Reserve University has developed and implemented several outreach programs in the African American community. The goal of the MRS is twofold: to increase awareness about Alzheimer's disease so that African Americans identify dementia early, seek diagnosis and treatment, and connect to appropriate services; and to increase the numbers of African Americans in research studies. The MRS program was chosen because it illustrates a different approach from those already described in this chapter.

MRS initially assigned a social worker, an African American, to build visibility and trust in Cleveland's large, diverse African American community through presentations at health fairs, church-based senior events, and community talks. Audiences were usually small and there were few contacts with families who had members with memory problems. After some reflection, we recognized that issues other than dementia might be more pressing for African American families. Members of the African American community often experience higher incidences of loss and death due to employment status, chronic illness, lack of resources for adequate health care, shorter life expectancy, violence, drugs, and infant mortality (Markides & Manuel, 1997). Therefore, many African Americans with family members who are impaired may be currently experiencing grief or be in a chronic grief state due to multiple losses or deaths that overlap (Ebersole, 1989).

In order to meet the needs of African American families in the community more effectively, we decided to expand beyond the typical dementia program to offer a workshop with broader appeal. As a first step, we partnered with the Nu Chi chapter of Chi Eta Phi sorority and produced a one-day grief workshop called "Matters of the Heart & Mind: A Grief Workshop" (Redd, 2000). The aim of this workshop was to help older African Americans cope with many types of losses, including cognitive losses, specifically dementia-related. The 1-day workshop included information about health, social, or functional problems that create a real loss for the individual, family, and community; understanding grief, how illness and death cause grief, and the grieving process. A panel of individuals who were grieving or have experienced grief shared their stories. Information on such topics as mourning, religious customs, support groups, and available services for individuals and families were provided. Time was allotted for the audience to discuss the ethical, spiritual, and psychosocial issues of grief. The day ended with a healing remembrance circle.

This program attracted senior and middle-aged women from the community who were undergoing various types of losses, church workers, and professional health care workers. We challenged the participants to be our advocates by providing accurate information to their communities about dementia, use of services and programs, and the importance of minorities participating in research. The program was viewed positively by the community, and other similar programs were recommended. A second workshop, held 6 months later, was expanded to a 2-day format. We retained the content of the first workshop and added a series of six break-out sessions, covering topics such as legal, estate, and burial planning. This content was added in response to the feedback from the original workshop. Recurrent themes of history, culture, and faith were included each day so participants could choose to come one day only.

The main emphasis of the second workshop was to provide information about grief, loss, and mourning and to create an atmosphere of healing and peace where emotions could be expressed and questions could be answered. It was important that the planning committee and speakers were conscious of the history, culture, and traditions of African Americans specifically, and of minorities in general. Although loss and grief are universal, being African American is not. The success of this workshop was contingent on presenters who were diverse and knowledgeable about issues relevant to dying, death, and grief, as well as preplanning legal and financial matters and social and emotional support through community programs and services.

The 2-day workshop attracted 90 people the first day and 75 people the second. Again, the audience was mainly from the lay public, with about one third made up of health care professionals. The conference was considered successful in that many individuals learned of available services offered in the community. Additionally, we received numerous inquiries about services through our research programs, and roughly a dozen African American families enrolled in our research program as a result of the two workshops.

Goals of the Program

This program was designed to educate and support African American families and professionals about grief, loss, and mourning related to Alzheimer's and other chronic conditions. By providing a safe, culturally sensitive environment, participants were open to sharing their personal beliefs, views, and feelings about loss and death and dying. Goals related specifically to dementia were to help families recognize grief related to cognitive losses, prepare in practical ways for end-of-life issues, and learn of available services to assist them in their time of need.

Outcomes to Date

The workshop evaluations indicated a positive educational and spiritual experience among the health care professionals and the African Americans who attended. Several ministers have changed their funeral services as a result. Others have requested extra copies of materials used at the workshop to share with their families. It also served to unite participants, to emphasize the similarities across cultures and faith traditions, while illuminating some of the purposes and traditions associated with African American death and dying rituals. New information (creating a legacy, preplanning, and distinguishing grief from depression) and new concepts (changing the traditional funeral customs and using bereavement services) were shared. These issues have increased awareness in some health care organizations about cultural and spiritual differences. Also, several churches have united to create a bereavement care program and have referred their members to existing church-based and community programs that can meet the needs of the grieving.

Challenges

The main challenge was overcoming the fear of dementia in the African American community. Creating a broader theme—loss and grief—attracted a larger audience that then was open to the content.

As stated earlier, the purpose of the MRS is to educate individuals and families about Alzheimer's disease and related memory disorders, related health and social issues, and the importance of minority participation in research. The grief workshop was not designed to be Alzheimer's-specific, although numerous references were made to dementia. So the second challenge was to create a program that was broad-based enough to include all types of caregivers while serving the goals of the MRS. The positive effect of this workshop in the community is that people remember us, see us as a community resource, and refer people to us for help and for research participation.

Case Examples

Mrs. L., a retired case manager, had experienced the recent death of her youngest daughter, Daphne, who had stomach cancer. Mrs. L. had been her daughter's caregiver for 26 months, initially caring for her in her own home and then in a residential hospice facility. Mrs. L. was experiencing tremendous episodes of sadness, tearfulness, and loneliness. She had not only lost her daughter, but also her role as caregiver, advocate, and, to some extent, her matriarchal position in the family. Because of the workshop experience she expressed that she was justifiably depressed and would see her family physician as soon as possible. She also stated that some of the practice suggestions about successful grieving were very helpful for her. At Christmas time several weeks later, Mrs. L. planned a family gathering to talk about and celebrate her daughter's life. She stated, "Daphne's spirit still lives and I want to keep it alive in a healthy way."

Mrs. W., a pastor and the caregiver to her husband who has been on dialysis for 7 years, was one of the speakers. She shared her caregiving experiences of dealing with his kidney disease and the dementia that has been a part of her husband's condition for the past 2 years. She shared that the workshop helped her to decide what legal documents she needed to complete and to start planning her husband's funeral with him. Being able to talk about the "loss" of her husband's ability and character and the change in her role from wife to "caregiver" made her feel supported and not so alone.

Mrs. C., widowed for 6 months, was inspired to plan a memorial service in honor of her husband of 42 years. Mrs. C., her family, and the church community created a wonderful celebration and remembrance of his life. The celebration started with the placing of his headstone and ended with a party.

How This Program Might Be Tailored to Other Groups

The task of introducing unfamiliar service programs (particularly those with a research theme) into a community can be difficult. In our case we built on a predominant theme of grief and loss in the community as a way to introduce our programs. Irish, Lundquist, and Nelsen (1997) state, "Normal grief and the normal understanding of death and life in other cultures may be quite odd, viewed by the standards of one's own culture. To work effectively with the dying and with bereaved people from other cultures it is necessary to step outside one's own culture and presuppositions." Thus, to implement novel service programs, one must first develop a thorough understanding of the community and culture. Second, programs must be tailored in ways that are consistent with the traditions of the culture. Local established agencies frequently can be helpful in this regard, such as the Alzheimer's Association, Hospice Bereavement Services, Bereavement support groups, American Red Cross, local Agency on Aging offices, and interfaith councils.

CONCLUSIONS

The programs described in this chapter have successfully delivered dementia education and services to specific ethnic communities that have not typically accessed such services previously. In examining the programs a number of commonalities emerge. Each of the organizations initiated a needs assessment prior to program development. Although the temptation is often to conduct business as usual by offering services such as caregiver support groups that are commonly used by Anglo families, these providers designed their programs specifically for the target community. An example of this was Kimochi's decision to abandon a traditional support group model in favor of an educational program. MRS, learning from past experience, opted to try a new, potentially less threatening approach by focusing on loss and grief associated with dementia rather than on dementia per se. This illustrates how a side-door approach can be more effective than a direct, dementia-specific program.

All of the projects carefully assessed the generally held beliefs about dementia before developing and implementing new programs. Addressing these preconceived beliefs about memory loss, caregiving duties, and the acceptance of community services is essential in attracting people to programs and *keeping* them involved. This is especially important in programs where translation from one language to another is needed. For example, in the programs at John XXIII, staff were careful to talk about dementia in terms of memory loss and to avoid using both written and spoken translations that connote "craziness" or "stupidity."

All the programs have relied on community partnerships. For El Portal, community ownership of the services is critical and makes it possible for the programs to continue after the grant funding is expended. The MRS project also effectively develops community partnerships through its outreach to community providers and gatekeepers. By offering continuing-education credits to providers they have attracted numerous senior service providers to the programs who then later refer families to the MRS center. Even more effective has been the impact on families in attendance. MRS has found that these participants later act as advocates, telling friends and family about dementia and the MRS programs and research studies.

In addition to these critical ingredients there are several common features of the programs described above that contributed to their success.

1.   Solicit input early on from professionals and caregivers from the community as to the types of services they prefer and providing those services. Many of the programs that we've seen fail can be attributed to skipping this step. Some of the typical services (e.g., lecture-style educational events) offered to dementia caregivers are not desirable in certain ethnic communities.

2.   Recruit and hire staff who are representative of the community you wish to serve. It is not, however, necessary to have staff who have a priori experience in dementia care and caregiving. It is possible to train and mentor culturally diverse staff about dementia so that they can act as leaders, though the reverse is not accomplished as easily.

3.   Offering culturally appropriate food and activities at programs is an easy way to demonstrate sensitivity to the community. Not doing so clearly demonstrates insensitivity.

4.   Discover the individual no matter what group you are working with. As is true whenever we talk about culture and ethnicity, we speak in generalities. It is critical to connect with people on the individual level to understand their perceptions, beliefs, and desires related to dementia care. It is also important to consider factors such as acculturation of the caregiver, patient, and other family members, as well as the preferred language and reading abilities.

ACKNOWLEDGMENT

The authors gratefully acknowledge the input of Jeannette Hilgert, MSG, MSW, Education and Outreach Coordinator and Rosa Ramirez, MSW, MPA, Director of Community Education of the Alzheimer's Association of Los Angeles and Anna Sawamura, Program Development Director at Kimochi, Inc. Also the authors wish to acknowledge that Dr. Redd's work is supported in part by the National Institute on Aging, Alzheimer Disease Research Center Grant AG08012. Both El Portal and the John XXIII programs are or were funded in part by the

California Department on Aging and the Administration on Aging Alzheimer's Disease Demonstration Grant to states.

REFERENCES

Brownlee, A. T. (1978). *Community culture and care: A cross-cultural guide for health workers.* St. Louis, MO: Mosby.

Ebersole, P. E. (1989). *Caring for the psychogeriatric client.* New York: Springer.

Elliott, K. S., Di Minno, M., Lam, D., & Tu, A. M. (1996). Working with Chinese families in the context of dementia. In G. Yeo & D. Gallagher-Thompson (Eds.), *Ethnicity and the dementias* (pp. 89–108). Washington, DC: Taylor & Francis.

Green, J. W. (1982). *Cultural awareness in the human services.* Englewood Cliffs, NJ: Prentice-Hall.

Irish, D., Lundquist, K., & Nelsen, V. J. (1997). *Ethnic variations in dying, death, and grief: Diversity in universality.* Washington, DC: Taylor & Francis.

Markides, K., & Manuel, M. (1997). *Minorities, aging and health.* Newbury Park, CA: Sage.

Redd, D. (2000) *Matters of the heart & mind: A grief workshop. Program planning manual.* Alzheimer Center, 12200 Fairhill Road, Cleveland, Oh, 44120.

Valle, R. (1981). Natural support systems, minority groups and the late life dementia: Implications for service delivery, research and policy. In N. Miller & G. D. Cohen (Eds.), *Clinical aspects of Alzheimer's disease and senile dementia* (pp. 287–299). New York: Raven Press.

Valle, R. (1989, Winter 1988–1989). Outreach to ethnic minorities with Alzheimer's disease: The challenge to the community. *Health Matrix, 6*(1), 13–27.

12

Male Caregivers: Challenges and Opportunities

Sean A. Lauderdale, James A. D'Andrea, and David W. Coon

Until recently, the average caregiver from demographic surveys of persons who are frail and elderly (Stone, Cafferata, & Sangl, 1987) and persons with dementia (Canadian Study of Health and Aging, 1994; Ory, Hoffman, Yee, Tennstedt, & Schulz, 1999) has been either an older woman caring for her husband or a middle-aged daughter caring for her parent (or parent-in-law). In general, men have comprised only a small proportion of these samples, accounting for approximately 25% of participants. However, changes in societal structure, such as decreasing family size, women's increasing presence in the work force, and increasing life expectancies (Dwyer & Coward, 1992), are expected to significantly impact caregiving demographics by placing more men in caregiving roles. These factors, combined with increased family mobility and larger numbers of single-headed households, will no doubt require more men to assume caregiving responsibilities in the future (Kaye & Applegate, 1990). Indeed, a recent survey of caregivers over the age of 18 providing at least some care to a chronically disabled or ill older person (National Family Caregivers Association, 2000) found that the number of men providing care accounted for almost half of that particular sample (44%). Moreover, many of these men (40%) are providing significant amounts of assistance with activities of daily living (e.g., toileting, bathing, dressing) and nursing care (e.g., administering medications). These findings call attention to the need for practitioners and service providers to consider gender a potential variable that significantly shapes caregiving experiences.

Unfortunately, despite increasingly complex theoretical models depicting a dynamic interplay of background characteristics (ethnicity, socioeconomic status, personality characteristics), stressors, appraisals, coping, and outcomes in caregiving (e.g., Haley, Levine, Brown, & Bartolucci, 1987; Pearlin, Mullan, Semple, & Skaff, 1990; Russo, Vitaliano, Brewer, Katon, & Becker, 1995), consideration of gender differences has received little attention in theories of caregiver distress and intervention. Naturalistic and intervention studies that consider or integrate gender differences in caregiving have been slow to emerge and often lack the methodological sophistication needed to garner support and acceptance, despite recurrent calls in the professional literature for the development and implementation of such important work (Gallagher-Thompson, Coon, Rivera, Powers, & Zeiss, 1998; Gwyther, 1992; Toseland & Rossiter, 1989). In addition, the inclusion of only small proportions of male caregivers in larger caregiving studies limits the statistical power to detect potential gender differences and in turn prohibits the examination of male subgroup differences (e.g., by relationship: husband versus adult son). Taken together, these issues have fostered a theoretical and practice-oriented one-size-fits-all approach that seemingly downplays how gender may influence multiple aspects of the caregiving process, including the types of stressors encountered, support sought and received, views and experiences of caregiving tasks, expectancies and experiences regarding psychosocial interventions, and the outcomes experienced as a result of caregiving.

This chapter explores a variety of challenges and opportunities in the development and implementation of psychosocial interventions for male caregivers. We discuss the limits of current theoretical explanations of gender differences in caregiving and key gender differences found in the extant caregiving literature, followed by an overview of male caregiver interventions in the literature and our experiences conducting psychoeducational-based male caregiver groups. Finally, we present a case example to highlight many of the issues raised and close with a discussion of future directions and additional opportunities in the development and implementation of male caregiver interventions.

THEORETICAL MODELS OF GENDER DIFFERENCES

Two general models have been used to describe caregiving gender differences: gender-role socialization and the social role conflict/stress process model. The gender-role socialization model posits that women are more vulnerable to stress associated with caregiving because socialization processes have fostered an affiliative orientation in which they identify themselves through their relationships with others and subsequently perform more nurturing behaviors to those in need. In turn, women are more vulnerable to the loss of the individual with dementia, more likely to express feelings of distress, and provide greater care than men. In contrast, men are theorized to place more emphasis on being autonomous and providing instrumental (e.g., financial support) forms of care (see Miller & Cafasso, 1992, and Walker, 1992, for review). Although this theory explains increased burden levels reported by women in comparison to men, the explanative mechanisms for these differences are vague and the theory ignores important intragender differences, such as findings that substantive proportions of men provide extensive care and report levels of distress comparable to those reported by women (Coward & Dwyer, 1990; Kaye & Applegate, 1994). Moreover, this model does not take into account related phenomena such as higher risk of suicide among older retired men, especially widowers, when compared to women (e.g., Templer & Cappelletty, 1986). Such related phenomena leave clinicians wondering if bereaved male caregivers may be in greater need of services than their female counterparts. Thus, the gender-role-socialization model is relatively insensitive to the unique experiences of individual men and women caregivers and does not provide clear directions for services for those who do not readily "fit" stereotypical gender roles.

The second model used to describe gender differences in caregiving is the social-role-conflict model, which posits that exposure to stressors such as care recipient behavioral problems, appraisals of those stressors and one's ability to manage them, participation in multiple social roles (e.g., caregiver, employee), and availability of resources (e.g., social support and formal care services), interacts in multiple ways to shape caregiving outcomes (e.g., Aneshensel, Pearlin, Mullan, Zarit, & Whitlach, 1995; Pearlin et al., 1990). Although this model includes gender as a potential background variable that may affect the stress process, little theoretical or empirical work has been conducted to help explain how gender may qualitatively influence outcomes or potential mediators such as appraisals of stressors or use of resources to cope more effectively.

Both these models identify potential gender differences that suggest men and women caregivers may want and desire different interventions to meet their unique needs, but they do little to inform intervention design or the tailoring of interventions for men across the progression of dementia. Yet it is conceivable that gender differences in the way dementia is conceptualized (Miller, 1987), the perceived benefits of caregiving (e.g., Neufeld & Harrison, 1998), and the manner in which care is provided (e.g., Corcoran, 1992) may shape the kinds of intervention programs that men need. In addition, little guidance is provided from either model in describing how to market various services for male caregivers. New models or modifications and extensions of these models needed to be tested across the entire caregiving career, either with larger samples of male caregivers or smaller samples of well-defined subgroups (younger versus older cohorts, sons versus husbands, specific minority ethnic and racial groups) of caregiving men.

GENDER DIFFERENCES IN THE CAREGIVING PROCESS

Although some significant gender differences in the literature have emerged, results have been mixed and oftentimes conflictual, providing less direction for interventions than expected.

Caregiver Burden and Depression

To date, a good deal of cross-sectional research examining gender differences in caregiving indicates that men report fewer symptoms of burden and depression when compared to women (e.g., Cohen et al., 1990; Fitting, Rabins, Lucas, & Eastham, 1986; Gallagher, Wrabetz, Lovett, Del Maestro, & Rose, 1989; Harper & Lund, 1990; Miller & Cafasso, 1992; Pruchno & Resch, 1989; Yee & Schulz, 2000). Although this may lead some to assume that male caregivers weather the caregiving process better and need less intervention or support, other findings suggest that professionals should exercise caution in adopting this view. For example, husbands providing assistance to physically ill wives were less happy, had less perceived emotional support, and reported greater symptoms of depression and lower levels of marital happiness than noncaregiving husbands (Kramer & Lambert, 1999). In a longitudinal study of caregivers, men became more depressed over time while women's depression level remained stable, suggesting that men become more similar to their female caregiving counterparts as caregiving continues (Schulz & Williamson, 1991). Likewise, caregiving sons who were an only child or from a single-gender sibling network (i.e., all brothers) reported similar levels of stress and burden compared to caregiving daughters (Coward & Dwyer, 1990).

Men and women caregivers of patients with dementia also report different levels of depressive symptoms at various stages of caregiving (Collins, Stommel, Wang, & Given, 1994), with men reporting increased depressive symptoms associated with bereavement when compared to male caregivers at other stages. In contrast, bereaved women caregivers reported fewer depressive symptoms compared to women providing in-home care or care to a relative in a nursing home. Most important, even when lower levels of burden (or other forms of stress or distress) are found among men, such a finding "does not equal inconsequential burden" (Kramer, 1997, p. 240). As Fuller-Jonap and Haley note, "comparisons to women caregivers in some cases are of limited value, given that even in the general community women have far higher rates of depression than men" (1995, p. 113). In their study comparing husband caregivers of AD spouses with noncaregiving husbands, they concluded that "depressive symptoms do exist among male caregivers even though men may be more hesitant to express them than women" (Fuller-Jonap & Haley, 1995, p. 113).

Predictors of Caregiving Mental-Health Outcomes

Some significant gender differences have also emerged here. For example, in caregiving husbands was related to their wives' wandering and memory loss, limited social support, and having others living in their home (Harper & Lund, 1990). In contrast, increased burden of caregiving wives was associated with more frequent behavior problems (agitation, emotional liability) and lower amounts of social support, income, and life satisfaction. More recently, Bookwala and Schulz (2000) compared models for predicting depression in husbands and wives caring for a spouse who was confused or needed assistance completing activities of daily living. For husbands, primary stressors stemming from caregiving (e.g., problem-behaviors) were not linked with symptoms of depression as they were for wives. However, husbands' activity restriction was negatively associated with the perceived quality of their relationships with their wives, which was not found to be the case for caregiving wives.

Sons and daughters appear to have different variables associated with negative caregiving outcomes. Although emotional strain was predicted for both by interference with their social and personal life, sons were more likely than daughters to experience increased strain from disruptive behaviors and having fewer people helping them with care. In contrast, daughters' emotional strain was predicted by their race (being White) and having a poor relationship with their parent (Mui, 1995). Similarly, different predictors of depression and emotional distress have been found for sons and daughters caring for a parent in a nursing home (Brody, Dempsey, & Pruchno, 1990). Although sons' and daughters' emotional distress was predicted by a time pressure and dissatisfaction with facility staff, sons' emotional distress was also predicted by lack of visitors while daughters' emotional distress was predicted by the number of illnesses their parent had. When assessing depression, sons' and daughters' depressive symptoms were both associated with the number of illnesses their parents had, but daughters' symptoms were also predicted by time pressure, their parent's need for assistance with instrumental activities of daily living, and dissatisfaction with facility staff.

Caregiver Coping Strategies

Although it has been implied that women may use fewer effective coping strategies than men do, thereby placing them at greater risk for psychological distress (e.g., Barusch & Spaid, 1989; Lutzky & Knight, 1994), the research is inconsistent and warrants additional attention (Yee & Schulz, 2000). For example, several studies comparing males and females have found no differences in the usage frequency of various coping strategies (e.g., Pratt, Schmall, Wright, & Cleland, 1985), while others suggest that coping strategies may indeed differ by gender (e.g., Devries, Hamilton, Lovett, & Gallagher-Thompson, 1997; Quayhagen & Quayhagen, 1988). However, the way in which coping is measured and the disregard for relationship differences (spouses versus adult children) may be misleading. Taking a more finely grained approach to measuring coping is more informative. For example, in their microanalysis of coping, DeVries and colleagues (1997) found considerable overlap in the strategies frequently used by male and female caregivers. However, women used a wider variety of strategies and appeared more likely to use coping patterns that encompassed perspective-taking, self-affirmation, social-support-seeking, and recreational support. Notably, these women did *not* use avoidant coping any more frequently than men. Similarly, Parks and Pilisuk (1991) found that in response to a stressful caregiving situation, sons and daughters did not differ in their use of coping strategies. Both objectively viewed the problem, sought solutions, created meaning, or detached themselves from the situation.

Informal and Formal Social Support

Gender differences have been reported in several studies of support provided to the care recipient, as well as informal and formal support received by the caregiver. With regard to help provided, one of the most often cited findings suggest that sons provide less hands-on assistance such as household chores, meal preparation, self-care activities, or transportation in comparison to daughter caregivers (Horowitz, 1985). Similarly, Miller and Cafasso's (1992) meta-analyses indicated that although male and female caregivers did not differ in total level of caregiver involvement, males were less likely to provide assistance with personal care activities and household chores when compared to females. Although this finding has been replicated (Dwyer & Coward, 1991), other findings suggest that these results are relationship-bound. Studies of spousal caregivers of the frail elderly (Bookwala & Schulz, 2000) and dementia patients (Pruchno & Resch, 1989) found that husbands did not differ from wives in the amount of caregiving tasks (i.e., instrumental and basic activities of daily living) performed. Furthermore, Bookwala and Schulz (2000) found that men provided their spouses significantly more help with eating, toileting, and heavy housework than wives did with husbands.

Comparisons of informal and formal social support received by caregivers have also revealed some gender differences. Husbands have reported receiving more assistance with caregiving from family members than wives did (Monahan & Hooker, 1995; Yee & Schulz, 2000) and more satisfaction with their social contact (Schulz & Williamson, 1991). Other studies have found no gender differences in informal support and in some, men actually reported less informal support and less formal service use than women (e.g., Barusch & Spaid, 1989; Collins &

Jones, 1997; Delgado & Tennstedt, 1997; Horowitz, 1985). Finally, some research has suggested that once husbands have adopted a primary caregiver role, gender differences lessen considerably across a broad spectrum of caregiver functions, with all caregivers receiving limited informal and formal support (e.g., Enright, 1991; Kaye & Appegate, 1994). Thus, the picture of gender similarities and differences in caregiver support provided and received is still not completely clear.

In sum, we believe the literature effectively points toward some emerging gender differences in terms of variables associated with caregiver distress (caregiver relationship to the care recipient, change in depression and burden across caregiving stages or time) that can be successfully integrated into male caregiver interventions. But more important, this review should remind interventionists of the heterogeneity of male caregivers and that those stereotypes of the male caregiver with ample informal and formal support and low levels of stress and distress are just that—stereotypes.

INTERVENTIONS FOR MEN

Taken together, results of this review suggest that men and women may require unique interventions to address negative caregiving outcomes they may experience. To date, only a few researchers have evaluated the experiences of men in support groups (Davies, Priddy, & Tinklenberg, 1986; Kaye & Applegate, 1993; Moseley, Davies, & Priddy, 1988) and psychoeducational groups (McFarland & Sanders, 2000) despite promptings from a number of researchers for gender-specific interventions (Gallagher-Thompson et al., 1998; Gwyther, 1992; Toseland & Rossiter, 1989). The low number of studies of male caregiver intervention is likely related to several variables, including the small number of men in caregiving roles (Stone et al., 1987), low rates of male participation in caregiving studies (Horowitz, 1985, 1992), and men's stereotypes regarding the use of psychological or mental health services (Brooks, 1996; Sprenkel, 1999). Other potential obstacles to men's participation may be the assumptions of researchers and mental health care professionals that men avoid seeking supportive services because it is a sign of weakness or failure and that men are resistive to sharing their emotional experiences (Kaye & Applegate, 1993). Nonetheless, evidence suggests that when men do participate in support groups they derive benefits (Kaye & Applegate, 1993).

Davies and colleagues (1986) developed a male support group at the behest of men in mixed-gender support groups. They had two groups, one of which was a problem-solving-skills group and the other a general discussion group, both of which were both time-limited (six weekly sessions). The latter evolved into a group that continued to meet (see Moseley et al., 1988, for follow-up). In contrast, McFarland and Sanders (2000) recruited 11 men for a weekly psychoeducational group that met for four sessions. Despite the diverse formats of these groups, several convergent themes emerged. For example, both groups of researchers used unique marketing strategies for recruitment that included emphasis on the educational component and the opportunity for group members to provide researchers feedback regarding the group experience. Group members emphasized the benefit of hearing and sharing caregiving experiences with other men and in some cases indicated a reluctance to do so in mixed-gender groups. They also stressed the importance of learning concrete caregiving skills and learning more about the course and progression of dementing illnesses. Both sets of authors conceptualized the groups as an opportunity for men to expand their social networks by interacting with experientially similar others. Both sets of authors discussed or alluded to the difficulty men had expressing their emotions during the course of the groups. Recommendations for future groups made by these clinicians included (a) maintaining small groups sizes so that sharing of emotional experiences resulting from caregiving is facilitated; (b) devoting group time to discussing concrete caregiving skills that men may not be familiar with (such as assisting others with self-care activities); (c) integrating other educational components such as an overview of dementing illnesses and identification of community resources; and (d) allowing time for discussing skills needed to manage distress resulting from caregiving.

In response to these recommendations and the results of the literature review above, we developed a psychoeducational group for men that emphasizes discussion of negative caregiving emotions, such as anger, frustration, and sadness, in a context that fosters the development of skills to manage these reactions through monitoring of specific thoughts and behaviors that occur in the individual's caregiving context.

COPING WITH CAREGIVING: A PSYCHOEDUCATIONAL GROUP FOR CAREGIVERS

The Coping with Caregiving program, like other manualized treatments, was designed to structure an approach to therapy that taught participants coping skills in a classroomlike environment, while at the same time providing them with social support from other caregivers participating in the classes. The format used in this study followed a modified version of the Coping with Caregiving psychoeducational group intervention developed by Gallagher-Thompson and her associates (Gallagher-Thompson, Ossinalde, & Thompson, 1996) for Resources for Enhancing Alzheimer's Caregiver Health (REACH), an NIA/NIH-funded multisite collaborative project (see Coon, Schulz, & Ory, 1999, for descriptions of the project). The theoretical foundation for the course rests on cognitive-behavioral theory (e.g., Beck, Rush, Shaw, & Emery, 1979; Lewinsohn, Muñoz,

Youngren, & Zeiss, 1986) that was adapted for application with older adults who need relief from the stress associated with caregiving and adjusting to progressive cognitive impairment and physical disabilities (see Table 12.1).

In class, caregivers were presented with an overview of the cognitive-behavioral model that illustrates the role of cognitions and behaviors as primary causative agents in affective states such as anger and depression. To deal with the negative emotions frequently experienced among caregivers, participants were taught various skills such as relaxation in stressful situations and self-monitoring negative thought patterns in consequent negative emotional states. The cognitive component of the workshop covered typical thought patterns that aggravated the

TABLE 12.1   Session Content for the "Coping with Caregiving" Psychoeducational Group for Male Caregivers

Sessions 1 and 2

Review goals and rules of classes
Overview of dementia
Sources of caregiver frustration
Purpose of relaxation and in-class exercise
Coping with unchangeable situations
Presentation of the ABC model
Six common unhelpful thoughts

Sessions 3 and 4

Relation between negative thoughts and affect
Physiological danger signals and visual stop-signs
Changing unhelpful thoughts and adaptive behaviors
How to change unhelpful thoughts
Case example: changing unhelpful thoughts

Sessions 5 and 6

Signs of depression
How life events affect mood
Identifying and increasing pleasant events
How to monitor mood and why
Assertive, passive, and aggression communication styles
Increasing and tracking pleasant events
Obstacles to pleasant events
Overcoming obstacles to pleasant events
Graphing the relationship between pleasant events and mood
Skills review

caregiving situation (such as seeing things in black-and-white, judging their own behavior against unrealistically high standards, personalizing the effects of difficult behaviors exhibited by the person with dementia, jumping to conclusions, discounting the positive, and mind-reading). Second, methods were presented for developing realistic appraisals of care-recipient abilities and maintaining positive thought patterns in the midst of facing stressful caregiving situations. Cognitive strategies were provided for countering negative thought patterns related to specific caregiving situations. These strategies included objectively examining the evidence for the negative beliefs, reframing the initial appraisal into more workable terms, weighing the pros and cons of various courses of action, conducting experiments to test the negative beliefs, and anticipating difficult situations that might arise in the future in order to develop strategies for coping with them before they actually occur.

The behavioral component of the program was based on the behavioral principle that obstacles to, or prolonged absences of, reinforcement lead to frustration and eventually to depression. Recognizing that caregivers spend the majority of their time fulfilling their caregiving responsibilities and consequently sacrifice time spent in pleasurable activities, the program emphasizes the need for caregivers to engage in pleasant events not only to return balance to their lives, but also to help them become more effective caregivers. Pleasant events are defined as activities that are enjoyable to the person, are realistically achievable, and can be scheduled or planned. Examples of pleasant events include having lunch with a friend, taking walks, and going to movies or shows. (A windfall, such as winning the lottery, would not be considered a pleasant event under this definition, because the likelihood of winning is highly improbable and cannot be scheduled.) Our experience has shown that participating in a minimum of three to four pleasant events each day provides enough reinforcement to buffer against daily stressors from caregiving.

Although the importance of engaging in pleasant events is sometimes met with resistance, participants in the class learn through homework exercises that the number of daily pleasant events they participate in is positively correlated with their subjective mood ratings. For example, after developing a list of 10 to 15 possible pleasant events, participants are asked to engage in as many pleasant events as possible each day and to monitor their daily mood using a simple Likert rating scale. In the next class, participants are asked to graph their daily mood rating scales against the number of pleasant events they did each day. The graphic representation that emerges is a salient depiction of the impact that pleasant events have on subjective feelings of well-being. For participants who were only able to perform a few pleasant events during the week, engaging in problem-solving and getting the group's support can help those who find it difficult to schedule time for increasing the number of pleasant events.

Other behavioral skills covered in the Coping With Caregiving program are assertiveness training and self-monitoring unpleasant mood states. The assertiveness-skills-training component teaches how to effectively communicate with care recipients who are difficult to engage in normal dialogue, as well as dealing with family members who are reluctant to provide assistance and government or health care bureaucracies. Ample time is devoted during class to practice these skills during role-playing exercises. The goal of the assertiveness training is to help caregivers negotiate a win-win situation without feeling compromised or losing composure. By increasing self-awareness of visceral signs of anger and frustration, participants will learn to take corrective action before losing behavioral control.

Recruitment

Fliers were posted in a local health care facility and in community service organizations and were inserted in newsletter mailings from the local Alzheimer's Association chapter. Reports from previous researchers (Davies et al., 1986) indicate that traditional methods that use printed advertisements in the form of fliers and advertisements yield low numbers of participants when the group is identified as a support group. This was consistent with our experience even when these advertisements were placed in locations and publications where caregivers seek services.

To increase the response rate, the language in the fliers was reevaluated in light of anecdotal evidence suggesting that gender-sensitive language that emphasizes education may be more successful at recruiting male caregivers (Gwyther, 1992; McFarland & Sanders, 2000). The program was described as a workshop for learning keys to caring for a person with memory loss, as opposed to a program of mutual support or idea sharing. This de-emphasized the emotional and supportive aspects of group process that are associated with support groups, and it highlighted the informational aspects of the programs, appealing to men's task-oriented approach to caregiving. Other male caregivers enrolled in the course at the urging of trusted individuals (such as an adult child or other health care provider) who were concerned for the caregiver's well-being. A very few inquired about the program after attending a presentation on caregivers stress that was held at a seminar center or other community location. Thus, our experience shows that printed announcements and presentations in the community met with modest success in getting male caregivers to attend a Coping With Caregiving workshop. A more fruitful approach was to work with relatives, friends, and health care workers who knew distressed male caregivers and encourage them to refer caregivers to the program.

Scheduling

The second issue was scheduling the class at that time convenient to all participants. Generally speaking, most of the caregivers felt that late morning was the
most convenient time for meeting because they could arrange for adult day care
or brief respite during those hours. In addition, symptoms of confusion in the
persons they were caring for seemed least problematic in the morning hours, so
the class participants were not overly distracted by safety concerns.

Session Format

The original format of the Coping With Caregiving class consisted of 10 weekly
sessions of 2 hours' duration each. This represented a significant time commitment for the caregivers; most expressed their wish for a shorter class period so
that it would not interfere with their other daily scheduled activities and caregiving
responsibilities. A balance was reached between the caregivers' need for a short-
ened class on the one hand and being able to cover key material in the program.
This resulted in a 90-minute class that met weekly for 6 consecutive weeks.

The session format is based upon a structured approach in which each session
builds upon lessons learned from the previous session. Homework assignments
are given to participants to practice the skills learned from each lesson and to
convey that the actual benefits from the program are achieved by putting the
skills into practice outside the workshop setting. Sessions began with a review of
the homework assignment from the previous session and ended with participants'
receiving another homework assignment for practicing the skills demonstrated
in that class. If participants had difficulty completing their homework assignments, group members would offer support and the investigator offered help in
problem-solving whatever obstacles there were to completing the assignments
successfully.

Evaluation of the Group Experience

Several themes emerged in feedback sessions from our male caregiver groups.
First, the emphasis the class placed on learning concrete skills appealed to them.
Many said that learning new approaches to deal with the challenges of caregiving
significantly improved their ability to manage stress. Second, group members
appreciated hearing the experiences of other men in the same situation and how
they dealt with common problems and concerns. Third, the group provided
participants with mutual support and decreased social isolation, which was a
complaint commonly heard from our participants. Close bonds were formed

between members within each group and friendships often were maintained after the program was completed. Last, a follow-up or booster session was requested by many group members to help them polish their skills after trying the new approaches on their own for a period of time.

CASE EXAMPLE

Mr. B. is a 74-year-old Caucasian man with a college degree who worked as an executive until about 20 years ago when he retired and started his own business. He closed this business approximately 2 years ago because his wife was getting "sloppy" managing the finances and scheduling appointments. He still has a substantial income but has cared for his wife of 53 years without assistance from formal services. Mr. B. feels obligated to care for his wife because "she stayed home and raised my daughters." On average, he spends 6 to 8 hours a day in care activities for his wife, such as cleaning and cooking meals, as well as helping her with self-care tasks like dressing.

Initially, Mr. B. believed his wife's confusion and indecision regarding everyday decisions was an intentional act used to keep him home. However, he credits his primary care physician for initially raising the possibility that the problems his wife was experiencing could be related to dementia. As her memory problems have continued to worsen, Mr. B. recognizes that she is "losing circuits . . . not connecting with present . . . in the part of the brain responsible for that." He also believes that his wife is depressed because she stopped participating in activities she used to enjoy, such as volunteering, and has isolated herself from friends she has known for many years. He does not believe that his wife recognizes the nature and severity of her impairments and does not have control over many of the problematic behaviors she displays. Despite obvious impairments in basic self-care tasks and memory, Mr. B.'s wife has not been diagnosed with dementia because she believes others are "trying to make her look crazy" and has refused to participate in medical and neurological assessment for dementia.

Mr. B. believes the greatest difficulty he has is managing his wife's memory and problem behaviors. He described her as having difficulty recalling the daily events they planned, the tasks they have completed, and misplacing objects (e.g., putting her jewelry in the freezer or peanut butter in the laundry hamper). She also experiences a significant amount of indecision and frequently asks him when she should do things, such as chores. As a result, Mr. B. reports that he spends countless hours each day reviewing their daily calendar with her, searching for lost or misplaced objects, and reassuring her that they have completed important tasks such as eating. Because he often gets involved in activities and has a "one-track mind," his wife becomes upset and explodes with anger when she believes he is ignoring her. Recently, she has begun to use profanity, threatened to harm him, and frequently brings up mistakes he has made in their marriage. During these times, Mr. B. and his wife "waste time having the same arguments again." Because of her memory problems and emotional labiality, he has become increasing vigilant and watches her closely throughout the day.

Emotionally, Mr. B. is torn between sympathy for his wife (because of her changes in mental functioning) and resentment for the burden his caregiving responsibilities place on him. In particular, he is frustrated because he is unable to do things he enjoys or planned on doing in his retirement, such as completing home remodeling projects. He believes not completing these tasks and others (paying bills, shopping for groceries) represents a failure on his part, especially because he has always set specific goals for himself each day and believes that this strategy was a key to helping him become a successful executive and business owner. He has also struggled learning new skills, such as learning to cook, clean, and help his wife with self-care activities (dressing) because he believes that accepting help from others would represent a failure on his part to fulfill his marital obligations. He also has become disgusted with himself for raising his voice at his wife when they have argued. In addition, he has become depressed and found himself thinking "what's the use?" At night, "the tape starts running" and he ruminates about the tasks he was unable to complete and is subsequently unable to fall asleep because of increasing anxiety and the feeling that "things are piling up."

When thinking about his future, he is fearful of the increasing demands that caring for his wife will place on his mental and physical health and on his time. He also is fearful of having to place his wife in a skilled-nursing facility as another member of his social group has done. He avoids thinking about this by becoming involved in other activities. Mr. B. believes placing his wife in tantamount to a divorce and "cutting a segment out of his life." He also fears the loneliness he'll experience without her at home "goading" him to get things done.

Prior to attending the caregiving classes, he coped with his emotional reactions to caregiving by finding activities that he could do outside their home but nearby so he could keep watch. He described himself becoming involved in completing heavy physical tasks, such as yard work, as a way of alleviating the frustration he experienced from caregiving. He relies on monthly phone calls with his daughters as a way of dealing with his stress. Although they do not help with any hands-on care, their willingness to listen and empathize with his experience is something he appreciates. Furthermore, his youngest daughter has taken his wife on one short trip away from home to give him respite. Although he was able to accomplish many tasks while his wife was away, he remarked that the pleasure and relief he experienced was short-lived and her return was a "reality check" that dragged him back into the emotional turmoil he has experienced being her caregiver. Finally, he credited his primary care physician for "pushing" him to balance his caregiving with time for himself in order to maintain his sense of well-being and health.

By attending the male caregiving group, he reported learning a number of specific skills that helped him manage his distress. First, learning the relaxation exercises has been crucial in keeping his frustration and anger at a manageable level so that these emotions do not interfere with his problem-solving skills. Frequent practice of the relaxation exercises has resulted in his simply being able to start deep breathing to lower his sense of frustration, even when he is in a difficult interaction with his wife. Second, monitoring his unhelpful thoughts in specific stressful situations has helped him identify those caregiving situations that cause him the most frustration and distress. He has used this awareness to anticipate and plan how to manage these events when they occur so he does not feel as unprepared. Third, as he has become more adept at identifying the negative thoughts he has regarding caregiving, he has struggled with identifying ways to change his thoughts so that they are adaptive. For example, he has worked on accepting that his wife will misplace objects and has become more watchful of where she puts them. He has also worked at revising his thoughts so that he acknowledges she does not misplace everything and that helping her find objects frees his time later in the day. To learn this skill, he needed frequent coaching from the class coleader and assistance from other class members. He described this portion of the class as the "most useful caregiving class" he has ever had, because it helped him increase his awareness of events that cause him difficulty and prepares him with a toolbox of strategies to use. Finally, Mr. B. was taught to recognize the importance of pleasant daily events and their impact on mood. By graphing this relationship based on his own schedule of activities (which he monitored), he learned that his mood and events were closely linked. Over the last sessions of the group, he incrementally increased his number of events and has reported feeling "recharged" when returning to care for his wife.

Mr. B.'s situation, and his response to the group, is fairly typical in our experience: Once the decision to seek help has been made, and appropriate services are available, male caregivers will participate actively and benefit.

FUTURE DIRECTIONS AND OPPORTUNITIES

Increasing awareness of men's needs as caregivers is an emerging area for clinicians and clinical researchers. Accordingly, service providers and researchers are confronting a number of challenges in meeting men's caregiving needs. In the following sections, we will review some potential areas that hold promise for broadening our understanding of male caregivers' service needs.

Diversity Among Men Providing Care

For a number of years, increasing attention has been paid to how kinship ties with the care receiver affect caregiving trajectories in a number of ways (see Montgomery, 1996, for review). Findings suggest that the relationship between the caregiver and patient (based on accepted social behaviors) can fundamentally influence caregiving at multiple levels such as the identification with the caregiving role, the degree of care provided, the type of care provided, the amount of care shared with others, and the duration of care. In addition to unique factors associated with the caregiver's personal history (e.g., cultural views and acculturation, quality of the premorbid relationship with the care receiver, personality characteristics), all of these factors undoubtedly interact to shape caregivers' reactions to providing care as well as their desire for services and the types of services sought (Montgomery, 1996). The implication for practitioners is that different marketing strategies and services need to be tailored to the needs of men from diverse caregiving roles (e.g., sons, husbands, siblings).

In addition, we must plan for variability in services needs across caregiving transitions (e.g., diagnosis, placement) (Aneshensel et al., 1995). Caregiving husbands who placed their wives in a nursing home experienced an increase in available time and physical energy, but reported no significant change in their level of depressive symptoms (Kramer, 2000). Similarly, mean burden levels were not significantly different between a group of men (husbands, sons, and other males) providing care to a relative with dementia after institutional placement, compared to a group of men (husbands, sons, and other male relatives) providing in-home care (Mathew, Mattocks, & Slatt, 1990). Taken as a whole, these findings indicate that the effects of caregiving are dynamic and this ebb and flow will subsequently shape the needs of male caregivers in different stages of the caregiving process. In terms of tailoring interventions to men at different caregiving stages, it may be that men who are providing care at home would benefit from learning skills such as managing problem behaviors, providing self-care assistance, and learning about community resources that provide respite. In contrast, men who place wives and mothers should benefit from interventions that focus on helping them to process feelings of guilt associated with placement and learning to reintegrate into a large social network to cope with feelings of loneliness and loss.

Finally, cultural experiences provide a lens through which dementia is conceptualized and experienced and care is provided (Yeo & Gallagher-Thompson,

1996). Our understanding of the caregiving experiences of men from diverse cultural backgrounds is limited (e.g., Harris & Long, 1999; Miller & Kaufman, 1996) and needs further attention so that services can be appropriately tailored to their needs.

Measuring Outcomes for Male Caregivers

In measuring caregiver outcomes, more attention needs to be paid to the effect of gender bias on commonly used measures. Recent studies (Cole, Kawachi, Maller, & Berkman, 2000; Stommel et al., 1993) found significant gender-biased responses to certain items of the Center for Epidemiologic Studies-Depression (CES-D) (Radloff, 1977), one of the most widely used measures of depression in the caregiving literature. Similar biased responding may also be found with other caregiving measures, such as the Zarit Burden Interview (Zarit, Todd, & Zarit, 1986), which were developed and normed with predominantly female samples. These findings suggest that measures may need to be adapted to decrease the impact of gender-biased responding (as has been done with the CES-D) (Stommel et al., 1993) or new measures created to tap adequately into men's experiences and reactions to caregiving.

Other avenues of evaluating caregiving outcomes should also be considered, especially those that are less subject to response bias, in order to identify multiple domains that caregiving impacts. Recent findings using physiological measures hold promise for providing understanding of the stress on men produced by caregiving. For example, several sources indicate that caregiving husbands (caring for a spouse with dementia) reveal changes on various physiological indicators, including cardiovascular responsivity (which did not reach statistical significance due to low power) (Lutzky & Knight, 1994); risk factors for cardiovascular disease (Vitaliano, Russo, & Niaura, 1995); and psychoneuroimmunological measures of chronic stress exposure (Scanlan, Vitaliano, Ochs, Savage, & Borson, 1998). Poor self-rated health has also been associated with subjective caregiver burden for husbands caring for their spouses (Kramer, 1997). An additional benefit of expanding awareness of the multiple effects of caregiving may provide directions for future interventions. Recently, investigators have found that a relatively short-term physical activity program for family caregivers (both men and women) reduced ambulatory blood pressure and increased duration on an exercise stress-test relative to controls (King & Brassington, 1997). Furthermore, both caregiving men and women in this study were interested in changing their level of physical activities through the use of supervised home-based programs that incorporated physical activity.

Finally, little qualitative work has explored in depth the experience of men in the caregiving role (e.g., Harris, 1993, 1995, 1998). Practitioners and clinical researchers alike need to consider that male caregivers may be best understood not in comparison to their female counterparts, but rather through investigations of their own experiences. This is especially important in light of the current literature that suggests they may conceptualize caregiving differently, express distress and adapt to the career differently, and may respond to interventions, programs, and services in a different manner than women (e.g., Harris 1995; Parsons, 1997).

Partnering With Primary Care Physicians

As Burns and his colleagues note in chapter 8 of this volume, the primary care physician is the first person families turn to when memory problems emerge in their loved ones. In addition, primary care is often the first place older cohorts turn to when they experience depression or high levels of anxiety and stress. Therefore, primary care could prove a particularly salient place for male caregiver intervention or intervention promotion.

When partnered with community service providers, primary care physicians and their staff may be able to provide male caregivers information and ongoing support throughout the caregiving process that circumvents the time and financial reimbursement demands imposed by managed care organizations (Perel, 1998). In particular, physicians and their staff can provide oral and written information describing the diagnosis and prognosis of dementing illnesses, raise safety and legal issues, and assist caregivers in making long-range care decisions (e.g., placement and end-of-life care) in advance. Furthermore, their familiarity with community service providers' logistical information (e.g., eligibility, duration of services, contact phone numbers, and alternative service providers) may enhance compliance with service recommendations (Gwyther, 1996), a finding that may be particularly relevant for men.

Primary care physicians and staff can also make referrals to community resources to provide ongoing support to men. A recent study found that more than three fourths of older adults who committed suicide visited their primary care physician within the month prior to suicide, with most also having moderately severe but undiagnosed depressive symptoms (Conwell, 1994). This is especially important to consider given that gender is the demographic variable with the greatest predictive power for completed suicide in the U.S., with widowed or divorced men demonstrating higher risks of suicide than married persons. Also, their own declining health and the impact of retirement on their quality of life can make it more difficult for men to manage effectively than women (Templer & Cappelletty, 1986). Thus, physicians and primary care staff are in a frontline position to evaluate affective distress symptoms in men. Although men are not asked about symptoms of caregiving distress at rates comparable to women

(Chopra, Perweiler, & Karenick, 1999), this is an important component to consider that can be readily incorporated into regularly scheduled appointments through the use of brief checklists or other informal assessments techniques.

Interventions for Grief and Loss

Caregiving is associated with loss in a number of domains. During our interviews with men, many have described the loss-of-life plans because of their caregiving responsibilities. Furthermore, men have described losses associated with changes in their social relationships with friends and relationships with family members as well as loss of leisure time, freedom, and job opportunities (Harris, 1998). They also have described experiencing the loss of the relationship with the care receiver and the experience of grieving for the spouse (in particular) prior to her death (Parsons, 1997). Ultimately, caregivers are faced with the death of the care receiver and some evidence suggests that the loss of a spouse can be detrimental to the mental and physical health of husbands, although these findings are equivocal (see Nolen-Hoeksema & Larson, 1999; Turk-Charles, Rose, & Gatz, 1996, for review). Overall, these findings strongly argue for clinicians to address such feelings with men during their caregiving role and when it ends.

CONCLUSIONS

The number of male caregivers will swell in the decades ahead due to changing demographics—including increased longevity for men and the even greater longevity of women—coupled with the association between age and dementia or other chronic illnesses and family geographic mobility and dispersion. However, the current socialization process in many cultures, including the "majority" culture of the U.S., presumes that it is inappropriate or out of character for men to assume the caregiver role, a role tightly aligned to "women's work." In order to be effective, interventions directed to male caregivers must be prepared to address the expectations long held by relatives of male caregivers, their employers, many service providers, and society as a whole, not to mention many of the men themselves. For example, interventions with older husbands of persons with dementia that help men combine their "workmanship and nurturant" qualities (Kaye & Applegate, 1994) may be more palatable and useful than those that don't help men face societal stereotypes and barriers. These challenges afford rich opportunities for clinicians and clinical researchers to develop creative (and appropriate) interventions to serve men at the various stages of their caregiving careers.

REFERENCES

Aneshensel, C. S., Pearlin, L. I., Mullan, J. T., Zarit, S. H., & Whitlatch, C. J. (1995). *Profiles in caregiving: The unexpected career.* San Diego, CA: Academic Press.

Barusch, A. A., & Spaid, W. M. (1989). Gender differences in caregiving: Why do wives report greater burden. *Gerontologist, 29,* 667–676.

Beck, A. T., Rush, J., Shaw, B., & Emery, G. (1979). *Cognitive therapy of depression.* New York: Guilford Press.

Bookwala, J., & Schulz, R. (2000). A comparison of primary stressors, secondary stressors, and depressive symptoms between elderly caregiving husbands and wives: The caregiver health effects study. *Psychology and Aging, 15,* 607–616.

Brody, E. M., Dempsey, N. P., & Pruchno, R. A. (1990). Mental health of sons and daughters of the institutionalized aged. *Gerontologist, 30,* 212–219.

Brooks, G. R. (1996). Treatment for therapy resistant men. In M. P. Andronico (Ed.), *Men in groups: Insights, interventions, and psychoeducational work* (pp. 7–20). Washington, DC: American Psychological Association.

Canadian Study of Health and Aging. (1994). Patterns of caring for people with dementia in Canada. *Canadian Journal on Aging, 13,* 470–487.

Chopra, A., Perweiler, E., & Karenick, G. (1999). Primary care physician practice patterns in diagnosis and management of dementia. *Journal of the American Geriatrics Society, 47,* S23.

Cohen, D., Luchins, D., Eisdorfer, C., Paveza, G., Ashford, J. W., Gorelick, P., Hirschman, R., Freels, S., Levey, P., Semla, T., & Shaw, H. (1990). Caring for relatives with Alzheimer's disease: The mental health risks to spouses, adult children, and other family caregivers. *Behavior, Health, and Aging, 1,* 171–182.

Cole, S. R., Kawachi, I., Maller, S. J., & Berkman, L. F. (2000). Test of item-response bias in the CES-D scale: Experiences from the New Haven EPESE study. *Journal of Clinical Epidemiology, 53,* 285–289.

Collins, C., & Jones, R. (1997). Emotional distress and morbidity in dementia carers: A matched comparison of husbands and wives. *International Journal of Geriatric Psychiatry, 12,* 1168–1173.

Collins, C., Stommel, M., Wang, P., & Given, C. W. (1994, July-August). Caregiving transitions: Changes in depression among family caregivers of relatives with dementia. *Nursing Research, 43,* 220–225.

Conwell, Y. (1994). Suicide in the elderly. In L. S. Schneider, C. F. Reynolds, B. D. Lebowitz, & A. J. Friedhoff (Eds.), *Diagnosis and treatment of depression in late life: Results of the NIH Consensus Development Conference.* Washington, DC: American Psychiatric Press.

Coon, D. W., Schulz, R., & Ory, M. G. (1999). Innovative intervention approaches for Alzheimer's disease caregivers. In D. E. Biegel & A. Blum (Eds.), *Innovations in practice and service delivery across the lifespan* (pp. 295–325). New York: Oxford Press.

Corcoran, M. A. (1992). Gender differences in dementia management plans of spousal caregivers: Implications for occupational therapy. *American Journal of Occupational Therapy, 46,* 1006–1012.

Coward, R. T., & Dwyer, J. W. (1990). The association of gender, sibling network composition, and patterns of parent care by adult children. *Research on Aging, 12,* 158–181.

Davies, H., Priddy, J. M., & Tinklenberg, J. R. (1986). Support groups for male caregivers of Alzheimer's patients. *Clinical Gerontologist, 5,* 385–395.

Delgado, M., & Tennstedt, S. (1997). Making the care for culturally appropriate community services: Puerto Rican elders and their caregivers. *Health and Social Work, 22,* 246–255.

DeVries, H. M., Hamilton, D. W., Lovett, S., & Gallagher-Thompson, D. (1997). Patterns of coping preferences for male and female caregivers of frail older adults. *Psychology and Aging, 12,* 263–267.

Dwyer, J. T., & Coward, R. T. (1991). A multivariate comparison of the involvement of adult sons versus daughters in the care of impaired parents. *Journals of Gerontology: Social Sciences, 46,* S259–S269.

Dwyer, J. W., & Coward, R. T. (1992). Gender, family, and long-term care of the elderly. In J. W. Dwyer & R. T. Coward (Eds.), *Gender, families, and elder care* (pp. 3–17). Newbury Park, CA: Sage.

Enright, R. B. (1991). Time spent caregiving and the help received by spouses and adult-children of brain-impaired adults. *Gerontologist, 31,* 375–383.

Fitting, M., Rabins, P., Lucas, M. J., & Eastham, J. (1986). Caregivers for dementia patients: A comparison of husbands and wives. *Gerontologist, 26,* 248–252.

Fuller-Jonap, F., & Haley, W. E. (1995). Mental and physical health of male caregivers of a spouse with Alzheimer's disease. *Journal of Aging and Health, 7,* 99–118.

Gallagher, D., Wrabetz, A., Lovett, S., Del Maestro, S., & Rose, J. (1989). Depression and other negative affects in family caregivers. In E. Light & B. D. Lebowitz (Eds.), *Alzheimer's disease treatment and family stress: Directions for research* (pp. 218–244). (DHHS Publication No. (ADM) 89–1569). Rockville, MD: National Institute of Mental Health.

Gallagher-Thompson, D., Coon, D. W., Rivera, P., Powers, D., & Zeiss, A. M. (1998). Family caregiving: Stress, coping, intervention. In M. Hersen & V. Van Hasselt (Eds.), *Handbook of clinical geropsychology* (pp. 469–494). New York: Plenum Press.

Gallagher-Thompson, D., Ossinalde, C., & Thompson, L. W. (1996). *Coping with caregiving: A class for family caregivers.* Palo Alto, CA: VA Palo Alto Health Care System.

Gwyther, L. P. (1992). Research on gender and family caregiving: Implications for clinical practice. In J. W. Dwyer & R. T. Coward (Eds.), *Gender, families, and elder care* (pp. 202–218). Newbury Park, CA: Sage.

Gwyther, L. P. (1996). Care for families facing Alzheimer's disease: Primary care practice implications from research. In Z. S. Khachaturian & T. S. Radebaugh (Eds.), *Alzheimer's disease: Causes, diagnosis, treatment, and care* (pp. 323–334). New York: CRC Press.

Haley, W. E., Levine, E. G., Brown, S. L., & Bartolucci, A. A. (1987). Stress, appraisal, coping and social support as predictors of adaptational outcome among dementia caregivers. *Psychology and Aging, 2,* 323–330.

Harper, S., & Lund, D. A. (1990). Wives, husbands, and daughters caring for institutionalized and noninstitutionalized dementia patients: Toward a model of caregiver burden. *International Journal of Aging and Human Development, 30,* 241–262.

Harris, P. B. (1993). The misunderstood caregiver? A qualitative study of the male caregiver of Alzheimer's disease victims. *Gerontologist, 33,* 551–556.

Harris, P. B. (1995). Differences among husbands caring for their wives with Alzheimer's disease: Qualitative findings and counseling implications. *Journal of Clinical Geropsychology, 2,* 97–106.

Harris, P. B. (1998). Listening to caregiving sons: Misunderstood realities. *Gerontologist, 38,* 342–352.

Harris, P. B., & Long, S. O. (1999). Husbands and sons in the United States and Japan: Cultural expectations and caregiving experiences. *Journal of Aging Studies, 13,* 241–267.

Horowitz, A. (1985). Sons and daughters as caregivers to older parents: Differences in role performance and consequences. *Gerontologist, 25,* 612–617.

Horowitz, A. (1992). Methodological issues in the study of gender within family caregiving relationships care. In J. W. Dwyer & R. T. Coward (Eds.), *Gender, families, and elder care* (pp. 132–150). Newbury Park, CA: Sage.

Kaye, L. W., & Applegate, J. S. (1990). Men as elder caregivers: A response to changing families. *American Journal of Orthopsychiatry, 60,* 86–95.

Kaye, L. W., & Applegate, J. S. (1993). Family support groups for male caregivers: Benefits of participation. *Journal of Gerontological Social Work, 20,* 167–185.

Kaye, L. W., & Applegate, J. S. (1994). Older men and the family caregiving orientation. In E. H. Thompson (Ed.), *Older men's lives* (pp. 218–236). Newbury Park, CA: Sage.

King, A. C., & Brassington, G. (1997). Enhancing physical and psychological functioning in older family caregivers: The role of regular physical activity. *Annals of Behavioral Medicine, 19,* 91–100.

Kramer, B. J. (1997). Differential predictors of strain and gain among husbands caring for wives with dementia. *Gerontologist, 37,* 239–249.

Kramer, B. J. (2000). Husbands caring for wives with dementia: A longitudinal study of continuity and change. *Health and Social Work, 25,* 97–107.

Kramer, B. J., & Lambert, J. D. (1999). Caregiving as a life course transition among older husbands: A prospective study. *Gerontologist, 39,* 658–667.

Lewinsohn, P. M., Muñoz, R. F., Youngren, M. A., & Zeiss, A. M. (1986). *Control your depression.* New York: Prentice-Hall.

Lutzky, S. M., & Knight, B. G. (1994). Explaining gender differences in caregiver distress: The roles of emotional attentiveness and coping styles. *Psychology and Aging, 9,* 513–519.

Mathew, L. J., Mattocks, K., & Slatt, L. (1990). Exploring the roles of men caring for demented relatives. *Journal of Gerontological Nursing, 16,* 20–25.

McFarland, P. L., & Sanders, S. (2000). Educational support groups for male caregivers of individuals with Alzheimer's disease. *American Journal of Alzheimer's Disease and Other Dementias, 15,* 367–373.

Miller, B. (1987). Gender and control among spouses of the cognitively impaired: A research note. *Gerontologist, 27,* 447–453.

Miller, B., & Cafasso, L. (1992). Gender differences in caregiving: Fact or artifact? *Gerontologist, 32,* 498–507.

Miller, B., & Kaufman, J. E. (1996). Beyond gender stereotypes: Spouse caregivers of persons with dementia. *Journal of Aging Studies, 10,* 189–204.

Monahan, D. J., & Hooker, K. (1995). Health of spouse caregivers of dementia patients: The role of personality and social support. *Social Work, 40,* 305–314.

Montgomery, R. J. V. (1996). The influence of social context on the caregiving experience. In Z. S. Khachaturian & T. S. Radebaugh (Eds.), *Alzheimer's disease: Causes, diagnosis, treatment, and care* (pp. 313–322). New York: CRC Press.

Moseley, P. W., Davies, H. D., & Priddy, J. M. (1988). Support group for male caregivers of Alzheimer's patients: A followup. *Clinical Gerontologist, 7,* 127–136.

Mui, A. (1995). Caring for frail elderly parents: A comparison of adult sons and daughters. *Gerontologist, 35,* 86–93.

National Family Caregivers Association. (2000, October). *Caregiver survey—2000.* Kensington, MD: Author.

Neufeld, A., & Harrison, M. J. (1998). Men as caregivers: Reciprocal relationships or obligations? *Journal of Advanced Nursing, 28,* 959–968.

Nolen-Hoeksema, S., & Larson, J. (1999). *Coping with loss.* Mahwah, NJ: Erlbaum.

Ory, M. G., Hoffman, R. R., Yee, J. L., Tennstedt, S., & Schulz, R. (1999). Prevalence and impact of caregiving: A detailed comparison between dementia and nondementia caregivers. *Gerontologist, 39,* 177–185.

Parks, S. H., & Pilisuk, M. (1991). Caregiver burden: Gender and psychological costs of caregiving. *American Journal of Orthopsychiatry, 61,* 501–509.

Parsons, K. (1997). The male experience of caregiving for a family member with Alzheimer's disease. *Qualitative Health Research, 7,* 391–407.

Perel, V. D. (1998). Psychosocial impact of Alzheimer's disease. *Journal of the American Medical Association, 279,* 1038–1039.

Pearlin, L. I., Mullan, J. T., Semple, S. J., & Skaff, M. M. (1990). Caregiving and the stress process. An overview of concepts and their measures. *Gerontologist, 30,* 583–594.

Pratt, C. C., Schmall, V. L., Wright, S., & Cleland, M. (1985). Burden and coping strategies of caregivers to Alzheimer's patients. *Family Relations, 34,* 27–33.

Pruchno, R. A., & Resch, N. L. (1989). Husbands and wives as caregivers: Antecedents of depression and burden. *Gerontologist, 29,* 159–165.

Quayhagen, M. P., & Quayhagen, M. (1988). Alzheimer's stress: Coping with the caregiving role. *Gerontologist, 28,* 391–396.

Radloff, L. S. (1977). The CES-D scale: A self-report depression scale for research in the general population. *Applied Psychological Measurement, 1,* 385–401.

Russo, J., Vitaliano, P. P., Brewer, D., Katon, W., & Becker, J. (1995). Psychiatric disorders in spouse caregivers of care-recipients with Alzheimer's disease and matched controls: A diathesis-stress model of psychopathology. *Journal of Abnormal Psychology, 194,* 197–204.

Scanlan, J. M., Vitaliano, P. P., Ochs, H., Savage, M. V., & Borson, S. (1998). CD4 and CD8 counts are associated with interactions of gender and psychosocial stress. *Psychosomatic Medicine, 60,* 644–653.

Schulz, R., & Williamson, G. M. (1991). A 2-year longitudinal study of depression among Alzheimer's caregivers. *Psychology and Aging, 6,* 569–578.

Sprenkel, D. G. (1999). Therapeutic issues and strategies in group therapy with older men. In M. Duffy (Ed.), *Handbook of counseling and psychotherapy with older adults* (pp. 214–227). New York: Wiley.

Stommel, M., Given, B. A., Given, C. W., Kalaian, H. A., Schulz, R., & McCorkle, R. (1993). Gender bias in the measurement properties of the center for epidemiologic studies depression scale (CES-D). *Psychiatry Research, 49,* 239–250.

Stone, R., Cafferata, G. L., & Sangl, J. (1987). Caregivers of the frail elderly: A national profile. *Gerontologist, 27,* 616–626.

Templer, D. I., & Cappelletty, G. G. (1986). Suicide in the elderly: Assessment and intervention. *Clinical Gerontologist, 5,* 475–487.

Toseland, R. W., & Rossiter, C. M. (1989). Group interventions to support family caregivers: A review and analysis. *Gerontologist, 29,* 438–448.

Turk-Charles, S., Rose, T., & Gatz, M. (1996). The significance of gender in the treatment of older adults. In L. L. Carstensen, B. A. Edelstein, & L. Dornbrands (Eds.), *The practical handbook of clinical gerontology* (pp. 107–128). Thousand Oaks, CA: Sage.

Vitaliano, P. P., Russo, J., & Niaura, R. (1995). Plasma lipids and their relationships with psychosocial factors in older adults. *Journals of Gerontology: Psychological Sciences, 50B,* P18–P24.

Walker, A. J. (1992). Conceptual perspectives on gender and family caregiving. In J. W. Dwyer & R. T. Coward (Eds.), *Gender, families, and elder care* (pp. 34–46). Newbury Park, CA: Sage.

Yee, J. L., & Schulz, R. (2000). Gender differences in psychiatric morbidity among family caregivers: A review and analysis. *Gerontologist, 40,* 147–164.

Yeo, G., & Gallagher-Thompson, D. (1996). *Ethnicity and the dementias.* Washington, DC: Taylor & Francis.

Zarit, S. H., Todd, P. A., & Zarit, J. M. (1986). Subjective burden of husbands and wives as caregivers: A longitudinal study. *Gerontologist, 26,* 260–266.

13

The Families We Choose: Intervention Issues With LGBT Caregivers

David W. Coon and L. McKenzie Zeiss

RECOGNIZING OUR LENS AND ITS PERCEPTIONS . . . FIRST

Who is in the mirror? Lesbian, gay male, bisexual, and transgender (LGBT) adults often report recognizing their sexual orientation as children or adolescents (e.g., Bell, Weinberg & Hammersmith, 1981; Wishik & Pierce, 1995). Although many racial and ethnic minority members observe, participate in, and learn about their cultures and identities as a normative part of growing up and experience themselves as part of a community of difference, LGBT youth cannot easily identify others of similar orientation and often end up feeling isolated by their difference. LGBT caregivers may continue to experience this aloneness as adults, shaped not only by their own lenses, but also by the realities of indifference and discrimination. They may therefore be struggling to identify clinicians and services that adequately address their needs. Similarly, we as practitioners, administrators, or clinical researchers need to look in our own mirrors and examine our own lenses. Past and present experiences clearly shape our views of who is competent to speak, teach, research, and write about LGBT individuals who help partners, family members, and friends live with dementia. Though our lenses also shape our views regarding research and practice with the "majority" and other minority groups, few issues in our society fuel as heated a debate with such strongly held opinions as the one of sexual orientation. These views lead some professionals and family caregivers to question whether raising the topic is really important or necessary. Are the services LGBT caregivers need truly different from those in the larger community?

In response, this chapter takes the position that until we live in a world where LGBT individuals no longer experience the discrimination and social isolation that create barriers to receiving competent care, we need to continue to educate ourselves and other service providers and researchers to develop increasing competence in our service provision to LGBT family caregivers. More specifically, we discuss key questions related to LGBT caregiver interventions, such as who are LGBT caregivers and what are the obstacles these caregivers face to service utilization? How can we engage members of the LGBT community with the services that we provide? How do we educate service providers to serve LGBT caregivers not merely out of increased awareness but also from ever-growing competence?

Most published accounts of LGBT caregiving are derived from the HIV/AIDS caregiving literature, which delineates outcomes associated with the heroic response to the epidemic by the LGBT community and their supporters (e.g., Fredriksen, 1999; Wrubel & Folkman, 1997). In response to the need for valid data on emerging issues within the aging LGBT community, the New York Community Trust and the Sam Wilmer Funds awarded a grant in December 1999 to the Pride Senior Network to conduct a qualitative study of caregiving provided in the older LGBT New York City community and to determine the community's present and future needs. The study will explore questions such as, Can the LGBT community provide the support that caregivers themselves will need? Has the community suffered a degree of burnout due to the level of caregiving demanded by the HIV/AIDS epidemic? Hopefully, this investigation as well as future studies will add to the regrettably sparse research and clinical literature currently available. Moreover, we hope it augments this chapter's information, which is based on current literature drawn from multiple disciplines and integrated with our own clinical experiences and the clinical impressions of colleagues.

Finally, many of the challenges and responses presented here are drawn from LGBT-caregiver and clinician experiences with larger LGBT communities in cities like San Francisco, New York, Dallas, Los Angeles, and Phoenix, suggesting that obstacles and issues faced by LGBT caregivers in smaller cities and rural areas may be exacerbated by more limited resources and greater isolation. However, we must caution readers about the tendency to stereotype or overgeneralize in discussions of the LGBT community, just as with any minority group, and instead recognize and celebrate its diversity. Many LGBT persons experience great joy as well as hardships and obstacles, and the difficulties discussed in this chapter should not be read as necessary truths about members of the LGBT community. For example, though many LGBT persons are isolated from their birth families, one LGBT caregiver recently reminded his support group

I know how lucky I am. My parents and siblings in rural [America] love Todd [his partner of more than 20 years]. My younger brother and [my] sister-in-law drove out last year and we traveled to the Coast together; them helping me watch out for Todd. . . . Of course, there were a few stressed moments. But, just like our gay and lesbian friends like Jill and Pat, they haven't abandoned us. Can't say that about everyone, of course . . . but I am lucky.

WHO ARE LGBT DEMENTIA CAREGIVERS?

Diversity

The LGBT experience cuts across cultural and experiential lines and, when considering the experiences of caregivers, it clearly cuts across age groups. Younger caregivers care for former partners, neighbors, and friendship network members who helped them during the coming-out process and are now older. There are also older LGBT caregivers caring for long-time partners or friends. Moreover, there are individuals of all ages who identify with the LGBT community and who provide care for older biological family members. LGBT caregivers represent a diverse group in terms of ethnicity, race, language, national origin, and physical challenges, as well. In our experience providing individual and couple therapy to dementia caregivers and their partners in the San Francisco Bay Area, as well as facilitating LGBT support groups for the local Alzheimer's Association chapter, clients and participants have self-identified as Latino and Mexican American, Filipino, Chinese, African American, Vietnamese, and White. Interracial as well as same-race couples have attended these groups and accessed these and related services. Although it is not the purpose of this chapter to debate whether LGBT identity serves as a separate culture, we do argue that it does function as a minority community with some unique caregiver needs. Still, when considering LGBT identification as constitutive of a community, providers must recognize that it is predominantly those individuals who self-identify as LGBT who use LGBT specific support services. Many of these caregivers, depending on their level of "outness" will be more reluctant to be out with providers and agencies not known for serving the LGBT community. This may be particularly true for members of older cohorts who faced many years of discrimination and intolerance, as well as other individuals in same-sex relationships who feel vulnerable as a result of heterosexism and whose feelings are compounded by issues of sexism, racism, ageism, or discrimination based on disabilities (Barón & Cramer, 2000). All this may be compounded further in areas of the country that lack strong LGBT communities.

Defining LGBT

Over the years a number of studies report ranges of LGBT prevalence from 2% or 3% upwards to about 18% to 20% (e.g., Sell, Wells, & Wypij, 1995; Tanfer, 1993). The number is hard to determine due to respondents' fear of social stigma and discrimination associated with LGBT self-identification, as well as complexities associated with defining LGBT status. Even the terminology is variable. "Sexual orientation" refers to emotional and sexual attraction to others of a particular sex. More recently, the term "sexual preference" has come to be viewed as inappropriate, because it implies that sexual orientation is a behavioral choice rather than an intrinsic personal characteristic. Sexual orientation is not synonymous with sexual behavior, despite being commonly defined as such in the United States (e.g., Dworkin, 2000; Herek, 1986). For example, a person identifying as gay male or lesbian may have sexual experiences with the opposite sex.

Current thinking really no longer describes sexual orientation as a dichotomy between homosexuality and heterosexuality (Fox, 1996; Markowitz, 1995). Rather, sexual orientation can be thought of as a continuum from exclusively heterosexual to exclusively homosexual. Sexual orientation is conceptualized as multidimensional, in that it not only encompasses sexual behavior but also affiliation, sexual and emotional feelings and desires, and spiritual components (Alquijay, 1997; Coleman, 1987). These dimensions are further developed along a temporal dimension from the past through the present and into thoughts of the future, with some individuals expressing flexibility in their sexual orientation, such as sequential bisexuality (Kimmel, 1978; Klein, Sepekoff, & Wolf, 1986; Money, 1988). Transgender individuals have a strong sense of incongruity between their birth sex and their gender identity. Some may be receiving hormonal treatments without a plan for reassignment surgery, while others actively may have sought surgical therapies to become physically congruent with their gender identities. Transgender individuals self-identify as heterosexual, gay male, lesbian, or bisexual and therefore can experience discrimination based on their sexual orientations as well as their gender identities. Finally, differences at the cultural, cohort, regional, and community level can also influence the acceptability of "labels" that LGBT members choose to describe themselves, ranging from homosexual, bisexual, gay, or lesbian to the reclamation of the term "queer." Because of the complexities involved, self-identifying as a member of the LGBT community is not always a clear-cut issue.

So do we care about pinning down these multidimensional, potentially shifting, and often hidden identities? Is it important for us to know how many caregivers in the general population identify as LGBT or how our own clients identify? From the standpoint of increasing therapist competency and effectiveness, it certainly is. LGBT clients may face discrimination or stress as a result of who they are and where they live, which affects the services or recommendations that are appropriate to provide. Knowing how many caregivers are likely to need similar types of services or referrals to LGBT-friendly medical, elder care, social, or psychological services is the cornerstone to the development and dissemination of useful community and organizational resources. Still, although this information would be useful, it is not required in order for service providers to increase their competence in the development and implementation of effective interventions tailored to meet LGBT caregiver needs. The key point to remember is that ignoring issues of sexuality and discrimination that LGBT clients face allows the pervasive heterosexist bias of our society to invade services by default, decreasing our helpfulness to clients (Garnets, Hancock, Cochran, et al., 1991; Winegarten, Cassie, Markowski, et al., 1994). Because of the obstacles and issues that caregivers in the LGBT community must face, we as providers need ongoing training and consultation, beginning with increasing our awareness of key socio-cultural influences that impact LGBT caregivers.

CONSIDERING THE SOCIOCULTURAL CONTEXT

The sociocultural context can significantly influence and shape beliefs and expectations about dementia and family caregiving, including who should serve as primary or secondary caregivers and who will hold the ultimate decision making power (Yeo & Gallagher-Thompson, 1996). It can influence how caregivers experience or express signs and symptoms of distress, how they understand their feelings, thoughts, and behaviors, and how they view others in their environments, including service providers. That, in turn, can alter their health-seeking behavior and treatment practices. The sociocultural context can also create other barriers including language barriers for caregivers whose first language is not English, culturally insensitive or dystonic services, and financial constraints for those services that are available (Coon, Davies, McKibbin, & Gallagher-Thompson, 1999; Gallagher-Thompson et al., 2000; see also chapter 3 in this book). In addition, it is important for us to remember that the therapist brings his or her own cultural background and assumptions to the encounter. Thus, service provision occurs not just in the larger present-day sociocultural context, but also in the context of the clients' relationship to the therapist, which is inevitably influenced by the personal histories of each. Several components of the larger sociocultural context surface for LGBT individuals in the course of caregiving that warrant further discussion.

FINANCIAL AND LEGAL CONTEXTS

LGBT caregivers of all backgrounds often face special financial and legal burdens. They can be deeply concerned about balancing career, work, and retirement issues with caregiving responsibilities. Employment discrimination is real, and there is very little protection for most against being laid off or denied opportunities because of sexual orientation (Alexander, 1997; Kimmel & Sang, 1995). Surveys of lesbian and gay male workers indicate that as many as two thirds said it would cause serious problems for them to be out at work, including both formal and informal forms of discrimination such as harassment, stunted promotion, termination, forced retirement, and loss of pension, as well as psychosocial losses and associated stress (e.g., Croteau, Anderson, Distefano, & Kampa-Kokesch, 2000). The positive side of this danger (if there is one) is that it may encourage LGBT caregivers and other community members to define themselves well beyond their careers and therefore expand their social support networks beyond the workplace.

LGBT caregivers also face legal hurdles, especially in caring for partners. Many privileges that are taken for granted by other members of society are difficult for LGBT persons to obtain. They can be prevented from visiting life partners or care recipients in hospitals or nursing homes if medical personnel or blood relatives choose to block them and be dismissed or ignored in the decision-making process. LGBT caregivers are typically excluded from their partners' health insurance; and they are frequently discriminated against, no matter how long their partnership, in matters of survival benefits, inheritance rights, and community property rights. They must pay extra legal fees to develop the documents to ensure that their wishes are carried out. Even then, these wishes may still be challenged effectively in many communities by blood relatives, because few laws on the books protect LGBT partners (Connolly, 1996; Ettelbrick, 1996). These experiences can lead to feelings of helplessness and depression, disrupting normative grief processes (Berger & Kelly, 1996; Slater, 1995).

SOCIAL SUPPORT

Although it is true that many LGBT care recipients might not have children to rely on for social support, physical security, and economic assistance as they grow older, it is a false stereotype that all LGBT elders do not have children or inevitably are alone. There may be biological children, grandchildren, or stepchildren from past heterosexual unions, in addition to other family members such as siblings, nieces, and nephews. Social science research (e.g., Berger, 1982; Grossman, D'Augelli, & Hershberger, 2000; Kimmel, 1978) supports the contention that many LGBT seniors have expanded, multigenerational social and professional networks in the community, which may help combat some of the discrimination they face, and adjust more easily to the aging process. However, the impact of social losses due to the AIDS epidemic may question such assumptions for future cohorts. For older LGBT persons, the positive adjustment to aging also appears to be related to increased social support from other gay males and lesbians, greater satisfaction with gay or lesbian identity, and lower levels of "closetedness" (Dorfman et al., 1995; Grossman et al., 2000).

LGBT care recipients who live independently may hold more realistic expectations of who will take care of them. They may not expect that blood relatives, neighbors, or friends will provide for them beyond a certain point, and they may have prepared for that (Kimmel, 1978; Quam & Whitford, 1992). Moreover, LGBT caregivers may have let go of rigid sex roles or divisions of labor early in their relationships and therefore may be more willing to do many of the things their partners can no longer manage, from cooking and cleaning to finances and lawn care. By contrast, some research indicates that among older heterosexual caregiving couples, performance of these tasks may be gender-role-driven (Yee & Schulz, 2000), with one partner having to learn "opposite role" behavior in the stressful course of caregiving. This greater flexibility may be a plus for LGBT caregivers, and, as with their expanded social networks, may lead to greater satisfaction with the overall aging process. However, older LGBT individuals historically have had to create support networks on their own, with few social or community resources at their disposal (Grossman et al., 2000). Such LGBT-specific resources have only emerged and strengthened in urban centers over the last couple of decades.

SPIRITUAL CONTEXTS

Religion and religiosity are often assumed to be key coping mechanisms for caregivers, as in the recent national survey conducted by the National Alliance for Caregiving and the American Association for Retired Persons (NAC/AARP, 1997). Even though many experts argue that LGBT people are in need of, and are open to, spiritual nourishment due to societal oppression (Davidson, 2000), institutionalized religion has been an agent of intolerance and oppression of the LGBT community since the early Middle Ages (Boswell, 1980). Though some religious organizations are reconsidering or changing their views on same-sex relationships, few religious organizations and their congregations truly welcome or accord full status to LGBT people who are out. Exceptions to this rule exist, of course, especially in urban areas with large LGBT populations where churches and temples serve the LGBT community, and some denominations have become inclusive to the point of supporting commitment ceremonies for same-sex couples. There are also churches, such as the Metropolitan Community Church, created for male gays, lesbians, and their biological and chosen families.

Still, many times LGBT persons struggle to maintain, adapt, or reject religious doctrine and spiritual beliefs that are discordant with their sexual orientation—a struggle most of their heterosexual contemporaries never face. Thus, current cohorts of LGBT caregivers may not feel they can turn to the religious or spiritual forms of coping often utilized by their heterosexual friends and family during personal crises and extended caregiving. Moreover, it is difficult or impossible to distance oneself from religion in some cultures where individuals must choose either to participate in the religious traditions and events of their cultures of origin or feel forced to give up their cultural identification. To better serve LGBT caregivers, it can be useful for practitioners to familiarize themselves with contemporary distinctions between religiosity on the one hand, and spirituality on the other. For example, spirituality often envelops the ideas described by Richards and her colleagues (1999) as "the facet of self that generates meaning and purpose in life, and provides the experience of individual transcendence and connection to universal order." In contrast, religiosity encompasses one's involvement with an organized system of traditions and codes that shapes one's attitudes, beliefs, and practices (Lukof, Lu, & Turner, 1992). Thus, many LGBT caregivers "may find meaning in non-traditional spiritualities or create a myriad of models and definitions within and outside of traditional religions, for spiritual expression" (Davidson, 2000, p. 416). Having said all this, it is crucial to remain mindful of the heterogeneity within the LGBT community. Many LGBT caregivers may find their religious communities and spiritual beliefs to be of tremendous importance in coping with caregiving and consider religion a primary source of support, and therefore we must not assume that LGBT identity alone determines a person's orientation towards spirituality or religiosity (e.g., Fukuyama & Ferguson, 2000).

CULTURAL CONTEXTS

Cultures differ in their openness about sexuality, what they designate as acceptable forms of sexuality, and the consequences for diverging from permissible sexual activities (e.g., Choi, Salazar, Lew, & Coates, 1995; Fox, 1996; Fukuyama & Ferguson, 2000; Herdt, 1990; Moore, 1997). In some Latino, Asian, and Native American cultures, women are not allowed to talk about sexuality, making it particularly difficult for lesbian or bisexual women to share such information with service providers. Sexuality is typically stigmatized when it violates other cultural rules, values, or conventions (Ross, Paulsen, & Stalstrom, 1988); therefore, societal disapproval derives not necessarily from sexual behavior, but rather from an individual's self-identification as gay male, lesbian, or bisexual. Many Asian and Pacific Islander cultures, for example, have deep-rooted social and cultural norms that allow the expression of same-sex behaviors within socially prescribed contexts, but public discussion of any kind of sexual behavior, especially same-sex behavior, is discouraged (Fukuyama & Ferguson, 2000). A recent study of Latin American men found that they could engage in sex with other men without stigma as long as they were the active partners (Zamora-Hernandez &

Patterson, 1996). Although these behaviors may be tolerated, the narrow sexual identities ascribed to these individuals do not allow for the development of a sexual identity as an LGBT person even when involved in long-term same-sex relationships or engaging for years in sexual relations with same-sex partners.

Cultural differences can also frequently arise in the context of dementia-caregiver service provision around the routine use of nontraditional therapies and healers (Gallagher-Thompson et al., 2000). Due to the HIV/AIDS crisis, many LGBT community members from a variety of cultural backgrounds also have become accustomed to seeking care from sources that traditional service providers may view with limited respect. Practitioners such as acupuncturists, herbalists, or spiritual advisors are consulted by growing numbers of LGBT patients with dementia and their caregivers who feel that their needs are inadequately met by the health care establishment. Service providers need to be prepared to work with such interests in ways that foster goal alignment between complementary or divergent approaches. In addition, we may need to provide education or referral information in a culturally sensitive manner (e.g., referrals back to their physicians or pharmacists or the Alzheimer's Association) on approaches that may exacerbate conditions or put patients with dementia or caregivers at risk.

Cross-cultural conflicts can also occur between the individualistic culture of mainstream America and more collectivist structures in other cultures. White gay males and lesbians may view it as their right to disclose their sexual orientations and to claim equal rights in the larger society. In contrast, the sociocultural contexts of some LGBT individuals of color stipulate that coming out is not an individual privilege, but rather is disrespectful and disruptive to the family, which thereby increases the perceived risk associated with disclosure to service providers (Fukuyama & Ferguson, 2000). In cultures where family is particularly important, such as the Latino, African American, and some Asian communities, individuals may have to choose between family and LGBT support. For many people of color, family helps protect against racism, so losing the support of family may be particularly traumatic (Moore, 1997). Some families of color, like some White families, tend to accept their LGBT family members as long as they don't openly disclose their sexual orientations. This form of denial allows the family to maintain its disapproval of same-sex orientations while keeping its connection with LGBT family members. This is especially true when increased caregiving responsibilities tie LGBT individuals more closely to biological kin both in terms of their time spent caregiving and their physical proximity to care recipients, whether they are same-sex partners or blood relatives. Thus, increasing our understanding of cultural influences on LGBT individuals, their interactions with their families, and the tensions they may face between self-disclosure and familial and culture proscriptions is critical for strengthening service provider competence. Given such high stakes, we must learn to read between the lines and accept that caregivers may present a distorted or very limited story, avoid our home visits, or prefer a telephone hot-line, on-line, or other more anonymous services.

MOVING FROM AWARENESS TO INCREASING CULTURAL COMPETENCE

Understanding sociocultural factors can help therapists begin to move from simple awareness of the LGBT community toward increasing competence in intervening with its members. Within the sociocultural contexts just discussed, service providers need to explore the physical, psychological, and social changes LGBT caregivers may face, by encouraging and respecting the sharing of their family stories. Thus, it is important to elicit and explore the target complaints of LGBT caregivers within their own varied contexts, using their labels and descriptors, rather than working solely from the service provider's frameworks that are shaped by his or her own cultural and professional background.

It is also crucial for service providers to recognize the meaning of social shifts and their effects on cohorts of LGBT caregivers. The sociocultural landscape has changed quite drastically for lesbians and gay males in a relatively short time, and this must be taken into account in moving from awareness to competence. In sharp contrast to years past, there are significant numbers of LGBT pride parades and LGBT film festivals today. At the same time, anti-LGBT ads appear in major newspapers, rising numbers of military personnel are discharged under the "don't ask, don't tell" policy, and programs and intervention models often funded and supported by the religious right encourage people to renounce their LGBT identities and take on heterosexual lifestyles. LGBT caregivers often need to research whether or not services and organizations will support them, ignore them, or even condemn them. Therefore, LGBT caregivers may still have extremely mixed feelings and deep misgivings about openly seeking help.

Older LGBT caregivers in particular have a legitimate interest in wondering how well service providers understand their particular contexts and concerns, which often differ dramatically from those of younger cohorts (Fassinger, 1997; Kimmel, 1995). For example, we need to consider that members of the cohort born in 1930 are now roughly 70 years old and were approximately 40 at the time of the Stonewall riot in 1969; they may have little in common with younger LGBT cohorts who haven't experienced life before the LGBT-rights movement (Kimmel & Sang, 1995). Older LGBT people, like their heterosexual contemporaries, experienced many large social shifts, such as the Great Depression, World War II, feminism and the Civil Rights movement. However, in contrast to their straight friends and families, they also lived much of their lives under the weight of a hostile society that regarded them as perverts, religious organizations that shunned them as sinners, psychologists and mental health professionals who diagnosed them as mentally ill, and police who harassed them as criminals (Kimmel & Sang, 1995).

It is only in the last couple of decades that the majority of health, mental health, and social service professional organizations have stopped labeling LGBT as mentally ill. Still, many professionals and lay people may continue to do so, and there is no guarantee that these hostile individuals are not also members of service communities, acting on their beliefs and biases regardless of the official stances of their professional organizations. Research suggests LGBT people have legitimate concerns about negative views held by medical and dental professionals and the impact these views can have on their health care (Kauth, Hartwig, & Kalichman, 2000). Knowledge of these views can and should affect service provider referral, treatment, and case management activities for both LGBT care recipients and caregivers. Given their histories and current hostilities, LGBT caregivers may not trust service providers and the health care and social service systems with information regarding their sexual orientation. Service providers need to be able to address this unfortunate yet well-founded concern in order to provide culturally competent care. For providers with limited training, books and literature are continually emerging and are oftentimes accessible through local LGBT community resources or on-line services. The American Society on Aging and its Lesbian and Gay Aging Information Network is a very valuable resource. Whether we live in LGBT-resource-rich environments or not, provider competence requires ongoing training through continuing education workshops and presentations at professional meetings, professional consultation with knowledgeable colleagues individually or at team meetings, and formal staff trainings by consulting groups that specialize in LGBT topics. Identifying obstacles to LGBT-caregiver service utilization and brainstorming ways to overcome or circumvent these obstacles is one of the most useful ways to keep strengthening our competence in developing and implementing interventions with LGBT caregivers.

IDENTIFYING OBSTACLES TO LGBT-CAREGIVER SERVICE UTILIZATION

Caregivers of patients with dementia can tackle numerous obstacles to service utilization in the course of the disease (e.g., Maslow & Selstad, 2001). However, LGBT caregivers typically confront additional barriers as a result of their sexual orientations and identities. These barriers cross multiple levels, from the individual or interpersonal level and the organizational or system level to the community level and the policy or legislative level.

Individual Barriers

LGBT individuals may be reluctant to seek services because of their own internalized beliefs about sexuality. Socialized in heterosexist societies, many gay males and lesbians struggle with internalized homophobia (e.g., Davison, 1991; Meyer, 1995; Meyer & Dean, 1998) and resist finding support for their specific concerns out of reluctance to confront their own discomfort with their sexual orientation and an LGBT identity. Coming out is a very personal choice and may be perceived as a benefit or an additional burden. The coming-out process involves a complex juggling of issues, including the redefinition of self and the management of parents, siblings and friends, and even at times spouse and children, who built an understanding of the LGBT person framed within a heterosexual context (Laird, 1996; Matteson, 1996). LGBT persons regularly face decisions about when to talk with whom about what and when to remain silent. LGBT caregivers, like all LGBT people, vary in their levels of outness, with some being out of the closet with friends but not work colleagues and siblings, and vice versa. Although coming out is associated with increased self-worth and other positive mental health effects (e.g., Gillow & Davis, 1987; Kurdek, 1988; Weinberg & Williams, 1974), the process may be too overwhelming for stressed caregivers. Service providers must watch for signs of stress and distress and help LGBT caregivers determine if they have sufficient coping resources or adequate amounts of social support to manage the process effectively.

Other LGBT caregivers may believe that sexuality is a private matter, not appropriate for public discussion, and therefore may resist approaching service providers who either self-identify as LGBT or who tailor their services to clients on the basis of sexual orientation and identity. This may be particularly true for older LGBT individuals or for caregivers from certain cultural backgrounds. Thus, the social service provider's responsibility is not to pull a person out, but to facilitate whatever process is needed and to respect the caregiver's level of outness. It is important for service providers to respect clients' beliefs and comfort levels, but we must also remain aware of the obstacles that internalized homophobia and reticence about issues of sexual orientation present to care providers trying to adequately serve LGBT patients and caregivers.

Organizational/System Barriers

Many of the barriers LGBT caregivers face in seeking services may stem not so much from individual interactions with care providers themselves, but rather from larger system and organizational barriers. Although we try to help caregivers manage their physical, mental, and sexual health, we must recognize that LGBT caregivers and care recipients may be reluctant to reveal their sexual orientations and behaviors to health care professionals for fear of discrimination from managed care systems and insurance companies or even the providers themselves (Kauth et al., 2000). This can be especially problematic for people in small or very well connected communities where the holders of the information may see one another frequently (D'Augelli & Garnets, 1995). Unfortunately withholding this information may lead to misdiagnosis and impede effective treatment and care management for patients with dementia and their caregivers. This is just one example of organizations and systems being set up in a way that interferes with meeting LGBT clients' needs.

Other common organizational barriers include such phenomena as health care systems deferring to estranged biological relatives rather than to longtime partners about decisions; and extended-care settings refusing to allow LGBT partners to visit care recipients or to openly express affection for fear that other patients and caregivers will be uncomfortable. Institutional barriers to care are common. They may be as subtle as brief expressions of discomfort or disapproval from staff or as overt as refusing to include LGBT issues as part of diversity committees and staff training; or discriminating against LGBT applicants for care-recipient placement in long-term care. Domestic partner benefits are not widely available in organizations, institutions, and other social systems, placing many LGBT caregivers and their care-recipient partners at risk for additional financial, social, and psychological stress.

LGBT Community Barriers

Unfortunately, the LGBT community shares many of the same prejudices as the larger society. Ageism is just as prevalent among gay males and lesbians as among heterosexuals and often presents a substantive obstacle for LGBT caregivers who are seeking support within their own communities. Formal support systems for older gay males and lesbians, let alone for caregivers of patients with dementia, are rarely in place, even among larger LGBT communities. Moreover, younger community members may often appear uninterested in, or reluctant to confront issues of, aging in dementia support-groups. Younger and older LGBT caregivers may disagree on the appropriate levels of outness versus closetedness necessary to be effective caregivers. If support-group facilitators are not aware of, and prepared to deal with, cohort differences like these, the rift can be quite significant.

LGBT persons of color may confront racial or ethnic discrimination from within the LGBT community as well (Gock, 1992; Greene, 1994). Discrimination can be overt and similar to that found in the larger community, sometimes taking the form of greater scrutiny in the workplace or in community clubs, restaurants, or stores. It can also be subtler, as in the absence of people of color in positions of power or leadership in LGBT community organizations. Because of these experiences of discrimination, LGBT caregivers of color may be reluctant to reach out to formal support programs in the LGBT community.

Hatred, Discrimination, Intolerance

In addressing the barriers to care, we need to consider the role of hatred, discrimination, and intolerance (DiPlacido, 1998; Herek, Gillis, & Cogan, 1999; Meyer, 1995) across multiple levels of possible caregiver interventions, from individualized treatments to organizational policy and governmental legislation. Ageism interacts with heterosexism in our society to create particularly negative stereotypes about LGBT older adults. This can place LGBT care recipients and caregivers in double, triple, or even quadruple jeopardy when they hold other minority status (for example, being a member of a racial or ethnic minority or having a physical disability) (Greene, 1994). The number of LGBT hate crimes continues to rise in the country (e.g., Herek et al., 1999); many LGBT caregivers fear that identifying themselves as such means placing themselves at risk. More than 80% of the respondents to a recent survey of more than 1,400 LGBT caregivers to family members, including caregivers to older family members, experienced harassment because of their sexual orientation (Fredriksen, 1999). In particular, LGBT care recipients as well as caregivers struggling with their own illnesses may feel themselves particularly vulnerable to hate crimes and other forms of discrimination that can encourage social isolation or withdrawal. It is very important for service providers to acknowledge these concerns and not pathologize clients, but rather consider these concerns as indicators of "healthy paranoia" or reasonable vigilance.

Fear of discrimination and intolerance interferes with LGBT care provision on many levels. Fears of hate crimes, loss of employment, and social stigma prevent many individuals from obtaining proper care, either because they do not seek out the services they need or because they withhold relevant information from medical, psychological, and social service providers. Therefore, it is important for us to discuss confidentiality (and its potential limits) and our respect for client privacy and to gain an explicit understanding of how and to whom clients want to be referred and what needs to be documented.

OVERCOMING OBSTACLES TO LGBT-CAREGIVER SERVICE UTILIZATION

In order to maximize the effectiveness of caregiver interventions with LGBT people, our change efforts must cross the multiple levels of obstacles just presented (Coon & Thompson, 2002). In this section, we present several approaches that program planners, clinicians, and other service providers might consider to foster the development and integration of effective interventions for their LGBT clientele.

Pulling Down Institutional Barriers

Sensitivity to personal and institutional heterosexism can help providers see and address specific instances of bias across multiple intervention levels. For example, organizations need to review their policies not just for clients but for their employees as well. Are their employment practices inclusive, encouraging the hiring and retention of LGBT staff? Does the organization have domestic partner benefits? Are training dollars adequately allocated for diversity training that encompasses LGBT concerns? Providers need to assess how their biases impact the way in which they communicate and the way in which they interpret LGBT caregivers' situations. Expression of heterosexist or homophobic bias can delay additional help-seeking behavior, censor the sharing of vital information with other providers, or stop help-seeking behavior completely. When service providers are not willing or cannot identify these biases and modify their service delivery practices, then LGBT caregivers and patients need to be referred to competent colleagues. Unfortunately, these biases need not be overt to impact outcomes significantly. Several studies have shown that provider biases regularly appear in therapeutic settings, impacting LGBT clients' assessments of the usefulness of services (Garnets et al., 1991; Phillips & Fischer, 1998; Winegarten et al., 1994).

Administrators should adopt a zero-tolerance policy for discrimination, either subtle or overt, that applies to all employees from top management to front-line staff. As part of the zero-tolerance policy, discriminatory language must be removed from all levels of care provision. Inclusive language and phrasing should be employed in all conversations, printed materials, and intake forms. Many service providers unintentionally overlook LGBT clients and fail to meet their needs simply because their language does not allow for the possibility of choices other than being in a heterosexual relationship or being single. Moreover, language should be inclusive and allow for a range of possible arrangements, behaviors, and identifications, rather than simply adding LGBT as an extra category of identity. Caregivers can engage in same-sex behaviors or have same-sex relationships but not identify as LGBT and may resist being pigeonholed into simplistically labeled categories. In order to communicate a safe environment, practitioners will need to become more skilled in helping caregivers tell their own stories and describe their relationships and caregiving situations in their own terms.

Choose Teachable Moments Wisely

Education is an ongoing process, and administrators, service providers, and caregivers alike cannot absorb all relevant and useful information at any one time. We have to choose teachable moments wisely. Discriminatory language and thinking should be challenged whenever possible, but how and when and in front of whom can substantially impact the outcomes. Just as other therapeutic feedback is "packaged" to maximize its palatability, comprehensibility, and usefulness to the recipient, education about LGBT issues should be presented in a consistent, planned, and open manner to maximize its reception and effectiveness. Case presentations and consultation in team meetings or supervision groups provide particularly salient opportunities to extend knowledge and expand skill sets.

Ongoing research suggests that even many graduate students are insufficiently trained in providing competent service to LGBT clients and feel little confidence in their abilities to work effectively with them (Allison, Crawford, Echemendia, et al., 1994; Buhrke, 1989; Glenn & Russell, 1986; Pilkington & Cantor, 1996). One strategy that supervisors and other instructors can use in training to increase provider competence with LGBT clients is simply to ask employees about their experiences with LGBT people. How many LGBT clients have they had? If none, why not? Could it be they failed to recognize LGBT clients by assuming heterosexuality and ignoring all hints to the contrary? Administrators and service providers must blend organizational policies with service procedures in order to provide a safe place for those who choose to come out to do so, without forcing unwelcome confrontations or demanding information that some people do not want to share. Several useful resources exist on incorporating LGBT issues into training and supervision (e.g., American Psychological Association, 2000; Buhrke & Douce, 1991; Cabaj & Stein, 1996; Greene & Croom, 2000; Hancock, 1995; Phillips, 2000). Interweaving training on LGBT issues with other issues of diversity can help build upon the shared skill sets that are necessary to serve diverse groups of caregivers effectively, while at the same time highlighting the unique issues faced by LGBT caregivers of various backgrounds.

Service Provider Outness, Acceptance, Competence

It is erroneous to assume that the most appropriate service providers for LGBT clients must be members of the LGBT community themselves. Such an assumption rests on the premise that LGBT functions as a simple, unitary category that bestows a fundamental similarity on all its members. Pigeonholing clients and service providers in this way hinders the effective development of treatments and interventions and may force together clients and providers with vastly different beliefs, comfort levels, and agendas on the basis of a categorized identification.

Service providers, like other LGBT community members, have widely varying comfort levels of outness. Although organizational policy and staff behavior should promote respect for LGBT employees and provide a safe place to be open, openness can only be fostered, not forced. Administrators and other staff must respect these individual levels of outness and recognize that closeted staff (especially those with limited LGBT experience or training) may be less effective than heterosexual staff who have established their comfort and competence with LGBT clients. As always, it is important to listen to the nuances of language used by providers and their level of experience and training in determining their suitability to work with specific clients.

Create a Safe Place Symbol

A "safe place symbol" system can be effectively instituted in many settings and contexts that caregivers frequent. A simple, easily identifiable symbol known to the LGBT community should be chosen, appear in newsletters and on intake forms, and be clearly posted to denote that the organization's staff and service providers are not only sympathetic to LGBT concerns but have received specific training in working with LGBT issues. Developing a symbol that could be shared across whole neighborhoods, service areas, or cities could prove particularly effective. Imagine LGBT seniors seeing such symbols in their doctors' offices, community centers, or short- and long-term-care facilities.

Add LGBT Information to Forms and Referral Lists

LGBT issues and information should be included as a matter of course in training, paperwork language, and referral materials. As already discussed, it is necessary to make language inclusive from the first moment of contact. Intake forms and client histories should make no assumptions about sexual orientation or history. To make services not only accessible but also useful to LGBT clients, it can be helpful to have magazines, newspapers, and brochures available that are inclusive of, and specific to, the LGBT community.

Providers must be comfortable referring caregivers to local LGBT resources; be mindful that LGBT clients often consider service providers' knowledge of LGBT community resources as an important factor when choosing providers (Liddle, 1997; Matteson, 1996). Therefore, interventionists and other service providers must educate themselves about available LGBT resources that are pertinent to caregiving by visiting with staff in these organizations. Such professional behavior is analogous to referring White, heterosexual older adults to mainstream senior centers, or referring individuals facing specific conditions such as Alzheimer's to their local Alzheimer's Association and other appropriate support groups.

It is a service provider's responsibility to seek out feedback on referrals. Sometimes a referral that is given so commonly it is not even thought about can turn out to be quite problematic for LGBT clients. For example, senior day-care centers that provide excellent care and have friendly, well-trained, caring staff may be extremely inhospitable to LGBT caregivers. A lesbian caregiver who sends her partner to pick up her elderly mother one afternoon may find the staff is no longer so friendly or caring when she brings her mother in the next morning. Service providers need to be aware of these possibilities and obtain the feedback necessary to make sure they are in fact providing appropriate, LGBT-friendly referrals. Conversely, when referring to LGBT resources, one must be sure that they welcome seniors. Many LGBT centers and organizations have no programs in place for elders or caregivers and may be decidedly unwelcoming to those individuals. Experiencing ageism from an LGBT referral can be just as distressing to clients as experiencing homophobia from elder-care or caregiver-support referrals. Again, encouraging LGBT caregivers and care recipients to provide feedback on community resources can help keep an organization's referral list up to date and its reputation in good standing.

Shift One Brick and Change the Wall

The number and complexity of the issues raised thus far may make it seem that the challenges of providing competent services to LGBT dementia caregivers and care recipients are insurmountable. Service providers face obstacles of socio-cultural discrimination and hostility, of justifiably suspicious and sometimes hard-to-identify target populations, and of the magnitude of caregiver stress, burden, and need for support and coping skills. However, we must remember that changing one factor shifts the relation and function of the rest. Shifting one brick, one obstacle, changes the face of the wall, and potentially helps caregivers' situations become more approachable. The first brick to shift for any intervention is simply to provide a safe place where LGBT caregivers can talk openly about the relationship between caregiving and their sexual orientation or identity. The opportunity for genuine honesty with providers who are trained in addressing issues of caregiver burden and stress and LGBT-specific concerns can make the difference between viewing the situation as one of overwhelming distress or seeing it as a set of more manageable problems.

Build on Strengths

Throughout this chapter, we have examined the difficulties of being an LGBT caregiver, the strengths of LGBT identities, and potential resources available to community members. It is important for service providers to keep these strengths in mind as well. To characterize LGBT identity as simply a source of stress and pain is to fall into one of the most insidious forms of lingering homophobia.

One resource available to many LGBT caregivers is the support of their chosen families. Even if they are painfully estranged from their biological families, living day-to-day in a chosen, like-minded family can be an incredible source of understanding and support, surpassing what many caregivers find available to them in their families of origin. As noted earlier, LGBT communities often evolve extended, multigenerational networks as part of their response to the hostility of the surrounding world. For some caregivers and care recipients, the LGBT community response to the AIDS crisis has created advanced networks of family and friends who are experienced with caregiving, end-of-life issues, and AIDS-related dementia. However, for other caregivers, the impact of social losses due to the AIDS epidemic is profound and the isolation of dementia care is painful. All existing and current informal networks, as well as formal care resources, need to be explored as potentially rich sources of support and practical assistance for LGBT caregivers, especially for older men who were often socialized to "go it on their own." Thus, social support can be reconceptualized beyond the family unit, not just by creating and relying on chosen "families," but by extending support contacts beyond the immediate group to a larger community with services that are sensitive to the needs of LGBT care recipients with dementia and their caregivers.

Finally, LGBT elders tend to have spent many years developing effective coping mechanisms just to live happily in a hostile world (Fassinger, 1997; Kimmel, 1995). Many of these coping skills are directly applicable to caregiving. Service providers should capitalize on extant effective coping skills, by redirecting familiar strategies toward caregiving stressors and then augmenting those strategies with whatever additional coping skills may be warranted.

The SURE 2 Framework

LGBT caregivers and other LGBT clients typically enter the service arena out of a desire to resolve growing stressors or conflicts. These conflicts occur at multiple levels of social interaction that are ripe for intervention. At the individual and interpersonal levels, the conflict may be a growing tension between self and an emerging self, which often centers around taking on new or additional aspects of the caregiving role. However, for some LGBT caregivers, it may also arise as they move out of the closet. This coming-out process may either involve revealing their sexual orientation to care recipients, employers, or others they had been closeted with in the past, or "coming out as a caregiver" with their LGBT families about their loved one's dementia. Conflicts at the interpersonal level can also emerge as a result of caregiving demands that create stressors between caregivers and their partners, friends, or employers who have limited understanding about dementia and caregiving. Tensions often occur between caregivers and their partner's estranged family members who never accepted the care recipient's homosexuality and the couple's relationship and who now do not acknowledge the caregiver's role, sometimes actively working to thwart efforts and limit their rights. As presented earlier, caregivers also face conflicts with organizations, the larger community, and their associated policies. Hatred, discrimination, and intolerance, both overt and subtle, create additional psychosocial and financial conflicts that bring LGBT caregivers to service providers' doors.

These multiple levels of obstacles and conflicts indicate the complementary need for multiple levels of intervention from the individual, interpersonal, organizational, community, and policy levels, with purposeful linkages developed between successful intervention elements identified at each level (Emmons, 2001). The SURE 2 Framework is a basic model directed at the individual and interpersonal levels that blends the elements of grassroots support groups with basic cognitive-behavioral therapy (CBT) techniques (e.g., Beck, Rush, Shaw, & Emery, 1979; Lewinsohn, Muñoz, Youngren, & Zeiss, 1986). The CBT perspective suggest that for groups to be most effective, they need to encourage participants to grow, learn, and change by maximizing their extant effective coping skills and trying out new skills and strategies presented by other participants or the facilitator (Thompson et al., 2000). Sharing emotional and spiritual support is very important but in the SURE 2 framework, support groups also function as an educational site where participants are encouraged to reframe unhelpful thoughts, to use consistently the healthy coping strategies that already work for them, and to explore new alternative coping strategies for additional support and stress reduction. Although directed at the individual and interpersonal levels, components of the framework help caregiving participants identify and share information that impacts stressors experienced across other levels and encourages use of the cognitive and behavioral techniques to manage stress associated with them. The first author's experience running an open-ended, drop-in support group for the LGBT community suggests it is a useful framework for facilitators to use. It has also been easily adapted for individual counseling and family consultation with LGBT caregivers that can allow for the intervention model to be more structured with traditional CBT homework assignments and consistent follow-up.

The letters in SURE 2 represent concepts that are easy for facilitators to remember throughout group meetings. These are presented from an empowerment perspective designed to encourage LGBT caregiving participants to empower one another and themselves.

Sharing and Support. In the tradition of caregiver support groups, the focus is on group members' sharing their feelings about caregiving and its impact on their lives. The first part of each meeting involves a traditional introduction and check-in, with caregivers putting items on a table to discuss during the second part of the meeting. Basic questions for clarification are allowed during check-in, but the focus on informational and emotional support occurs later when items on the table are shared more fully. In a demonstration of support for the most pressing concerns, group members help the facilitator prioritize the items for discussion. Often these items can be grouped together, with caregivers' drawing relationships between one another's situations.

Unhelpful Thoughts/Behaviors and Understanding. During the second part of the meeting, caregivers often discuss the conflicts or stressors that brought them to the group, whether it be a conflict between them and significant others, including the care recipient, or conflicts with health care systems or legal problems and difficulties. Whatever the case, group members and the facilitator encourage other caregivers to identify what isn't working, and they share their empathy and understanding of how easy it is to get caught up in negative thinking about themselves, to reach for unhelpful behaviors (worrying, eating, working, drinking, or smoking too much), and to not take care of themselves.

Reframes and Referrals. Caregivers are also encouraged to consider ways to reframe their thinking and their situations through basic cognitive restructuring techniques (e.g., basic problem solving, cost-benefit analyses, avoiding black-and-white thinking, and positive reframing) and to elicit ideas or perspectives from the group. These ideas also include recognizing the obstacles LGBT people face as a result of their sexual orientation or identity, such as difficulty finding LGBT-sensitive in-home health- or day care or appropriate placement situations, and sharing referrals when competent professionals and organizations are identified.

Education and Exploration. The groups regularly include updates and education about the disease, the course of caregiving, and upcoming educational seminars sponsored by the local Alzheimer's Association and other organizations. Each session reviews recent explorations of alternative coping strategies, recent referrals tried and feedback to one another about those referrals, and closes with an exploration of at least one strategy or referral that each group member will try to help them take care of themselves in the course of caregiving.

CASE EXAMPLE

Stan, a 72-year-old retired plumber, had been actively participating in the group for more than a year, seeking information and emotional support while caring for his partner of 41 years. Stan's partner, Burt, had been diagnosed with Alzheimer's disease 5 years earlier. Until he found the group, Stan had been "so alone in the disease . . . just going crazy." Burt had run a hardware store until he suffered a stroke and then received the Alzheimer's disease diagnosis almost 6 years later. Burt was a few years older than Stan, and they had met at the hardware store and refurbished the house they now lived in. Through other group members, Stan was encouraged to interview companies that might have gay-friendly in-home health workers to help him lift and bathe Burt. And group members helped him locate an attorney who was familiar with the concerns of LGBT older adults and their partners. Burt became less communicative and slept more and more. Many days Stan wondered if Burt recognized him anymore. Stan and Burt had been regular members of a gay-friendly church in their neighborhood for many years, but Burt was unable to last through a service or church outing anymore. Support group members had encouraged Stan to continue attending both for the spiritual support he felt he needed as well as the social connection it provided. At one group meeting many months later, Stan shared that he was struggling with something he never thought would happen again in his life. He had met a new church member, Richard, a recently retired insurance salesman who had moved to the area, and they had fallen in love. Stan shared that Burt and he had been a monogamous couple, and though he still loved Burt, he definitely loved Richard now, too. The reactions of the group members varied, ranging from clear support of polyamory to more cautious approaches. One member encouraged him to take it slowly and another shared that while it might not work for him, Stan needed to determine what was right for both Burt and him. Interestingly enough, some group members spontaneously turned to the SURE 2 model during Stan's sharing of his dilemma, First they provided emotional support, but then they began to ask, "What is really bothering you most? What are you thinking and how can you look at it differently?" Through the process, Stan decided to check out assumptions he was holding about what close friends and family might think of him. Instead of beating himself up about "not loving Burt enough," he also reviewed conversations he'd had with Burt soon after the stroke, in which each wanted the other to consider "remarrying" if one partner were to die. Through that review and conversations with Burt's closest friends and his sister, Stan believed he would have Burt's blessing to develop a new relationship. Stan and Richard continued dating, with Richard helping Stan more and more with Burt's caregiving, and they were both with Burt when he died 6 months later. Stan returned to the group for several months after Burt's death, providing ongoing support, caregiving information, and books and education material that he thought other group members could use. He also handed out contact information for the gay-friendly home-health agency he hired. At his last meeting he thanked the group for helping him out of the isolation of caregiving and for helping him to "always look for another alternative."

CONCLUDING COMMENTS

To be a member of the LGBT community is to be overwhelmed with the attitudes of other people, and in order to free ourselves from that we have to put those aside and develop our own sense of what is right (Harry Britt as cited in Crisp, 1989). As practitioners and program developers, we must develop our interventions in ways that not only maximize LGBT caregivers' support from their biological families, but also that honor and support the LGBT family members they choose and help them find ways to cherish the overlap. As the caregiver who was quoted at the start of this chapter said, "We often talk about that book [Kath Weston's *Families We Choose: Lesbians, Gays, Kinship*]. My family is really both: it's my nuclear, my blood family, and it's the gay and lesbian family Todd and I chose together here in the city and from back home, years ago. Many of them are still with us. They are our champions."

Perhaps, as Barón (1991) suggests in citing Quentin Crisp (1989), the ultimate challenge is to make same-sex relationships boring—not in the sense of dull, but in the sense of being an inconsequential part of everyday life, similar in that respect to heterosexuality. As the lesbian poet Elsa Gidlow asks in her autobiography, "Who has ordained, and on what authority, that we must supply the world with script and justification of our intimate interactions?" (Gidlow, 1986, p. 301). However, until LGBT clients and professionals alike "no longer need to explain, justify, enlighten and otherwise ask for understanding" (Barón, 1991, p. 239) about how sexual orientation impacts their daily lives, including their caregiving roles and their need for LGBT-sensitive referrals and services, practitioners and researchers need to share information on the topics we begin to address in this chapter. Practitioners need to be aware of, and be prepared to address competently, the particular needs of all their clients.

Although services will always be provided within the context of the larger culture and under the shaping influence of service providers' own sociocultural backgrounds—making the ideal of "culture-free" services both unrealistic and irrelevant—by consciously working to eliminate homophobic bias and insensitivity from our services we can in turn contribute to changing the surrounding culture to better suit our own ideals of acceptance and diversity. In this way, service providers' actions echo beyond the moment of client contact to make them agents of change in a much larger sense. Only through first increasing our awareness of the particular issues and needs of LGBT caregivers and then continuing to develop our competence through ongoing education, training, and consultation can we strive for a level of competence wherein sexual orientation will no longer put caregivers at risk of receiving inappropriate or inadequate services.

RESOURCES

- American Society on Aging's Lesbian and Gay Aging Issues Network, San Francisco, CA; (415)974-9600; www.asaing.org/lgain
- *Outword: Newsletter of the Lesbian and Gay Aging Issues Network of the American Society on Aging.* San Francisco: American Society on Aging.
- New Leaf Outreach to Elders (formerly GLOE/Gay & Lesbian Outreach to Elders), San Francisco, CA. (415)255-2937
- Pride Senior Network, New York, NY, (212)757-3203; www.pridesenior.org
- Senior Action in Gay Environments, New York, NY, (212)741-2247; www.sageusa.org

REFERENCES

Alexander, C. J. (1997). *Growth and intimacy for gay men.* New York: Harrington Park Press.

Allison, K., Crawford, I., Echemendia, R., Robinson, L., & Knepp, D. (1994). Human diversity and professional competence: Training in clinical and counseling psychology revisited. *American Psychologist, 49,* 792–796.

Alquijay, M. A. (1997). The relationships among self-esteem, acculturation and lesbian identity formation in Latina lesbians. In B. Greene (Ed.), *Ethnic and cultural diversity among lesbians and gay men* (pp. 249–265). Newbury Park, CA: Sage.

American Psychological Association. (1992). Ethical principles and code of conduct. *American Psychologist, 47,* 1597–1611.

American Psychological Association. Division 44/Committee on Lesbian, Gay, and Bisexual Concerns Joint Task Force. (2000). Guidelines for psychotherapy with lesbian, gay, and bisexual clients. *American Psychologist, 55,* 1440–1451.

Barón, A. (1991). The challenge: To make homosexuality boring. *Counseling Psychologist, 19,* 239–244.

Barón, A., & Cramer, D. (2000). *Potential counseling concerns of aging lesbian, gay, and bisexual clients. Handbook of counseling and psychotherapy with lesbian, gay, and bisexual clients.* Washington, DC: American Psychological Association.

Beck, A. T., Rush, A. J., Shaw, B. F., & Emery, G. (1979). *Cognitive therapy of depression.* New York: Guilford Press.

Bell, A. P., Weinberg, M. S., & Hammersmith, S. K. (1981). *Homosexualities: A study of diversity among men and women.* New York: Simon and Schuster.

Berger, R., & Kelly, J. (1996). Gay men and lesbians grown older. In R. Cabaj & T. Stein (Eds.), *Textbook of homosexuality and mental health* (pp. 305–316). Washington, DC: American Psychiatric Press.

Berger, R. M. (1982). *Gay and gray: The older homosexual man.* Urbana: University of Illinois Press.

Boswell, J. (1980). *Christianity, social tolerance and homosexuality.* Chicago: The University of Chicago Press.

Buhrke, R. (1989). Female student perspectives on training in lesbian and gay issues. *Counseling Psychologist, 17,* 629–636.

Buhrke, R., & Douce, L. G. (1991). Training issues for counseling psychologists in working with lesbians and gay men. *Counseling Psychologist, 19,* 216–239.

Cabaj, R. P., & Stein, T. S. (1996). *Textbook of homosexuality and mental health.* Washington, DC: American Psychiatric Press.

Choi, K. H., Salazar, N., Lew, S., & Coates, T. J. (1995). AIDS risk, dual identity, and community response among gay Asian and Pacific Islander men in San Francisco. In B. Greene & G. M. Herek (Eds.), *AIDS identity and community: The HIV epidemic and lesbians and gay men* (pp. 115–134). Thousand Oaks, CA: Sage.

Coleman, E. (1987). Assessment of sexual orientation. *Journal of Homosexuality, 14,* 9–24.

Connolly, L. (1996). Long-term care and hospice: The special needs of older gay men and lesbians. In K. J. Peterson (Ed.), *Health care for lesbians and gay men: Confronting homophobia and heterosexism* (pp. 77–91). New York: Harrington Park Press.

Coon, D. W., Davies, H., McKibbin, C., & Gallagher-Thompson, D. (1999). The psychological impact of genetic testing for Alzheimer's disease. *Genetic Testing, 3,* 121–132.

Coon, D. W., & Thompson, L. W. (2002). Family caregiving for older adults: Emergent and ongoing themes for the behavior therapist. *The Behavior Therapist, 25,* 17–20.

Crisp, Q. (1989). *Quentin Crisp's book of quotations: 1000 observations on life and love, by, for, and about gay men and women.* New York: Macmillan.

Croteau, J. M., Anderson, M. Z., Distefano, T. M., & Kampa-Kokesch, S. (2000). In R. Perez, K. A. DeBord, & K. J Bieschke (Eds.), *Handbook of counseling and psychotherapy with lesbian, gay, and bisexual clients.* Washington, DC: American Psychological Association.

D'Augelli, A., & Garnets, L. (1995). Lesbian, gay, and bisexual communities. In A. D'Augelli & C. Patterson (Eds.), *Lesbian, gay, and bisexual identities over the life span: Psychological perspectives* (pp. 293–320). New York: Oxford University Press.

Davidson, M. G. (2000). Religion and spirituality. In R. Perez, K. A. DeBord, & K. J Bieschke (Eds.), *Handbook of counseling and psychotherapy with lesbian, gay, and bisexual clients* (pp. 409–434). Washington, DC: American Psychological Association.

Davison, G. (1991). Constructionism and morality in therapy for homosexuality. In J. Gonsiorek & J. Weinrich (Eds.), *Homosexuality: Research implications for public policy* (pp. 137–148). Newbury Park, CA: Sage.

DiPlacido, J. (1998). Minority stress among lesbians, gay men, and bisexuals: A consequence of heterosexism, homophobia, and stigmatization. In G. Herek (Ed.), *Psychological perspectives on lesbian and gay issues: Vol. 4. Stigma and sexual orientation: Understanding prejudice against lesbians, gay men, and bisexuals* (pp. 138–159). Thousand Oaks, CA: Sage.

Dorfman, R. A., Lubben, J. E., Mayer-Oakes, A., Atchison, K., Schweitzer, S. O., DeJong, I. J., & Matthias, R. E. (1995). Screening for depression among a well elderly population. *Social Work, 40,* 295–304.

Dworkin, S. H. (2000). Individual therapy with lesbian, gay, and bisexual clients. In R. Perez, K. A. DeBord, & K. J. Bieschke (Eds.), *Handbook of counseling and psychotherapy with lesbian, gay, and bisexual clients* (pp. 157–181). Washington, DC: American Psychological Association.

Emmons, K. M. (2001). Behavioral and social science contributions to the health of adults in the United States. In B. D. Smedley & S. L. Syme (Eds.), *Promoting health: Intervention strategies from social and behavioral research* (pp. 254–321). Washington, DC: National Academy Press.

Ettelbrick, P. L. (1996). Legal issues in health care for lesbians and gay men. In K. J. Peterson (Ed.), *Health care for lesbians and gay men: Confronting homophobia and heterosexism* (pp. 77–91). New York: Harrington Park Press.

Fassinger, R. (1997). Issues in group work with older lesbians. *Group, 21,* 191–210.

Fox, R. (1996). Bisexuality in perspective: A review of theory and research. In B. Firestein (Ed.), *Bisexuality: The psychology and politics of an invisible minority* (pp. 263–291). Thousand Oaks, CA: Sage.

Fredriksen, K. L. (1999). Family caregiving responsibilities among lesbians and gay men. *Social Work, 44,* 142–155.

Fukuyama, M. A., & Ferguson, A. D. (2000). Lesbian, gay, and bisexual people of color: Understanding cultural complexity and managing multiple oppressions. In R. Perez, K. A. DeBord, & K. J. Bieschke (Eds.), *Handbook of counseling and psychotherapy with lesbian, gay, and bisexual clients* (pp. 81–105). Washington, DC: American Psychological Association.

Gallagher-Thompson, D., Solano, N., Coon, D., & Árean, P. (in press). Recruitment and retention of Latina dementia family caregivers in intervention research: Issues to face, lessons to learn. *Gerontologist.*

Gallagher-Thompson, D., Árean, P., Coon, D., Menéndez, A., Takagi, K., Haley, W., Argüelles, T., Rubert, M., Loewenstein, D., & Szapocznik, J. (2000). Development and implementation of intervention strategies for culturally diverse caregiving populations. In R. Schulz et al. (Eds.), *Handbook of dementia caregiving: Evidence-based interventions for family caregivers* (pp. 151–185). New York: Springer.

Garnets, L., Hancock, K., Cochran, S., Goodchilds, J., & Peplau, L. (1991). Issues in psychotherapy with lesbians and gay men: A survey of psychologists. *American Psychologist, 46,* 964–972.

Gidlow, E. (1986). *I come with my songs.* San Francisco: Booklegger Press.

Gillow, K. E., & Davis, L. L. (1987). Lesbian stress and coping methods. *Journal of Psychosocial Nursing, 25,* 28–32.

Glenn, A., & Russell, R. (1986). Heterosexual bias among counselor trainees. *Counselor Education and Supervision, 25,* 222–229.

Gock, T. (1992). The challenges of being gay, Asian, and proud. In B. Berzon (Ed.), *Positively gay* (pp. 247–252). Millbrae, CA: Celestial Arts.

Greene, B. (1994). Ethnic minority lesbians and gay men: Mental health and treatment issues. *Journal of Consulting and Clinical Psychology, 62,* 243–251.

Greene, B., & Croome, G. (Eds.). (2000). *Psychological perspectives on lesbian and gay issues: Vol. 5. Education, research, and practice in lesbian, gay, bisexual, and transgendered psychology: A resource manual.* Thousand Oaks, CA: Sage.

Grossman, A. H., D'Augelli, A. R., & Hershberger, S. L. (2000). Social support networks of lesbian, gay, and bisexual adults 60 years of age and older. *Journal of Gerontology, 55B,* P171–P179.

Herdt, G. (1990). Developmental discontinuities and sexual orientation across cultures. In D. P. McWhirter, S. A. Sanders, & J. M. Reinisch (Eds.), *Homosexuality/heterosexuality: Concepts of sexual orientation* (pp. 208–236). New York: Greenwood Press.

Herek, G. (1986). On heterosexual masculinity: Some psychological consequences of the social construction of gender and sexuality. *American Behavioral Scientist, 29,* 563–577.

Herek, G. M., Gillis, J. R., & Cogan, J. C. (1999). Psychological sequelae of hate crime victimization among lesbian, gay, and bisexual adults. *Journal of Consulting and Clinical Psychology, 67,* 945–951.

Kauth, M. R., Hartwig, M. J., & Kalichman, S. C. (2000). Health behavior relevant to psychotherapy with lesbian, gay, and bisexual clients. In R. Perez, K. A. DeBord, & K. J. Bieschke (Eds.), *Handbook of counseling and psychotherapy with lesbian, gay, and bisexual clients.* Washington, DC: American Psychological Association.

Kimmel, D. C. (1978). Adult development and aging: A gay perspective. *Journal of Social Issues, 43,* 113–120.

Kimmel, D. C., & Sang, B. E. (1995). Lesbians and gay men in midlife. In A. R. D'Augelli & C. J. Patterson (Eds.), *Lesbian, gay, and bisexual identities over the lifespan: Psychological perspectives* (pp. 190–214). New York: Oxford University Press.

Kimmel, D. (1995). Lesbians and gay men also grow old. In L. Bond, S. Cutler, & A. Grams (Eds.), *Promoting successful and productive aging* (pp. 289–303). Thousand Oaks, CA: Sage.

Klein, F., Sepekoff, B., & Wolf, T. (1986). Sexual orientation: A multi-variable dynamic process. *Journal of Homosexuality, 11,* 35–49.

Kurdek, L. A. (1988). Perceived social support in gays and lesbians in cohabitating relationships. *Journal of Personality and Social Psychology, 54,* 504–509.

Laird, J. (1996). Invisible ties: Lesbians and their families of origin. In J. Laird & R. J. Green (Eds.), *Lesbians and gays in couples and families: A handbook for therapists* (pp. 89–122). San Francisco: Jossey-Bass.

Lewinsohn, P. M., Muñoz, R. F., Youngren, M. A., & Zeiss, A. M. (1986). *Control your depression.* New York: Prentice-Hall.

Liddle, B. (1997). Gay and lesbian clients? Selection of therapists and utilization of therapy. *Psychotherapy, 34,* 394–401.

Lukoff, D., Lu, F., & Turner, R. (1992). Toward a more culturally sensitive DSM-IV: Psychoreligious and spiritual problems. *Journal of Nervous and Mental Disease, 180,* 673.

Maslow, K., & Selstad, J. (2001). Chronic care networks for Alzheimer's disease: Approaches for involving and supporting family caregivers in an innovative model of dementia care. *Alzheimer's Care Quarterly, 2,* 33–46.

Markowitz, L. (1995). Bisexuality: Challenging our either/or thinking. *In the Family, 1,* 6–11, 23.

Matteson, D. (1996). Counseling and psychotherapy with bisexual and exploring clients. In B. Firestein (Ed.), *Bisexuality: The psychology and politics of an invisible minority* (pp. 185–213). Thousand Oaks, CA: Sage.

Meyer, I. (1995). Minority stress and mental health in gay men. *Journal of Health and Social Behavior, 7,* 9–25.

Meyer, I., & Dean, L. (1998). Internalized homophobia, intimacy, and sexual behavior among gay and bisexual men. In G. Herek (Ed.), *Psychological perspectives on lesbian and gay issues: Vol. 4. Stigma and sexual orientation: Understanding prejudice against lesbians, gay men, and bisexuals* (pp. 160–186). Thousand Oaks, CA: Sage.

Money, J. (1988). *Gay, straight, and in-between: The sexology of erotic orientation.* New York: Oxford University Press.

Moore, E. S. (1997). *Does your mama know? An anthology of Black lesbian coming out stories.* Decatur, GA: Red Bone Press.

National Alliance for Caregiving and the American Association of Retired Persons. (1997). *Family caregiving in the US: Findings from a national survey. Final Report.* Bethesda, MD: National Alliance for Caregiving.

Perez, R., DeBord, K. A., & Bieschke, K. J. (2000). *Handbook of counseling and psychotherapy with lesbian, gay, and bisexual clients.* Washington, DC: American Psychological Association.

Phillips, J. (2000). Training issues and considerations. In R. M. Perez, K. A. DeBord, & K. J. Bieschke (Eds.), *Handbook of counseling and psychotherapy with lesbian, gay and bisexual clients* (pp. 337–358). Washington, DC: American Psychological Association.

Phillips, J., & Fischer, A. (1998). Graduate students? Training experiences with lesbian, gay, and bisexual issues. *Counseling Psychologist, 26,* 712–734.

Pilkington, N., & Cantor, J. (1996). Perceptions of heterosexual bias in professional psychology programs: A survey of graduate students. *Professional Psychology: Research and Practice, 27,* 604–612.

Quam, J. K., & Whitford, G. S. (1992). Adaptation and age-related expectations of older gay and lesbian adults. *Gerontologist, 32,* 367–374.

Richards, T. A., Acree, M., & Folkman, S. (1999). Spiritual aspects of loss among partners of men with AIDS: Postbereavement follow-up. *Death Studies, 23,* 105–127.

Ross, M. W., Paulsen, J. A., & Stalstrom, O. W. (1988). Homosexuality and mental health: A cross-cultural review. *Journal of Homosexuality, 15,* 131–152.

Sell, R. L., Wells, J. A., & Wypij, D. (1995). The prevalence of homosexual behavior and attraction in the United States, the United Kingdom and France: Results of national population-based samples. *Archives of Sexual Behavior, 24,* 235–248.

Slater, S. (1995). *The lesbian family life cycle.* New York: Free Press.

Tanfer, K. (1993). National survey of men: Design and execution. *Family Planning Perspectives, 25,* 83–86.

Thompson, L., Powers, D., Coon, D., Takagi, K., McKibbin, C., & Gallagher-Thompson, D. (2000). Older adults. In J. R. White & A. S. Freeman (Eds.), *Cognitive behavioral group therapy for specific problems and populations* (pp. 235–261). Washington, DC: American Psychological Association.

Weinberg, M. S., & Williams, C. (1974). *Male homosexuals: Their problems and adaptations.* New York: Oxford University Press.

Weston, K. (1991). *Families we choose: Lesbians, gays, kinship.* New York: Columbia University Press.

Winegarten, B., Cassie, N., Markowski, K., Kozlowski, J., & Yoder, J. (1994, August). *Aversive heterosexism: Exploring unconscious bias toward lesbian psychotherapy clients.* Paper presented at the 102nd Annual Convention of the American Psychological Association, Los Angeles, CA.

Wishik, H., & Pierce, C. (1995). *Sexual orientation and identity: Heterosexual, lesbian, gay and bisexual journeys.* Laconia, NH: New Dynamics.

Wrubel, J., & Folkman, S. (1997). What informal caregivers actually do: The caregiving skills of partners of men with AIDS. *CARE, 9,* 691–706.

Yee, J. L., & Schulz, R. (2000). Gender differences in psychiatric morbidity among family caregivers: A review and analysis. *Gerontologist, 40,* 147–164.

Yeo, G., & Gallagher-Thompson, D. (Eds.). (1996). *Ethnicity and the dementias.* Washington, DC: Taylor & Francis.

Zamora-Hernandez, C. E., & Patterson, D. G. (1996). Homosexually active Latino men: Issues for social practice. In J. F. Longres (Ed.), *Men of color: A context for service to homosexually active men* (pp. 69–91). New York: Harrington Park Press.

4

Recommendations for the Future

14

Future Directions in Dementia Caregiving Intervention Research and Practice

Larry W. Thompson,
Dolores Gallagher-Thompson,
and William E. Haley

The impetus for this edited book was our interest in describing the various strategies employed by different professionals to assist family members in their role as caregivers for loved ones who no longer have the capability to care for themselves. At this point, little needs to be said about the stress and strain experienced by those held "captive" in this new and often strenuous "career." Frequently, significant lifestyle changes are required, and invariably at one or more points over the course of this lengthy journey, many different forms of assistance have proven beneficial in improving or maintaining quality of life for both caregivers and care recipients alike.

Numerous professional groups have accepted the challenge of providing services to family caregivers, and each has come forth with its own strategies, tackling the problem from multiple levels with different tools and models to guide them. Given the diverse nature and intensity of the problems encountered, it seems reasonable to assume that such a multifaceted approach covering a wide range of interventions is justified. Lack of communication and coordination among the various specialties, however, could conceivably become a potential barrier to optimal implementation of services. One hopes that increased exchange of information about the interventions used by different professional specialties will foster greater coordination in the application of multilevel interventions. The present volume reviews some of these strategies, ranging from direct work with individual caregivers in their home setting to local, regional, and national policy changes that are reported to be effective in assisting caregivers. In part 1, Coon and coworkers laid the groundwork by summarizing several models that are employed to tie research evidence to policy and practice, in terms of both assessment and intervention. The authors emphasized the practical and theoretical importance of developing interventions that are targeted for multiple levels of impact, and in so doing they remind the reader that caregiver needs and problems are continually changing as health-related changes occur in the care recipient. Gottlieb and his associates continue to develop this premise, while focusing on the methodological requirements for evaluating and monitoring both proximal and distal changes due to interventions. Gallagher-Thompson and her colleagues emphasize the impact of multicultural influences on outcomes and their importance in the development of effective interventions.

In part 2, more specific information was provided by professionals from a variety of disciplines. Each chapter contains detailed theoretical and clinical material reflecting the authors' experience with approaches they found to be helpful with family caregivers. Several common problem areas or intervention targets that were mentioned include the numerous losses experienced by caregivers as their loved one deteriorates; the burdens of care resulting from innumerable stressful challenges; the inadequacies of current instrumental and social resources; and the depletion of caregivers' physical and psychological capabilities over time. Careful consideration of the array of interventions described in this section should alert the interested professional that one or more specific assistance programs may be called for at any given moment in time, depending on the functional level of the care recipient, the personal characteristics of the caregiver, and the existing social, emotional, and instrumental resources that are available. In part 3, greater attention is focused on the practical application of interventions to specific caregiving groups, including men and ethnic and racial minorities, as well as caregivers from the lesbian, gay male, bisexual, and transgender community.

INTERVENTIONS ARE NEEDED ON A VARIETY OF LEVELS FOR MAXIMAL EFFECTIVENESS

The material presented in this volume leads us to five major points we would like to make in this closing chapter. First, we wish to underscore the importance of thinking of future intervention research and practice that is not focused solely on the primary caregiver. Work with other members of the family, including the care recipient and significant friends of the family (whenever possible), may provide assistance that is critical to the welfare of caregivers and their essential support systems, both in and around the family unit. Furthermore, researchers and practitioners should expand their concept of intervention to encompass more indirect influences within their communities at large. This could include, for example, involvement in policy development at the local, state, and national levels; being a presence at community-sponsored special events for caregivers, such as health screening fairs; and membership or voluntary service in special interest groups that focus on empowering caregivers, such as a local Alzheimer's Association chapter. Such efforts should enable us to develop models that encourage provision of assistance to caregivers in a coordinated manner, at multiple levels, and at the same time, that minimize excessive costs and avoid duplication of services.

DIFFERENT INTERVENTIONS ARE NEEDED AT DIFFERENT POINTS IN THE CAREGIVING PROCESS

Aneshensel and colleagues (Aneshensel, Pearlin, Mullan, Zarit, & Whitlatch, 1995) have developed a model of the "caregiving career" that progresses through various phases, including role acquisition (at the beginning of providing care), role enactment (providing care in the home and if necessary through placement in a facility), and then role disengagement including the final loss of the care receiver through death and the subsequent bereavement process of the caregiver. Over the course of several years, caregivers typically progress from assisting with the performance of activities of daily living (such as balancing the checkbook or issuing reminders to keep appointments) to managing behavior problems common in the middle stage of dementia (such as wandering and inappropriate social behavior). In the final stage of most dementing disorders, caregivers manage bedridden, totally dependent adults either at home or through placement in an extended-care facility. Although it may seem intuitively correct to assume that caregiving stress increases as the dementing disorder worsens (and as the number of years spent caregiving increases) most longitudinal studies addressing this issue have not found that to be case. Goode, Haley, Roth, and Ford (1998), for example, found little direct effect of care-receiver deterioration on caregivers' depression or self-reported physical health over time. Similar results were reported by Powers, Gallagher-Thompson, and Kraemer (2002) who found stability both in caregivers' level of depressive symptoms and their reported preferred strategies for coping with caregiving stress, over the 2-year period of study. Using a validated measure of the frequency and "bother" of a variety of memory and behavioral problems, McCarty et al. (2000) found an inverted-U-shaped curve such that the highest bother scores were observed for care recipients with cognitive function scores toward the middle of the distribution (i.e., care recipients with moderately severe dementia). A corollary to this is the observation by McCarty et al. (2000) that fewer behavioral problems are actually reported as cognitive functioning declines.

Unfortunately, findings such as these have been slow to inform the intervention literature. Most studies have lumped together caregivers at various points along the continuum of care and have given them whatever particular intervention program was under study, with little regard for their place along the caregiving continuum. Our own work proceeded in much the same fashion until serendipity created a unique finding in one of our intervention studies. Gallagher-Thompson and Steffen (1994) compared the efficacy of individually administered brief cognitive-behavioral therapy compared to brief psychodynamic therapy for the treatment of clinically significant depression in family caregivers. They predicted that the former would be more appropriate for caregivers in the earlier stages of their career because specific coping strategies were taught for managing difficult caregiving situations, whereas the latter would be more appropriate for later-stage caregivers who were dealing with issues of grief and loss (which were a focus of the particular form of psychodynamic therapy used in that study). Contrary to expectations, the opposite results were found: Early stage caregivers responded more strongly to the psychodynamic therapy, while the cognitive-behavioral approach was more effective for later-stage caregivers on several relevant outcome measures. Posttreatment interviews with participants indicated that in the early stages they were coping with the impending loss of their loved one as they knew that person, while in the later stages, being able to learn effective coping strategies for dealing with their own negative emotions about caregiving was perceived to generate hope in an otherwise hopeless landscape. Statistically, the authors determined that 44 months was the recommended cut-off point for decision-making regarding treatment modality. To our knowledge these results have not been replicated, yet the data are persuasive as to the differential utility of these specific interventions at different times in the care-giving process.

Similarly, Zarit and colleagues (Zarit, Stephens, Townsend, & Greene, 1998) conducted a carefully controlled study examining the effects of adult day-care use on perceived stress in dementia family caregivers. They observed that prior studies reporting negative results included caregivers who did not actually use day-care at a sufficiently intense level for it to impact their well-being. To ensure that caregivers in their own study were in fact distressed enough by their loved one's memory and behavioral problems to need this level of care, Zarit et al. (1998) required at least twice-weekly day-care use by the care receiver over a 3-month period in order for the caregiver to be eligible to participate in the research. The investigators found that caregivers who met that criteria improved on measures of depression, role overload, and strain, compared to those in the control condition whose care receiver did not participate in a day care program. Positive results found at the 3-month assessment point were maintained, by and large, 1 year later. This study underscores the point that it is both appropriate and effective to provide interventions that are specific to the kinds of stresses that caregivers are actually experiencing, based on where they are in their overall caregiving career.

GENDER AND ROLE DIFFERENCES SHOULD INFORM INTERVENTION CHOICES

A related issue is the growing (but still limited) body of knowledge about the intervention preferences of different family members, based on their gender and their relationship to the care receiver. For example, some studies have shown that spousal caregivers (typically wives) report more fatigue, less energy, and more sleep disturbances than nonspousal caregivers (Teel & Press, 1999). This suggests that intervention programs that have a health promotion or wellness focus may be well-received and effective for this group. Whether they would be more effective when directly compared to intervention programs that focus on enhancing psychological status remains to be seen and should be the subject of future research.

Research is just beginning to emerge in which intervention effectiveness is compared for wife versus adult-daughter caregivers. In one novel study comparing the differential impact of participation in a physical activity program with participation in an information-oriented control condition that provided nutritional data, King, Baumann, O'Sullivan, Wilcox, and Castro (2002) found that both wife and adult-daughter caregivers over the age of 50 benefited from both programs. Greater benefit on a set of physiological variables was found among those who were in the in-home exercise intervention program. This involved moderate intensity workouts (e.g., brisk walking) an average of four times per week for 30 to 40 minutes, over a 1-year period. For these caregivers, sleep improved, more energy was reported, and blood pressure reactivity values were reduced over time. However, caregivers in both conditions reported improved levels of depression and stress by the end of the program. It should be noted that results were similarly positive for wives and daughters, suggesting that health promotion programs may be very appropriate for older, primarily sedentary female caregivers. These intriguing findings surely warrant replication and extension in future research. Because the mean age of the sample overall was about 63 years, age and relationship status are somewhat confounded in this particular project. Future research will need to examine whether similar results are found with young and middle-aged daughters, who comprise (demographically speaking) the largest group of informal caregivers in this country at the present time.

Regarding the issue of the differential appropriateness of interventions for husbands (compared to wives) and older sons (compared to daughters), the existing literature is quite sparse, and results are not consistent from one study to the next. For example, Bookwala and Schulz (2000) found that stress is significantly associated with depression for caregiving wives but not caregiving husbands, even though both groups performed the same kind and amount of caregiving tasks on a daily basis. In contrast, other studies (cf. Neal, Ingersoll-Dayton, & Starrels, 1997) found that men provided less hands-on care than women, and that in turn was associated with less distress overall on psychological measures of stress and depression. Differences in correlates of caregiver stress have also been found for sons and daughters caring for older parents. In one frequently cited study by Mui (1995), sons' emotional strain was found to be predicted by the parents' level of disruptive behaviors, while for daughters, poor relationship quality and interference with work responsibilities were more predictive of distress.

Lauderdale and Gallagher-Thompson (in press) describe an intervention program designed with these findings in mind. For example, it utilized a small-group approach that included information about a wide array of support services, how to access them, and how to select appropriate in-home care workers. Also, rather than focusing on depression (as many of our small-group programs with women caregivers do), this program taught skills for modifying problem behavior in the home environment. Finally, the group atmosphere created a "safe place" for feelings to be expressed if that was appropriate, but sharing of feelings was not a required element of group participation. Both adult sons and husbands joined this program. At the completion of six sessions, most reported improved well-being and more confidence about their ability to handle caregiving stress. Interestingly, in postintervention interviews, they indicated that the most important aspect of the program was the opportunity to get support from other men in a similar situation. This apparently was truly a unique experience for the majority of participants.

Taken together, these studies suggest that men and women may require unique interventions to address the particular ways in which caregiving is stressful for them. So, in order for knowledge to advance, future research must seriously address differences in intervention program specifics based on timing (the point in the ongoing process at which the caregiver seeks help), gender, and relationship status.

ETHNIC, RACIAL, AND CULTURAL DIFFERENCES SHOULD INFORM INTERVENTION CHOICES

It is good to remember that caregivers live in an ever-changing sociocultural context. This includes such factors as their ethnic and racial identification, values and beliefs about health care that have their basis in cultural traditions, cohort differences, demographic differences rooted in education, occupational status and income, and linguistic preferences, particularly for those caregivers for whom English is a second language. In our opinion, future research needs to evaluate these factors systematically in order to enrich the theoretical underpinnings of intervention models and better understand how various factors interact to effect outcomes. In brief, the field of caregiving intervention research has just begun to study the impact of ethnic, racial, cultural, and other differences (e.g., sexual orientation) on how caregiving is viewed and experienced, particularly with regard to levels of stress, preferred coping mechanisms, and preferred kinds of interventions (Hinton, Fox, & Levkoff, 1999).

Yet there is an empirical base of studies comparing the experiences of stress and coping among different racial or ethnic groups of caregivers from which to draw valuable information that should be useful in the design of intervention research in the years ahead. For example, numerous studies have found that African American family caregivers are less susceptible than Caucasian caregivers to the emotional distress associated with dementia caregiving and in general report fewer symptoms of depression or other stress-related indices (see reviews in Aranda, 2001; Connell & Gibson, 1997; Janevic & Connell, 2001; Navaie-Waliser et al., 2001). This seems to be related to their more frequent use of religious beliefs and practices to assist in the coping process, which is markedly more common among African Americans than other groups.

In contrast, studies in which Hispanic and Latino caregivers were compared to White caregivers generally find markedly higher levels of distress in the Latino group. For example, Harwood et al. (1998) found high levels of depressive symptoms, as did Adams, Aranda, Kemp, and Takagi (in press). In fact, in the latter study, Hispanics had the highest rates of depression among four caregiver groups studied (Japanese, African American, Caucasian, and Latinos). This is true despite the fact that reported caregiver burden is generally less among Latinos than among Whites (John & McMillian, 1998). This is believed to reflect the cultural value of self-sacrifice, meaning that individuals should not complain about the "crosses" they bear but instead should accept such challenges with grace. Other studies have found that when Latinos and African Americans are compared, the former report higher levels of personal and role strain than the latter. Still other studies reported that minority caregivers received less informal support than Caucasians, and less than would be anticipated, given the generally larger size of their immediate and extended families. This lack of an extensive social support network when it comes to caregiving is associated with increased distress for Latinos in particular (Janevic & Connell, 2001).

Considerably less is known about caregiving stress and coping among the various Asian groups in this country. The few studies that have been done with Chinese family caregivers have found a greater likelihood of distress being experienced in the form of somatic (rather than psychological) symptoms, along with minimal reported burden and caregiving stress (reviewed in Janevic & Connell, 2001). A handful of studies with Korean caregivers found higher levels of caregiving-associated burden, less use of active coping strategies to deal with this sense of burden, less available instrumental and social support, and less gratification from caregiving compared to Caucasians in the same studies (reviewed in Janevic & Connell, 2001). A recent book edited by Yeo and Gallagher-Thompson (1996) on the topic of ethnicity and dementia contained chapters reflecting both clinical and empirically based information on caregiving among several Asian groups, including Chinese, Japanese, and Filipino families. However, other Asian groups, such as Vietnamese and Hmong, were not included in that volume due to lack of information about their experiences with dementia caregiving. Note that in the same book several chapters described caregiving among Native Americans in both rural and urban settings. To our knowledge the literature available on Native Americans with regard to dementia caregiving has expanded little since that time.

Given all this, a key question for future intervention planners and researchers seems to be: How then can this and related information (e.g., about coping styles and preferences) be used to develop and implement appropriate interventions for members of specific ethnic, racial, and cultural groups? Clearly there is no simple answer to this question; in fact, attempts to address it are just beginning. Two recent papers from our laboratory discuss our own efforts and those of colleagues in different parts of the country to tailor existing interventions to meet some of the unique needs of African American and Latino caregivers, specifically (Gallagher-Thompson et al., 2000; Gallagher-Thompson et al., in press). These papers recommend a number of modifications that may be useful to others who are working with these particular groups. In addition, work is under way at our center to engage in a similar process (e.g., beginning with focus groups and consultations with community gatekeepers) to develop and implement intervention programs specifically for Chinese family caregivers. However, much work remains to be done, as our studies will only sample a limited number of caregivers from a particular region in the U.S. There is little reason to expect that interventions that are successful with Mexican Americans in northern California, for example, will be able to be used as-is with Cuban Americans in Florida or with Puerto Rican Americans in New York City.

In summary, a crucial point in this entire discussion is the specificity of intervention for specific target groups. As Valle (1998) points out so eloquently, "Culture filters how a message is heard and interpreted; conditions how a person responds to the message; plays a role in help-seeking and help-accepting communications and behaviors; influences individual and group attitudes and actions; and influences future actions" (p. 33). For these reasons, interventions must be rooted in appropriate cultural contexts and implemented in culturally syntonic ways.

INTERVENTION PROGRAMS OF THE FUTURE NEED TO INCLUDE DIFFICULT ISSUES

Our final point is a call to action for intervention researchers and clinicians to include more complex and emotionally laden content in their programs, as appropriate, given the various individual difference considerations that have been noted throughout this chapter. One topic that has received little attention in the intervention literature to date but that is associated with considerable family caregivers' stress is that of end-of-life planning and decision making. Although national groups such as the Alzheimer's Association have produced some literature (e.g., pamphlets in the English language) on this topic and are increasing their coverage of it in family-oriented workshops and lecture presentations, it is rarely (if ever) explicitly included in the intervention programs that have been utilized in the various settings described in this volume, and to our knowledge it has not been a definite component of any of the programs for which research data are available at the present time. Yet this is an area of significant concern to families (and of frequent conflict among family members) when the disease of the individual who is demented progresses to the point that he or she is bedbound and in need of continuous nursing care and supervision. When that time comes, difficult decisions about the use of tube feeding, for example, or a ventilator to assist with breathing, will need to be made. Very likely, significant financial resources will have to be allocated if life is prolonged under these circumstances, and many will question whether this is appropriate, given the futility of the situation. In the absence of explicit information about how the care receiver wishes to be treated as death nears, family members are burdened with the task of deciding what should and should not be done, and under what circumstances, to prolong life or terminate it (Haley et al., in press).

In our society there is an ever-increasing focus on preparing for the end of life in that adults are encouraged to execute wills to dispose of their estates and to file advance directives with their families and physicians so that their preferences for end-of-life medical care can be clearly stated. However, though the vast majority of older adults surveyed agree that it is desirable to have advance directives, few actually have them and even fewer seem to understand them. When asked about this, the most common reason given is the assumption that their family knows them best and can be trusted to make appropriate health care choices when the time comes (Hopp, 2000). Studies with African Americans and Chinese Americans have found that this belief is particularly strong among those groups, thus putting an additional burden on family caregivers (Haley et al., in press). In fact, the caregiver may not wish to shoulder this responsibility and may actually wish the older adult to prepare an advance directive but at the same time, may feel it is culturally inappropriate to ask them to do so. For example, it is considered disrespectful by older Chinese to speak openly about end-of-life decision making. Adult children are not supposed to bring up this topic, thus rendering communication difficult and adding to the stress of the situation. Perceived stress was noted as well by Silliman (2000) who observed that discussions about end-of-life care often do not occur until very late in the process, if at all, for most families. Yet when there are no clear verbal or written statements about desired end-of-life care, family members (regardless of ethnicity) experience more stress compared to family members who know their older relatives' care preferences.

Other research with minority groups has found a strong preference (especially among older generations) for the use of heroic methods to prolong life, even for persons with advanced dementia, rather than participate in any kind of decision making that could hasten death (American Psychological Association, 2000). Thus, the issues are quite complex and, once again, are heightened by the interplay of cultural values and beliefs with the medically driven need to make health care decisions when chronic illnesses such as dementia reach their terminal stage.

It seems to us that families would benefit from the opportunity to discuss this situation and to explore their options in a nonjudgmental manner with empathic professionals who can help them weigh the pros and cons and then decide how to proceed. Based on our clinical experience (i.e., counseling caregivers in distress and eliciting caregivers' comments in focus group discussions), we recommend that a component such as this be included in future intervention research studies. This would permit the empirical determination of whether or not there is any "added value" (in terms of improved outcomes) to the inclusion of this kind of material, and it would highlight cultural and ethnic issues that would need to be addressed.

There are other difficult issues that have not typically been included in existing intervention research programs. One that is particularly salient to us is exploration of the ongoing process of loss that is involved in dementia caregiving. In this we include the goal of better characterization of "anticipatory grieving" and its impact on subsequent bereavement reactions. Many caregivers report feeling conflicted because they have begun to grieve but cannot fully grieve and "get on with their lives" while the care recipient is still alive. At the same time, a significant number of their needs (e.g., emotional and physical intimacy, companionship, etc.) are not being met in the relationship. This is very true for spousal caregivers who can be characterized as "funny kinds of widows" (Davidson, in press). Would these caregivers benefit from intervention programs expressly designed to address this situation? Should opportunities be provided for developing new coping strategies to deal with grief and loss while caregiving is ongoing? One hopes that future research will answer these and related questions.

One final future direction for caregiving research is the inclusion of studies designed to bridge the scientist-practitioner gap, going "from bench to bedside" (Horton, 1999). Recently, the National Institutes of Health has made this kind of "translational" research a priority area for funding, to encourage the creation of strong bridges among efficacy research, effectiveness (real-world) studies, and practice and service delivery systems (National Institutes of Health, 1999). This movement reflects that historically, research results have been slow to inform clinical practice. For example, the value of empirically supported therapies for depression has been known for more than a decade, yet practitioners generally continue to employ the method of therapy in which they were trained in graduate school even when there are data that reveal the greater efficacy of a different approach. The same situation may well occur in the caregiving research field unless translational studies are conducted in the near future.

Although we have learned much in the past decade about how to intervene to improve caregivers' quality of life, clearly there is much, much more to learn in the future. It is our hope that this chapter in particular (and the book in general), will facilitate the readers' engagement in clinically informative research and practice to assist this ever-growing group of individuals who deserve the very best care we can provide.

REFERENCES

Adams, B., Aranda, M., Kemp, B., & Takagi, K. (in press). Ethnic and gender differences in distress among Anglo-American, African-American, Japanese-American and Mexican-American spousal caregivers of persons with dementia. *Journal of Clinical Geropsychology.*

American Psychological Association. (2000). *Working group on assisted suicide and end of life decisions. Report to the board of directors.* Washington, DC: Author. (Available: www.apa.org/pi/aseolf.html).

Aneshensel, C. S., Pearlin, L. I., Mullan, J. T., Zarit, S. H., & Whitlatch, C. J. (1995). *Profiles in caregiving: The unexpected career.* San Diego, CA: Academic Press.

Aranda, M. P. (2001). Racial and ethnic factors in dementia caregiving research in the US. *Aging and Mental Health, 5*(Suppl. 1), S116–123.

Bookwala, J., & Schulz, R. (2000). A comparison of primary stressors, secondary stressors, and depressive symptoms between elderly caregiving husbands and wives: The caregiver health effects study. *Psychology and Aging, 25,* 607–616.

Connell, C. M., & Gibson, G. D. (1997). Racial, ethnic, and cultural differences in dementia caregiving: Review and analysis. *Gerontologist, 37,* 355–364.

Davidson, A. (in press). *A funny kind of widow.* Secaucus, NJ: Carol Publishing.

Gallagher-Thompson, D., Árean, P., Coon, D., Menendez, A., Takagi, K., Haley, W., Argüelles, T., Rubert, M., Loewenstein, D., & Szapocznik, J. (2000). Development

and implementation of intervention strategies for culturally diverse caregiving populations. In R. Schulz (Ed.), *Handbook on dementia caregiving* (pp. 151–185). New
York: Springer.

Gallagher-Thompson, D., Haley, W., Guy, D., Rubert, M., Argüelles, T., Zeiss, L. M.,
Tennstedt, S., & Ory, M. (in press). Tailoring psychological interventions for ethnically
diverse dementia caregivers. *Clinical Psychology: Science and Practice.*

Gallagher-Thompson, D., & Steffen, A. (1994). Comparative effectiveness of cognitive/
behavioral and brief psychodynamic psychotherapies for the treatment of depression
in family caregivers. *Journal of Consulting and Clinical Psychology, 62,* 543–549.

Goode, K. T., Haley, W. E., Roth, D. L., & Ford, G. R. (1998). Predicting longitudinal
changes in caregiver physical and mental health: A stress process model. *Health
Psychology, 17,* 190–198.

Haley, W. E., Gallagher-Thompson, D., Reynolds, S., Allen, R. Chen, H., & Burton, A.
(in press). Family issues in end-of-life decision making and end-of-life care. *American
Behavioral Scientist.*

Harwood, D. G., Barker, W. W., Cantillon, M., Loewenstein, D. A., Ownby, R., & Duara,
R. (1998). Depressive symptomatology in first-degree family caregivers of Alzheimer
disease patients: A cross-ethnic comparison. *Alzheimer Disease and Associated Disorders, 12,* 340–346.

Hinton, W. H., Fox, K., & Levkoff, S. (1999). Introduction: Exploring the relationships
among aging, ethnicity, and family dementia caregiving. *Culture, Medicine and Psychiatry, 23,* 403–413.

Hopp, F. P. (2000). Preferences for surrogate decision makers, informal communication
and advance directives among community-dwelling elders: Results from a national
study. *Gerontologist, 40,* 449–457.

Horton, B. (1999). From bench to bedside. *Nature, 402,* 213–215.

Janevic, M. R., & Connell, C. M. (2001). Racial, ethnic, and cultural differences in the
dementia caregiving experience: Recent findings. *Gerontologist, 41,* 334–347.

John, R., & McMillian, B. (1998). Exploring caregiver burden among Mexican Americans:
Cultural prescriptions, family dilemmas. *Journal of Aging and Ethnicity, 1,* 93–111.

King, A. C., Baumann, K., O'Sullivan, P., Wilcox, S., & Castro, C. (2002). Effects of
moderate-intensity exercise on physiological, behavioral, and emotional responses to
family caregiving: A randomized controlled trial. *Journal of Gerontology: Medical
Sciences, 57A,* M26–M36.

Lauderdale, S., & Gallagher-Thompson, D. (in press). Older men providing care: Experiences from a psychoeducational group for men. *Clinical Gerontologist.*

McCarty, H. J., Roth, D. L., Goode, K. T., Owen, J. E., Harrell, L., Donovan, K., &
Haley, W. E. (2000). Longitudinal course of behavior problems during Alzheimer's
disease: Linear and curvilinear patterns of decline. *Journal of Gerontology: Medical
Sciences, 55A,* M200–M206.

Mui, A. (1995). Caring for frail elderly parents: A comparison of adult sons and daughters.
Gerontologist, 35, 86–93.

National Institutes of Health. (1999). Bridging science and service: A report by the
National Advisory Mental Health Council's Clinical Treatment and Services Research
Workgroup (NIH Publication No. 99-4353). Washington, DC: Author.

Navaie-Waliser, M., Feldman, P. H., Gould, D. A., Levine, C., Kuerbis, A. N., & Donelan, K. (2001). The experiences and challenges of informal caregivers: Common themes and differences among Whites, Blacks, and Hispanics. *Gerontologist, 41,* 733–741.

Neal, M. B., Ingersoll-Dayton, D., & Starrels, M. E. (1997). Gender and relationship differences in caregiving patterns and consequences among employed caregivers. *Gerontologist, 37,* 804–816.

Powers, D. V., Gallagher-Thompson, D., & Kraemer, H. (2002). Coping and depression in Alzheimer caregivers: Longitudinal evidence of stability. *Journals of Gerontology: Psychological Sciences, 57B,* P205–P211.

Silliman, R. A. (2000). Caregiving issues in the geriatric medical encounter. *Clinics in Geriatric Medicine, 16*(1), 51–60.

Teel, C. S., & Press, A. N. (1999). Fatigue among elders in caregiving and noncaregiving roles. *Western Journal of Nursing Research, 21,* 498–520.

Valle, R. (1998). *Caregiving across cultures: Working with dementing illness and ethnically diverse populations.* Washington, DC: Taylor & Francis.

Yeo, G., & Gallagher-Thompson, D. (Eds.), (1996). *Ethnicity and the dementias.* Washington, DC: Taylor & Francis.

Zarit, S. H., Stephens, M. A. P., Townsend, A., & Greene, R. (1998). Stress reduction for family caregivers: Effects of adult day care use. *Journal of Gerontology: Social Sciences, 53B,* S267–S277.

Index